FREEDOM AND PROSPERITY IN THE 21st CENTURY

A Multinational Compendium

FIRST EDITION
Georgian International University Press

GEORGE P. STASEN
ZVIAD KLIMENT LAZARASHVILI
GARI T. CHAPIDZE
CHIEKE E. IHEJIRIKA
VALERIAN RAMISHVILI

Edited by Zviad Kliment Lazarashvili

Printed in the United States of America
GEORGIAN INTERNATIONAL UNIVERSITY PRESS
Visit us on the web:
www.GIUAmerica.org

General Editor: Zviad Kliment Lazarashvili
Editor of the citations, quotations and annotations used in the book:
Chieke E. Ihejirika

Cover Design by Demetre Dekanosidze
Graphic designer, illustrator and the sole responsible party on copyright issues
for the pictures, illustrations and graphics used in the book:
Demetre Dekanosidze

DEDICATION

The authors of this book would like to thank most profoundly Georgian International University and the Laissez-faire Fraternity for their support and encouragement.

ACKNOWLEDGEMENTS

EDITORIAL COMMITTEE:

General Editor: Zviad Kliment Lazarashvili, Ph.D.

Editor of Citations: Chieke E. Ihejirika, Ph.D.

Cover Designer: Demetre Dekanosidze

Graphic Designer-illustrator: Demetre Dekanosidze

APPRECIATION LIST: Winford B. Johnson, Ph.D. Yale University

                                Janet Mathewson, Ph.D. Yale University

                                Guram Tavartkiladze, Ph.D.
                                Founder and Rector President of Tbilisi State
                                University of Economic Relations & Law

                                Prof. Robert Goodell, Strayer University

                                George L. Frunzi, Ph.D. Temple University

                                Levi Nwachuku, Ph.D.
                                Michigan State University

                                Dean Judith A.W. Thomas, Ph.D.
                                Lincoln University

                                Dean Izzeldin Bakhit, Ph.D.
                                Strayer University

                                Daniel Terfassa, Ph.D. Strayer University

                                Prof. Cynthia Orth, Strayer University

                                Gordian Ndubizu, Ph.D. Drexel University

                                Elaine Delancey, Ph.D. Drexel University

                                Julie Mostov, Ph.D. Drexel University

                                James J. Munnis, Esq, West Chester, PA

                                Shota Agladze, Ph.D.
                                Javakhishvili Tbilisi State University

                                Peter Stercho, Ph.D. Drexel University

                                Jan Lutjes, Ph.D. Drexel University

Nugzar Tsereteli, Ph.D.
Javakhishvili Tbilisi State University

Aryeh Botwinick, Ph.D. Temple University

Benedict Stavis, Ph.D. Temple University

Dean Besik Aladashvili

Tbilisi State University of Economic
Relationsand and Law

Olga Metreveli, Ph.D.
Georgian Technical University

Rev. Dr. Theophilus Okere, Professor Emeritus
Whelan Research Institute Owerri

Rev. Kingsley Ihejirika, Doctoral Candidate
Pontifical Urbaniana University, Rome

Scudder G. Stevens, Esq, Kennett Square, PA

Lawrence Okere, Ph.D.
University of Arkansas, Pine Bluff

Ewa Unoke, Ph.D.
Kansas City Kansas Community College

Alphonso Ogbuehi, Ph.D.
Park University Kansas City Missouri

Emmanuel Ihejirika, Ph.D.
Argosy University

Richard Deeg, Ph.D. Temple University

Joseph Schwartz, Ph.D. Temple University

Educational University Rvali, Rustavi, Georgia

Carol Smith-Williamson, JD.
Lincoln University

Prof. Chris Mbah, Ph.D.
Olive College North Carolina

TABLE OF CONTENTS

ABOUT THE AUTHORS

Dr. GEORGE P. STASEN
Georgian International Academy, Ph.D.
Drexel University, LeBow College of Business, MBA
Drexel University, LeBow College of Business, BS

George P. Stasen has served as a director and/or advisor to government units, foundations, mutual funds, investment companies, private companies and public corporations, as well as professor of economics and corporate finance. He has structured and provided financing and investment guidance to major corporations, investment companies, developing enterprises and municipalities.

Dr. Stasen serves as general partner of Mentor Special Situation Fund, L.P., a highly successful venture capital fund and also serves as Chairman of CoreCare Systems, a publicly held corporation; Chairman and cofounder of SBC Corporation, the developer and manufacturer of the world's fastest and most accurate tracking technology; and Chairman and cofounder of RAPC Corporation, a designer and manufacturer of highly durable high capacity computers for the defense industry. Since 2011 Dr. Stasen also serves as the Vice President of Georgian International Academy – a premier postgraduate research and educational institution in Georgia. Dr. Stasen is one of the founders of Georgian International University. He also serves as a faculty member at the university's Hayek School of Economics.

Dr. Stasen earned his BS from Drexel University with a concentration in Economics and was subsequently awarded a fellowship and earned an MBA from Drexel University. Mr. Stasen earned his Ph.D. in Economics from Georgian International Academy. In 2011 Dr. Stasen coauthored the 3rd edition of the book *Pantheon of Political Philosophers*.

George P. Stasen would like to dedicate this labor of love to Dr. Peter Stercho, a Ukrainian Professor of Economics at the Drexel University LeBow College of Business, in Philadelphia, Pennsylvania, for his inspiration, superb scholarship and wisdom in seeing the true value of free markets, as well as Drexel University where Dr. Stasen developed his love of economics and commerce. He would also like sincerely to thank the Georgian International Academy for encouraging his continuous study of economics and education. May God Bless those hallowed halls.

George P. Stasen would also like to thank Montgomery County Community College where he spent several wonderful years teaching Economics as an adjunct faculty member.

Dr. ZVIAD KLIMENT LAZARASHVILI

Georgian International Academy, Academician
Georgian International Academy, Ph.D.
Educational University Rvali, Ph.D. (HON)
Strayer University, MBA
Educational University Rvali, JD
Tbilisi State University of Economic Relations and Law, BS

Zviad Kliment Lazarashvili is the author of several books in literature, philosophy, economics and political science. Dr. Lazarashvili is the Executive Vice President at Selective Broadcasting Corporation, the developer and manufacturer of the world's fastest and most accurate tracking technology. Dr. Lazarashvili is the Executive Vice President at RAPC National Security Division, Inc., a designer and manufacturer of highly durable high capacity computers for the defense industry. He has served as a Capital Markets analyst for Merrill Lynch on Wall Street. He has served as a consultant at several universities, high-technology and financial companies, including Georgian International University, Educational University Rvali and Mentor Special Situation Fund, L.P. He has served as a visiting professor at Tbilisi State University of Economic Relations and Law of Georgia and at Educational University Rvali of Georgia, and also as a Distinguished Lecturer in political science, economics and finance at Lincoln University of Pennsylvania. Since 2011 Dr. Lazarashvili also serves as the Vice President of Georgian International Academy – a premier postgraduate research and educational institution in Georgia. Dr. Lazarashvili is one of the founders of Georgian International University. He also serves as a faculty member at the university's Hayek School of Economics. His academic researches and financial analyses were published in *Friedrich Ebert Foundation of Germany, Journal of Business Management (1998), Scholar Magazine, Washington, DC (2008)* and *Lincolnian, Lincoln University, PA (2009)*. Dr. Lazarashvili's previous literary works include *Manhope (2004)* and *Invictus-Pathos (2003)*. He also collaborated on several academic treatises and historical theses on social, political and philosophical issues with Dr. Janet Mathewson of Yale University: *Political Economy of the 19th Century New England (2000), Treatise on Christianity and Capitalism (2001)* and *American Conservatism (2001)*. In 2009-2010 Zviad Kliment Lazarashvili co-authored two academic books, *Political Philosophy: A Global Approach (2009)* and *Political Theory Made Simple (2010)*. Since fall of 2009 the books are used as undergraduate text books in political theory and political science in several universities.

Zviad Kliment Lazarashvili is the first Georgian translator of Henry David Thoreau's political essays. His pioneering translations, historical analyses and commentaries on Thoreau's works were introduced in Georgia as an academic treatise, *Hero of the American Nation (2008)*. In 2010 the second edition of the book was published in the U.S., *Henry David Thoreau: Essays (2010)*. The book is bilingual and contains five of Henry David Thoreau's best known political essays in both, English and Georgian languages: *Civil Disobedience, Slavery in*

Massachusetts, A Plea for Captain John Brown, Life Without Principle, and *The Last Days of John Brown*. It is the first scholarly, fully annotated edition of Thoreau's political essays in the world. It contains some 700 footnotes which explain Thoreau's ideas, Slavery, Abolitionism and the 19th century American politics in broad historical context. The second edition offers an abundance of detailed annotations. It also includes an extended introduction by Dr. Lazarashvili, and the translator's biography by George P. Stasen, Ph.D. The book also contains illustrations and copies of historical documents relevant to the 19th century Abolitionism.

In 2011 Dr. Lazarashvili authored the book *American Heroes (2011)*. Besides Thoreau's five political essays, the book contains prison letters of John Brown, Brown's speeches, interviews and his Provisional Constitution, rare biographical information obtained from archives, and extensive commentaries of John Brown's hagiographer, Franklin Benjamin Sanborn. The book also contains illustrations and copies of historical documents relevant to the 19th century Abolitionism and New England. The book is bilingual and is intended for graduate students of history of Abolitionism and political philosophy in the United States and Georgia. In 2011 the book was recognized by the National Academy of Sciences of Ukraine and Dr. Lazarashvili was awarded Plato Gold Medal for his "immense contributions to the science of philosophy".

In 2011 Dr. Lazarashvili coauthored the 3rd edition of the book *Pantheon of Political Philosophers*. The book presents broad and comprehensive descriptions of prominent political theorists and a unique approach to their concepts. Every notion is shown not only as a philosophical hypothesis, but as a corollary of diverse personal, cultural and even ethnic experiences, which all men, and especially men of keen observation, undergo throughout their lives. Dr. Lazarashvili is a polymath who easily connects political issues to economic problems and philosophical doctrines to religious concerns. Thus he creates a cross-disciplinary picture of political science, which is closely knit with other disciplines and many aspects of human existence.

Dr. GARI T. CHAPIDZE
Fazisi Academy of Sciences, Academician
Georgian National Academy of Sciences, Academician
Lomonosov Moscow State University (MGU), BA, MS

Dr. Gari T. Chapidze is the world renowned academic figure in political science, pedagogy and journalism. He is an Academician and a full member of several national academies of sciences of Georgia and Ukraine. He is the author of over seventy scholarly books which have been widely accepted in scientific and academic circles of Georgia, Russia, Ukraine, Europe and now the United States. Dr. Chapidze is the author of the first and only Georgian-Ukrainian Dictionary and the first and only Georgian-Belarusian Idiomatic Dictionary.

Dr. Gari T. Chapidze has served as a Rector of Chiatura Academy of Liberal Sciences (1993-2003). Since 2003 he serves as the President of Georgian International Academy. Since 2008 he serves as the Rector of Georgia-Ukraine Institute of Social Relations. Since 1997 he serves as the Chief Editor of the academic monthly newspaper "Chiragdani". Since 2011 he serves as the President of the Gogebashvili Society of Georgia.

Dr. Gari Chapidze is the winner of several national and academic prizes and medals: Medal of Honor of Georgia (2003), Gogebashvili Medal (1993), Gogebashvili Medal (2000), Ilia Chavchavadze Prize and Medal (2003), Akaki Tsereteli Prize and Medal (2003), Tabidze Prize and Medal (2005), Plato Gold Medal of Ukraine (2010), Guramishvili Prize and Medal (2010), Georgia-Ukraine Medal of Friendship (2010), International Science Medal of Georgia (2007), International Science Medal of Georgia (2008), Gold Medal of Georgia for Accomplishments in Public Education (2008).

In this particular book Dr. Chapidze offers the global view on political science and political economy. He advocates economic freedom, capitalism, political justice and explains their precedence throughout the world and throughout history. With Dr. Chapidze's initiative the book will be used as a standard academic textbook for the disciplines of political economy and political theory at Georgian International Academy, Georgian International University, and Georgia-Ukraine Institute of Social Relations.

Dr. CHIEKE E. IHEJIRIKA
Temple University, Ph.D.
University of Waterloo, Canada, MA
Catholic University of Leuven, Belgium, BA, MA
Alvan Ikoku College of Education, B. Ed.

Dr. Chieke E. Ihejirika is an Associate Professor of Political Science at Lincoln University, Pennsylvania. In the last fifteen years he has served as a graduate teaching fellow at Temple, Adjunct Professor at Drexel, Avila University in Kansas City and Political Science professor at Kansas City Kansas Community College. Some of his publications include: *Ndiigbo in Nigeria: A Quest for Survival and Prosperity (2010); US-Africa Relation from Nixon to Reagan (2008); African-American Elitism: A liberal and Quantitative Perspective (2008). Pan Africanism: A Survey (2006); Africa's Utopia: Economic Development without Political Development? (2002); The Communal Nature of Igbo Aesthetics (1994); Nigerian foreign policies, 1960-1983 sources and patterns, Ottawa: National Library of Canada (1988).*

Dr. Ihejirika has a unique capacity of making some of the very arcane subjects readily comprehensible to even freshmen students. He is an avid advocate of political justice and economic freedom. He is an idealist with infectious optimism believing that market economy and fair politics, more than anything else, can restore faith in our common humanity. Concurring with Aristotle that politics is at the same time the most nurturing and most dangerous human endeavor, he believes that with good politics human suffering could be drastically reduced. He brings the African fairness based on intrinsic spirituality to the understanding of politics and economics. He is very committed to spreading the uniquely African humanism that is quintessential to the building of a more humane world. The need to understand the various attitudes about the acquisition, and use of power over the millennia and across the world has become imperative in this era of globalization.

DR. VALERIAN RAMISHVILI
Georgian Academy of Philosophical Sciences, Academician
Highest Attestation Commission of Georgia, Ph.D.
Ivane Javakhishvili Tbilisi State University, MS
Ivane Javakhishvili Tbilisi State University, BA

Doctor Habilitatus Valerian Ramishvili is the world renowned expert in philosophy, theology and political science, and he has authored several pioneering books in these disciplines. He is a member of Georgian Academy of Philosophical Sciences. Currently Dr. Ramishvili is a professor at Ivane Javachishvili Tbilisi State University. He has served as the Deputy Head of the Study and Research Center for Regional Politics and Management of the President of Georgia, and as the Senior Researcher at the Institute of Political Sciences, prominent think tanks and national policy institutes in Georgia. Dr. Ramishvili has served as the Dean of faculty of philosophy and sociology at Ivane Javachishvili Tbilisi State University, as the Dean of faculty of social sciences at Euro-Caucasus University (Georgian-German university) and as an associate professor at the Rvali University. His academic researches have been published in Romania, Russian Federation and Ukraine, including: *Man and Destiny (2002)*, *Absurd and Responsibility (2008)*, and *Philosophy (2010)*. He has co-authored several monographs, including *Local Democracy and Regional Development as Elements of Political Order (2008)*, and *Handbook for Local Self Government Servants (2007)*.

Dr. Ramishvili's articles have been published worldwide. The long list includes *Christian Democracy and New Orientation (1999)*, *Dilemma of Political Consciousness (2005)*, *Global Transformation and Global Challenges (2009)*, *European Regional Politics (2010)*, *Georgian Political Culture (2005)*, *Transformation of Society and Political Consciousness (2006)*, *Culture of Post Modernity and Experience with Freedom (2006)*, *Georgian Political Culture and Responsibility(2008)*, *Religion Hermeneutics and Dialogue of Culture (2008)*, *Global World, Culture and Responsibility (2008)*, *Paradigm of Christ and Martin Heidegger's Ontology (2008)*, and *Ilia Chavchavadze and Change of the Paradigm of Georgian Culture (2005)*.

INTRODUCTION

"Those who would give up essential Liberty, to purchase a little temporary safety, deserve neither Liberty nor safety."

Benjamin Franklin (1706-1790)

Economics is the study of resource allocation, – *Resources are scarce but human wants are insatiable.* Early man recognized that rules were necessary for survival. If food was scarce who would eat, who would go hungry, who would die, or who would be invaded?

Until the 18th century, philosophers, rulers and leaders devised schemes to allocate resources and maintain power. They invoked mandate, expropriation and taxation. However, with the arrival of the new merchant class and the industrial revolution, the world changed and those without power or privilege had an alternative to subsistence living.

By the early 20th century freedom and prosperity reshaped parts of the world, while in other nations people remained poor and powerless. Was this dichotomy due to the nature and quantity of resources or the method of resource allocation? In some nations the government allocated resources and in others the market determined quantity, price and allocation. In those nations that offered freedom, wealth ensued but some were left behind. Is there a perfect system? No! And there never will be a perfect system!

This book examines economic development and related economic theory, the truth and the tradeoff, the rhetoric and the reality. It is presented from different perspectives and from different parts of the world. The Authors are from Georgia, Ukraine, Nigeria and the United States. The European Union economics is also discussed in depth.

The lessons provided are essential for understanding freedom and prosperity, now and in the future.

Enjoy the journey.

"Those who cannot remember the past are condemned to repeat it."

George Santayna (1863-1952)

ECONOMIC PERSPECTIVE AND THE USA

CICERO'S OBSERVATIONS

The following extract is from Cicero's famous *De Republica*, written in 54 BC.

"We are taxed on our bread and our wine, on our incomes and our investments, on our land and on our property, not only for base creatures who do not deserve the name of men, but for foreign nations, for complaisant nations who will bow to us and accept our largesse and promise us to assist in the keeping of the peace – these mendicant nations who will destroy us when we show a moment of weakness or our treasury is bare, and surely it is becoming bare! We are taxed to maintain legions on their soil, in the name of law and order and the Pax Romana, a document which will fall into dust when it pleases our allies and our vassals. We keep them in precarious balance only with our gold. Is the heart-blood of our nation worth these? Shall one Italian be sacrificed for Britain, for Gaul, for Egypt, for India, even for Greece, and a score of other nations? Were they bound to us with ties of love, they would not ask our gold. They would ask only our laws. They take our very flesh, and they hate and despise us. And who shall say we are worthy of more?"

Elsewhere Cicero wrote:

"But when a government becomes powerful it is destructive, extravagant and violent; it is an usurer which takes bread from innocent mouths and deprives honorable men of their substance, for votes with which to perpetuate itself."

INTRODUCTION

My purpose is to help the reader grasp important concepts in economic thought and economic development. We will explore economic theory and economic reality through the eyes of great economic philosophers, including Adam Smith, Karl Marx and John Maynard Keynes. Their work shaped economic thought from the beginning of the industrial revolution to the present. We shall also examine their strengths, their weaknesses, their character and their contribution to economic thinking and society. They were prolific and brilliant.

Great civilizations remained great because they understood their economic environment and the limitation of their resources. Did the Egyptians build pyramids in preparation for the afterlife or did some ancient Egyptian philosopher/economist conceive of pyramid building to prevent cyclical unemployment caused by Nile River seasonal flooding. Employment provides wages, which stimulates the economy and calms civil unrest. By the same reasoning the magnificent cathedrals of Europe and the Great Wall of China also created jobs. The famous Sun Tzu, *The Art of War* (China, approximately 600 BC), understood economic policy as a tool of politics and war.

Economics, in western tradition, began with the Greeks. They were the first philosophers (Greek: philo sophia – love of wisdom). Plato (418-347 BC) published many works, but is best known for his famous *Republic*. The central theme of *the Republic* was the question; how could society be reshaped so that man might realize the best that is in him. Plato also offered a hierarchical collectivist utopia run by philosopher Kings.

His student, Aristotle (384-322 BC) developed the concept of natural law and wondered about exchange and value. During this period an ancient Greek produced the first document whose theme was economics (Greek *oikonomia* – household management). There was Hesiod who wrote a famous poem about scarce resources and abundant human desires. The ancient Greek philosophers debated a famous paradox. Why were diamonds more valuable than water when water was essential for life? For modern economic man the answer was obvious – diamonds are scarce and water is abundant. Of course, there can be exceptions. Markets can be time and location specific. Water is very valuable to someone lost in the dessert.

THE TWENTIETH CENTURY LABORATORY

The twentieth century was a comprehensive "economics laboratory". The century began with the first airplane and ended with pocket computers and rocket ships. It was also a period of volatile economic growth and political change. The early part of the century was characterized by world war and a depression and was followed by world war and wealth that could not have been envisioned.

We have been provided a framework to examine and analyze economic theory in "the real world", not simulations, not games, not models, but a "true test" with real outcomes driven by human behavior. In the real world, economic decisions are not always rational, leaders are not always enlightened and politicians do not seek optimal economic outcomes. This environment is not static, it is a world of vast uncertainty.

The 20th century began with the physicist Albert Einstein, and the mathematician turned economist John Maynard Keynes, each seeking a "theory of everything" in their respective disciplines. In both cases they postulated a "General Theory". Keynes did not want to work in any one's shadow, particularly the great economist Alfred Marshall and certainly not anyone from the Great Austrian School of Economics. As an economist, I would say that the physicists have the easier task, as physics is pure science and mathematics. Economics is not science and the mathematical models used by economists are useless as a forecasting tool. As Albert Einstein said, "God does not play dice with the universe". Economists, lawyers and legislators do play dice with the universe – such is the cost of hubris. They seek to employ and impose their craft, which, more often than not, is counterproductive and frequently restricts liberty. My favorite cartoon is a scene from a "Cold War" May Day parade in Red Square. The cartoon depicts miles of troops and weapons followed by an open car with several old men. A Russian General asks the Premier, "who is in the car"? The Premier responds, "our most devastating weapon against the West, they are the economists"!

Every economic crisis that has plagued the United States for the past 100 years has its roots in the government "trying to help". This laboratory has given us the ability to examine the global economic system and see actual results of alternative economic and political systems. It is unfortunate that an examination will upset economists and politicians alike.

Politicians are like female tarantulas. They kill their mate after an intimate encounter.

American politicians are fond of saying "sunlight is the best disinfectant" but they wear very dark "sun" glasses and frequently have their important meetings in the evening. By examining our economics laboratory we can enable economic man to seek better economic outcomes. However, among the political class, ideology is always more important than truth or facts.

The free market is the most efficient method to allocate resources, and the laws of supply and demand are the cornerstone of the market mechanism. At the equilibrium price there is neither shortage nor surplus. Smith saw the market as essential, Keynes did not embrace it, and Marx believed that only government could and should allocate resources.

It was the great economist Alfred Marshall, Keynes' professor, who detailed the laws of supply and demand with illustration and mathematical precision. He created what would later become known as microeconomics. Keynes formulated what would become known as macroeconomics.

As stated previously, economics is not a pure science. Granted, there are some aspects of economics that can be modeled with mathematical precision, but attempt to model an entire economic system is an exercise in futility. Among other things, there are exogenous events that can cloud the finest crystal ball, such as a natural disaster. Switzerland, a closed economy, can export excess workers, but they cannot export a natural disaster.

At this point it is important to define key concepts in political thought since many of the readers are from European and African nations. In the eighteenth and early nineteenth centuries the concept of "liberalism" emphasized freedom as the ultimate goal of man and society. It meant a reduced role of the state and a Laissez-faire approach to commerce. It placed liberty above the state. However, in the late 1800s, and after the 1930s in the United States, the concept of liberalism took on a new meaning. It came to represent reliance on the state to achieve objectives desired by the state. The term "liberalism" was usurped by the progressives and replaced by the term liberal. The true meaning of liberal has been replaced with conservative and libertarian, which can be confusing. Consequently, we shall use the terms "left and right". Left shall represent those that seek more government and a reduction of freedom and the term right shall represent those seeking less government and more freedom. In this regard communism, socialism and the Nazi movement are regarded as left, and free market capitalism shall be regarded as a movement of the right.

Economics is a social science whose emissaries are influenced by ideology. In the United States legislature, members of the Republican Party (generally right) and members of the Democrat Party (generally left) have diametrically opposed solutions to the same economic problems. In the early part of the 20th century, Hitler, Mussolini and Stalin rose to power and large influential American newspapers, like the New York Times, praised their leadership, wisdom, nationalism, central planning and the glory of enlightened socialism. The truth about the Union of Soviet Socialist Republics was hidden by the American "intelligentsia" out of fear that there would be a misunderstanding about the true goodness of communism. When Stalin was informed that five million Kulaks, landed peasants from Ukraine, were starved to death under the guise of land reform, Stalin expressed surprise that the death toll was not materially higher. Stalin rapidly achieved two goals. He increased the per capita GDP and accelerated the collectivization of agriculture. The "economic achievements" of socialism in China and other communist states were also achieved through savage brutality. God is not permitted in communism, since the government is the "almighty power" and those who do not support the government are killed for the greater good of the society. In the later part of the 20th century socialism began to die a slow death due to economic failure. Vestiges of ideological absurdity remain in Cuba and North Korea.

Those that seek economic growth through central planning are not engaged in optimizing the distribution of resources but in controlling the means of production for political purposes. The end result is always the same; freedom is confiscated along with private property. "Economic Freedom is a necessary but not sufficient condition for political freedom.... Political freedom in turn is a necessary condition for the long term maintenance of economic freedom."[1] War is assuredly a quest for resources and history is a time line of war.

History

As we examine history we can see that industrial society has gradually and tediously transformed the human condition from a subsistence agrarian culture to centers of wealth unimaginable a century ago. To understand this phenomenon we must examine the nature of the

---

[1] Friedman, Milton. (1982). *Free Markets and the Generals.*

human condition. The path has not been a straight line; change and growth are never linear. Change comes about through new ideas. And with each new development society seeks an outcome that provides the best results. This is universal unless there are religious or cultural taboos. Great rivers do not move in a straight line, they take the path of least resistance. Despots achieve leadership by the sword and not the will of the people. Freedom can only exist in a democracy supported by a free market system. Change not supported by the free will of the people is like a bridge over water with a weak foundation. It will only survive if the current is weak.

Economic man seeks to improve his life and government seeks to control economic man. Government always tries to control society and taxes are a weapon of choice. That is not to say that all taxation is bad. Government must have funds to maintain the "rule of law" and to protect "the state". A nation cannot be an economic power without being a military power – wealth must be protected from those who want to take wealth rather than create wealth. And government itself does not create wealth, it only confiscates it. Advocates of big government always want more power and more money to achieve governmental control at the cost of freedom. They also want the populace to believe that they are smarter and morally superior. But the result is less freedom and the justification is racist.

THE JOURNEY BEGINS: ADAM SMITH

"Experience should teach us to be most on our guard to protect liberty when the Government's purposes are beneficent. Men born to freedom are naturally alert to repel invasion of their liberty by evil-minded rulers. The greatest dangers to liberty lurk in insidious encroachment by men of zeal, well-meaning but without understanding."

Louis D. Brandeis (1856-1941)
Supreme Court Justice
Olmstead v. United States 1928

Adam Smith (1723-1790) published *The Wealth of Nations* in 1776. The book had a truly profound impact on the world of his time and remains a mainstay of economic thought to this day. Some however, believe that modern economics began with Richard Cantillon (1680s-

1734), not Smith. Cantillon was a French-influenced Irish merchant and banker. It has been said that an economist is someone who knows everything about money, but has none. On this measure Cantillon failed. He died a multimillionaire. After becoming very rich as a speculator he returned to France, his adopted home.

In 1730 Cantillon wrote his great work, *Essai sur la nature du commerce en general*. The book was circulated widely and published in 1755. In 1734, while living in London, this mysterious man died in his house as it burned to the ground. W. Stanley Jevons called Cantillon's *Essai* the first treatise on economics and its author – the historian of economic thought. Charles Gide considered it the first clearly mapped work on political economy. Over a century later the famous Austrian economist F. A. Hayek called it the first work of what we now call economics. Among other things Cantillon provided the first sophisticated modern analysis of market pricing. He was also the first to propose the importance of an entrepreneur. Although some economic historians believe that Adam Smith received more praise than he deserved, and economic writers before him dealt with price and introduced the concept of laissez-faire, most maintain that Smith was an intellectual giant and the founder of modern economics.

Smith was a Scottish moral philosopher and pioneer in the study of political economy. He studied social philosophy at the University of Glasgow and the University of Oxford. He was considered a key figure of the Scottish enlightenment. He published *The Theory of Moral Sentiments* while a professor at Glasgow, and then published *An Inquiry into the Nature and Causes of the Wealth of Nations*, usually abbreviated as *The Wealth of Nations*. Smith spent ten years writing his magnum opus, the first modern economics book according to most economists.

Prior to the industrial revolution mankind struggled to maintain a subsistence lifestyle. Existence consisted of starvation, disease and war for all but those born to privilege. This situation remained unchanged for hundreds of years. With the enlightenment a new industrial dawn arrived where workers could earn sufficient wages to eat and clothe their families. Wages, which had been stagnant for hundreds of years, began to rise. Smith's *Wealth of Nations* ignited the world. But most important, his treatise on markets, trade, and wages, as well as other topics provided a guide to economic growth and independence. That year the United States signed the *Declaration of Independence*, which was influenced by the economic philosopher John Locke (1632-1704). Smith also influenced numerous leaders of the American Revolution.

Smith was seeking a guide to "universal prosperity", not utopia. He called his framework the "system of natural liberty". It is ironic that Sir Isaac Newton inspired Smith, just as Albert Einstein inspired John Maynard Keynes. *The Wealth of Nations* was a huge blow to mercantilism – an economic model that kept continental Europe and, of course England, in poverty.

Mercantilism viewed commerce as a "zero sum game" where only one nation could grow at the expense of another. Since wealth was viewed as constant, a pie of fixed size to divide, wealth could only increase for one nation by exploiting mankind through slavery and war. The concept of increasing the size of the pie was inconceivable. Smith clearly understood that the tariffs, duties, and the quotas of mercantilism restrained trade, which restrained production and, in turn, economic growth. Mercantilism only benefited monopolists, rulers and those who owned the means of production. But even they were restrained by the system. His message was clear, "if a foreign country can supply us with a commodity cheaper than we ourselves can make it, better it of them." Smith understood that the key to prosperity was production and exchange. J. B. Say clearly understood the importance of production also, – we will visit Say later.

One of Smith's great contributions to economic thought and the industrial revolution was "the division of labour". I have provided an excerpt from the Wealth of Nations, which describes his famous analysis of the pin factory and the division of labor. I have also included this because it demonstrates the clarity of Smith's writings and thought:

> To take an example, therefore, from a very trifling manufacture; but one in which the division of labour has been very often taken notice of, the trade of the pin-maker; a workman not educated to this business (which the division of labour has rendered a distinct trade), nor acquainted with the use of the machinery employed in it (to the invention of which the same division of labour has probably given occasion), could scarce, perhaps, with his utmost industry, make one pin in a day, and certainly could not make twenty. But in the way, in which this business is now carried on, not only the whole work is a peculiar trade, but it is divided into a number of branches, of which the

greater parts are likewise peculiar trades. One man draws out the wire, another straights it, a third cuts it, a fourth points it, a fifth grinds it at the top for receiving the head; to make the head requires two or three distinct operations; to put it on is a peculiar business, to whiten the pins is another; it is even a trade by itself to put them into the paper; and the important business of making a pin is, in this manner, divided into about eighteen distinct operations, which, in some manufactories, are all performed by distinct hands, though in others the same man will sometimes perform two or three of them. I have seen a small manufactory of this kind where ten men only were employed, and where some of them consequently performed two or three distinct operations. But though they were very poor, and therefore but indifferently accommodated with the necessary machinery, they could, when they exerted themselves, make among them about twelve pounds of pins in a day. There are in a pound upwards of four thousand pins of a middling size. Those ten persons, therefore, could make among them upwards of forty-eight thousand pins in a day. Each person, therefore, making a tenth part of forty-eight thousand pins, might be considered as making four thousand eight hundred pins in a day. But if they had all wrought separately and independently, and without any of them having been educated to this peculiar business, they certainly could not each of them have made twenty, perhaps not one pin in a day; that is, certainly, not the two hundred and fortieth, perhaps not the four thousand eight hundredth part of what they are at present capable of performing, in consequence of a proper division and combination of their different operations. [2]

The division of labor – specialization – is the cornerstone of manufacturing today, as well as a key to decision making. If an enterprise has a financial problem, it is not resolved by a plant manager, but by a financial officer. In a successful enterprise experts are nurtured. In all endeavors we want the best-qualified person to handle the task or to make the decision. Adam Smith's concept of specialization and comparative advantage is not restricted to the factory floor. In today's world schools of business teach the importance of group decision making as a tool to problem solving. Although this concept is frequently appropriate, it is often misguided. For example, if a large jar of coins is placed in the front of a classroom the mathematical average of the class

[2] Smith, Adam. (1991, original 1776), *The Wealth of Nations*. Page 4.

will be closer to the actual result than any individual result. However, if a solution to a mathematical problem is required, the best mathematics student should always be selected. Managers that rely on consensus decision making become hostage to the least competent team member. Alternatively, if a majority decision is required, the manager is forced to seek a decision that embodies the lowest common denominator. In each of the two aforementioned decisions the result was suboptimal when compared to seeking the advice of an unbiased expert, a specialist. A superior Chief Executive Officer can be worth his weight in gold. There is no substitute for knowledge, intelligence and insight for critical decisions. There is no substitute for leadership and decision making skills in guiding an enterprise. However, elected officials are typically the winners of a popularity contest. I am certain that the average IQ in the corporate boardroom is materially higher than the legislature of the United States.

In *The Wealth of Nations* we also realize that Smith was advocating a world of abundance and freedom, – not utopia, but the elimination of abject poverty through trade and free markets. Smith believed in "natural liberty", and he objected to government policies that impeded the right to work or the right to choose a profession. At that time government in many countries imposed licensing requirements or certification. He further argued against policies that restricted worker mobility and the right of the worker to charge a market wage. He understood that these policies inhibited economic growth and freedom. He understood that the elimination of import restrictions, as well as the restrictions on labor and prices, would initiate prosperity through lower prices and higher wages. In one of his most memorable statements he declares, "It is not from the benevolence of the butcher, the brewer, or the baker, that we expect our dinner, but from their regard to their own interest."

Frequently government impedes economic growth and the law of "unintended consequences" creates an additional set of problems. In the final decades of the twentieth century, the United States legislature created policies that enabled and encouraged the poor and others to buy homes they could *not* afford. The legislators were well intentioned, but they were *naïve* and lacked an understanding of *basic* economics. We must remember that the path to hell is paved with good intentions. Their action, along with an "easy money federal reserve policy", created a boom – bust cycle, misdirected capital flows, forced investment in unproductive activities, billions of dollars in losses, large scale unemployment and inhibited mobility which acerbated the unemployment problem. Since workers and professionals, alike, occupied homes they couldn't sell, they couldn't relocate, which caused a structural unemployment problem.

Smith was eccentric, as well as reclusive, and exemplified the "absent minded professor", but his vision was clear. Smith began *The Wealth of Nations* with a discussion of how wealth and prosperity are created from democratic free markets. His "classical model" was built on three points:

1. Freedom – individuals must have the right to produce and exchange products, labor, and capital;

2. Competition – individuals must have the right to compete in the production and exchange of goods and services;

3. Justice – the actions of individuals must be just and honest according to the rules of society.

In today's climate those successfully engaged in international business emulate Smith's thinking without knowing it. They understand that a nation in order to prosper must provide: free markets for trade and a judicial system to enforce the law. It is axiomatic that many poor nations remain poor because they do not provide these prerequisites for growth. Examine the difference between the living standards of North Korea and South Korea. Prior to the division of the country the Korean nation was one of the poorest nations in the world with a GDP per capita in line with the nations of sub-Saharan Africa. Today South Korea is prosperous while North Korea and the African states remain poor. South Korea flourished because it opened its borders and markets, and established a legal structure which protects private property and the rule of law. Also consider the difference in living standards between East Germany and West Germany prior to the collapse of the Berlin wall. The message is simple and so is the path to freedom and prosperity.

Smith's enlightened self-interest is frequently referred to as the "invisible hand." Smith's message is magnificent. The individual "intends only his own gain" but is "led by an invisible hand to promote an end which was not part of his intention." Smith only uses the term "invisible hand" once in the Wealth of Nations; nonetheless, the now famous term has come to represent free market capitalism. Many economists consider the invisible hand the epicenter of economics. The complete quotation follows:

> As every individual, therefore, endeavors as much as he can both to employ his capital in the support of domestic industry, and so to direct that industry that its produce may be of the greatest value; every individual necessarily labours to render the annual revenue of society as great as he can. He generally, indeed, neither intends to promote the public interest, nor knows how much he is promoting it. By preferring the support of domestic to that of foreign industry, he intends only his own security; and by directing that industry in such a manner as its produce may be of the greatest value, he intends only his own gain, and he is in this, as in many other cases, led by an invisible hand to promote an end which was no part of his intention. Nor is it always the worse for society that it was not part of it. By pursuing his own interest he frequently promotes that of the society more effectively than he really intends to promote it. I have never known much good done by those affected to trade for the public good. It is affection, indeed not very common among merchants, and very few words need be employed in dissuading them from it.[3]

Those who have not read Smith presume that Smith endorsed greed. That is *not* the case. Smith did not attend church, but believed that upon death there would be a final accounting. He always supported a system of natural liberty, which presumed moral values. He firmly maintained that all exchange must benefit both parties to a transaction and that the invisible hand only works among those that have a goal of continuous success. He knew that individuals of character realize that unfair practices undermine sound business practices and success. In this belief he may be viewed as a forerunner of "Pareto efficiency".[4] Smith also knew that monopoly distorts price and that competition is essential in a self-regulating society. The concept of a self-regulating society is a key

---

[3] Smith, Adam. (1991, original 1776), *The Wealth of Nations*. Page 399.

[4] Pareto efficiency or Pareto optimality is a concept in economics with applications in engineering and social sciences. The term is named after Vilfredo Pareto, an Italian economist who used the concept in his studies of economic efficiency and income distribution. Given an initial allocation of goods among a set of individuals, a change to a different allocation that makes at least one individual better off without making any other individual worse off is called a Pareto improvement. An allocation is defined as "Pareto efficient" or "Pareto optimal" when no further Pareto improvements can be made.

to maximizing growth and freedom for all of society, the rich and the poor, as we shall see later. Critics of capitalism argue that only the rich benefit from a free market system. They believe that the rich get richer and the poor get poorer. However research clearly demonstrates that this is not the case. The poor also get richer. If the published data does not convince you, carefully view the increased standard of living for all people over time in a free society.

Smith clearly understood that big government was inherently bad, driven by inefficiency and fueled by excessive taxation and hypocrisy, which undermine growth and freedom. His core beliefs laid the foundation for the classical model of economics: free markets, limited government, balanced budgets and sound money accompanied by thrift and hard work. This is quite different from the Keynesian model, which viewed saving as bad, government spending as good, and taxation as a social policy tool. Keynesian policy has led to budget deficits and the creation of welfare states that cannot sustain themselves. Greece in 2010 and 2011 is a primary example of Keynesian policy at work.

In order to understand the magnitude of Smith we must also view his stand on money and wages. In regard to money, Smith took the following position:

The sole use of money is to circulate consumable goods. By means of it, provisions, materials, and finished work, are bought and sold, and distributed to their proper consumers. The quantity of money, therefore, which can be annually employed in any country, must be determined by the value of the consumable goods annually circulated within it. These must consist either in the immediate produce of the land and labour of the country itself, or in some thing, which had been purchased with some part of that produce. Their value therefore must diminish as the value of that produce diminishes, along with it the quantity of money, which can be employed with circulating them. But the money, which by this annual diminution of produce is annually thrown out of domestic circulation, will not be allowed to lie idle. The interest of whoever possesses it requires that it should be employed. But having no employment at home, it will, in spite of all laws and prohibitions, be sent abroad, and employed in purchasing consumable goods, which may be of some use at home. Its annual exportation will in this manner continue for some time to add something to the annual consumption of the country beyond the value of its own annual produce.[5]

The foregoing, along with the following excerpt, lays the foundation for an early quantity theory of money. Smith continues (page 304) with this wonderful insight:

> The quantity of money, on the contrary, must in every country naturally increase as the value of the annual produce increases. The value of the consumable goods annually circulated within the society being greater will require a greater quantity of money to circulate them.

In order to demonstrate clearly the brilliance and clarity of Smith, particularly in comparison to Marx and Keynes, we must view Smith's views on wages, particularly when compared to the labour theory of value promulgated by Marx. Again I choose to quote Smith whose prose best conveys his mastery of expression:

> In that original state of things, which precedes both the appropriation of land and the accumulation of stock, the whole produce of labour belongs to the labourer. He has neither landlord nor master to share with him.[6]

> As soon as land becomes private property, the landlord demands a share of almost all the produce, which the labourer can either raise, or collect from it.[7]

This is in all likelihood a paragraph that influenced Marx, who spent most of his entire adult life in a library. From the perspective of Marx, private property denies the workingman the value of his labor. However, Smith continues and explains the symbiosis between landowner and labor:

> It seldom happens that the person who tills the ground has wherewithal to maintain himself till he reaps the harvest. His maintenance is generally advanced to him from the stock of a master, the farmer that employs him, and who would have no interest to employ him, unless he was to share in the produce of

---

[5] Smith, Adam. (1991, original 1776), *The Wealth of Nations*. Page 302.
[6] Smith, Adam. (1991, original 1776), *The Wealth of Nations*. Page 56.
[7] Smith, Adam. (1991, original 1776), *The Wealth of Nations*. Page 57.

his labour, or unless his stock was to be replaced by him with a profit.................. In all arts and manufactures the greater part of the workmen stand in need of a master to advance them the materials of their work, and their wages and maintenance till it be completed. He shares in the produce of their labour, or in the value, which it adds to the materials upon which it is bestowed; and in this share consists his profit. It sometimes happens, indeed, that a single independent workman has stock sufficient both to purchase the materials of his work, and to maintain himself till it be completed. He is both master and workman, and enjoys the whole produce of his own labour, or the whole value, which it adds to the materials upon which it is bestowed. It includes what are usually two distinct revenues, belonging to two distinct persons, the profits of stock, and the wages of labour.

Smith understood that this is not the rule but the exception; the landlord holds the upper hand because the landlord has capital to sustain himself and he can let the land remain fallow for a prolonged period of time. During this time it would be common for the landowners to agree among themselves to maintain a wage ceiling. In this perspective we see the foundation of tacit oligopoly, which Smith saw as unethical and immoral:

What are the common wages of labour depends everywhere upon the contract usually made between those two parties, whose interests are by no means the same. The workmen desire to get as much, the masters to give as little as possible. The former are disposed to combine in order to raise, the latter in order to lower the wages of labour.[8]

In order to bring the point to a speedy decision, they [the workmen] have always recourse to the loudest clamor, and sometimes to the most shocking violence and outrage. They are desperate, and act with the folly and extravagance of desperate men, who must either starve, or frighten their masters into an immediate compliance with their demands. The masters upon these occasions are just as clamorous upon the other side, and never cease to call aloud for the assistance of the civil magistrate, and the rigorous execution of those laws which have

---

[8] Smith, Adam. (1991, original 1776), *The Wealth of Nations.* Page 58.

been enacted with so much severity against the combinations of servants, labourers, and journeymen.[9]

At this point we can see the early communists and Marx sitting in the library with a vision of revolution led by the proletariat. Smith continues:

> A man must always live by his work, and his wages must be sufficient to maintain him. They must even upon most occasions be somewhat more; otherwise it would be impossible for him to bring up a family, and the race of such workman could not last beyond the first generation.

> ......The scarcity of hands occasions a competition among masters, who bid against one another, in order to get workmen, and thus voluntarily break through the natural combination of masters not to raise wages.......

> It is not the actual greatness of national wealth, but its continual increase, which occasions a rise in the wages of labour. It is not, accordingly, in the richest countries, but in the most thriving, or in those, which are growing rich the fastest, that the wages of labour are highest. England is certainly, in the present times, a much richer country than any part of North America. The wages of labour, however, are much higher in North America than in any part of England.[10]

Smith was well informed and had great insight. He recognized that wages in the early United States were much higher than in England. The wealth of the United States was found in many forms, but two proved critical: the Early Americans ate very well since there was an abundance of land for farming and raising livestock, as well as new types of fruits and vegetables. However the astonishing abundance of fish and timber was more than the English could envision. As a result, the output per capita was amazing and the well-fed workers were highly productive.

> But though North America is not yet so rich as England, it is much more thriving, and advancing with much greater rapidity to the further acquisition of riches. The most decisive mark of

---

[9] Smith, Adam. (1991, original 1776), *The Wealth of Nations*. Page 59.
[10] Smith, Adam. (1991, original 1776), *The Wealth of Nations*. Page 60.

the prosperity of any country is the increase of the number of its inhabitants….. Notwithstanding the great increase occasioned by such early marriages, there is a continual complaint of the scarcity of hands in North America. The demand for labourers, the funds destined for maintaining them, increase, it seems, still faster than they can find labourers to employ…..

The price of provisions is everywhere in North America much lower than in England.[11]

Advocates of free market policies have celebrated Smith as the founder of free markets, a view reflected in the naming of such bodies as the Adam Smith Institute, Adam Smith Society and the Australian Adam Smith Club. Also, Dr. George Stasen and Dr. Zviad Kliment Lazarashvili, contributors to this book, founded *The Laissez-faire Fraternity* in honor of Adam Smith. Alan Greenspan, a disciple of Ayn Rand and former Chairman of the Federal Reserve Bank of the United States of America maintains, "The wealth of Nations is one of the great achievements in human intellectual history. Smith has his detractors but his brilliance cannot be denied."

THE ERA OF KARL MARX

Since the publication of *Utopia* by Sir Thomas More (1478-1535) "the Worldly Philosophers"[12] have endeavored to conceive of a world without poverty. Karl Marx (1818-1883) was consumed with the economic disparity that existed between the owners of the means of production and those who laboured for them.

Classical economics after Adam Smith had a flaw. Smith went to great lengths to explain production and trade, but he did not address the nature of prices and how they were determined in the market place. The diamond / water paradox remained an enigma. This flaw served as kindling for the socialists and communists. Since they did not have an answer either, they concluded that "the market place" was immoral. The famous English political economist David Ricardo (1772-1823) – a follower of Smith's laissez-faire policies – added fuel to the socialist fire.

---

[11] Smith, Adam. (1991, original 1776), *The Wealth of Nations*. Page 62.
[12] The Worldly Philosophers – a term coined by an American economist and historian of economic thought, Robert Heilbroner (1919-2005), to describe the great minds of economics.

He proposed that limited resources would keep workers at subsistence levels. And in 1798 Thomas Malthus (1766-1834) – another follower of Smith's laissez-faire philosophy – published *Essays on Population*, which concluded that population would grow faster than the food supply, creating starvation. Ricardo and Malthus painted a dim picture, which helped to ameliorate Smith's optimism and expansion of wealth. Their view helped to form the notion that economics was "the dismal science".

Ricardo was a major contributor to economic thought and was seen as a financial economist. His reasoning was superb and he became very wealthy as a government securities trader. He developed "comparative advantage" and the "quantity theory of money", major achievements in the history of economic thought. He also contributed to the "labour theory of value" and other concepts, adopted by Marx. Ricardo's work provided Marx a legitimate stage.

Smith developed a model of economic growth, but Ricardo examined the division of wealth among the classes. Smith saw harmony where Ricardo saw conflict. Some economists believe that Ricardo, a securities broker, was blinded by his occupation. He understood money, but not how goods were produced or how an economy functioned. The same thing could be said today about government officials, most economists and the "wizards" of Wall Street.

1848 was an important year in the history of economic thought. It was the year of the "1848 rebellion" in Europe, the year *The Communist Manifesto* was published by Karl Marx (1818-1883) and Friedrich Engels (1820-1895) and the year the textbook *Principles of Political Economy* was published by the famous John Stuart Mill (1806-1873). Mill's publication dominated the western world for fifty years with amazing thirty-two editions. He was a major contributor to social and political theory, as well as political economy. However, Mill was a man of contradiction. He supported the freedom of individuals against the tyranny of the state, but questioned the validity of private property. He is best known for his famous libertarian book *On Liberty*. Mill's attack on wealth and private property provided another plank for the Marxian stage.

Karl Marx – Introduction

Karl Marx remains one of history's most influential scholars. His impact on history, philosophy, sociology and political economy has been profound. Karl Marx was a German of Jewish ancestry born May 5, 1818 in Trier, Prussia. His family converted to Christianity so that his father could practice law. However, Karl Marx became an atheist, which was essential to his ideology. He studied philosophy at universities in Bonn and Berlin, but transferred to Jena due to his radical views. Jena, unlike other universities, accepted his dissertation and awarded him his doctorate in Greek Philosophy. In 1843 Marx fled to Paris due to his radical views, but later returned to Germany to take part in the "1848 revolution". When the revolution failed he moved to London in 1849.

Two radical philosophers contributed to Marx' views while he was a university student; G. W. F. Hegel (1770-1831) and Ludwig Feuerbach (1804-1872). From Hegel Marx adopted "dialectical materialism", all human progress is achieved through conflict, and from Feuerbach he adopted the claim that man created God. Feuerbach also argued that worshipping God was a distraction from productive activities, which was another view that Marx adopted. From this Marx famously stated, "the philosophers have only interpreted the world, and the point is to change it."

Marx was prolific and brilliant rhetorician. And as all vain rhetoricians, he was also a deeply disturbed hypocrite whose life was full of contradiction and self-centered exploitation of those around him. He deeply loved his children, but two starved to death since he did not work and two committed suicide. These are details seldom found in print. He also fathered an illegitimate son, despite the love he professed for his wife and family. He was disturbed by the plight of the factory worker, but never set foot on a factory floor. He was preoccupied with money, but never held a real job. He berated exploitation but exploited everyone he knew. He cursed the bourgeoisie, but lived a bourgeoisie life style later in life with inherited money. Smith and Marx were polar opposites. Smith espoused free markets, while Marx sought to destroy them. To Marx Europe was a battlefield. War had to be waged between the wealthy bourgeoisie and the destitute proletariat. Marx was insane, as were many of his followers.

According to Marx, capitalism in Europe developed when peasants began to sell their labor and they became an alienated commodity because they did not own the land they worked. They became "proletarians", a term Marx invented. According to Marx, the buyers of labor became the capitalists; and the landowners, as well as the owners of machines, became the bourgeois.

Beliefs of Marx were expressed in his vast writings. In the *Economic and Political Manuscripts of 1844* he argued that the conditions of modern industrial societies alienated workers from their own labor. *On the Jewish Question* (1848) Marx attacked the influence of religion over politics and proposed a revolutionary restructuring of European society. Despite being Jewish by birth, Marx used anti-Semitic slurs against his enemies and accused Jews of worshipping money. He never renounced his anti-Semitic comments and is seen as an elitist and racist by many. In *The Communist Manifesto* (1848) Marx describes the class struggle that exists between the proletariat and bourgeoisie. Later Marx provided a complete explanation of his economic theories in his famous *Capital* (*Das Capital* 1867) and his *Theory of Surplus Value* (1862). Marx was viewed as a scholar of remarkable ability by many and the first to develop his own school of economic thought, even though it is universally accepted that his ideas lacked economic validity and he knew nothing of economics.

The Scholarship of Marx

In Paris Marx met his future colleague, Friedrich Engels. Engels was quite Teutonic in appearance, particularly when compared to Marx. He was also rich, his father was a wealthy German industrialist. Although Engels despised his father and everything his father represented, Engels became wealthy managing one of his father's enterprises in Manchester, England. Like Marx, Engels was a hypocrite. Despite Engels' vociferous pronouncements in support of the worker, he never tried to improve the working conditions of his factory. Engels was bright and he shared Marx' idealism and fervor. He was also a gifted manager of details and money, as well as a much better economist than Marx. As a result, he became Marx' compatriot, private banker, and he transformed Marx into a revolutionary communist.

Marx and Engels were commissioned by the London headquartered Communist League to write their famous *Communist Manifesto*. The following paragraph is from the introduction of the *Manifesto*:

With the exception of Great Britain most countries in Western Europe and Central Europe experienced some kind of revolutionary upheaval around the year 1848. (Two generations earlier the French Revolution had broken the old aristocratic order in France, but the effects of that revolution had been contained by the restoration of the Monarchy in 1814). Now Europe's disenfranchised classes – the peasants, parts of the bourgeoisie, and the proletariat – once more articulated their demands through strikes, mass demonstrations, and acts of resistance. This was the context in which Karl Marx and Friedrich Engels composed *der Kommunistischen Partei* (*Manifesto of the Communist Party*, mostly known as the *Communist Manifesto*) in 1847. It was first published in London in February 1848 only weeks before the outbreak of the first phase of the 1848 revolution in France, the so-called February Revolution. The primary purpose of the manifesto was to announce and publicize that the communists had given up on the conspiratorial activities of the past and were entering the scene of politics through an open declaration of principle.[13]

In the *Manifesto* Marx argued that capitalism, like previous systems would inevitably self-destruct due to internal tensions. He argued that just as capitalism replaced feudalism, socialism would replace capitalism, leading to a stateless society called pure communism.

Marx was a marvelous writer whose words stirred emotions. Consider these moving quotations from the *Communist Manifesto*:

A specter is haunting Europe – the specter of communism. All the Powers of Old Europe have entered into a holy alliance to exorcise this specter: Pope and Tsar, Metternich and Guizot, French Radicals and German Police Spies.[14]

The history of all hitherto existing society is the history of class struggles. Freeman and slave, patrician and plebeian, lord and serf, guild master and journeyman, in a word, oppressor and oppressed, stood in constant opposition to one another, carried on an uninterrupted, now hidden, now open fight, a fight that

---

[13] Marx, Karl and Engels, Friedrich. (2005, Original 1848). *The Communist Manifesto*. Barnes & Noble.
[14] Marx, Karl and Engels, Friedrich. (2005, Original 1848). *The Communist Manifesto*. Barnes & Noble. Page 5.

each time ended either in a revolutionary reconstitution of society at large or in the common ruin of the contending classes. In the earlier epochs of history we find almost everywhere a complicated arrangement of society into various orders, a manifold gradation of social rank. In ancient Rome we have patricians, knights, plebeians, slaves; in the Middle Ages, feudal lords, vassals, guild masters, journeymen, apprentices, serfs; in almost all of these classes, again, subordinate gradations. The modern bourgeois society that has sprouted from the ruins of feudal society has not done away with class antagonisms. It has but established new classes, new conditions of oppression, and new forms of struggle in place of the old ones.[15]

Let the ruling classes tremble at the communist revolution. The proletarians have nothing to lose but their chains. They have a world to win. Working men of all countries, unite.[16]

Like William Shakespeare, Marx invented his own vocabulary to make his point. He introduced: surplus value, bourgeoisie, proletarian, capitalism and monopoly capitalism. He was also responsible for labeling Laissez-faire the "Classical School".

Like most "intellectuals", Marx was very good at finding fault, but not solutions. The works of Marx and Engels contained very little about the "wonderful world" of communism, but extensively criticized capitalism.

To illustrate the clarity and appeal of the Manifesto I have provided an additional key section that describes the agenda of the communist movement:

These measures will of course be different in different countries. Nevertheless in the most advanced countries, the following will be pretty generally applicable:

1. Abolition of property in land and application of all rents of land to public purposes.

---

[15] Marx, Karl and Engels, Friedrich. (2005, Original 1848). *The Communist Manifesto*. Barnes & Noble. Page 7.
[16] Marx, Karl and Engels, Friedrich. (2005, Original 1848). *The Communist Manifesto*. Barnes & Noble. Page 41.

2. A heavy progressive or graduated income tax.

3. Abolition of all right of inheritance.

4. Confiscation of the property of all emigrants and rebels.

5. Centralization of credit in the hands of the State, by means of a national bank with State capital and an exclusive monopoly.

6. Centralization of the means of communication and transport in the hands of the State.

7. Extension of factories and instruments of production owned by the State; the bringing into cultivation of wastelands and the improvement of the soil generally in accordance with a common plan.

8. Equal liability of all to labor. Establishment of industrial armies, especially for agriculture.

9. Combination of agriculture with manufacturing industries; gradual abolition of the distinction between town and country by a more equable distribution of the population over the country.

10. Free education for all children in public schools. Abolition of children's factory labor in its present form. Combination of education with industrial production, etc. etc.

[NOTA BENE! The aforementioned agenda remains the agenda of the left – the "progressive" movement of the United States.]

When in the course of development class distinctions have disappeared and all production has been concentrated in the hands of a vast association of the whole nation, the public power will lose its political character.

In place of the old bourgeois society, with its classes and class antagonisms, we shall have an association in which the free development of each is the condition for the free development of all.[17]

By bourgeoisie is meant the class of modern Capitalists, owners of the means of social production and employers of wage labor. By proletariat, the class of modern wage-laborers who, having no means of production of their own, are reduced to selling their labor power in order to live [Engels' note, 1888].

As stated previously, after the failure of the workers' revolution, Marx moved to London permanently in 1849 with his wife and three children. He was 34 years old and for the next six years he and his family lived in squalor and poverty. Although he never worked, he did write a few articles for the New York Dailey and other newspapers. In London Marx devoted his energy to organizing revolutionary activities and spent years in the British Library trying to understand political economy and capitalism.

In 1856 his wife inherited money and Engels granted him an annuity. As a result of this largesse, Marx and his family lived a lavish Bourgeoisie lifestyle. He wrote Engels about making a killing speculating in London. This is ironic since a basic tenant of communism was abolishing the stock exchange. By 1857 he had prepared 800 pages of notes and short essays on capital, land, wage labour, the state, foreign trade and the world marketplace. This work did not appear in print until 1941. In 1859 he published *Contribution to the Critique of Political Economy*, his first significant work. And in 1867 he published *Das Kapital* (*Capital*). Marx completed the first of three volumes; Engels begrudgingly finished the last two volumes.

A Flawed Theory

"When I put a question to [Lenin] about socialism and agriculture, he explained with glee how he had incited the poorer peasants against the rich ones – and they soon hanged them from the nearest tree – ha!

---

[17] Marx, Karl and Engels, Friedrich. (2005, Original 1848). *The Communist Manifesto*. Barnes & Noble. Page 27-28.

ha! ha! – his guffaw at the thought of those massacred made my blood run cold."

Bertrand Russell (1872-1970)
– referring to a 1920 interview.

"It doesn't matter a jot if three-fourths of mankind perish! The only thing that matters is that, the remaining fourth should become communist."

Lenin (1870-1924)[18]

In his *Capital* Marx endeavors to offer an alternative to Adam Smith's classical economics. He saw capitalism as a flawed system that served the capitalists, the bourgeoisie and those that exploit the workers. He saw a system that would inevitably self-destruct. In order to save humanity, Marx proposed the revolutionary destruction of capitalism, to be replaced by the communist state.

According to Marx, the difference between the input costs and output prices was "surplus value", therefore the difference is between the subsistence wage for labour and the value of their output (profit). It is simple to transform capitalists into exploiters of labour intellectually, if all profits and interest are viewed as surplus value – theft from the working class. Marx continues his flawed reasoning by stating that the utilization of machinery, which increases output, increases the magnitude of exploitation. And according to Marx' convoluted and totally illogical mathematics, an increase in machinery drives down profits, which reduces wages and creates unemployment. He then sees large firms driving smaller capitalists out of business creating more unemployment, more devastation and deeper and more frequent cycles of economic collapse leading to the demise of capitalism. No one has ever found this to be true!

Although Marx believed that the rise of Communism was inevitable, he insisted that violent revolution was both, necessary and inevitable to assure the success of the communist transformation. Marx truly loved violence and killing. This appears to be a requirement for devout communists.

---

[18] Fulop-Miller, Rene. (1935). *Leaders, Dreamers and Rebels.*

It is a bit ironic that communism established its roots in agrarian societies, like Russia and China, as opposed to industrial societies as Marx predicted. Was it because they were societies held in check by mass agrarian deprivation or was it because Mao and Lenin were power hungry madmen who saw Marxism as a doctrine to subjugate the population and seize control. Lenin, Mao and others understood the power of their new god, Karl Marx.

As stated in the *Manifesto*, Marx was in favor of abolishing private property, which, in his mind, brought about slavery. Of course, if private property were abolished, all property would be owned by the state. As previously stated, Marx would also abolish the traditional family. It has become fashionable in the United States for those on the left to claim that it takes a village to raise a child. No! It takes two responsible parents to raise a child. Those that choose to leave that responsibility to the state should not have children, since the absence of love and family will assuredly doom children to jail. The consequences of the state raising children must have been the catalyst for the book *Brave New World*. Marx also required a Godless state. If God cannot exist, then everything must emanate from the state. Again we have the basis for the great books, *1984* and *Animal Farm*. Marx understood the power that could be obtained without God.

Despite Marx' pronouncements, capitalism is not self-destructive. It renews itself. In a capitalist society capital increases output per man-hour, which creates supply, which creates jobs, which creates wages, which creates demand, which creates profit, which creates capital.

Capital is the life-blood of enterprise. Capital for the purpose of expanding an enterprise is obtained through profit, a loan or the sale of equity (ownership) in the enterprise. Government does not provide permanent capital. Business and investors provide capital, they take risks. Profit, which is viewed with disdain by some members of the intellectual "elite", is the essential lifeblood of economy. Such "intellectuals" lack the knowledge or capacity to understand how an economy works or how jobs are created. For those that believe that nonprofit organizations serve the community more effectively than for-profit institutions, they should evaluate the efficiency and salaries of major charitable organizations, universities, hospitals, schools and numerous other organizations. Then ask why the cost of a college education in the United States has been growing faster than the rate of inflation for more than thirty years. Is the obscene cost of higher education in the US a form of social engineering, gross incompetence or both? Nonprofit institutions do *not* have to be efficient and, therefore, they waste resources. After all, they are not subject to taxation and they can solicit donations from the public to masquerade their ineptitude. Government hides its ineptitude by raising taxes. An inefficient enterprise or an enterprise that is not profitable will fail in a capitalist society. Therefore, resources are conserved. Failure is beneficial; it redirects capital towards a more productive purpose. The famous economist, Joseph Schumpeter (1883-1950) coined the term "creative destruction" to describe the way inefficient or unnecessary enterprise is destroyed and replaced with a better way of doing things. This is the great strength of capitalism.

In a communist or socialist state, antiquated industries may be supported by the state in order to maintain jobs, despite the fact that the enterprise may be arcane or inefficient. Since there is no price system or profit motive, the government may not realize that resources are being squandered or misdirected or may not care. In the former Soviet Union the Lada automobile was rolling junk, but without a free market to provide feedback or market for their currency the Soviets continued to support inefficiency. In a free market society, a country that cannot produce a good efficiently will import that good. Commencing in the 1970s the US began to import a substantial number of foreign automobiles, which adversely impacted market share for US automobile producers. However, the American consumer benefited. The American automobile industry was forced to provide a better quality vehicle at a lower price.

To paraphrase Adam Smith, the capitalist works in his own selfish interest and all of mankind benefits. Marx maintained that capital was "frozen" labor and that all of the proceeds of production should go to wages. As the mid-nineteenth century passed, the deficiencies of Ricardo and Marx became more apparent. Marx maintained that his theories were based on science and the laws of economics. However, neither the laws of science, nor economics supported his theories. The labor theory of value, a cornerstone of Marx' theories, was denounced by the community of economists. Gold is not valuable because men dig for it; men dig for it because it is valuable. Further undermining of Marx' theories was the "Transformation Problem". It was never resolved. Marx stated that capital equipment reduces surplus value (profit). Marx maintained that prices varied with labor time; therefore, in accord with his theory, capital-intensive industries should be less profitable than labor-intensive industries. However, that is not the case and research demonstrates that there is no direct relationship between the two variables. This was another nail in Marx' coffin, and the theory died. Apologists for Marx have tried to reconcile the "Transformation Problem", but they all failed. As clearly stated by the Austrian School of Economics, the application of capital raises wages and therefore gross output for a nation.

The first major economist to confront Marx' theories was the famous Austrian Eugen Bohm-Bawerk (1851-1914) in his *Capital and Interest*, which was published in 1884. His reasoning was so sound that Marx never regained the respect of the economics community. Bohm-Bawerk's attack on surplus value, the labor theory of value and exploitation theory was decisive. He was also among the first to point out that capitalists take risk that workers do not take, which creates opportunity.

In all of his writings Marx fails to say that capitalism is unjust or that communism is just. In fact, Marx avoids the discussion of morality or justice in any form. Upon its publication, *Capital* received mediocre reviews, but, through the efforts of Engels and other supporters, the book was kept alive. Originally only one thousand copies were printed. However, Engels had it published in Russian in 1872, where Vladimir Ilich Ulyanov, also known as V. I. Lenin, read it. Lenin became Marx' most ardent follower and kept Marx' name alive to the detriment of the rest of the world. Karl Marx and the communist movement caused human suffering on a scale beyond comprehension, ultimately bringing about the death of possibly 30 million people through followers such as Lenin, Mao, Pol Pot, and other psychopathic devotees.

In search of abundance the following nations at some point adhered to Marxist dogma: Albania, Afghanistan, Angola, Bulgaria, China, Cuba, Cyprus, Czechoslovakia, East Germany, Ethiopia, Hungary, Laos, Moldova, Mongolia, Nepal, Mozambique, Nicaragua, North Korea, Poland, Romania, the Soviet Union, Yugoslavia and Vietnam. In addition, the Indian States of Kerala, Tripura, and West Bengal have had Marxist Governments. In all of these nations food and freedom were scarce. This alone should prove the folly of socialism, central planning and progressive politics.

In London Marx continued to write about economics until his death in 1883. Only eleven people attended his funeral and upon his death he was almost forgotten.

With the collapse of the Soviet Union and other communist states, the theories of Marx and the role of central planning have moved to the trash bin of economic thought and Adam Smith's star again became bright in the heavens.

"Socialism in general has a record of failure so blatant that only an intellectual could ignore it".

Thomas Sowell
The great Economist and Social Scientist
From the University of Chicago

THE DAWN OF A NEW ERA

"Economic freedom is a necessary but not sufficient condition for political freedom.... Political freedom in turn is a necessary condition for the long term maintenance of economic freedom"

Milton Friedman[19]

Jean-Baptiste Say (1767-1832) established himself as a great economist and supporter of Adam Smith with the publication of his treatise on political economy, *Traite d'Economie Politque* (1803). His discourse supported Adam Smith's views with clarity and introduced the important role of the entrepreneur and market forces. Say also demonstrated that the division of labor requires capital to achieve specialization. He recognized that specialization is not limited to the factory but applied to all endeavors in society.

Say was born in France to a family of textile merchants and spent his early life in Geneva and then London, where he became an apprentice to a commercial enterprise. He then returned to Paris, employed by an insurance company, and later in life became a major force in

---

[19] The closing paragraph of *Free Markets and the Generals* by Milton Friedman.

manufacturing. Napoleon had banned Say from publishing the second edition of the *Traite*, but, with the fall of Napoleon in 1814, Say was able to publish it in 1819. Upon its successful publication, he became an acclaimed academic with prominent French academic institutions. In fact, Thomas Jefferson was so enamored by Say's works that he offered a professorship to Say at the newly established University of Virginia.

J. B. Say's thinking, particularly his "law of markets" – "supply (production) creates its own demand (consumption)" – became crucial to the foundation of classical economics. Simply stated, when something is produced, it is consumed, which creates jobs, which in turn creates spending. This is a sharp departure from Keynes who focused his energies on the importance consumption.

In America most jobs are created by small business. An entrepreneur invests capital and time in order to create a product or service that is hopefully purchased. The sale of the good initiates an economic event. We shall see that this is critical for economic growth in every country. Say stated: "it is the aim of good government to stimulate production, of bad government to encourage consumption." Keynes studied Say and knew that Say, who anointed the entrepreneur, had to be discredited if Keynes was going to assume the mantle of economic leadership.

Say, in contrast to Marx, understood that capital increased human productivity, which reduced the cost of production, which improved the product and improved the standard of living, which in turn removed the worker from a subsistence existence. This of course is diametrically opposed to the view held by Marx. Aside from "Say's Law", Say has not been provided the respect he deserves from the economic community. Critics argue that overproduction creates an economic glut, which we now call recession. The Keynesian solution for a glut is to reduce production, inflate the money supply and incur deficits to create consumption. This prescription does not necessarily cure the patient. It is at times analogous to giving the patient a stimulant when sleep and rest are required. This nostrum did not reverse the great depression or the recent *great* recession. To Say the solution was obvious. Allow prices to fall and the market will be cleared. Sometimes, time is needed. Say also understood that misperception and speculation add to the problem, which is another symptom of easy money and government interference. He understood that boom and bust cycles would occur. Did Say have a comprehensive solution for glut (recession)? He did not, nor has anyone else. Say's law became bastardized by his critics, particularly by John Maynard Keynes, whose criticism of Say became central to promoting his own theories. If Say is right, then Keynes was wrong. We believe that Say was right. Say never received the accolades he deserved. He remains however an intellectual giant.

The Marginalist Revolution

By the late 1800s the goal of economists was to transform the dismal science into a scientific discipline. Political economy was viewed as a branch of philosophy and law. To accomplish this goal they needed tools that produced precision. The chief tool-maker was the great Cambridge economics professor, Alfred Marshall (1842-1924). But he had help from other brilliant "worldly philosophers", William Stanley Jevons (1835-1882), Carl Menger (1840-1921), and Leon Walrus (1834-1910).

Marshall's first impact was naming his textbook "Principles of Economics", not Political Economy. His unique 1890 publication introduced supply and demand curves, elasticity of demand, markets, production, money, credit, trade, diminishing marginal utility, price theory, cost of production, and other concepts including the use of advanced mathematics. He also included a brief history of economic thought. It was a marvelous textbook that made a major contribution to economics.

Marshall's predecessor, William Jevons was a cornerstone of the "Marginalist Revolution" – introducing graphical and mathematical presentations of marginal utility theory. Jevons realized that utility theory represented a major contribution to economics and the theory of demand, and it would replace the labor theory of value promulgated by Ricardo and Marx. In *A General Mathematical Theory of Political Economy*, a minor paper he published in 1863 and in *The Theory of Political Economy*, published in 1871, Jevons concluded that value depends entirely on utility. Menger, working independently, reached a similar conclusion and is considered a cofounder of the marginal utility revolution and founder of the Austrian school of economics. The famous Leon Walras was also a leading scholar of the marginalist revolution. Strangely, Walras did not know Jevons and Menger, and developed his theories independently.

The introduction of utility theory to economics was as important as Newton's introduction of calculus to physics. With diminishing marginal utility theory, the paradox of water and diamonds was explained. Water is abundant and its marginal utility is low. Diamonds are scarce and, hence, the marginal utility is high. As a result, "ceteris paribus", all things being equal, diamonds are more valuable than water.

For example, the fourth Burger King cheeseburger consumed has less marginal utility than the first one consumed. But if the price is low enough or reduced, you may nonetheless consume one more cheeseburger. However, this may result, in an increase in the marginal utility of a doctor's visit.

As the study of economics expanded beyond market theory to include distribution theory, an American, John Bates Clark (1847-1938) made a major contribution to economics. In his work, *The Distribution of Wealth* (1899), Clark argued that each factor of production – Land, Labor, and Capital – is paid according to the value added to the total revenue of the product; thereby creating "Marginal Product". Each factor gets what it creates. This subsequently became an essential component to economic theory.

However, a key factor was missing if economics was going to address the expanding and changing climate of the twentieth century. A theory of money was needed, and the famous Yale Professor, Irving Fisher (1867-1947) would fill the void. Fisher devoted his life to the study of money and credit and became the founder of the "Monetarist" School of Economics. Among his many contributions to economics, Fisher developed the Quantity Theory of Money from the equation of exchange. In his famous presentation $MV=PT$, M represents the quantity of money in circulation, V represents the velocity of money, P represents the annual price level and T represents the total number of transactions during the year. Since V and T remain largely stable, then changes in the money supply M must account for changes in the price level P. This remains a foundation of monetary theory.

Fisher is a reminder of one of the many definitions of an economist, "Someone who knows everything there is to know about money but does not have any". Fisher lost all of his money in the stock market crash of 1929-1933. His theory, although brilliant, was incomplete. He did not anticipate the ensuing economic crisis. He focused on price levels and not the monetary aggregates and the ineptitude of the new Federal Reserve Bank and the government.

However, not everyone was surprised by the economic collapse. The prescience pundits were the famous "Austrian School Economists" Ludwig von Mises (1881-1973) and Friedrich Hayek (1899-1992). They understood that the prevailing easy money policies in the US were a precursor to a boom and bust cycle. When their wisdom became obvious, the world came to their door to learn from the new masters of the dismal science. They, along with Milton Friedman (1912-2006) of the University of Chicago, were the greatest economists of the twentieth century.

THE GREAT DEPRESSION: A CROSSROAD IN ECONOMIC POLICY

The Great Depression of the 1930s was as important to the world of economics, as Einstein's "Theory of Relativity" was to the world of physics. It altered the state of the universe and created an opportunity for the famous John Maynard Keynes (1883-1946), a student of Alfred Marshall. Although Marshall recognized that Keynes was brilliant, he did not view him as a brilliant economist.

In the 1930s Keynes led a revolution in economic thinking which was adopted by main stream American economists. He maintained that aggregate demand determined the overall level of economic activity and that insufficient aggregate demand led to prolonged unemployment. After World War II the "western nations" adopted the "Keynesian" approach to economic policy. It is important to note that during the 1930s capitalism was at a crossroad. The perceived failure of capitalism provided the American Socialist and the American Communist movements with an opportunity to denounce capitalism. As a result, Marxism, which had been dismissed by the economic community, had new followers. Needless to say they had no understanding of basic economics or enterprise. The left and "progressives", who had supported Marxist dogma, found an opportunity to resurrect their false messiah. It is important to recognize, that Hitler and Mussolini were influenced by the communist movement and their henchmen were former communists. They believed in "National Socialism." They were a movement of the left and not the right, as portrayed by the left, academia and the media. The left was busy hiding the atrocities of the Soviet Russia and didn't want another stain on their mask. A movement of the right would have sought less government and more liberty and not an authoritarian regime. Like Stalin, Hitler was a godless mass murderer on a mission of ethnic cleansing. Hitler and Stalin had more in common than generally acknowledged

In the United States the stock market declined eighty five percent, the national output declined by thirty percent and the unemployment rate climbed to twenty five percent. This also contributed to the abysmal economic and political conditions in Europe and the Great Britain. In the United States, numerous books and the media frequently cite the stock market crash as the cause of the great depression. That is clearly not the case and there is no conclusive evidence to support that view. This is a myth of the left and government. The stock market was merely reflecting economic reality. The depression was caused by government ineptitude, government interference, the Smoot-Hawley Tariff Act and the disastrous performance of the newly formed Federal Reserve System (The Central Bank of the United States). However, new research establishes the President of the United States, Franklin Delano Roosevelt (FDR) as the focal point of the carnage.

As previously stated, the Brilliant Austrians, Von Misses and Hayek and others anticipated the crisis. But Keynes, according to Keynes, had the right medicine. Faced with despair people will take any medicine. The medicine of Germany was Adolph Hitler. Hitler did create full employment in Germany, and it was World War II that created full employment in the United States. Contrary to popular belief, WWII did not end the depression in the US. The depression ended after WWII. The War and war time controls masked the continuing economic malaise. Hayek and von Misses believed in orthodox neoclassical solutions, such as market induced wage and price reduction, a reduction in taxes, and a reduction in government interference. This remedy was considered insufficient for the "Great Depression" according to the government, Keynes and Roosevelt. However, the classical solutions did serve the nation well in the previous century.

The Great Depression

"The great threat to freedom is the concentration of power".

> Milton Friedman
> Introduction
> *Capitalism and Freedom.*

In order to understand Keynes and his times, we must revisit the history and chronology of the great depression.

The following excerpt is from "The Forgotten Man", – a nationally acclaimed work by Amity Shlaes. Amity Shlaes is a senior fellow in economic history at the Council on Foreign Relations and a syndicated columnist for Bloomberg – Business & Financial News. She has written for the *Financial Times* and the *Wall Street Journal*, where she is an editorial board member.

The book is a marvelous treatise on what the "New Deal" did and did not accomplish. The book was published by Harper in 2007. This excerpt is from pages 3 to 14, the introduction to the book:

> The standard history of the Great Depression is one we know. The 1920s were a period of false growth and low morals. There was certain godlessness – the Great Gatsby image – to the decade. The crash was the honest acknowledgment of the breakdown of capitalism and the cause of the Depression. A dangerous inflation caused by speculating margin traders brought down the nation. There was a sense of a return to a sane, moral country with the crash. A sense that the economy of 1930 or 1931 could not revive without extensive intervention by Washington. Hoover, it was said, made matters worse through his obdurate refusal to take control, his risible commitment to what he called rugged individualism. Roosevelt, however, made things better by taking charge. His New Deal inspired and tided the country over. In this way, the country fended off revolution of the sort bringing down Europe. Without the New Deal, we would all have been lost.

> The same history teaches that the New Deal was the period in which Americans learned that government spending was

important to recoveries; and that the consumer alone can solve the problem of "excess capacity" on the producer's side. This explanation acknowledges that the New Deal did not bring the country to recovery fast, but emphasizes that the country got there eventually—especially with the boost of military spending in the late 1930s. The attitude is that the New Deal is the best model we have for what government must do for weak members of society, in both times of crisis and times of stability. And that the New Deal gave us splendid leaders and characters: Roosevelt himself, a crippled man who bravely willed us all back into prosperity and has been called the apostle of abundance. The brain trust, thoughtful men whose insights validated their experiments. The Hundred Days—that period at the start of his first term when Roosevelt legislated unprecedented reforms—was a thrilling period. From Adolf Berle, the expert on corporations to Frances Perkins, the pioneering social reformer, to Tugwell, the New Dealers displayed a sort of dynamism from which today's moribund politicians might learn.

Without the New Deal, the country would have followed a demagogue, Huey Long, or worse, Father Coughlin. The rightness of Roosevelt's positions was only validated by what followed; FDR saved the country in peace, and then he saved it in war. *Or so the story line goes.*

The usual rebuttal to this from the right is that Hoover was a good man, albeit misunderstood, and Roosevelt a dangerous, even an evil one. The stock market of the 1920s was indeed immoral, too high, and inflationary—and deserved to crash. Many critics on the right focus on monetary policy. Another set of critics focuses on Roosevelt's early social programs. They argue that New Deal programs such as the Works Progress Administration of the Civilian Conservation Corps spoiled the United States and accustomed Americans to the pernicious dole. Yet a third set of critics, an angry fringe, has argued that Roosevelt's brain trusters reported to Moscow. Stalin steered the New Deal and also pulled us into World War II, in their argument. For many years, now, these have been the parameters of the debate.

It is time to revisit the late 1920s and the 1930s. Then we see that neither the standard history nor the standard rebuttal entirely captures the realities of the period. The first reality was that the 1920s was a great decade of true economic gains, a period whose strong positive aspects have been obscured by the troubles that followed. Those who placed their faith in laissez-faire in that decade were not all godless. Indeed religious piety moved some, including President Calvin Coolidge, to hold back, to pause before intervening in private lives.

The fact that the stock market rose high at the end of the decade does not mean that all the growth of the preceding ten years was an illusion. American capitalism did not break in 1929. *The crash did not cause the Depression.* It was a necessary correction of a too-high stock market, but not a necessary disaster. The market players at the time of the crash were not villains, though some of them – Albert Wiggin of Chase, who shorted his own bank's stock – behaved reprehensibly. There was indeed an annihilating event that followed the crash, one that Hoover never understood and Roosevelt understood incompletely; deflation.

Hoover's priggish temperament, as much as any philosophy he held, caused him to both misjudge the crash and fail in his reaction to it. And his preference for Germany as a negotiating partner over Soviet Russia later blinded him to the dangers of Nazism. Roosevelt by contrast had a wonderful temperament, and could get along, when he felt like it, with even his worst opponent. His calls for courage, his Fireside Chats, all were intensely important. "The only thing we have to fear is fear itself" – in the darkness, Roosevelt's voice seemed to shine. He allowed Cordell Hull to write trade treaties that in the end would benefit the U.S. economy enormously. Roosevelt's dislike of Germany, which dated from childhood, helped him to understand the threat of Hitler and, eventually, that the United States must come to Europe's side.

Still, Hoover and Roosevelt were alike in several regards. Both preferred to control events and people. Both underestimated the strength of the American economy. Both doubted its ability to right itself in a storm. Hoover mistrusted the stock market. Roosevelt mistrusted it more. Roosevelt offered rhetorical optimism, but pessimism underlay his policies. Though Americans associated Roosevelt with bounty, his insistent emphasis on sharing – rationing, almost – betrayed a conviction that the country had entered a permanent era of scarcity. Both presidents overestimated the value of government planning. Hoover, the Quaker, favored the community over the individual. Roosevelt, the Episcopalian, found laissez-faire economics immoral and disturbingly un-Christian.

And both men doctored the economy habitually. Hoover was a constitutionalist and took pains to intervene within the rules – but his interventions were substantial. Roosevelt cared little for constitutional niceties and believed they blocked progress. His remedies were on a greater scale and often inspired by socialist or fascist models abroad. A number of New Dealers, Tugwell included, had been profoundly shaped by Mussolini's Italy and, especially, Soviet Russia. That influence was not parenthetical. The hoarse-voiced opponents of the New Deal liked to focus on the connections between these men, the Communist Party, and authorities in Soviet Russia. And several important New Dealers did indeed have those connections, most notably Lauchlin Currie, Roosevelt's economics adviser in later years, and Harry Dexter White, at the Treasury. White's plan for the pastoralization of Germany takes on a new light when we know this. Lee Pressman and Alger Hiss duped colleagues in government repeatedly.

But few New Dealers were spies or even communists. The emphasis on that question is in any case misplaced. Overall, the problem of the New Dealers on the left was not their relationship with Moscow or the Communist Party in the United States, if indeed they had one. Senator McCarthy was wrong. The problem was their naïveté about the economic value of Soviet-style or European-style collectivism – and the fact that they forced such collectivism upon their own country. Fear of being labeled a red-baiter has too long prevented historians from looking into the Soviet influence upon American domestic policy in the 1930s.

What then caused the Depression? Part of the trouble was indeed the crash. There were monetary and credit challenges at the young Federal Reserve, and certainly at the banks. Deflation, not inflation, was a big problem, both early on and also later, in the mid-1930s. The loss of international trade played an enormous role—just as both Hoover and Roosevelt said at different point. If the United States had not raised tariffs at the beginning of the decade and Europe had not collapsed in the 1930s, the United States would have had a trading partner to help sustain it. Part of the problem was the challenge of the transition to industrialization from agriculture. Part was freakish weather: floods and the uncanny Dust Bowl seemed to validate the sense of apocalypse. With money and the weather breaking down, men and women in America felt extraordinarily helpless. They were willing to suspend disbelief.

But the deepest problem was the intervention, the lack of faith in the marketplace. Government management of the late 1920s and 1930s hurt the economy. Both Hoover and Roosevelt misstepped in a number of ways. Hoover ordered wages up when they wanted to go down. He allowed a disastrous tariff, Smoot-Hawley, to become law when he should have had the sense to block it. He raised taxes when neither citizens individually nor the economy as a whole could afford the change. After 1932, New Zealand, Japan, Greece, Romania, Chile, Denmark, Finland, and Sweden began seeing industrial production levels rise again—but not the United States.

Roosevelt's errors had a different quality but were equally devastating. He created regulatory, aid, and relief agencies based on the premise that recovery could be achieved only through a large military-style effort. Some of these were useful – the financial institutions he established upon entering office. Some were inspiring – the Civilian Conservation Corps, for example, which created parks, bridges, and roads we still enjoy today. From Wyoming, whose every county saw the introduction of projects, including the dramatic Guernsey State Park, to Greenville, Maine, whose CCC Road still bears the program's name today, the CCC heartened young Americans and found a place in national memory. CCC workers planted a total of three billion trees across the country. Establishing the Securities and Exchange Commission, enacting banking reform – as well as the reform of the Federal Reserve System – all had a stabilizing effect. Roosevelt's desire to control tariff law worked to the benefit of the economy, for, through Cordell Hull, he undid some of the damage of the Smoot-Hawley tariff.

Other new institutions, such as the National Recovery Administration, did damage. The NRA's mandate mistook macroeconomic problems for micro problems – it sought to solve the monetary challenge through price setting. NRA rules were so stringent they perversely hurt businesses. They frightened away capital, and they discouraged employers from hiring workers. Another problem was laws like that which created the NRA – and Roosevelt signed a number of them – were so broad that no one knew how they would be interpreted. The resulting hesitation in itself arrested growth.

Where the private sector could help to bring the economy back – in the arena of utilities, for example – Roosevelt and his New Dealers often suppressed it. The creation of the Tennessee Valley Authority snuffed out a growing – and potentially successful – effort to light up the South. The company that would have delivered that electricity was Willkie's company, Commonwealth and Southern. The *New Yorker* magazine's cartoons of the plump, terrified Wall Streeter were accurate; business was terrified of the president. But the cartoons did not depict the consequences of that intimidation: that business decided to wait Roosevelt out, hold on to their cash, and invest in future years. Yet Roosevelt retaliated by introducing a tax – the undistributed profits tax – to press the money out of them.

Such forays prevented recovery and took the country into the depression within the Depression of 1937 and 1938, the one in which William Troeller died and Willkie worried. One of the most famous Roosevelt phrases in history, almost as famous as "fear itself," was Roosevelt's boast that he would promulgate "bold, persistent experimentation." But Roosevelt's commitment to experimentation itself created fear. And many Americans knew this at the time. In autumn 1937, the *New York Times* delivered its analysis of the economy's downturn: "The cause is attributed by some to taxation and alleged federal curbs on industry; by others, to the demoralization of production caused by strikes." Both the taxes and the strikes were the result of Roosevelt policy; the strikes had been made possible by the Wagner Act the year before. As scholars have long noted, the high wages generated by New Deal legislation helped those workers who earned them. But the inflexibility of those wagers also prevented companies from hiring additional workers.

Hence, the persistent shortage of jobs in the latter part of the 1930s. New Deal laws themselves contributed to the sense of lost opportunity. This sense is what led to the famous description of the period that we have all heard – "the Depression was not so bad if you had a job." John Steinbeck described the same sense of futility more poetically in 1945 in *The Red Pony*: "No place to go, Jody. Every place is taken. But that's not the worst – no, not the worst. Westering had died out of the people. Westering isn't a hunger any more. It's all done." The trouble, however, was not merely the new policies that were implemented but also the threat of additional, unknown, policies. Fear froze the economy, but that uncertainty itself might have a cost was something the young experimenters simply did not consider.

The big question about the American depression is not whether war with Germany and Japan ended it. It is why the Depression lasted until that war. From 1929 to 1940, from Hoover to Roosevelt, government intervention helped to make the Depression Great. The period was not one of a moral battle between a force for good – the Roosevelt presidency – and forces for evil, those who opposed Roosevelt. It was a period of a power struggle between two sectors of the economy, both containing a mix of evil and virtue. The public sector and the private sector competed relentlessly for advantage. At the beginning, in the 1920s, the private sector ruled. By the end, when World War II began, it was the public sector that was dominant.

The contest was a brutal one, fought across the land, through famines and floods, and in a Washington that knew neither air-conditioning nor angiograms. Roosevelt was clear about it. As he put in his second inaugural address, he sought "unimagined power." He, his advisers, and his congressional allies instinctively targeted monetary control, utilities, and taxation because they were the three sources of revenue whose control would enlarge the public sector the most. Since the private sector – even during the Great Depression – was the key to sustained recovery, such bids did enormous damage. Today we even have an economic theory, public choice economics, which sheds light on this. Public choice economics says that government is not higher than the private sector but rather a coequal combatant. Public choice theory tells us as much about the New Deal as the traditional economics Americans have been taught.

This particular school postdates the Depression, but the notion that something destructive was going on was evident, even to Roosevelt's allies. A number of them tried to articulate the problem. Ray Moley and Tugwell, two of Roosevelt's original brain trusters, dedicated years to grappling with the hypocrisy and damage of Roosevelt's actions. Wendell Willkie, at first a Democrat and enthusiastic reformer, would demonstrate that the contest between the TVA and his Commonwealth and Southern was not merely about electric power but also about control of the American future.

There remains a question. If so much of the New Deal hurt the economy, why did Roosevelt win reelection three times? Why, especially, the landslide of 1936? In the case of the third and fourth Roosevelt terms the answer is clear: the threat of war, and war itself. Roosevelt, unlike his narrow-minded Republican opponents, understood the dangers that Nazi Germany represented. In 1936, however, the reason for victory was different.

That year Roosevelt won because he created a new kind of interest-group politics. The idea that Americans might form a political group that demanded something from government was well known and thoroughly reported a century earlier by Alexis de Tocqueville. The idea that such groups might find mainstream parties to support them was not novel either: Republicans, including the Harding and Coolidge administrations, had long practiced interest-group politics on behalf of big business. But Roosevelt systematized interest-group politics more generally to include many constituencies – labor, senior citizens, farmers, union workers. The president made groups where only individual citizens or isolated cranks had stood before, ministered to those groups, and was rewarded with votes. It is no coincidence that the first peace-time year in American history in which federal spending outpaced the total spending of the states and towns was that election year of 1936. It can even be argued that one year – 1936 – created the modern entitlement challenge that so bedevils both parties only.

Roosevelt's move was so profound that it changed the English language. Before the 1930s, the word "liberal" stood for the individual; afterward, the phrase increasingly stood for groups. Roosevelt also changed economics forever. Roosevelt happened on an economic theory that validated his politics and his moral sense: what we now call Keynesians. *Keynesians, named after John Maynard Keynes, emphasized consumers, who were also voters. The theory gave license for perpetual experimentation – at least as Roosevelt and his administration applied it.*

Keynesianism also emphasized government spending. Yet focusing on consumers meant that Washington neglected the producer. Focusing on the fun of experiments neglected the question of whether unceasing experimentation might frighten business into terrified inaction. Admiring the short-term action of spending drew attention away from its longer-term limits – economies often go into recession when the spending disappears. Supplying generous capital to government made government into a competitor that the private sector could not match. Keynesians provided the intellectual justification and the creation of constituencies.

Too much attention has been paid to what political polls said about the New Deal. Too little has been paid to two other measures, both also polls, in their way. One was the unemployment rate, which did not return to precrash levels until the war. The other was the stock market. It told a heartbreaking story. Uncertainty about what to expect from international events and Washington made the Dow Jones Industrial Average gyrate, both daily and over longer periods, in a fashion not repeated through the rest of the century: seven out of the ten biggest "up" days of the twentieth century took place in the 1930s. The uncertainty made Americans doubt themselves as investors. The Dow did not return to 1929 levels until nearly a decade after Roosevelt's death. The goodwill of the New Dealers, and there was enormous goodwill, could not excuse such consequences.

About half a century before the Depression, a Yale philosopher named William Graham Sumner penned a lecture against the progressives of his own day and in defense of classical liberalism. The lecture eventually become an essay, titled "The Forgotten Man." Applying his own elegant algebra of politics, Sumner warned that well-intentioned social progressives often coerced unwitting average citizens into funding dubious social projects. Sumner wrote:

"As soon as A observes something which seems to him to be wrong, from which X is suffering, A talks it over with B, and A and B then propose to get a law passed to remedy the evil and help X. Their law always proposes to determine…what A, B, and C shall do for X." But what about C? There was nothing wrong with A and B helping X. What was wrong was the law, and the indenturing of C to the cause. C was the forgotten man, the man who paid, "the man who never is thought of."

In 1932, a member of Roosevelt's brain trust, Ray Moley, recalled the phrase, although not its provenance. He inserted it into the candidate's first great speech. If elected, Roosevelt promised, he would act in the name of "the forgotten man at the bottom of the economic pyramid." Whereas C had been Sumner's forgotten man, the New Deal made X the forgotten man—the poor man, the old man, labor, or any other recipient of government help.

Roosevelt's work on behalf of his version of the forgotten man generated a new tradition. To justify giving to one forgotten man, the administration found, it had to make a scapegoat of another. Businessmen and businesses were the targets. Roosevelt's old mentor, the Democrat Al Smith, was furious. Even Keynes was concerned. In 1938 he wrote to Roosevelt advising him to nationalize utilities or leave them alone—but in any case cease his periodic and politicized attacks on them. Keynes saw no point "in chasing utilities around the lot every other week." Roosevelt and his staff were becoming habitual bullies, pitting Americans against one another. The polarization made the Depression feel worse. Franklin Roosevelt's forgotten man, the constituent X, perpetually tangled with Sumner's original forgotten man, C.

Among the people whom the New Deal forgot and hurt were great and small names. The great casualties included the Alan Greenspan figure of the era, Andrew Mellon, treasury secretary for the Harding, Coolidge, and Hoover administrations—a figure so towering it was said that "three presidents served under him." Another was Samuel Insull, a utilities magnate and innovator to whom the New Dealers assigned the blame for the crash. Yet another was James Warburg, a Roosevelt adviser who became so angry with the president that he penned book after book to express his range. George Sutherland and James McReynolds, two of the four justices on the Supreme Court who fought back against Roosevelt, were also important. It was Willkie who spoke out most explicitly for the forgotten man on the national stage.

Others were of humbler background: those farmers who found themselves forced to kill off their piglets in a time of hunger because FDR's Agricultural Adjustment Administration ordained they must; a family of kosher butchers named Schechter who believed in Roosevelt but fought the New Deal all the way to the Supreme Court; a black cult leader named Father Divine; Will W., the founder of Alcoholics Anonymous, who taught Americans that the solution to their troubles lay not with a federal program but within a new sort of entity – the self – help community.

Of course the Hoover and Roosevelt administrations may have had no choice but to pursue the policies that they did. They may indeed have spared the country something worse – an American version of Stalin's communism, or Mussolini's fascism. That is the position that author Sinclair Lewis was taking when, in 1935, he published It Can't Happen Here, a fantasy version of the United States under fascist leaders remarkably similar to Roosevelt's opponents. The argument that democracy would have failed in the United States without the New Deal stood for seven decades, and has been made anew, by scholars of considerable quality, quite recently. But it is not right that we permit that argument—even if it is correct—to obscure some of the consequences of the two presidents' policies. Nor is it right that we overlook the failures of their philosophies. Glorifying the New Deal gets in the way of getting to know all the Cs, the bystanders, the third parties. They spoke frequently of the forgotten man at the time—the phrase "forgotten man" recurred throughout the decade—but eventually became forgotten men themselves. Going back to the Depression is worthwhile, if only to retrieve their lost story.

Nota Bene!

The Appendix contains a time line of The Great Depression reprinted from The Forgotten Man.

JOHN MAYNARD KEYNES

John Maynard Keynes (1883-1946) was born to a middle class family in Cambridge, England on June 21 1883. His father John Neville Keynes was an economist and lecturer at Cambridge University; his mother Florence was a social reformer. Throughout his education, starting from his early school years, teachers almost always described Keynes as brilliant, although he missed school frequently due to poor health. While at the prestigious Eton, which he attended on a scholarship, he distinguished himself in mathematics, classics and history. In class-conscious England, despite his middle class roots, Keynes was well received by the upper-class students. In 1902 Keynes left Eaton to study at King's College, Cambridge, on a mathematics scholarship. Alfred Marshall recognized Keynes brilliance and encouraged him to study economics; Keynes declined and received his degree in Mathematics in 1904. Keynes always believed in his ability to solve problems and had a strong belief in the ability of government to solve problems and work for the good of mankind. Keynes, however, was not the egalitarian he pretended to be; he believed that society should be governed by culture and not expertise. He also served on the board of the British Eugenics Society in 1945. Eugenics is commonly viewed as the utilization of government to improve the racial, genetic and biological health of a nation. Keynes, along with Julian Huxley, maintained that Eugenics was the most important branch of sociology.

In 1906 Keynes began his civil service career as a clerk in the India Office. In 1908 he returned to Cambridge to work on probability theory. His father and the famous economist Arthur Pigou provided the funding. He published his first work in 1909 about the effects of the global economic downturn on India. He also accepted a lectureship in economics established by Alfred Marshall.

With the outbreak of the First World War Keynes went to London at the request of the government to provide advice and joined the British

Treasury Department. At that post he served brilliantly and he was appointed to the position of Treasury Representative to the 1919 Versailles Peace Conference. Keynes was correct in trying to reduce the reparations payments that were demanded of Germany. He realized that it would take a huge toll on the German people with repercussions for the entire world. His opinions however did not sway the outcome. In 1919 he published *The Economic Consequences of Peace*, which is considered his best work. His predictions of disaster came true when the German economy suffered from the hyperinflation in 1923, the collapse of the Weimer Republic and the rise of Hitler. Keynes published his work, *A Treatise on Probability* in 1921, which introduced new methods of statistical analysis. In 1924 Keynes encouraged the government to create jobs by spending on public works and eliminating the constraints of the gold standard.

By the 1920s Keynes began a theoretical work, which examined the economic relationship between unemployment, prices and money. The two-volume book, *Treatise on Money* was published in 1930, and at the peak of the depression in 1933 Keynes published *The Means to Prosperity*. The books respectively dealt with the problem of excess saving and the benefit of counter cyclical government spending. The books were studied by the American and British governments and paved the way for Keynes to propose remedies for a global recession. However, mainstream economists remained opposed to fiscal intervention until the outbreak of World War II.

Keynes' most significant work, *The General Theory of Employment Interest and Money* was published in 1936. The book was Keynes' rationale for government management of economic policy. It was a complete attack on neo-classical economic theory. Keynes set himself apart from his contemporaries, his predecessors and the entire economic establishment. *The General Theory* argued that demand, not supply as proposed by Say, stirred economic activity.

From the onset of his career Keynes worked diligently and courted influential members of society to set himself apart from those around him and those who preceded him. In September 1941 he filled a vacancy in the court of directors in the Bank of England and in June 1941 Keynes was rewarded with a hereditary peerage. His title was Baron Keynes of Tilton in the county of Sussex, and he took his seat in the House of Lords and sat with the Liberal Party. Towards the end of WW II Keynes participated in discussions regarding the Bretton Woods System and proposed a single world currency.

However, upon his death, Keynes told his friend, Henry Clay, a professor and advisor to the Bank of England, "I find myself relying more on the invisible hand which I tried to reject from economic thinking twenty years ago". I have seldom found this comment in print.

KEYNES THE MAN

John Maynard Keynes was a legend in his own mind and an intellectual elitist from the day he started school. When asked how he pronounced his name he would always reply "Keynes as in brains". He was a pompous, arrogant dandy who worked diligently to preserve that reputation. But no one could deny his brilliance and if they did – he would set them straight. While attending Cambridge, Keynes was invited to join the Apostles, an elite Cambridge secret society with a long list of noteworthy members from the British elite. The Apostles were a radical organization with contempt for Victorian and upper class values. Keynes spent his life denouncing those values, but worked diligently for acceptance by the upper class and the aristocracy. The Apostles also advocated and practiced homosexuality as a morally superior virtue. Keynes *reportedly* abandoned his homosexual lifestyle in 1925 when he married the famous Russian Ballerina, Lydia Lopokova. Homosexuality in Victorian England was seen as complete moral deprivation and perversion. Keynes biographers spent considerable effort trying to conceal his homosexual adventures.

Although Keynes' reputation as a successful speculator is legendary, history tends to obfuscate his investment failures. Like the famous Yale professor, Irving Fisher, Keynes was very bullish prior to the crash and he predicted a major bull market. This misstep cost him dearly; both, his reputation and pocketbook suffered. His Austrian contemporaries, whom he viewed with disdain, realized that Keynes' exuberance was misplaced. Keynes was almost ruined by the ensuing decline in the stock and commodities markets.

However, Keynes was a skilled investor and he recovered a substantial portion of his net worth. He was however given a "helping hand" with a loan that enabled him to continue investing when his assets were essentially depleted. This is seldom mentioned. A key to Keynes' financial recovery was his ability to recognize out of favor stocks which had potential. Like Warren Buffet and Buffet's Mentor, Benjamin Graham, Keynes became a contrarian investor. His subsequent success as an investor enabled him to earn a very attractive return. Keynes regained his reputation and accumulated a substantial estate by his death in 1946, although he was philosophically opposed to investing and the stock market, as was Marx. Keynes, like many members of the left, supported estate taxes *after* they inherited money.

Keynes was a successful and a respected economist, but the economic community and his supporters have remained silent about the shortcomings of his theories and his hypocrisy. He rejected laissez-faire as an economic principal, and the crash led him to reject classical economics and the stock market. After all he must have been right, and the speculators who drove the market down must have been wrong. He was the "wizard of Cambridge" and the money he lost blurred his vision and his thinking.

Keynes and the Emperor's Clothes

Keynes has been proclaimed the greatest economist of the 20th century by the economics community of Great Britain and the United States. Keynes is in fact the only man who has had an entire school of thought named after him, – "Keynesian Economic Theory." Just as Charlemagne crowned himself, Keynes inducted himself. We must remember that his economic policies placed his supporters in power and empowered the left. Acceptance of Keynes' economic beliefs has enabled government to justify what they do best, – tax and spend, – and the more that is spent, the greater the power of government. As spending for entitlements increases, government creates a population indebted to government, which creates a voting block of mindless supporters addicted to the world's strongest opiate, – the government dole. And as the programs expand, the electorate becomes further hooked and government must again ratchet up taxes to pay the immense debt that has been created. The sympathizers bleed for every cause regardless of the consequences. In the words of former British Prime Minister, Margaret Thatcher, "Socialism works until the rich run out of money". Government cannot create wealth, it can only destroy wealth.

In regard to Keynes' revolutionary General Theory, I am compelled to commit economic heresy by raising a few questions. Did Keynes renounce classical economics because he failed to anticipate the great depression? Did Keynes endeavor to preserve his reputation by seeking a scapegoat, – the speculators? Did Keynes, a believer in the moral superiority of government, establish his theories to justify government control of resources and policy? Did Keynes develop a theory that would support his conclusions? Did Keynes insist on driving aggregate demand theory because Say maintained that economic growth was predicated on supply? Did Keynes see himself as the only one capable of guiding his brave new World? Did Keynes see himself as the ultimate Philosopher King? A careful analysis of the man and his times would indicate that the answer may be YES to all the above.

Keynes was an *influential* economist, but was he *correct*? It is my firm belief that future economists will view Keynesian Economic Theory as a mechanism that mired the world in excessive debt, excessive taxation, excessive government, high unemployment, low growth, limited freedom and a denial of human dignity.

KEYNESIAN ECONOMIC THEORY

Among other things, Keynes' *The General Theory of Employment, Interest and Money* is poorly organized, cumbersome and poorly written. The following excerpt is typical:

Chapter 2 – The Postulates of the Classical Economics

Most treatises on the theory of value and production are primarily concerned with the distribution of a *given* volume of employed resources between different uses and with the conditions which, assuming the employment of this quantity of resources, determine their relative rewards and the relative values of their products.

The question, also, of the volume of the available resources, in the sense of the size of the employable population, the extent of natural wealth and the accumulated capital equipment, has often been treated descriptively. But the pure theory of what determines *the actual employment* of the available resources has seldom been examined in great detail. To say that it has not been examined at all would, of course, be absurd. For every

66

discussion concerning fluctuations of employment, of which there have been many, has been concerned with it. I mean, not that the topic has been overlooked, but that the fundamental theory underlying it has been deemed so simple and obvious that it has received, at the most, a bare mention.

The classical theory of employment – supposedly simple and obvious – has been based, I think, on two fundamental postulates, though practically without discussion, namely:

i.   The wage is equal to the marginal product of labor.

That is to say, the wage of an employed person is equal to the value which would be lost if employment were to be reduced by one unit (after deducting any other costs which this reduction of output would avoid); subject, however, to the qualification that the equality may be disturbed, in accordance with certain principles, if competition and markets are imperfect.

ii.   The utility of the wage when a given volume of labor is employed is equal to the marginal disutility of that amount of employment.

That is to say, the real wage of an employed person is that which is just sufficient (in the estimation of the employed persons themselves) to induce the volume of labor actually employed to be forthcoming; subject to the qualification that the equality for each individual unit of labor may be disturbed by combination between employable units analogous to the imperfections of competition which qualify the first postulate. Disutility must be here understood to cover every kind of reason, which might lead a man, or a body of men, to withhold their labor rather than accept a wage, which had to them a utility below a certain minimum.[20]

---

[20] Keynes. (2008, original 1936). *The General Theory of Employment, Interest and Money*. Barnes and Noble Publishing, page 10.

Keynes the Socialist

Keynes firmly believed that government should play an active role in the management of the economy, but he disdained Karl Marx and Marx' theories and he correctly saw Marx as cruel and without a moral compass. Keynes also understood that Marxist theories were inconsistent with human nature and economics. Nonetheless, as stated previously, Keynes did not believe in laissez-faire and Marxists had little regard for Keynes' economic theories or his bourgeoisie lifestyle. This should not be a surprise. Despite his decidedly socialist ideology, many economists believe that Keynes saved capitalism by offering a government friendly economic alternative to Marx. Labor and the intellectual elite had turned to Marxist dogma as a shining light during the great depression. Keynes may have stemmed the tide. By the 1930s Keynes was completely disillusioned with capitalism and saw it as an immoral neurosis. However, he remained a "limousine liberal".[21] However, Keynes continued to accumulate wealth and could not find a feasible alternative to capitalism.

Keynes believed that classical economic theory was a special case only applicable to periods of normalcy and the economic conditions of the 19th century. Classical economists endorsed free-markets and Say's Law, "supply creates its own demand", as a guiding principal of economic activity. Classic theory holds that prices and wages adjust during an economic slowdown. However, Keynes believed that prices, particularly wages, were "sticky", and therefore not responsive to an economic slowdown. Keynes insisted that demand was the driving force of economic activity and that government should stimulate "aggregate demand" (the sum of all consumption and investment) during an economic slowdown. Critics and many advocates of Keynes recognized that Keynesian spending included paying one group of workers to dig a hole and another group to fill the hole. The mainstream economic community refuted Keynes' ideas, but they were incorporated in American economic thinking. The original introduction of Keynes' works became the cornerstone of a new branch of economics – Macroeconomics.

During the late 1930s and 1940s several prominent economists, including Franco Modigliani and Paul Samuelson, mathematically modeled Keynesian economic theory and classical economics. This

---

[21] A member of the left that maintains an elitist posture and covets wealth.

"neoclassical synthesis" became Neo-Keynesian economics. It must be stated that Keynes never studied economics and apparently did not understand how markets worked. This explains numerous shortcomings of Keynesian theory. Keynes intellectually was a wolf in sheep's clothing – the perfect socialist.

By the 1950s the economically developed world had adopted a Keynesian view of economics. The welfare state was becoming mainstream and the 1950s and 1960s produced growth and low unemployment. But was it due to Keynesian policy or in spite of Keynesian policy? Government tends to forget that business is the engine of growth and the creator of the income and wealth necessary to support government spending.

JOSEPH SCHUMPETER

The great Joseph Schumpeter was born in Moravia (now the Czech Republic, then part of Austria-Hungary) in 1883 to catholic-born ethnically German parents. He earned his Ph.D. in 1906 and became a professor of economics and government. He taught at several European Universities and moved to the United States in 1932, where he taught at several very prestigious American Universities until his death in 1950. Although Schumpeter did not have high standing among his peers, he was a critic of Keynesian economic theory, and developed a loyal following. Schumpeter claimed that he had set three goals for himself: to be the greatest economist in the world, the best horseman in all of Austria and the greatest lover in all of Vienna. He said he reached two of his goals, but never said which two. It was Schumpeter who conceived of "creative destruction" to describe the magnificent efficiency of capitalism. The concept became world famous and describes "the process by which the old ways of doing things are destroyed and replaced by new ways."

The following excerpt entitled *Schumpeter* from the May 23, 1983 issue of *Forbes* magazine, page 128, is both, brilliant and prophetic:

But Schumpeter's real contribution during the 32 years between the end of World War I and his death in 1950 was as a political economist. In 1942, when everyone was scared of a world-wide deflationary depression, Schumpeter published his best-known book, *Capitalism, Socialism and Democracy*, still, and deservedly, read widely. In this book he argued that capitalism would be destroyed by its own success. This would breed what we would now call the "new class": bureaucrats, intellectuals, professors, lawyers, journalists, all of them beneficiaries of capitalism's economic fruits and, in fact, parasitical on them, and yet all of them opposed to the ethos of wealth production, of saving and of allocating resources to economic productivity. The 40 years since this book appeared have surely proved Schumpeter to be a major prophet.

And then he proceeded to argue that capitalism would be destroyed by the very democracy it had helped create and made possible. For in a democracy, to be popular, government would increasingly become the "tax state," would increasingly shift income from producer to non-producer, would increasingly move income from where it would be saved and become capital for tomorrow to where it would be consumed. Government in a democracy would thus be under increasing inflationary pressure. Eventually, he prophesied, inflation would destroy both democracy and capitalism.

When he wrote this in 1942, almost everybody laughed. Nothing seemed less likely than an inflation based on economic success. Now, 40 years later (69 years to date), this has emerged as the central problem of democracy and of a free-market economy alike, just as Schumpeter had prophesied.

The Keynesians in the Forties ushered in their "promised land," in which the economist-king would guarantee the perfect equilibrium of an eternally stable economy through control of money, credit, spending and taxes. Schumpeter, however, increasingly concerned himself with the question of how the public sector could be controlled and limited so as to maintain political freedom and an economy capable of performance, growth and change.

THE BENEFIT OF FREE MARKETS

Creative Destruction at Work

In the December 18, 1999 issue of *Forbes* magazine there was an article by Guy Kawasaki entitled *Darwinism*. Mr. Kawasaki points out that in the 1800s ice harvesting was a thriving business in New England where hardy Yankees shipped ice around the world. But that business only lasted until the development of ice factories and ice factories only lasted until the development of refrigeration. The refrigerator was a "killer application". However, the revolution did not come from those in the ice harvesting business. Companies typically focus on their core competence and become blindsided. Of the countless horse and buggy companies that existed in the early 1900s only one made the transition to automobiles. The engineers making Friedman calculators and Underwood typewriters stubbornly stuck to their mechanical devices. Kawasaki made a great observation about the evolution of technology. There would be a long list of similar stories if Kawasaki was asked to update and expand his article. Nike started in the running shoe business eclipsing the long established shoe companies. And Apple Computer which started in a garage almost put IBM out of business, despite the fact that IBM was the company that destroyed the mechanical calculator and mechanical typewriter industry. There are countless examples of new companies that evolve to destroy existing technology. *That's* the strength of capitalism! During the 1950s and 1960s, new industries sprang up virtually overnight in the US. Despite the pronouncements of the government and the Keynesian community, the government was not responsible for the growth. The growth took place despite the government and Keynesian policy.

If corporate America, with their vast pool of talent, can be blindsided, it is no wonder that the government is always late to the party. The typical elected official has never held a real job, has never had to meet a payroll, was trained as an attorney and has no concept of the complexity of business. Furthermore, they frequently view profit with disdain and have no knowledge of the role of the entrepreneur in creating jobs and an enterprise. And for that matter, neither do most economists.

Growth and Employment

To create prosperity in a poor nation; dismiss the World Bank, the IMF and the economists, and establish a free market system, impose the rule of law, and replace the politicians with highly successful executives, like Lee Iacocca (formerly of Chrysler Corporation) or Jack Welch (formerly of General Electric). When this is accomplished capital will flow from all over the world. The outcome will most assuredly bring jobs, growth and prosperity for the entire nation; if capital flow is not restricted and tax policy is rational.

ECONOMISTS, POLICY WONKS, AND THOSE WHO HAVE WORKED FOR THE GOVERNMENT NEED NOT APPLY.

An economist from Ghana, who now works for a prominent US investment bank, blames much of the poverty in Africa on foreign aid. The proposition is that US financial aid has turned Africa into a welfare state. The solution, according to this economist, is to phase out the aid. After the conclusion of WWII Germany was receiving a substantial amount of US aid. German officials requested a halt to the aid. The West German government understood that a cessation of aid would cause pain for the people, but continuing the aid would cause economic death. When the aid stopped Germany began its march to becoming the engine of Europe. Reducing welfare in the US during the Clinton administration did not cause the poverty, hunger and unemployment envisioned by welfare advocates. The result was quite the opposite.

In the United States today (March 2011) we have unemployment in excess of 9% and the length of time a person can remain on unemployment has been extended to 59 weeks. However, studies show that a large percentage of unemployed workers find jobs within a reasonable period after benefits expire. A market solution is necessary. We must create an inducement to find a job. For example, we could gradually reduce the unemployment payment each month a worker is unemployed and allow workers to keep a declining portion of their unemployment benefits after they find a job. Everyone benefits.

The entrepreneurial dream is the engine of American growth. Small companies create most of the jobs in the United States in spite of the endless barriers that government places before them. When the government spends money to "stimulate economic growth", where does it get the money and what does it do with it? It gets the money from raising taxes and through deficit spending. Tax money is extracted from those who create jobs, and deficit spending destroys the economy. Government spending programs are counterproductive and many of Keynes' assertions have more holes than Swiss cheese.

PERSPECTIVE

Let's take a look at government spending in the United States. According to an article that appeared in the March 1, 2011 edition of the *Wall Street Journal* entitled *Billions in Bloat Uncovered in Beltway*: "The U.S. government has 15 different agencies overseeing food safety laws, more than 20 separate programs to help the homeless and 80 programs for economic development......The GAO has identified between $100 billion and $200 billion in duplicate spending......The agency found 82 federal programs to improve teacher quality; 80 to help disadvantaged people with transportation; 47 for job training and employment; and 56 to help people understand finances......On teacher quality, the report identified 82 programs that often have similar descriptions and goals and are spread across 10 federal agencies". And the list continues. This reminds me of a famous movie title, *Ship of Fools*.

If the United States economy had to depend on government to direct enterprise, the personal computer, along with countless other devices and products would not exist. After the development of ENIAC (Electronic Numerical Integrator and Computer), the first general purpose electronic computer, which was developed at the University of Pennsylvania during World War II, the government did not see the need for more than a few computers. And government would indeed vote against any labor saving device in order to save jobs. Also keep in mind that the Chilean miners would have died if the US government was directing the economy. A small entrepreneurial company in Pennsylvania developed the drilling technology that saved their lives.[22] The best and the brightest of the former Soviet Union and other socialist states worked for the central planning establishment; the result was empty shelves, substandard housing and hunger.

---

[22] An article entitled *Capitalism Saved the Miners* appeared in The Wall Street Journal on October 14, 2010 – See Appendix B.

Remember, Keynes was against saving. He believed that saving would reduce consumption and therefore reduce growth. However this does not hold up empirically or mathematically since saving increases consumption through accumulation and investment return. And enterprise, the engine of growth requires capital. As an aside, numerous studies have demonstrated that there is an inverse relationship between government regulation and economic growth. There is also an inverse relationship between government regulation and freedom. I'm sure the impoverished Cubans and North Koreans would leave their communist paradise tomorrow if they were not prisoners.

Was Keynes' admonition against saving because he had an insidious agenda devoted to promoting government dependency or because he wanted to justify the "Multiplier" and "Keynesian Theory." The Multiplier theory maintains that, as the "marginal propensity to consume" (MPC) increases (the portion of income spent), the impact on domestic output and income will increase by an amount greater than the amount spent (multiplier =1 / (1 – marginal propensity to consume)). Simply, if you spend 80% of your money the multiplier is 5 and if you spend 90 % of your money the multiplier is 10. This is an essential component of Keynesian theory. However, I have never seen a study that conclusively demonstrated a multiplier greater than two. In addition, the formula would lead us to believe that if 100% of income was spent, the multiplier would approach infinity. That creates a bit of a problem.

Keynes believed that all spending was good regardless of the purpose. That is not only foolish, but the history of the 20th century and the early 21st century clearly demonstrates the fallacy of that reasoning. As of this date, March 2011, the Obama administration has spent huge amounts of money to stimulate the economy and create jobs, to no avail. The solution to job creation is to reduce corporate and individual taxes. In addition, as stated previously, small business is the principal creator of jobs in the US. But excessive bureaucracy and other obstacles to small business are killing the job machine. As always, politics trumps sound reasoning.

In 1980, as a result of the theoretical foundations established by Austrian economists, Friedrich von Hayek and Ludwig von Misses, along with the help of a brilliant young American economist, Milton Friedman, Keynes lost his battle for economic sainthood. Friedman's *A Monetary History of the United States 1867 – 1960*, published in 1963, established him as the premier critic of Keynes and America's top economist. The Austrians and Friedman were free market advocates that relished freedom from every perspective, and did not suffer from Keynesian Narcissism. Their work proved that Keynes no longer reflected reality. Friedman firmly proclaimed that Keynesian policies would produce high unemployment and inflation – stagflation. He was correct. Of course there are those who have adhered to Keynesian dogma in spite of overwhelming evidence to the contrary. Like the French soldier Chauvin, who maintained allegiance to Napoleon despite threats of harm, the Keynesian economic community remained loyal to Keynes. Chauvin could not believe that Napoleon was anything other than a truly great Frenchman and patriot. And from Chauvin the word chauvinism became part of the English lexicon. It is descriptive of Keynesian apologists and the current administration in Washington

During the decade of the 1980s Keynesian economics remained under attack by the Chicago School of Monetarism and the Austrian Economic School. However, the financial crisis of 2008 enabled Keynesian advocates to resurrect Keynes again. But when the counting is done, it will be found that Keynesian economic policy and government intervention created the crisis and extended the recession. Consequently, the US will wake up, and the wisdom and efficiency of market-based solutions, along with sane tax policy, will enable us to grow and prosper. It is ironic that the policies of Keynes and the Roosevelt administration, which prolonged the great depression, are being called upon by the Obama administration during the Great Recession. Doesn't anyone in Washington study history?

Milton Friedman, in conjunction with his wife Anna J. Schwartz, coauthored *A Monetary History of the United States 1867-1960*, which was published by the prestigious National Bureau of Economic Research and Princeton University in 1963. Friedman's highly acclaimed work completely contradicted the Keynesian view that monetary policy was ineffective. Friedman's work also explained the nature of the American economic cycle. Friedman clearly demonstrated that Keynesian theory was wrong when Keynes proclaimed that "money doesn't matter". It was Friedman who discovered the true cause of the Great Depression. "From the cyclical peak in August 1929 to the cyclical trough in March 1933, the stock of money fell by over a third." Friedman conclusively pinned the blame on the Federal Reserve. In his landmark work, *Capitalism and Freedom*, published by the University of Chicago Press in 1962, Friedman clearly states on page 44 of the Fortieth Anniversary Edition: "The stock of money, prices, and output was decidedly more unstable after the establishment of the Federal Reserve System than before." The most dramatic period of instability in output was of course the period between the two wars which include the severe contractions of 1920-21, 1929-33, and 1937-38. No other twenty-year period in American history contains as many as three such sever contractions. Although the Federal Reserve was still in its infancy at the inception of the Great Depression and the monetary aggregates M1 and M2 were not available until they were developed by Friedman in his historic publication, the Fed and the government nonetheless acted recklessly. The Roosevelt administration did not have a clue regarding polices they were adopting, and the praise Keynes received for his work had no basis in fact or theory. The congress of the United States assured the collapse of the stock market and the economy by passing the Smoot-Hawley Tariff Act of 1930. The levels of tariffs under the act were the second highest in US history, exceeded only minimally by the Tariff of 1928. The ensuing retaliatory tariffs by US trading partners reduced American exports and imports by more than half. Today economists recognize that these "Beggar thy Neighbor Policies" were immensely destructive and reinforced the wisdom of Adam Smith and other classical economists. As the act was being circulated for review and passage, the stock market descended lockstep as the number of votes needed for passage gathered momentum. The great depression, as well as the financial crisis facing the United States at that time, was not a failure of the free market system, as has been frequently portrayed, it was a failure of government, caused by improper intervention and interference. The economic axiom – you get more of that which you subsidize and less of that which you tax – is always true. Government frequently proclaims that they know what is best for the people, despite the outrage of the voters. Actions of this nature are an abridgement of freedom and the ultimate act of hubris. There is no such thing as one size fits all.

In order to continue our examination of Keynes, we must analyze the basic tenets of Keynesian theory. Just as Friedman maintained that inflation was "always a monetary phenomenon," Keynesian theory maintained that all economic downturns were the result of insufficient aggregate demand, which could be stimulated by printing money, government spending, and government borrowing. Keynes further believed that thrift was bad and interest rates should be reduced to zero. Many critics of Keynes believe that *the General Theory* was merely a random series of thoughts without justification or proof. Possibly Keynes wanted to justify the need for government *and* Keynes. Keynes believed in and wanted to structure an egalitarian society. He never indicated whether that was good or bad economics. He believed in a progressive tax structure, but never provided the economic benefits of such structure other than to reduce economic inequality.

Communism everywhere has produced starvation, substandard housing, shortages of necessary goods, death, torture and prison for dissidents. Without free markets, private property, freedom, and the rule of law economic failure is assured. Socialism is also a failure and yet some nations continue to endorse more government when the secret to economic growth and wealth is less government. Critics of the free market system maintain that capitalism leaves some citizens behind, due to its competitive nature. In every system some get left behind, but it is always better to be poor in a rich nation than in a poor nation. In Cuba, essentially everyone is hungry. It is folly to kill the goose that laid the golden egg. Only a communist, socialist or madman would destroy a successful economic system to assure equality for all. Everyone is not equal. In addition, if everyone was equal we would not enjoy economic prosperity or cultural diversity. Imagine a life where everyone was a musician or everyone was a scientist. Everyone was equal in the former East Germany, but no one wanted to move from West Germany to East Germany. The flow was always east to west. As stated by workers in the former Soviet Union, "we pretend to work and the government pretends to pay us".

Keynes believed that estate taxes and income taxes were insufficient to create a just society or sufficient funds for government spending. Keynes' solution was print more money. The money would stimulate the banking system, and inflation would be kept in check through further taxation. This is a prescription for hyperinflation. A favorite cartoon from US newspapers is the Wizard of Id. In the cartoon the Wizard is standing before the King, proclaiming that the kingdom is facing a monetary crisis. The King exclaims, – are we out of gold? It is much worse your majesty, – the Wizard proclaims, – we are out of paper. When examining Keynes' personal correspondence and not his *General Theory,* we find an interesting truth. He despised those that earned money by engaging in business. How can a man with this bias develop economic policy whose purpose is to create economic growth? He can't. Keep in mind that business, and not government, produces wealth, creates real jobs and pays for the government.

The Stock Market

Keynes' self-serving naiveté also manifests itself in his view of the stock market. When Keynes lost money in the stock market, as a result of the crash, he blamed the rapacious speculators. He did not find fault with his view of the economic world. He saw the stock market as irrational, chaotic and a bit like gambling. When he made money in the stock market he did not see it as gambling. In the short run, the market may be a bit irrational; it is a manifestation of herd psychology. But it correctly anticipated the great depression, while Fisher and Keynes failed to do so. This was not a shortcoming of the market; it was a shortcoming of the prognosticators. Keynes also maintained that investing must be kept from private hands and left to the government. How? – By printing more money of course. Keynes' prescription for almost every economic problem was to drive interest rates to zero and to print more money. Aside from destroying the currency, history clearly demonstrates the inability of government to invest intelligently. Furthermore, leaving investment in the hands of private investors not only produces more goods and services, but the risk is carried by the investor, not the government, and the government should not be in the "bail out" business. Warren Buffet has become one of the richest men in the world by devoting his time to investing in stocks. His key to success may well rest in his ability to avoid economists. A favorite definition of an economist is one who learns more and more about less and less until he knows everything about nothing. A legislator is one who learns less and less about more and more until he knows nothing about everything. The financial crisis of the late 1990s was partially due to economists. The firm Long Term Capital Management employed Myron Scholes and Robert C. Merton, recipients of the Nobel Memorial Prize in Economics. However, they committed the sin of economic hubris, – they engaged in modeling and forecasting. The firm mathematically modeled economic scenarios and hedged against adverse financial outcomes. However, a perfect hedge only produces the risk free return, which is the Treasury bill return. They were in fact taking huge risks seeking huge returns. Despite their intellectual assertions, they were "making bets." They had achieved high returns from time to time, but in the end they lost, and lost *big*. They almost destroyed the financial system and they had to be bailed out by the Federal Reserve Bank in order to prevent a horrific financial domino effect.

The housing crisis in the United States, and the ensuing great recession were precipitated by bad government policy (i.e. providing mortgage financing to essentially *anyone* who could sign their name – X, must have been accepted). By employing leverage and derivatives strategies to "maximize profits while minimizing risk" assured capital availability by investors. Investors want to believe in the "golden fleece". But they were fleeced. Mathematics in finance and economics is seductive. It creates a false assurance for everyone involved.

As a member of the American Economic Association, I receive numerous scholarly journals on a regular basis. At times I read the topics to friends that are successful executives. The laughter is deafening. All economic modeling and obscure mathematics should be confined to the economic journals and the classrooms of doctoral students in economics, and economic journals should contain a warning similar to the warning on a pack of cigarettes. I was pleased to learn that a prime cause of poverty was an absence of capital. Keynes would have a solution. Print more money

Those that endeavor to become "Masters of the Universe"[23] will frequently fall to earth like Daedalus and Icarus. Markets are rational in the long run. For purposes of this text we are not referring to the Keynesian long run "when we are all dead" but a practical long run, a period of approximately ten years, a market cycle. Investment markets cause the greatest pain to the greatest number. This is more proof of market efficiency and investor hubris. They are rational over complete market cycles. It is human optimism and pessimism that drives markets to extremes which creates opportunities for the patient rational investor.

ECONOMIC SALVATION

The fiasco of communism and socialism has forced the world to examine their abysmal failure. The socialist experiment conclusively proved that socialism is not an economic system. Socialism was and remains a political system conceived of and administered by those who lack understanding of economics, human nature, resource allocation, decision-making, logic or any skill essential for the survival of the human race. But its greatest sin and downfall is that it robs the populace of dignity and freedom. It is a state sponsored prison camp.

---

[23] A Wall Street jargon for those that seek financial power and wealth.

The rapid growth of Asian countries, which quickly grew from poverty to highly developed nations, demonstrates the wisdom of adopting policies that are market friendly. These nations have forced the World Bank and International Monetary Fund to take notice and recognize that their success was due to a rejection of handouts. Handouts sap the strength of the people and the entrepreneurs, and prevent wealth formation. Yet the Marxists continue their rhetoric. Again ideology trumps reality. Consequently, I must conclude that the only mechanism to deal with the supporters of Marx is to introduce them to the supporters of Freud.

Occam's[24] Razor, although misunderstood and inappropriately used, is a useful guide to decision-making. In truth, the famous maxim suggests that we should accept that hypothesis which makes the fewest assumptions, and, whenever possible, substitute constructions out of known entities for inferences to unknown entities. If William of Ockham was alive today, he would examine socialism and free market capitalism, and form the following conclusion: socialism employs a great army of bureaucrats to determine: what should be produced, how it should be produced, what should be charged and who should get the production. This is an extremely complex process, even for a small village. He would most certainly conclude that this is a very expensive process which misdirects scarce resources from their most productive use creating both, surplus and shortage; a surplus of that which the administrators favor and a shortage of that which people need: food, clothing and housing. Ockham would see that a market-based society does not require government decisions regarding production, price and distribution. The market leaves neither surplus nor shortage. How Marvelous!

The primary criteria for economic growth follow: thrift, a stable monetary policy, minimal or no fiscal policy intervention, free trade, the rule of law, private property and an independent judicial system. Please note that freedom was not listed. That is because such a system provides freedom and without freedom such a system could not exist. Find a poor country and you will find widespread corruption and Swiss bank accounts with an abundance of money.

---

[24] William of Ockham (1285-1349) – an English Franciscan friar and scholastic philosopher, who is believed to have been born in Ockham, a small village in Surrey. He is considered to be one of the major figures of medieval thought and was at the center of the major intellectual and political controversies of the fourteenth century. Although he is commonly known for Occam's razor, the methodological principle that bears his name, William of Ockham also produced significant works on logic, physics, and theology.

Supply Side Economics – A Transition

The path to economic stability is a crooked road with numerous detours. Again, the path is foremost about ideology, more government vs. less government. Supply-side economics supports the proposition that minimally regulated markets offer the most efficient method of providing and distributing goods and services. The theory fell out of favor during the great depression due to government mismanagement of the economy and the rise of Keynesian theory.

During the 1970s, in response to the tax and spend policies of the US government and a resurgence of Keynesian economic policy, the right-leaning Republican party supported a policy of tax cuts to provide non-inflationary expansion. The Republicans were seeking an alternative to the stagflation that was undermining the economies of the US and Western Europe. The oil crisis of 1973 added fuel to the fire. Stagflation (slow growth and high inflation) ushered in a return to the Austrian school of thought, and the pivotal role of entrepreneurship and new classical economics. The movement was led by the right-leaning Republicans. Supply side policy proposed that production or supply was the key to economic growth, and that demand is a secondary consequence. Supply side economics was a rebuttal to Keynesian theory and a return to Say's Law and classical economics.

In 1978 Jude Wanniski published *The Way the World Works*, which described the nature of supply side economics and the failure of the progressive income tax system and associated policies. Wanniski also advocated a return to the gold standard. The debate also provided a forum for Arthur Laffer and his Laffer Curve. The Laffer Curve described the tradeoff between high marginal tax rates and disincentives to work. This was important. It supported the posture of supply side economics. Supply side theory advocated reducing tax on income and reducing the capital gains to spur investment and economic growth. The effectiveness of supply side economics, the Laffer Curve and tax policy are admittedly effected by political perspective. Supply side economics and Keynesian policy do not mix.

For additional information regarding supply side economics see Appendix C, which is a *Wall Street Journal* reprint entitled *Supply Side Economics and How It Grew From a Theory to a Presidential Program*. The article appeared on February 18, 1981. Also refer to Appendix D which contains a review of the book *Econoclasts* by Brian Domitrovic. The book "chronicles the history of supply-side economics." The review appeared in the June 217, 2011 issue of Forbes magazine.

The following quotation is from an article entitled *There's No Escaping Hauser's Law*. It is presented as Appendix E and concerns US tax policy. "Over the past six decades, tax revenue as a percentage of GDP (Gross Domestic Product) has averaged just under 19% regardless of the top marginal income tax. The top marginal tax has been as high as 92% (1952-53) and as low as 28% (1988-90)." This article is essential to understanding the true nature of tax policy. Higher marginal tax rates do not enhance economic growth but in fact deter growth. High state tax rates chase productive industries and productive individuals to other states, and high federal tax rates chase them to another country. Where is the wisdom of excessively taxing those that provide the jobs and provide the bulk of all tax revenue? As the often-quoted refrain goes – no one ever got a job from a poor person. The primary purpose of tax policy, as enunciated by Marx and Keynes, is to redistribute the wealth. As of this date Cuba is still not paradise.

MILTON FRIEDMAN

From our perspective, and in the opinion of many prominent economists, Milton Friedman (1912-2006) was the greatest economist of the 20th century. The *Economist* magazine declared that Milton Friedman was the most influential economist of the second half of the 20th century. Unlike Keynes, Friedman provided solid research and sound theories to support his views.

Milton Friedman was born in Brooklyn, New York in 1912. His parents were Jewish immigrants from a province of what was then part of the Austro-Hungarian Empire (now part of Ukraine). He received a B.A. from Rutgers University in 1932, an M.A. from the University of Chicago in 1933 and a Ph.D. from Columbia University.

Friedman was an advocate of deregulation, supply side economics, free markets, minimal government involvement and liberty. He understood the folly of Keynesian tax and spend polices, and fine-tuning the economy. When reading Friedman's works, if you listen carefully, you can hear him laughing at the hubris of his critics. Friedman has been proven correct, yet the policymakers of this period, under the Obama administration, have approached unemployment and other problems from a Keynesian perspective. This will be their undoing. I have never seen an economics book that endorsed deficit spending to create jobs or prosperity. It is a misdirection of assets with negative consequences. The Fed has worked hard to deal with speculative bubbles, – which they created through overly accommodative monetary policy. And the Government has worked hard to deal with fiscal problems, – which they created through reckless spending. So far Schumpeter, Hayek, Mises and Friedman are correct and the Keynesian advocates are wrong. Friedman understood the power of markets and the complexity of the economic system. Unlike Keynes, whose work was disorganized, difficult to read, ambiguous, not supported by evidence and sometimes contradictory, Friedman's writings were clear, logical, well-written and supported by facts and solid research.

I have selected specific passages form Friedman's famous book, *Capitalism and Freedom*, Fortieth Anniversary Edition (2002), originally published in 1962 by The University of Chicago Press, to demonstrate his clarity of thought and brilliance:

Page 3 Introduction Excerpt:

The preservation of freedom is the protective reason for limiting and decentralizing governmental power. But there is also a constructive reason. The great advances of civilization, whether in architecture or painting, in science or literature, in industry or agriculture, have never come from centralized government. Columbus did not set out to seek a new route to China in response to a majority directive of a parliament, though he was partly financed by an absolute monarch. Newton and Leibnitz; Einstein and Bohr; Shakespeare, Milton, and Pasternak; Whitney, McCormick, Edison, and Ford; Jane Addams, Florence Nightingale, and Albert Schweitzer; no one of these opened new frontiers in human knowledge and understanding, in literature, in technical possibilities, or in the relief of human misery in response to governmental directives. Their achievements were the product of individual genius, of strongly held minority views, of a social climate permitting variety and diversity.

Government can never duplicate the variety and diversity of individual action. At any moment in time, by imposing uniform standards in housing, or nutrition, or clothing, government could undoubtedly improve the level of living of many individuals; by imposing uniform standards in schooling, road construction, or sanitation, central government could undoubtedly improve the level of performance in many local areas and perhaps even on the average of all communities. But in the process, government would replace progress by stagnation, it would substitute uniform mediocrity for the variety essential for that experimentation which can bring tomorrow's laggards above today's mean.

Page 13 Economic Freedom and Political Freedom Excerpt:

Fundamentally, there are only two ways of coordinating the economic activities of millions. One is central direction involving the use of coercion – the technique of the army and of the modern totalitarian state. The other is voluntary co-operation of individuals – the technique of the market place.

The possibility of co-ordination through voluntary co-operation rests on the elementary – yet frequently denied – proposition that both parties to an economic transaction benefit from it, *provided the transaction is bi-laterally voluntary and informed.*

Exchange can therefore bring about co-ordination without coercion. A working model of a society organized through voluntary exchange is a *free private enterprise exchange economy* – what we have been calling competitive capitalism......

Page 14-15 Excerpt continued:

......So long as effective freedom of exchange is maintained, the central feature of the market organization of economic activity is that it prevents one person from interfering with another in respect of most of his activities. The consumer is protected from coercion by the seller because of the presence of other sellers with whom he can deal. The seller is protected from coercion by the consumer because of other consumers to whom he can sell. The employee is protected from coercion by the employer because of other employers for whom he can work, and so on. The market does this impersonally and without centralized authority.

Friedrich Hayek's *The Road to Serfdom* and Malcolm Gladwell's *The Tipping Point*, both point out a marvelous aspect of competition – it is blind of prejudice. Indeed, a major source of objection to a free economy is precisely that it does this task so well. It gives people what they want instead of what a particular group thinks they ought to want. Underlying most arguments against the free market is a lack of belief in freedom itself.

The existence of a free market does not of course eliminate the need for government. On the contrary, government is essential both as a forum for determining the "rules of the game" and as an umpire to interpret and enforce the rules decided on. What the market does is to reduce greatly the range of issues that must be decided through political means, and thereby to minimize the extent to which government need participate directly in the game. The characteristic feature of action through political channels is that it tends to require or enforce substantial conformity. The great advantage of the market, on the other hand, is that it permits wide diversity. It is, in political terms, a system of proportional representation. Each man can vote, as it were, for the color of tie he wants and get it; he does not have to see what color the majority wants and then, if he is in the minority, submit.

Page 39 The Control of Money Excerpt:

There is also widespread recognition that control over money can be a potent tool for controlling and shaping the economy. Its potency is dramatized in Lenin's famous dictum that the most effective way to destroy a society is to destroy its money. It is exemplified in more pedestrian fashion by the extent to which control of money has, from time immemorial, enabled sovereigns to exact heavy taxes from the populace at large, very often without the explicit agreement of the legislature when there has been one. This has been true from early times when monarchs clipped coins and adopted similar expedients to the present with our more sophisticated modern techniques for turning the printing press or simply altering book entries. The problem is to establish institutional arrangements that will enable government to exercise responsibility for money, yet at the same time limit the power thereby given to government and prevent this power from being used in ways that will tend to weaken rather than strengthen a free society.

Page 79 Fiscal Policy Excerpt:

I should like to discuss the view, now so widely held, that an increase in governmental expenditures relative to tax-receipts is necessarily expansionary and a decrease contractionary. This view, which is at the heart of the belief that fiscal policy can serve as a balance wheel, is by now almost taken for granted by businessmen, professional economists, and laymen alike. Yet it cannot be demonstrated to be true by logical considerations alone, has never been documented by empirical evidence, and is in fact inconsistent with the relevant empirical evidence of which I know.

Milton Friedman helped shape the modern free market system. Originally a Keynesian supporter of the New Deal and government intervention, Friedman reexamined Keynesian theory in the 1950s. His reinterpretation of the Keynesian consumption function challenged the Keynesian Model. At the University of Chicago he became the principal critic of Keynes. He promoted an alternative macroeconomic theory known as "monetarism". He argued that the government could not adjust the economy, since people would change their behavior to offset government actions. This is analogous to stock market efficient market theory. Friedman firmly believed that disciplined monetary policy could have prevented the great depression. The argument for that conclusion has become stronger each year, which is relevant for future policy analysts. Although he is given full credit for monetarism, its origins can be traced back to the 16th century School of Salamanca and possibly further. Friedman maintained that there is a close and stable relationship between price inflation and the money supply.

Friedman, always a free market advocate, was most proud of his work in eliminating conscription in the US military and his vision regarding "school choice" to improve inner city schools through competition and competence. His school choice position was enunciated years before the movement took roots. He passed away on November 16, 2006 at the age of 94 after a truly illustrious career. Friedman won the Nobel Memorial Prize in Economics in 1976 for his achievements in the fields of consumption analysis, monetary history, and demonstrating the complexity of stabilization policy. Friedman was also a supporter of supply-side economics, which dominated economic policy during the latter part of the 20th century. Friedman always advocated minimal intervention, free markets, market deregulation and disciplined monetary policy. Under president Ronald Reagan Friedman served as an economic advisor and saw his theories popularized.

Friedman's policies also influenced British Prime Minister Margaret Thatcher. The political left, as expected, viewed Friedman's policies with disdain. Reagan and Thatcher saw the wisdom of deep cuts in government spending and the privatization of government assets. The implementation of these policies induced growth and stability for both nations.

At the time of his passing, Dr. Ben Bernanke, Chairman of the Federal Reserve System under the Obama administration, stated that Friedman had "no peer" among economic scholars. Bernanke continued: "The direct and indirect influences of his thinking on contemporary monetary economics would be difficult to overstate. Milton conveyed to millions an understanding of the economic benefits of free, competitive markets, as well as the close connection that economic freedoms bear to other types of liberty."

THE ECONOMIC ENVIRONMENT

The economic outlook is uncertain. It is always uncertain. An economic forecast cannot anticipate earthquakes, natural disasters or failures of government policies. Economic forecasting is impossible, and given the variables, the permutations approach infinity. Anyone who can demonstrate that the economy can be accurately modeled should retire the Nobel Memorial Prize in Economic Science. Yet economists continue to profess their ability to fine tune monetary and fiscal policies. It can't be done. There is only one solution – adopt a Laissez-faire market-based society. However, government does not want to improve society, it wants to alter society.

At this moment the world economic system is awash in debt, the nations of the common market are bound together with string, Japan has experienced a monumental catastrophe, the middle-east is in turmoil, South America remains in a state of flux and China is growing rapidly, but requires a large external market to absorb its output.

For the benefit of the nation, I have a modest proposal: have the president of the United States appoint me Chairman of the Federal Reserve System. In regard to Fed policy I will have one meeting per year to announce staff cuts and the money supply target for the ensuing twelve months. In addition, and most important, banks would be allowed to fail. I would also provide a comfortable jail cell for bankers whose appetite for risk caused a failure. They don't care because it's not their money. Compensation for banking executives would be tied to risk and credit quality, as well as profit. In addition, leverage would be limited to prescribed guidelines, and capital requirements would be increased. Since depositors and shareholders would understand that failure was an option, only banks with a conservative capital structure and sound risk posture would attract capital and large depositors. As a result shareholders and depositors, and not the government, would suffer from a bank failure. The market would reward prudence and punish imprudence.

Just as a forest fire thins an overgrown forest, business failure eliminates inefficient business and redirects capital to efficient industries. "Creative destruction" constantly reinvigorates a free market economy.

FORECAST

Economists should never forecast economic events such as GDP, interest rates, the level of inflation or anything else for that matter without a warning that "forecasts can be hazardous to your wealth." Wall Street economists are paid to forecast and they adjust their forecasts with regularity to obfuscate their errors. Having said that and having provided the obligatory disclaimer, I shall provide a few thoughts regarding the future. If proven wrong, I shall blame my colleague, friend, former student and co-author Dr. Zviad Kliment Lazarashvili.

In the future I see the United States flourishing. I envision a free market revival led by the followers of Milton Friedman and freedom loving capitalists. This will take place because it must, if we are going to survive. It will become obvious that this is the only way to restore prosperity, freedom and economic stability to Western Europe and the United States. But it will take time and it will be painful. The damage caused by huge government deficits, massive federal government debt, state and local government debt, excessive government benefits, and massive government entitlement programs, will impose some suffering on the US population. But the population will adjust, just as the Germans and the Japanese adjusted to the ravages of WWII. Printing and borrowing money, the Keynesian solution, will not fix the problem, it *shall* only make it worse. Politicians will eventually recognize that postponing the day of reckoning will only exacerbate the problem. Greece and other nations are learning that lesson.

The common market countries will adapt faster than the United States, with Germany pulling the train *as always*. The Scandinavian nations will eventually realize that someone must pay the piper. Their socialist tendencies will cost them dearly, but they will adjust by adopting a reduced standard of living without complaint. That is their marvelous nature. The common market will be divided into currency sectors, the strong nations will continue to utilize the Euro, while Italy, Spain, Portugal and Greece will be forced to adopt their former currency, until they become fiscally responsible. The weaker members of the common market will adjust or they will be sent adrift, like a Viking Funeral, by the stronger nations. Alternatively, the euro will be abandoned. The cultural and economic disparities may be too large to reconcile.

It is my belief that the US secretly wants to preserve the Euro in order to establish the Euro as the world's reserve currency. This will simplify US monetary policy.

CONCLUSION

Attempts to improve or abandon the free market system and capitalism through socialism and government activism have failed and left a trail of despair, hunger, cruelty and death. No free market economy has ever experienced famine. Certainly the free market system is not perfect. Even nature is not perfect, – forest fires have a purpose. The poor need not be poor. Jobs are the universal panacea, not welfare checks or dependency. Dependency is government-supported slavery. Ronald Reagan famously stated, in his first inaugural address, January 20, 1981, when referring to the unemployment and inflation brought about by the application of Keynesian policy during the previous administration, "In this (economic) crisis, government is not the solution to our problem. Government is the problem."

Our journey began with Adam Smith and concluded with Milton Friedman. The path is clear. Government must stop governing when their actions interfere with markets and personal freedom.

Adam Smith's "classical model" was built on three points:

1. Freedom – individuals must have the right to produce and exchange products, labor, and capital;

2. Competition – individuals must have the right to compete in the production and exchange of goods and services;

3. Justice – the actions of individuals must be just and honest according to the rules of society.

The goal of every nation is to achieve economic growth, full employment and stability. Only free enterprise can provide the tools to achieve the desired outcome.

The best government is that which governs least.[25]

EPILOGUE

According to Gary S. Becker, the 1992 Nobel Economics Laureate and professor of economics at the University of Chicago, George P.

---

[25] "The best government is that which governs least", motto of the *United States Magazine, and Democratic Review*, 1837-1859. The motto appears on the title page. The quotation comes from the introductory essay to the first issue of this monthly journal (October issue, 1837). This essay was written by the editor, John Louis O'Sullivan. In 1843 Thoreau published the third essay in this collection. The essay was called *Paradise (To Be) Regained.* "the less government we have, the better" – a similar phrase is also used in Ralph Waldo Emerson's *Politics* (1844), sometimes mistakenly attributed to Thomas Jefferson.

Shultz, Secretary of Labor (1969-1970), Secretary of the Treasury (1972-1974) and John B. Taylor, professor of economics at Stanford University, "Credible Actions that reduce the rapid growth of federal spending and debt will raise economic growth and lower the unemployment rate. Higher private investment, not more government purchases, is the surest way to increase prosperity. When private investment is high, unemployment is low. In 2006 investment- business fixed investment plus residential investment – as a share of GDP – was high, at 17% and unemployment was low, at 5%. By 2010 private investment as a share of GDP was down to 12% and unemployment was up to more than 9%. In the year 2000, investment as a share of GDP was 17% while unemployment averaged around 4%. This is a regular pattern. In contrast, higher government spending is not associated with lower unemployment."[26]

Despite the overwhelming evidence that government spending does not produce growth and reduce unemployment, the US, along with many other nations, remains committed to useless spending. It is destructive and another failure of Keynesian economic theory, left wing politicians and the policies of the Obama administration. But why do nations continue down this road? There is only one rational explanation – ideology. The defenders of Marx, Keynes, the welfare state and other left leaning zealots will go to their grave defending these ideas despite their overwhelming failure. Is this a case of cognitive dissonance or chauvinism? Absolutely not! Unfortunately the reasons are sinister. The defenders of excessive government spending don't care if their policies reduce freedom, increase unemployment, lower the standard of living or establish the government as the employer of the last resort; so long as the state is "egalitarian" and the pillars of capitalism crumble. The denizens of the former Soviet States understand reality. They lived in Soviet Utopia and prayed for the collapse of the Soviet Union.

Freedom and Prosperity will be the hallmark of the 21st century because rational human beings seek liberty and opportunity above all else.

---

[26] This quotation appeared in the April 4, 2011 edition of the Wall Street Journal in an article titled *Time for a Budget Game – Changer*.

BIBLIOGRAPHY

Clark, John, Bates. (1908, original 1899). *The Distribution of Wealth.* The Macmillan Company.

Dornbusch, R., Fischer, S. Startz, R. (2004). *Macroeconomics.* McGraw-Hill.

Friedman, Milton. (2002, original 1962). *Capitalism and Freedom.* The University of Chicago Press.

Friedman, Milton. (1963). *A Monetary History of the United States, 1867-1960.* Princeton University Press.

Griffin, Edward, G. (2004). *The Creature from Jekyll Island: A Second Look at the Federal Reserve.* Barnes & Noble.

Harrod, F. R. (1951). *The Life of John Maynard Keynes.* Macmillan.

Hayek, Friedrich, August von. (1931). *Reflections on the Pure Theory of Money of Mr. J.M. Keynes.* Economica.

Hayek, F. A. (2007, original 1944). *The Road to Serfdom.* The University of Chicago Press.

Hazlitt, Henry. (1995). *The Critics of Keynesian Economics.* Irvington-on-Hudson, NY: Foundation for Economic Education.

Heilbroner, Robert. (1953). *The Worldly Philosophers.* New York: Simon & Schuster.

Kamenka, Eugene. (1983). *The Portable Karl Marx.* Viking.

Keynes, J. M., Moggridge, D. (1980). *The Collected Writings of John Maynard Keynes.* McMillan.

Keynes, John, Maynard. (2008, original 1936). *The General Theory of Employment, Interest and Money.* Barnes & Noble.

Keynes, John, Maynard. (1932). *A Short View of Russia.* London: Hogarth.

Lewis, Hunter. (2009). *Where Keynes Went Wrong*. Mount Jackson, Virginia: Axios Press.

Loucks, William. (1965, original 1938). *Comparative Economic Systems*. Harper & Row.

Marshall, Alfred. (2009, original 1890). *Principles of Economics: Unabridged Eighth Edition*. New York: Cosimo, Inc.,

Marx, Karl. Engels, Friedrich. (2005, original 1848). *The Communist Manifesto*. Barnes and Noble Classics.

Newman, Michael. (2005). *Socialism*. Oxford University Press.

Rothbard, Murray, N. (1995). *Classical Economics: An Austrian Perspective of the History of Economic Thought*. Auburn: Edward Elgar Publishing, Ltd.

Rothbard, Murray, N. (1995). *Economic Thought Before Adam Smith*. Auburn: Edward Elgar Publishing Ltd.

Say, Jean, Baptiste. (2001, original 1803). *A Treatise on Political Economy; or the Production Distribution and Consumption of Wealth*. Translated from the fourth edition of the French. Batoche Books.

Schumpeter, Joseph. (2003). *Ten Great Economists*. Simon Publications.

Shlaes, Amity. (2007). *The Forgotten Man*. New York: Harper Perennial.

Singer, Peter. (1980). *Marx*. Oxford, New York: Oxford University Press.

Skidelsky, Robert. (2010). *Keynes*. Oxford, New York: Oxford University Press.

Skousen, Mark. (2007). *The Big Three in Economics*. Armonk, New York: M.E. Sharpe, Inc.

Smith, Adam. (1991, original 1776). *The Wealth of Nations*. Everymans Library.

Sowell, Thomas. (1973). *Say's Law: An Historical Analysis*. Princeton University Press.

Wanniski, Jude. (1998, original 1978). *The Way the World Works*. Regency Gateway.

PERIODICALS

Friedman, Milton. (March 1968). The Role of Monetary Policy. *American Economic Review*.

Drucker, Peter. (May 23, 1983). Schumpeter. *Forbes*, page 128.

Kawasaki, Guy. (December 18, 1999). Darwinism. *Forbes*, page 280.

Domitrovic, Brian. (June 27, 2011). Econoclasts. *Forbes*.

Paletta, Damian. (March 1, 2011) Billions in Bloat Uncovered in Beltway. *The Wall Street Journal*.

Gary, Becker. Schultz, George. Taylor, John. (April 4, 2011). Time for a Budget Game-Changer. *The Wall Street Journal*.

Henninger, Daniel. (October 14, 2010). Capitalism Saved the Miners. *The Wall Street Journal*.

Merry, R. W., Bacon, K. C. (February 18, 1981). Supply-Side Economics and How It Grew from a Theory to a Presidential Program. *The Wall Street Journal*.

Hauser, W, Kurt. (November 26, 2010). There's No Escaping Houser's Law. *The Wall Street Journal*.

Friedman, Milton. Becker, Gary, S. (February 1, 2008). Milton Friedman on Economics: Selected Papers. *University of Chicago Press Journals*.

APPENDIX A

Timeline of the Great Depression from
The Forgotten Man by Amity Shlaes

1929

March 4: Herbert Clark Hoover is inaugurated as President of the United States. He announces that "government should assist and encourage these movements of collective self-help."

June 15: Hoover signs the Agricultural Marketing Act, establishing the Federal Farm Board to raise prices and revitalize the farm market.

July 19: Common stock in Insull Utility Investments, a holding company, hits a new high of 94, a full sixfold increase over its level of 15 just a few weeks before.

September 3: Dow Jones industrial average reaches a historic high of 381.

October 24: Black Thursday. Nearly thirteen million shares change hands, but Dow recovers most of losses by the end of the day.

October 29: Black Tuesday. Dow Jones Industrial Average drops to 230 from 261.

November 4: Samuel Insull's Civic Opera House opens with a performance of *Aida*. Attendance totals 3,740.

November 21: Hoover rallies business. With Hoover's support, Henry Ford announces wage hike at Ford to correct "an undersupply of purchasing power."

November 23: Hoover exhorts governors of all forty-eight states to expand public works and keep employment high.

1930

January 5: Stalin announces all farms must be collectivized by 1932.

June 17: President Hoover signs the Smoot-Hawley Tariff Act, raising U.S. tariffs to a historic high and triggering an international tariff war.

June 24: Hoover kills $102 million of additional funding in congressional package for veterans as "just bad legislation." Much smaller compromise package is created.

July 8: Hoover signs executive order creating Veterans Administration with annual budget of $800 million.

September 9: State Department announces it will curb immigration until unemployment lessens.

November 17: League of Nations opens the second International Conference on Concerted Economic Action in Geneva to discuss the spreading depression.

December 11: The Bank of United States, with 60 branches in New York that serve immigrants, closes doors. Some 1,350 banks will fail in 1930.

1931

January 7: Hoover's Emergency Committee for Employment Relief reports the number of unemployed is close to five million.

June 20: Hoover proposes a one-year moratorium on international debts, hoping to ease the effects of the spreading depression.

September 18: Japan launches invasion of Manchuria, breaching the Kellogg-Briand Pact of 1928.

September 20: Bank of England goes off the gold standard. Gold flows to France, regarded as the financial center least likely to abandon the gold standard.

October 7: Hoover proposes plan for the creation of the National Credit Corporation in an attempt to ease effects of the Depression.

October 8: Federal Reserve Bank of New York raises rediscount rates from 1.5 percent to 2.5 percent, a move "made advisable by the fact that the previous easy-money policy had failed," the *New York Times* sums up. A week later the Federal Reserve Bank of New York raises the rate again to 3.5 percent.

1932

February 2: Reconstruction Finance Corporation, entity created to lend billions to ailing businesses and banks, opens for business.

March 12: President Hindenburg receives several million more votes than Adolf Hitler of the Nazis in election contest, virtually guaranteeing that Hindenburg will be victorious in a runoff. *New York Times* describes the election as "the heaviest and quietest election the German republic has ever known."

Early April: A desperate Sam Insull travels to New York seeking rescue for his utilities empire – in vain. Combined shares were valued as high as $3 billion just a few years earlier during the electricity magnate's heyday.

May 29: Sixteen truckloads of veterans arrive in Washington as Bonus March appeal for early pension payment to veterans. Thousands of others will follow.

June 21: Samuel Insull arrives in Paris, having fled creditors and prosecution in the United States; begins lengthy period as fugitive.

July 28: Hoover orders eviction by U.S. Military of Bonus Marchers; officers leading the action, which involve the cavalry and the use of tear gas, includes General Douglas MacArthur, Major Dwight Eisenhower, and Major George Patton.

November 8: Franklin D. Roosevelt of New York wins presidential election.

1933

January 5: Calvin Coolidge dies of a heart attack at age sixty at the Beeches, his home in Northampton, Massachusetts.

January 24: Wendell Willkie is elected president of Commonwealth and Southern, a young utility.

January 30: Adolf Hitler becomes chancellor of Germany.

March 4: Franklin D. Roosevelt inaugurated as president. In his inaugural address, Roosevelt offers his famous line: "Let me assert my firm belief that the only thing we have to fear is fear itself." Proclaims bank holiday for following week.

March 9: Roosevelt begins his first One Hundred Days, the legislative period in which the New Deal is unfurled. Financial officials sort through banks; after bank holiday, financial institutions reopen with new confidence.

March 15: Dow climbs from 15 points to 62 points, a greater percentage than any single-day move since.

March 29: Congress passes bill establishing the Civilian Conservation Corps, creating jobs for approximately 250,000 young men.

April 19: FDR announces that the United States will abandon the gold standard, devaluing the dollar internationally.

May 18: Congress passes bill to establish the Tennessee Valley Authority in an attempt to raise the social and economic standards of residents in seven southern states.

May 19: Roosevelt names social worker Harry Hopkins of New York as Federal Emergency Administrator, a job created under the just passed Federal Emergency Relief Act. In the same month Congress and FDR create the Agricultural Adjustment Administration, to lower output and push up prices in order to help farmers.

May 27: Roosevelt signs the Securities Act of 1933, requiring a number of measures, including that stocks and bonds for public sale be filed with the Federal Trade Commission.

June 12: The International Economics Conference convenes in London to discuss the global depression.

June 16: As finale to the One Hundred Days, Congress passes the Farm Credit Act; the Banking Act of 1933, establishing the Federal Bank Deposit Insurance Corporation; and the National Industry Recovery Act, establishing the National Recovery Administration and the Public Works Administration.

August 5: FDR establishes the National Labor Board, which enforces the right to collectively bargain for organized labor.

December 29: Dow Jones Industrial Average closes year at 99, below the highs of the preceding summer of 1933.

1934

January 2: The Dow starts the year at 100. It will end the year a few points higher.

January 8: Supreme Court upholds the legality of the Minnesota Mortgage Moratorium Act in *Home Building & Loan Assn. v. Blaisdell*. Passed in response to the farm foreclosures resulting from the Depression, the Act allows individuals unable to make prompt payments to turn to courts and alter their payment schedule.

January 31: Roosevelt returns the dollar to the gold standard. The new price for fine troy ounce of gold is $35.00, up from $20.67.
FDR signs the Farm Mortgage Refinancing Act, assisting farmers with their mortgage payments.

February 2: FDR establishes the Export-Import Bank in an effort to facilitate international trade.

March 5: The Supreme Court holds in *Nebbia v. New York* that the 1933 Milk Control Law, a price control regulation adopted by New York State, is constitutional, since price control is not "arbitrary, discriminatory, or demonstrably irrelevant" to legislative policies aimed at promoting general welfare.

March 29: Turkish police board Greek steamer *Maoitis* in Bosporus, preventing Insull from disembarking. Insull is arrested shortly thereafter.

April 27: FDR signs amendment to Home Owners Loan Act of 1933. The *New York Times* reports that an additional $300 million is allotted for the remodeling and rebuilding of homes.

May 8: Samuel Insull spends night in Cook County jail rather than posting $200,000 bail before trial for fraud in Chicago.

May 28: U.K. economist John Maynard Keynes meets FDR on his visit to America. Roosevelt tells Labor Secretary Frances Perkins that Keynes confused him with a "rigmarole of figures."

June 6: FDR signs the Securities and Exchange Act, establishing the Securities and Exchange Commission.

June 12: FDR signs Reciprocal Trade Agreement Act, giving the president authority to lower tariffs by as much as 50 percent to countries with most-favored-nation status. Modern multilateralism in trade is born.

June 19: FDR signs Communications Act, establishing the Federal Communications Commission, a body of seven that will supervise telegraph, telephone, cable, and radio.

June 28: Roosevelt signs the National Housing Act, establishing the Federal Housing Administration. New Federal Farm Bankruptcy Act permits moratoria on mortgage foreclosures.
  FDR works with Marriner S. Eccles, who will become Chairman of the Board of Governors of the Federal Reserve.

November 6: Democrats win two-thirds majority in Senate and make significant gains in house, strengthening Roosevelt's position.

November 18: Roosevelt speaks at Tupelo, Mississippi, announcing that the TVA's work there "is going to be copied in every state of the union."

November 19: Wendell Willkie of Commonwealth and Southern calls Roosevelt "obviously misinformed" about utilities.

November 24: Federal jury in Chicago acquits Insull and others of mail fraud. "This is the beginning of my vindication," Insull says.

December 30: *New York Times* reports that Japan has publicly denounced the Washington Naval Treaty of 1922.

1935

January 27: The Supreme Court upholds that Section 9(c) of the NIRA is unconstitutional because it violates the separation of powers in *Panama Refining Co. v. Ryan*. Granting the president authority to prohibiting interstate shipment of petroleum products if the goods are in excess of state quotas, the NIRA provision had given legislative powers to the executive.

April 8: Roosevelt signs the Emergency Relief Appropriation Act leading to the establishment of the Resettlement Administration which aims to move poor families to the more productive Greenbelt regions.

April 27: Roosevelt signs bill to create the Soil Conservation Service in the U.S. Department of Agriculture.

May 6: FDR establishes Works Progress Administration (WPA), providing millions with work through construction projects; WPA also provides jobs for artists and academics.

May 11: FDR establishes the Rural Electrification Administration to finance the construction of utility projects in areas undeveloped by private companies.

May 27: The Supreme Court rules the National Industrial Recovery Act unconstitutional in *A.L.A. Schechter Poultry Corp. v. United States*. On the same day, the Court finds that President Roosevelt did not have the power to dismiss Hoover appointee William Humphrey from the office of commissioner at the Federal Trade Commission merely over policy differences and that such an action is a breach of executive power. In the same period Dow Jones industrial average begins broad rally that will last through the summer of 1937.

July 5: FDR signs the Wagner Act, establishing the national Labor Relations Board, which ensures the right to collective bargaining and paves the way for millions to join unions.

August 14: Social Security Act becomes law, ensuring pensions for Americans aged sixty-five and over. At signing, Roosevelt says that "We can never insure 100 percent of the population against 100 percent of the hazards and vicissitudes of life, but we have tried to frame a law which will give some measure of protection to the average citizen and to his family."

August 30: Roosevelt signs Revenue Act, raising estate and gift taxes, the marginal rate on individuals, and corporate income tax. Act taxes dividends received by corporations, formerly untaxed.

August 31: Roosevelt signs Neutrality Resolution, calling its purpose "wholly excellent." Law embargos arms sales to warring states.

November 9: John L. Lewis establishes the Committee for Industrial Organization in the American Federal of Labor to advocate for the organization of rubber, steel, and autoworkers.

November 15: The Philippines becomes a commonwealth of the United States.

1936

January 6: "Farm Act is Swept Away," reads *New York Times*, reporting Supreme Court decision to strike down the Agricultural Adjustment Act as unconstitutional. Shortly thereafter Congress will pass the Soil Conservation and Domestic Allotment Act, which subsidizes farming in different fashion.

February 17: The Supreme Court backs the Tennessee Valley Authority in its finding on *Ashwander v. Tennesssee Valley Authority*, affirming that the government's sale of excess electricity to consumers is constitutional.

May 9: Ethiopian emperor Haile Selassie flees his country, already occupied by Mussolini.

June 1: In *Morehead v. New York ex rel. Tipaldo*, the Supreme Court strikes down a New York minimum wage law as unconstitutional.

July 20: "Spain is saved," and "They will be punished," declares General Francisco Franco, as Civil War between Franco and Spanish government begins. War will last until 1939.

August 15: The Federal Reserve Bank raises required reserves by 50 percent, from 7 to 10.5 percent, with the new rate effective the next day. Future increases in the requirement will amount to an overall doubling.

November 3: FDR carries forty-six of forty-eight states, winning reelection.

1937

January 20: Roosevelt's second inaugural. He says that "we are fashioning an instrument of unimagined power for the establishment of a morally better world."

February 1: The United States' first free trade port opens on Staten Island.

February 5: In reaction to the Supreme Court's recent decisions against New Deal programs, FDR announces the Federal Court Reorganization bill, his court-packing proposal.

March 29: In *West Coast Hotel Co. v. Parrish*, the Supreme Court upholds the legality of a state minimum wage law for women, overruling the Court's 1923 finding in *Adkins v. Children's Hospital*.

April 12: In *National Labor Relations Board v. Jones & Laughlin Steel Corp*, the Supreme Court upholds the constitutionality of the National Labor Relations Act, maintaining that the federal government has the right to penalize corporations engaged in interstate commerce that discriminate against unionized employees.

May 24: The Supreme Court upholds the Social Security tax in *Steward Machine Co. v. Davis*.

July 7: Chinese and Japanese military clash at the Marco Polo Bridge near Beijing, marking the beginning of the Sino-Japanese War. Japan will occupy Beijing by July 28, as the war continues to spread to other parts of China. The massacre known as the "Rape of Nanking" will begin in December.

August 2: Dow, now at 187, begins a long slide.

August 26: Andrew Mellon dies while visiting his daughter Ailsa in Southampton.

November 10: Treasury Secretary Henry Morgenthau Jr. speaks at Hotel Astor, announcing that Treasury is "determined" to balance budget.

December 11: The Italian government withdraws from the League of Nations.

December 28: The Dow hits low of 119.

1938

February 12: Agriculture Secretary Henry Wallace celebrates "positive and universal production control" for government in new agriculture law.

March 18: Mexico nationalizes oil industry, expropriating over $400 million in holdings from foreign companies.

May 9: *New York Times* announces series of new efforts to revive economy including fiscal pump priming and a $1 billion in cash for Works Progress Administration.

May 27: Roosevelt delivers speech assailing Congress for voting to cut taxes and accuses lawmakers of abandoning principle of progressive taxation.

June 1: House passes food and drug bill that extends powers of Department of Agriculture and includes regulation of heretofore unregulated cosmetics and therapeutic devices. Lawmakers also at work on law that will create a wage and hour division within the Department of Labor.

June 25: FDR signs the Fair Labor Standards Act (FLSA), instituting minimum wage and maximum work hours.

July 16: Insull drops dead in Place de la Concorde station of Paris metro.

September 29: Germany gains Sudetenland via the Munich Pact.

1939

February 3: Willkie's name publicly bruited as possible presidential candidate.

March 2: Pollster George Gallup notes that public backs recent Supreme Court ban of sit-down strikes.

May 22: Germany and Italy sign the Pact of Steel, forming a military alliance.

July 1: FDR cleans the New Deal house, signing Reorganization Plan No. 1 of 1939, establishing the Federal Works Agency through the consolidation of five existing agencies.

September 1: Germany invades Poland. Within days Britain and France will declare war on Germany.

November 30: The Soviet Union invades Finland, marking the beginning of the Russo-Finnish War.

1940

May 10: Germany invades Luxembourg, the Netherlands, and Belgium. Winston Churchill becomes Prime Minister of England. In the following year, German forces will invade Soviet Union without warning.

May 10: Germany argues invasion of Netherlands was necessary because country favored "Germany's enemy."

June 22: France surrenders to Germany.

June 28: Willkie nominated on sixth ballot as Republican candidate for president.

August 20: Leon Trotsky is assaulted in Mexico and dies the following day.

September 27: Germany, Japan, and Italy enter into the Axis Pact.

November 5: FDR wins third term, defeating Republican candidate Wendell Willkie. The next day, the Dow closes at 132.

APPENDIX B

The Wall Street Journal
Capitalism Saved the Miners
October 14, 2010

It needs to be said. The rescue of the Chilean miners is a smashing victory for free-market capitalism.

Amid the boundless human joy of the miners' liberation, it may seem churlish to make such a claim. It is churlish. These are churlish times, and the stakes are high.

In the United States, with 9.6% unemployment, a notably angry electorate will go to the polls shortly and dump one political party in favor of the other, on which no love is lost. The president of the U.S. is campaigning across the country making this statement at nearly every stop:

"The basic idea is that if we put our blind faith in the market and we let corporations do whatever they want and we leave everybody else to fend for themselves, then America somehow automatically is going to grow and prosper."

Uh, yeah. That's a caricature of the basic idea, but basically that's right. Ask the miners.

If those miners had been trapped a half-mile down like this 25 years ago anywhere on earth, they would be dead. What happened over the past 25 years that meant the difference between life and death for those men?

Short answer: The Center Rock drill bit.

This is the miracle bit that drilled down to the trapped miners. Center Rock Inc. is a private company in Berlin, PA. It has 74 employees. The drill's rig came from Schramm, Inc. in West Chester, PA. Seeing the disaster, Center Rock's president, Brandon Fisher, called the Chileans to offer his drill. Chile accepted. The miners are alive.

Longer answer: The Center Rock drill, heretofore not featured on websites like Engadget or Gizmodo, is in fact a piece of tough technology developed by a small company in it for the money, for profit. That's why they innovated down-the-hole hammer drilling. If they make money, they can do more innovation.

This profit innovation dynamic was everywhere at that Chilean mine. The high-strength cable winding around the big wheel atop that simple rig is from Germany. Japan supplied the super-flexible, fiber-optic communications cable that linked the miners to the world above.

A remarkable Sept. 30 story about all this by the Journal's Matt Moffett was a compendium of astonishing things that showed up in the Atacama Desert from the distant corners of capitalism.

Samsung of South Korea supplied a cell phone that has its own projector. Jeffrey Gabbay, the founder of Cupron Inc. in Richmond, VA, supplied socks made with copper fiber that consumed foot bacteria, and minimized odor and infection.

Chile's health minister, Jaime Manalich, said, "I never realized that kind of thing actually existed."

That's right. In an open economy, you will never know what is out there on the leading developmental edge of this or that industry. But the reality behind the miracles is the same: Someone innovates something useful, makes money from it, and re-innovates, or someone else trumps their innovation. Most of the time, no one notices. All it does is create jobs, wealth and well-being. But without this system running in the background, without the year-over-year progress embedded in these capitalist innovations, those trapped miners would be dead.

Some will recoil at these triumphant claims for free-market capitalism. Why make them now?

Here's why. When a catastrophe like this occurs – others that come to mind are the BP well blowout, Hurricane Katrina, various disasters in China – a government has all its chips pushed to the center of the table. Chile succeeds (it rebuilt after the February earthquake with phenomenal speed). China flounders. Two American administrations left the public agog as they stumbled through the mess.

Still, what the political class understands is that all such disasters wash away eventually, and that life in a developed nation reverts to a tolerable norm. If the Obama administration refuses to complete free-trade agreements with Colombia, South Korea and Panama, no big deal. It's only politics.

But that's not true. Getting a nation's economics right is more important than at any time since the end of World War II. Chile, Colombia, Peru and Brazil are pulling away from the rest of their hapless South American neighbors. China, India and others are simply copying or buying the West's accomplishments.

The U.S. has a government led by a mindset obsessed with 250K-a-year "millionaires" and given to mocking "our blind faith in the market." In a fast-moving world filled with nations intent on catching up with or passing us, this policy path is a waste of time.

The miners' rescue is a thrilling moment for Chile, an imprimatur on its rising status. But I'm thinking of that 74-person outfit in Berlin, PA, whose high-tech drill bit opened the earth to free them. You know there are tens of thousands of stories like this in the U.S., as big as Google and small as Center Rock. I'm glad one of them helped save the Chileans. What's needed now is a new American economic model that lets our innovators rescue the rest of us.

APPENDIX C

Supply-Side Economics and
How It Grew From a Theory to a Presidential Program
The Wall Street Journal
February 18, 1981

Economist Norman Ture has been following public-policy debates since the Truman administration and has never seen anything like the rapid emergence of the idea called supply-side economics.

"It's one of the most dramatic, revolutionary developments I've ever seen," he says. "I don't know the like of it."

Mr. Ture should know; he is a supply-sider himself. Five years ago, most other economists dismissed him as something of a dreamer. Some still consider him that, but they can't disregard him today. Mr. Ture is the Reagan administration's undersecretary of the treasury for tax policy.

In that post he is working to apply the supply-side doctrine that sharp cuts in tax rates will simultaneously spur higher economic growth and lower inflation. Several years ago Mr. Ture was part of a small, largely ridiculed band of supply-side guerilla fighters battling an army of Keynesian economists who for a generation have guided government policy more towards controlling economic consumption than promoting production.

President Reagan and his cabinet now lead the supply-side movement. Today Mr. Reagan will announce to Congress and the nation a program of individual income-tax cuts, combined with extensive budget reductions and a call for tighter monetary policy by the Federal Reserve Board.

The program will be controversial in Congress, and many conventional economists still doubt that supply-side nostrums can produce the fast economic growth and low inflation that Mr. Reagan will forecast. The President's program thus will provoke an epic economic debate.

"We're at one of those great moments where the opportunity to reverse the steady slide of our economic system exists and where new ideas are being offered to accomplish the turnaround," says Otto Eckstein, a Harvard economics professor and president of Data Resources, Inc., a forecasting firm. But he warns that much of the supply-side theory hasn't been tested, and he worries that its rapid adoption "would be a gamble with our economic system."

At the heart of the debate is a fundamental question: What drives an economy? To the followers of the famous British economist John Maynard Keynes, the answer is aggregate demand – the willingness of people to trade their dollars for goods and services. In this view, if the government puts dollars in people's pockets through spending programs or tax cuts, they will spend much of the money, creating incentives for production. In other words, demand creates supply.

Not so, say the supply-siders. People produce not *only* because other people are ready to buy. They produce, in the words of New York's Rep. Jack Kemp, a leading supply-sider, "for after-tax income, after-tax profit, after-tax rewards." Individual tax cuts help, but they help more in brackets where people are more apt to invest and produce than they are to spend. If the rewards of production are stifled through high taxes and burdensome government regulations, potential producers won't engage in productive enterprises. Instead of working, saving and investing, they will spend their money – or dump it into nonproductive tax shelters and inflation hedges, such as gold.

That is happening in the U.S. now, the supply-siders argue, and it is stifling economic growth. They call for sharp cuts in tax rates designed to make both work and investment more rewarding, and thus to stimulate production, increase the supply of goods and services, and cool inflationary pressure.

Supply-siders reject the Keynesian idea that government can manage the economy by adjusting taxes and spending to achieve a balance between inflation and growth. They argue that increasing government spending to fight unemployment when taxes are high spurs inflation by increasing the demand for goods without increasing the supply. They also contend that tax increases to suppress demand and cool inflation – a policy sometimes advocated by Republicans – only produce recessions.

"Over the past several years, economic policy has been used to fight short-term swings in economic activity rather than to promote long-term growth of productive capacity," says Treasury Secretary Donald Regan. The Reagan team thinks it can produce simultaneous economic growth and milder inflation, rather than trade one for the other as the Ford and Carter administrations tried to do.

"None of the standard Keynesian policy models, with government as the central instrument for economic improvement, seems to work," concludes David Stockman, President Reagan's budget director and an ardent supply-sider.

He and other supply-siders also criticize the argument – long posed by Republicans but more recently by Democrats as well – that taxes shouldn't be cut until the budget is balanced. Although balanced budgets are desirable, in the supply-side view, it is impossible to eliminate government deficits as long as high taxes stifle economic growth.

President Reagan agrees. In his recent economic address, he complained of "those who always told us taxes couldn't be cut until spending was reduced." He added that "excessive taxation of individuals has robbed us of incentive and made overtime unprofitable." And Secretary Regan, who says "I was a supply-sider before I ever heard the term," argues that holding tax cuts "hostage" to budget-balancing efforts would only continue "business-as-usual" no-growth policies.

Capturing the Executive Branch of government was an amazing victory for the supply-side movement, which hardly existed a mere eight years ago. It emerged in the thinking of two economists – Arthur Laffer, now at the University of Southern California, and Robert Mundell of Columbia – whose ideas captured the imagination of an editorial writer for this newspaper, Jude Wanniski.

Mr. Wanniski, who now runs his own economic-consulting firm, combed Washington for receptive politicians and finally found his man – Rep. Kemp, who in 1977 was co-author of the Kemp-Roth bill to slash individual income-tax rates 30% over three years. Soon, Republican staffers on Capitol Hill were picking up supply-side ideas and guiding converted legislators in pushing alternatives to the ruling Democrats' economic programs.

Meanwhile, Mr. Kemp set out to convert Mr. Reagan, whom he considered the most receptive of the potential Presidents. It wasn't difficult. "Reagan has understood this stuff all the way along," says Mr. Wanniski.

But the supply-side outlook has some passionate critics. President Reagan's own vice president, George Bush, called it "voodoo economics" when he was running against Mr. Reagan in last spring's primaries. Walter Heller, former chairman of the Council of Economic Advisers, says the theory is supported by only "a few thimblefuls of questionable evidence." Sen. Paul Tsongas, a Massachusetts Democrat, derides it as "bumper-sticker economics."

Many economists reject the supply-siders' view that the best way to spur productivity is through deep cuts in individual income-tax rates. Even many Republicans in Congress argue that cutting individual taxes so sharply would merely generate new demand without immediately expanding supply and thus would worsen inflation. They prefer tax breaks for business and investors.

But supply-siders contend that people react quickly to reductions in their "marginal" tax rates, the amount of tax they pay on increased income. The theory is based on an abundant faith in Americans' work ethic, entrepreneurial spirit and investment savvy. When people realize they can keep more of each additional dollar earned, they will "shift into work out of leisure and into investment out of current consumption," says Paul Craig Roberts, a former Wall Street Journal editorial writer soon to become assistant treasury secretary for economic policy.

Many economists doubt, however, that cuts in marginal rates would produce an explosion of new work and investment. Mr. Heller says, "the eager beavers will work harder, and the laid-back people will work less."

Mr. Heller was chairman of the Council of Economic Advisers when the last major cuts in marginal rates took place. Although he concedes that the 1964 Kennedy-Johnson tax cuts spurred economic growth and thereby increased tax revenues even at the lower rates, he worries that sharp rate cuts now would encourage demand more than supply – and hence worsen inflation. The inflation rate was only 1.2% when the 1964 tax reductions occurred, compared with about 13% today, he notes, adding:

"The enormous preponderance of evidence is that there's a relatively slow and modest supply response."

Supply-siders retort that Keynesian economists are prisoners of their conventional demand-side computer models, which can't predict the future because they ignore supply-side incentive effects. The Reagan team predicts that its tax cuts, combined with sharp federal spending curtailments and a tight monetary policy, will lead to a rapid reduction in inflation even as the economy booms. Its projections for 1984 are bright: inflation, between 5% and 6%; economic growth after inflation, over 4%. In 1980, consumer prices rose 13.5% and the gross national product, adjusted for inflation, slipped by 0.1%.

"The world is dominated nine to one" by people who believe that the momentum of inflation can't be slowed as quickly as the administration predicts, says John Rutledge, president of Claremont Economics Inc. and a Reagan adviser. He contends that the President's program will quickly convince people that inflation will slow, causing rapid declines in interest rates and an easing in wage and price pressures as lenders, workers and everyone else become less frantic about keeping ahead of inflation.

Besides, the Reagan team assumes that the Federal Reserve Board will curb money-supply growth so as to moderate inflation, which Treasury Secretary Regan defines as "primarily a monetary phenomenon." He adds, "Stable prices are impossible if money-growth rates outstrip the growth of goods and services."

And so the Reagan team predicts that its program will quickly lower inflationary expectations, affecting prices "much faster than any of those white-coated econometricians would guess," in the words of Mr. Rutledge. The standard economic models, he adds, don't properly account for the boom in financial markets that will result from lowered inflation expectations and the willingness of people to forgo consumption in favor of investment.

Although many economists are skeptical, they're beginning to pay attention. For example, Richard Berner of Wharton Econometric Forecasting Associates Inc. is designing a new economic model that incorporates some of the supply-side thinking. Others may soon follow. "A new element has been injected into the ongoing economics debate," says Lawrence Klein, who won the Nobel Prize for developing the Wharton econometric models.

APPENDIX D

Econoclasts
by Brian Domitrovic
A Forbes Magazine Review
June 27, 2011

Brian Domitrovic chronicles the extraordinary history of supply-side economics: how it came into being, gathered traction in the 1970s and then triumphed with the election of Ronald Reagan. He tells this neglected but enormously important story with sympathetic verve, superb research and acutely drawn sketches of the principal characters. It has sharp relevance today and for the 2012 elections.

And what a story it is. Without the supply-side movement the U.S. in the 1980s and 1990s would have become a sluggish western European-style economy, with anemic growth and a dearth of innovation – which would have had profoundly negative geopolitical implications. The nation could never have financed Ronald Reagan's rapid and muscular military buildup, which, combined with an ever more dazzling cornucopia of new technologies and Reagan's robust diplomacy, won the Cold War for the Free World. Our standard of living – and those of everyone else – would be far meaner today. But because of supply-side economics we, followed by the rest of the globe, experienced two-plus decades of economic miracles.

Keep three numbers in mind – 3.3, 1.8 and 3.3. They tell an astonishing tale. Between the end of World War II and the early 1970s the U.S. economy grew, on average, at an impressive real rate of 3.3%. In the 1960s, with President John Kennedy's pledge to keep the dollar as good as gold and the passage of sweeping, across-the-board tax cuts, average growth exceeded 5% a year.

But then, like today, the U.S. went on a money-printing binge, and the gold standard, which had been in place for 180 years, was killed. Government spending erupted like a volcano. Taxes went up and up. Unemployment surged to higher levels than today, innovation withered. Through the terrible 1970s and early 1980s our growth rate collapsed to 1.8%. And even that feeble performance, based as it was on riotous speculation in commodities, land and commercial and residential real estate, exaggerated the actual health of the economy.

By the early 1980s, Japan and western Europe had virtually caught up with the U.S. economically. But then Ronald Reagan took office and supply-side economics was sitting firm in the saddle. The U.S. surged ahead again, achieving an average yearly growth rate of 3.3% until the recent financial crisis. Now, thanks to a reversion to 1970s-like policies – made worse by the semi nationalization via regulation of the health care and financial sectors – we have returned to 1970s-like stagnation and disturbingly high unemployment...

While the media conjure up visions of the 1930s when they discuss the current economic crisis, a more apt comparison, Domitrovic makes clear, is the stagnant and inflationary 1970s. We've forgotten how discouraging and unnerving that period was. The U.S. seemed in an unbreakable grip of ever rising inflation, unemployment and economic malaise. Economists were befuddled. They'd been taught that increased government spending and the Federal Reserve's printing more money would stimulate the economy. Economists believed there was an inverse relation between inflation and unemployment, exemplified by the Phillips Curve. If you wanted less inflation, you had to accept higher unemployment; lower unemployment meant accepting more inflation. But in the 1970s we were getting more of both inflation and unemployment. The professional was at a loss as to why its Keynesian-oriented theories weren't working, yet most economists adhered to them with Stalinist ferocity.

Two economists who defied the party line were Robert Mundell, winner in 1999 of the Prize in Economic Sciences, and the now iconic Arthur Laffer. They turned Keynesian orthodoxy on its head. Policymakers had it all wrong, they pointed out. The way to create an environment for growth and innovation was by reducing the tax burden through cutting income tax rates and by making the dollar strong and stable. Let producers, innovators and risk takers increase the supply of products and services, and the economy would boom. Hence the name "supply-side economics."

Given the ironclad Keynesian conventional wisdom that reigned then (and does again in the current White House), the supply-side victory was something of a miracle. "In the early 1970s all of two academic economists [Mundell and Laffer] could be counted in the movement. The rest of the first 'supply-siders' comprised a subterranean crew of journalists, congressional staffers and business forecasters."...

In the late 1960s and early 1970s Laffer was seen as a brilliant up-and-comer in the world of economics…

However, Paul Samuelson, the eminence grise of the profession, lashed out at the young and obscure economist in a lecture delivered at the University of Chicago, where Laffer was a tenured professor (Samuelson was ensconced at MIT). The lecture was entitled, "Whey They Are Laughing at Laffer." Even by the catty and nasty standards of academic political backbiting that was a stunning low blow. What offended Samuelson was obviously not the forecast but Laffer's free-market, sound-money principles. Samuelson's message to young economists: If you want academic success, don't associate yourself with the views of a man like this. Samuelson, who always had a soft spot for communist economies, was pining for an academic version of the Gulag…

But the desperate 1970s gave supply-siders their opening. Congress – including many Democrats – was ready to try something new. Supply-siders won their first major victory in 1978 with the astounding passage – despite intense White House opposition – of a major cut in the capital gains tax, engineered by an obscure Wisconsin congressman, Bill Steiger. The maximum rate was reduced from almost 50% to 28%. Despite the steep reduction, the next year's receipts from the capital gains levy easily exceeded those of previous years.

APPENDIX E

There's No Escaping Hauser's Law
The Wall Street Journal
November 26, 2010

Even Amoebas learn by trial and error, but some economists and politicians do not. The Obama administration's budget projections claim that raising taxes on the top 2% of taxpayers, those individuals earning more than $200,000 and couples earning $250,000 or more, will increase revenues to the U.S. Treasury. The empirical evidence suggests otherwise. None of the personal income tax or capital gains tax increases enacted in the post-World War II period has raised the projected tax revenues.

Over the past six decades, tax revenues as a percentage of GDP have averaged just under 19% regardless of the top marginal personal income tax rate. The top marginal rate has been as high as 92% (1952-53) and as low as 28% (1988-90). This observation was first reported in an op-ed I wrote for this newspaper in March 1993. A wit later dubbed this "Hauser's Law."

Over this period there have been more than 30 major changes in the tax code including personal income tax rates, corporate tax rates, capital gains taxes, dividend taxes, investment tax credits, depreciation schedules, Social Security taxes, and the number of tax brackets among others. Yet during this period, federal government tax collection as a share of GDP have moved within a narrow band of just under 19% of GDP.

Why? Higher taxes discourage the "animal spirits" of entrepreneurship. When tax rates are raised, taxpayers are encouraged to shift, hide and underreport income. Taxpayers divert their effort from pro-growth productive investments to seeking tax shelters, tax havens and tax-exempt investments. This behavior tends to dampen economic growth and job creation. Lower taxes increase the incentives to work, produce, save and invest, thereby encouraging capital formation and jobs. Taxpayers have less incentive to shelter and shift income.

On average, GDP has grown at a faster pace in the several quarters after taxes are lowered than the several quarters before the tax reductions. In the six quarters prior to the May 2003 Bush tax cuts, GDP grew at an average annual quarterly rate of 1.8%. In the six quarters following the tax cuts, GDP grew at an average annual quarterly rate of 3.8%. Yet taxes as a share of GDP have remained within a relatively narrow range as a percent of GDP in the entire post-World War II period.

This is explained once the relationship between taxes and GDP growth is understood. Under a tax increase, the denominator, GDP, will rise less than forecast, while the numerator, tax revenues, will advance less than anticipated. Therefore the quotient, the percentage of GDP collected in taxes, will remain the same. Nineteen percent of a larger GDP is preferable to 19% of a smaller GDP.

The target of the Obama tax hike is the top 2% of taxpayers, but the burden of the tax is likely to fall on the remaining 98%. The top 2% of income earners do not live in a vacuum. Our economy and society are interwoven. Employees and employers, providers and users, consumers and savers and investors are all interdependent. The wealthy have the highest propensity to save and invest. The wealthy also run the lion's share of small businesses. Most small business owners pay taxes at the personal income tax rate. Small businesses have created two-thirds of all new jobs during the past four decades and virtually all of the net new jobs from the early 1980s through the end of 2007, the beginning of the past recession.

In other words, the Obama tax increases are targeted at those who are largely responsible for capital formation. Capital formation is the lifeblood for job creation. As jobs are created, more people pay income, Social Security and Medicare taxes. As the economy grows, corporate income tax receipts grow. Rising corporate profits provide an underpinning to the stock market, so capital gain and dividend tax collections increase. A pro-growth, low marginal personal tax rate stimulates capital formation and GDP, which triggers a higher level of tax receipts for the other sources of government revenue.

It is generally accepted that if one taxes something, one gets less of it and if something is subsidized one gets more if it. The Obama administration is also proposing an increase in taxes on capital itself in the form of higher capital gains and dividend taxes.

The historical record is clear on this as well. In 1987 the capital gains tax rate was raised to 28% from 20%. Capital gains realizations as a percent of GDP fell to 3% in 1987 from about 8% of GDP in 1986 and continued to fall to below 2% over the next several years. Conversely, the capital gains tax rate was cut in 1997, to 20% from 28% and, at the time, the forecasts were for lower revenues over the ensuing two years.

In fact, tax revenues were about $84 billion above forecast and above the level collected at the higher and earlier rate. Similarly, the capital gains tax rate was cut in 2003 to 15% from 20%. The lower rate produced a higher level of revenue than in 2002 and twice the forecasted revenue in 2005.

The Obama administration and members of Congress should study the record on how the economy reacts to changes in the tax code. The president's economic team has launched a three-pronged attack on capital. They are attacking the income group that is the most responsible for capital formation and jobs in the private sector, and then attacking the investment returns on capital formation in the form of dividends and capital gains. The out-year projections on revenues from these tax increases will prove to be phantom.

CASE STUDY EUROPE

GLOBAL DEVELOPMENTS AT THE TURN OF THE CENTURY

Unprecedented global economic growth – although positive in many regards – will continue to put pressure on a number of highly strategic resources, including energy, food, and water. Demand for these essential resources is projected easily to outstrip available supplies over the next decade. This is especially problematic to the European economy, since Europe has very limited resources. It is largely dependent on Russia and other oriental countries with whom its relationship is, and has *always* been, taciturn *at best*. Call it healthy fear or paranoia, Europeans are concerned.

The World Bank estimates that demand for food will rise by 50 percent by 2030, as a result of growing world population, rising affluence, and the shift to Western dietary preferences by a larger middle class in both, Europe and Asia. Lack of access to stable supplies of water is reaching critical proportions, particularly for agricultural purposes, and the problem will worsen because of the rapid urbanization worldwide, to which approximately 1.2 billion persons will be added over the next 20 years. Today, experts consider 21 countries, with a combined population of about 600 million, will be either cropland or freshwater scarce. Call it healthy fear or paranoia, Europeans are concerned.

Europeans remain optimistic about the *long-term* prospects for greater democratization, even though advances are likely to be slow and globalization is subjecting many recently democratized countries to increasing social and economic pressures with the potential to undermine liberal institutions. The greatest hindrance to this global democratization is worldwide corruption. A great majority of Europeans thinks that many countries will be democratic on paper, but will remain autocratic *in-deed* and, therefore, *in essence*. As a result, a proper form of capitalism, that is competitive capitalism, will not flourish around the world, instead we will have its perversion, such as in Russia. It is a popular belief of many Europeans that collusive dealings between corrupt governments and dishonest businessmen will result in sheer plutocracy. Call it healthy fear or paranoia, Europeans are concerned.

Climate change is expected to exacerbate resource scarcities. Although the impact of climate will change varying by region, a number of regions will begin to suffer harmful effects, particularly water scarcity and loss of agricultural production.[27] Both, out of egalitarianism (whether it is sincere or not), as well as out of sheer economic, i.e. utilitarian concerns, which range from increased influx of immigrants from devastated areas to shortages in wheat output in Ukraine and Buckwheat harvest in Australia, Europeans worry that climate change may seriously obstruct the high standards of living of citizens of the European Union. Call it healthy fear or paranoia, Europeans are concerned.

We are witnessing an unprecedented moment in human history. Over the next several decades the number of people considered to be in the "global middle class" is projected to swell from 440 million to 1.2 billion or from 7.6 percent of the world's population to 16.1 percent, according to the World Bank. Most of the new entrants will come from China and India. Here the usual egalitarian sentiment of Europeans seems to vanish at once and serious concerns over global competition arise. For once I understand the reasons behind the constant fear and paranoia of the Europeans, – they want to keep the global supply of Beef Bourguignon, Jamon Iberico[28] and Foie Gras exempt from the increasing global demand. And as expected, they would like to secure such exclusive economic positions while maintaining their image of egalitarians, even though this would be taxing on the rest of the world – preaching equality, but striving for exclusivity – such is, and has been for quite some time, the strange hypocrisy of Europe! Call it healthy fear or paranoia, but it is evident that Europeans are concerned.

Modern economic life is full of competitive challenges, and it seems to me that's *precisely* what Europeans fear, – greater global competition and greater challenges produced by free market capitalism. And as "In time we hate that which we often fear",[29] it seems to me that Europeans, fearing free competition, started to hate that same hand which feeds them, – capitalism. Just as a side note from European history, I'd like to remind my European friends that "in the Dutch Republic, merchants who imported unprocessed salt from France, Portugal, and Spain gained

---

[27] Global Trends 2025: A Transformed World
http://www.dni.gov/nic/PDF_2025/2025_Global_Trends_Final_Report.pdf
[28] Iberian ham.
[29] Shakespeare, William. (2005). *The Yale Shakespeare: Complete Works*. Barnes & Noble.

control of the refining industry once exploitation of local salt marshes was halted for fear that dikes would be undermined."[30]

These negative constraints and positive developments will become the ultimate test of capitalism in the 21st century for Europe, as well as the rest of the newly developed world. Looking at the fast-developing economies of those countries which not too long ago made a shift from communism to capitalism, from command economy to free market economy, it becomes evident that capitalism is a superior form of administration, which, beyond economic growth, encourages self-governance and political freedom. It is also evident that capitalism is capable of creating wealth. But the two cardinal questions remain:

1. Will Europe (as well as Asian countries) resort to fierce protectionism out of fear for global competition?

2. Can competitive capitalism sustain the wealth and economic growth it produced in the past two decades and convince Europeans that they must follow capitalism in order to be wealthy, or else they shall perish?

These concerns are easily discarded and overlooked by many ardent supporters of laissez-faire capitalism, but most of Europe does not share such confidence. Perhaps Europeans have valid reasons. They have seen wealth-creation for a decade or two even in the Soviet Union, but the communist bubble soon burst and the Soviet failures became evident. On the other hand, there is no doubt, even among the most conservative Europeans, that capitalism is the superior economic system and, at least so far, no other alternative has been discovered. A process of elimination and deduction leaves capitalism as the only long-term road to wealth and prosperity, but... in spite of it all, the European doubt still remains.

Furthermore, Europeans are not like Americans, – they will *not* consume either American "cheese" or American "enriched" flour, – they do not deem these, and many other staple products of American diet, as nourishment, but rather as hazardous materials (for once I agree with them *wholeheartedly*). But beyond that, as mentioned in a preceding paragraph, Europeans like their foie gras to the point that they may forget their feeding hand, – competitive capitalism, – and resort to stark

---

[30] Duplessis, Robert, S. (1997). *Transitions to Capitalism in Early Modern Europe.* Cambridge University Press.

protectionism in order to limit the world demand for duck or goose livers. I am not surprised, – if an American is willing to risk it all and go out Alaska King Crab fishing, a risky occupation, then the European community is certainly entitled to risk its economic and political freedoms for a bit or a lot of Foie Gras, and the fancy European lifestyle. But I think that if such things did happen, a crab fisherman would be taking a more justifiable risk than a European protectionist. I'd only suggest that both of their boats to be inscribed with a warning motto: "BEWARE OF SERIOUS CONSEQUENCES!"

EUROPEAN PERSPECTIVE ON THE NATURE OF CAPITALISM

European society has a specific set of problems, and it matters *not* whether such concerns are rational or irrational, right or wrong. The concerns of Europe are different from the ones facing the American people. Different objectives require different approaches, as well as solutions. Hence, expectations of an average European significantly differ from expectations of an average American. Although both, people of Europe and people of America expect capitalism to provide opportunities for the realization of their hopes and aspirations.

Even most purely economic concerns of the continental Europe, historically speaking, have always been socio-economic, while American concerns tend to concentrate largely on economic objectives. Through research we have determined some of the most common cardinal socio-economic issues that concern a modern European:

1. Eradication of poverty in the European Union;

2. Eradication of extreme poverty and hunger throughout the world (staple product of the European egalitarian mindset);

3. Achieving universal primary education in the EU;

4. Promoting gender equality and empowering women in the EU and elsewhere;

5. Reducing child mortality;

6. Combatting HIV, AIDS, cancer and other diseases – advancing genetic research;

7. Ensuring sustainability at a workplace – decent wages and number of hours regardless of the line of work, plus vacation time (it seems that these are the issues almost unheard of in the United States);

8. Ensuring environmental sustainability – maintaining highest standards in farming and agriculture – no genetic engineering, no agricultural hormones and no chemicals.

Glancing over the list makes it crystal clear that European priorities vastly differ from American. That is not a chance outcome, but rather a reflection of historical mindset, which had been forming in the collective European psyche over the course of many generations, including the two World Wars, and at last found its realization in 1993 as the result of different processes at work, which began in 1991 in Maastricht, Netherlands, where the Treaty of Maastricht was signed and, subsequently, the European Union was founded upon its entry into force.

As already stated, economic issues are rarely strictly economic for Europeans. Then it must naturally follow that their understanding of capitalism must vastly differ from the American understanding of the concept. Europeans see capitalism as a socio-economic policy, rather than an economic mode or strategy. For Europeans the most important characteristics of capitalism, as a system of socioeconomic relationships, are:

1. Free trade,

2. Profit and desire to have a lot of money,

3. Free competition and freedom of speech,

4. Developing new technologies and realizing creative potential of an individual citizen,

5. Respect for private property,

6. Respect for individual human rights,

7. Law and order,

8. Deriving human benefits and personal happiness.

Correlations and associations that are reflected in this list cannot be overlooked. For example, note that free competition is correlated and associated with freedom of speech. Developing new technologies goes hand in hand with individual creativity, as a result helping to realize this creative element in its citizens is of major interest to the average European, as well as the European government. Also note that the list commences with *free trade* and culminates in *personal happiness*. I do not think this is random.

Towards the last quarter of the 20th century capitalism clearly proved its superiority over communism, by demonstrating to the people of Europe that the long-term benefits of freedom could not be matched in any respect by the welfare of *vulgar equality*. East and West Germany were a battlefield of the two forces, but the examples beyond Germany were even more persuasive, – from Czechoslovakia to the Baltic States and all the way to the edge of Europe. Entire nations were most passionately trying to defect from Russian-imposed communism, as well as socialism. They became ardent followers of capitalism.

The causes for such an enthusiastic following are not strictly based on economics. These people realized something which perhaps is rarely appreciated by the Western nations, – the relationship between capitalism and liberty, between prosperity and freedom. But this relationship goes beyond correlation. There is a definitive causation between capitalism and liberty, i.e. between economic freedom and political freedom. As Francis Fukuyama stated it was "The End of History" – capitalism had won decisively, and once and for all. We have plenty of reasons to believe he *could* be right to an extent if, and only if, mankind would listen to the voice of reason and capitalize on all that capitalism has to offer. We earnestly doubt if much of Fukuyama's prediction shall ever come true: "What we may be witnessing is not just the end of the Cold War, or the passing of a particular period of postwar history, but the end of history as such... That is, the end point of mankind's ideological evolution and the universalization of Western liberal democracy as the final form of human government."[31]

---

[31] Fukuyama, Francis. (1980). *The End of History and the Last Man*. Free Press.

CAPITALISM, MARKET, COMPETITION AND DEMOCRACY

Markets and capitalism are not necessarily identical concepts. Many markets currently exist without capitalism. Many markets shall exist without ever knowing the benefits of capitalism. Capitalism is a phenomenon destined to be the cornerstone *only* of the worthiest markets comprised of free and independent men. Markets can exist without capitalism, but capitalism cannot exist without a market. But... what capitalism does for the market is something transcending and truly amazing: capitalism is not merely an instrument for making money and accumulating capital, as some would like to persuade us. O no! It is much more than that! Capitalism is culture of freedom and courage. It is an economic lifestyle of free and courageous men and women. Capitalism fosters competition, and with this capitalism also encourages risk-taking, innovation, success, discipline, self-reliance and, eventually, self-governance. If we were to describe capitalism with one word, and one word only, it would be *competition*. Let's explore the essence of competition.

Competition is a peaceful battle, a placid challenge, a nonviolent war. Competition is readiness to take risk and its consequences, – success or failure. Risk is no small matter. It is the birth child of competition, but it is larger than competition in many regards. Risk is something only a free (or at least freedom-aspiring) man may experience in life. Perhaps the strength of this argument can be demonstrated with the following example from not too long ago:

Russian communists always feared risk, because the Soviet Union was politically unsound, and most risk-averse: The U.S.S.R. was an *empire*, and, like all empires, it consisted of the oppressor, – the Russian Federation, and the oppressed – Georgia, Ukraine, Lithuania, Latvia, Estonia, etc. The oppressor represented a willful element in this social contract; the oppressed represented a coerced element. That said, the Soviets, meaning Russians, always feared both, external, as well as internal competition. If you only knew how many games between the superior Dinamo Tbilisi[32] and the vastly inferior Dynamo Moscow were

---

[32] Dinamo Tbilisi was one of the most prominent clubs in Soviet football and a major contender in the Soviet Top League almost immediately after it was established in 1936. The club was then part of one of the leading sport societies in the Soviet Union, the All-Union Dynamo sports society which had several other divisions besides football, and was

blatantly fixed in order to impose pseudo Russian superiority, you would be shocked. Similarly, international competition was a huge threat to the Russians, both, in sports, as well as in economics. They were afraid of cardinal international failures which would further destabilize them politically and result in the breakdown of the dismal union. So they resorted to eliminating the element of risk in their economy. The result was dire, – the most unbearable equality – legislated equality. True, capitalist countries had their share of failures, inherent in risk-taking. As the line from a popular American film, *Some Like It Hot*, goes, "nobody's perfect". And neither is capitalism, – there will be some who will lose their shirts, and some will lose their livelihoods. Our argument is that it is best if *some* lose their shirts and livelihoods, than all of us losing. Perhaps Winston Churchill said it best: "The inherent vice of capitalism is the unequal sharing of blessings; the inherent virtue of socialism is the equal sharing of miseries."

The fact that capitalism has been flourishing in totalitarian China for two decades raises a valid question: is a union between democracy and capitalism necessary? Considering the sequential order of the cardinal elements of the question, the answer is NO! The question entails an element of anachronism – capitalism does not necessarily follow democracy. But if we pose the question in a chronologically correct sequence: is a union between capitalism and democracy necessary? The answer would be still no. *However*, it is most likely that capitalism will be followed with a greater democratization, meaning, economic freedom will bring about greater individual political freedom, and with that greater independent political participation. And *that's* precisely what has been taking place in China. Don't get me wrong, China is still a long way from democracy, but we believe that capitalism is the only thing that is inching it closer to it.

---

sponsored by the Soviet Ministry of Internal Affairs. Its main claim to European fame was winning the Cup Winners' Cup in 1981, beating FC Carl Zeiss Jena of East Germany 2–1 in the final in Düsseldorf. Throughout its history, FC Dinamo Tbilisi produced many famous players: Boris Paichadze, Avtandil "Basa" Gogoberidze, Shota Iamanidze, Tengiz Sulakvelidze, Vitali Daraselia, Vladimer Gutsaev, David Kipiani, Mikheil Meskhi, Ramaz Shengelia, Alexandre Chivadze, Slava Metreveli, Murtaz Khurtsilava. After the break-up of the Soviet Union, it would later produce some of the finest Georgian players, such as Temur Ketsbaia, Kakha Kaladze, Shota Arveladze, Giorgi Kinkladze. FC Dinamo Tbilisi was one of a handful of teams in the Soviet Top League (along with FC Dynamo Moscow and Dynamo Kyiv) that were never relegated. Their most famous coach was Nodar Akhalkatsi, who led the team to the Soviet title in 1978, two Soviet cups (1976 and 1979), and the UEFA Cup Winners' Cup in 1981.

A POOR BARGAIN:
SECURITY FOR THE PRICE OF FREEDOM

In order to understand the past, current or future European approaches to capitalism, as well as the socio-economic tendencies of the European Union, first, we must understand what Europe was and what it has become; what were the reasons and forces that created the European Union; and why is the likelihood so high for the European integration to continue even further and even at a faster pace, at least for a while.

European war history did not commence with the two World Wars. Europe was plagued with constant and constantly taxing full scale wars and smaller armed conflicts way before the 20th century. However, the two World Wars made Europeans realize: one, an armed conflict disrupts every aspect of life for all nations involved, winners and losers alike; two, a large armed conflict between economic and political powerhouses has a high propensity of becoming a global armed conflict, i.e. a world war. The end results of the two World Wars were so dismal that Europeans went past learning proper lessons from them, – beyond developing aversion for an armed conflict, they developed phobia of competition. The dismal effects of the wars forced the European mindset to view international competition and global political economy as a zero sum game, and, hence, as a hair-trigger for war. Europeans wanted to avoid another such war, so they created a union, where all the economic and political powerhouses of Europe have shared interests, shared infrastructures, shared laws, shared currency, shared international policies and shared economies. We believe that Europe went from one extreme to another, – from recklessness of war to conservative, conformist and most bureaucratic integration, – although we fully recognize that some, including many of our readers, may see this otherwise. But let's dig deeper into the essence of the European Union and, instead of relying on common beliefs, let's decide for ourselves what the EU truly is.

Imagine supporting communism, meaning, communal ownership, only because you fear hunger. Imagine what that would require, – surrendering your current, past and future property rights and earnings. Also imagine that out of fear of an invasion you surrender all your political and economic freedoms to a common union you have just formed with a *potential* invader. These two reasons must do in our book, although we could offer an almost endless list of similar reasons. Fear of

famine, fear of war, fear of global competition, fear of inner conflict…
and fear in general could be easily made into perpetual boogiemen,
which in turn would compel men, and lately entire nations, to surrender
their liberties to a union. Now, in the case of the EU the union is not only
political, or economic, or legal, or military, or social, but *all of the above*,
plus…

The European Union is a union of nations whose citizens had to
sacrifice their personal and national liberties for the sake of stability and
common prosperity of the region in order to avoid or to handle more
expediently the following boogiemen perpetuated by European
demagogues and bureaucrats:

- Another war between European nations;
- Another war with Russia;
- Economic competition from China;
- American dominance in *every* respect;
- Global competition in *every* respect from Asia;
- …and the list goes on…

Are such fears justifiable? – Sure. Will the EU be a successful
enterprise? – Only history can provide a conclusive answer to that, but
we believe it will be a failed conglomerate, precisely because it is *not* an
enterprise by *any* means, it is an unnatural concoction which is averse to
all natural forces, including competitive capitalism both, between its
member states, as well as globally.

The European *Union*, just as all the unions in the world, is a
protectionist entity, a discriminatory alliance, an anti-competitive
padlocked environment, a bubble, which is highly exclusive and
therefore highly stagnant. Such exclusivity also results in unfair
discrimination, not only for the outsiders, but especially for the insiders.
An exclusive union denies an opportunity to conduct economic
transactions freely. If nowadays Chinese are manufacturing better purses
at a cheaper price than Italians, the union would not only deny a Chinese
manufacturer his right to succeed, but it would also deny an Italian
manufacturer his God-given right to *fail*. Without failures life is not
worth living, and free market capitalism cannot evolve. Without failures,
without risks, without consequences, in short, without that "creative
destruction" Schumpeter most adequately spoke about, life becomes one
constant irrelevance, one stagnant immortality, and one perpetual
nothingness.

CONCLUSION

The European Union is an elitist club created through socio-political engineering on the grandest scale. It usurps nationality and diversity. It is a protectionist special interest group with a bias against non-members and even bigger lack of confidence for its members; that is, it expresses zero confidence in the ability of its members to compete freely and fairly. It is an artificial element, and like all artificial elements, it will be dissolved. This dissolution will be brought by nature, which promotes freedom over conformity, and, given due time, it has the ability to correct all artificial engineering done by men. It will not be surprising if nature utilizes economic freedom, i.e. competitive capitalism, to accomplish this latest, but by no means last, task. In the end, European nations will emerge as stronger and economically more viable fully independent, sovereign states than ever before, *especially* (to use a Wall Street jargon originally invented in Brussels) the PIGS – Portugal, Italy, Greece and Spain, with Italy and Greece leading the pack.[33]

---

[33] Dainotto, Roberto, M. (2007). *Europe (In Theory)*. Duke University Press.

BIBLIOGRAPHY

Dainotto, Roberto, M. (2007). *Europe (In Theory)*. Duke University Press.

Duplessis, Robert, S. (1997). *Transitions to Capitalism in Early Modern Europe*. Cambridge University Press.

Fukuyama, Francis. (1980). *The End of History and the Last Man*. Free Press.

Global Trends 2025: A Transformed World
http://www.dni.gov/nic/PDF_2025/2025_Global_Trends_Final_Report.pdf

McCormick, John. (2008). *Understanding the European Union: A Concise Introduction*. Palgrave Macmillan.

Nugent, Neill. (2010). *The Government and Politics of the European Union*. Palgrave Macmillan.

Rifkin, Jeremy. (2005). *The European Dream: How Europe's Vision of the Future Is Quietly Eclipsing the American Dream*. Tarcher.

Shakespeare, William. (2005). *The Yale Shakespeare: Complete Works*. Barnes & Noble.

CASE STUDY AFRICA

"Competition is the engine of a productive society, and that self-interest will eventually come to enrich the whole community, as if by an 'invisible hand'"

Adam Smith

Adam Smith's landmark treatise on the free market paved the way for modern capitalism, which has been variously defined by economists. The pioneer, Adam Smith defines capitalism as a system where the forces of supply and demand regulate the market, or the going prices for goods and services are maintained by the free market or under a government-leave-alone or *laissez faire* system.[34] According to George Reisman (1998) "capitalism is a social system based on private ownership of the means of production. It is characterized by the pursuit of material self-interest under freedom, and it rests on a foundation of the cultural influence of reason."[35] Immanuel Wallerstein describes capitalism as a "historical system defined by the priority of endless accumulation of capital."[36] What seems common to all definitions of capitalism is that capitalism is the economic principle which promotes private ownership and control of the means of production, and the economic freedom of the individual to manage his own affairs. In short, capitalism is the archetypal progressive model, because it is the only social system that leaves the individual free to pursue and achieve his own happiness.

Capitalism is the ethical ideal, because it is the only social system that leaves man free to be moral – to live by the use of his own mind. According to Ayn Rand "the moral justification for capitalism lies in the fact that it is the only system consonant with man's rational nature, in that it protects man's survival qua man."[37] Arguably, capitalism as free economic choice is the economic equivalent of democracy, because both, capitalism and democracy are distinguished by freedom of action and the ascendency of the individual. Both are anchored on human rationality,

---

[34] Smith, Adam. (1776). *The Wealth of Nations.*
[35] Reisman, George. (1998). *Capitalism: A Treatise on Economics.* Ottawa, IL: Jameson Books.
[36] Wallerstein, Immanuel. (1976). *World Systems Analysis: An Introduction.*
[37] Rand, Ayn. (1966). *Capitalism: the Unknown Ideal.* New York: New American Library.

which is the principal faculty sustaining human autonomy. The two principles are also based on rational choice according to Anthony Downs.[38]

This chapter first attempts to establish what the author sees as the extricable link between capitalism, democracy and rationality, meaning the pursuit of democratic capitalism as the only rational endeavor. Second, it attempts to delineate the fact that capitalism is the most wealth-producing of all available economic principles. Third, the chapter illustrates how capitalism is not an uncommon practice in traditional Africa. Finally, it presents a unique type of capitalism, termed micro-capitalism, as a blueprint for Africa's economic emancipation in the 21st century.

THE LOGIC OF CAPITALISM AS A RATIONAL ENDEAVOR

Being the sole rational beings in the familiar universe, mankind can claim to be the greatest of all creation. According to the stoics, reason is the quality that man shares with the gods, and man is at his best when acting rationally. Hence, Socrates categorically opted for a life of reason when he declared that: "The unexamined life is not worth living." The unexamined life is the same as the irrational life. Rationality gives man both, the right and means of fulfilling his divine mission of subduing the earth. This same rationality also guides both, his political and economic freedoms. It is reason that gives freedom, that is, autonomy, and meaning to human existence. Therefore, man must use his reason in order to attain pleasure and comfort in the world. This pursuit of comfort, pleasure or happiness, as compelled by reason due to self-interest, is what leads him to wealth creation and accumulation, and that is what capitalism is all about.

John Locke stated that "All men are created equal and endowed with the natural rights of life, liberty and property."[39] Later Thomas Jefferson quite appropriately called property "the pursuit of happiness."[40] So wealth and happiness can never be strange bedfellows. Some moralists argue that money does not guarantee happiness, but it surely

---

[38] Downs, Anthony. (1957). *An Economic Theory of Democracy*. New York: Harper.

[39] John Locke. (1980, orig. 1690). *Second Treatise of Government*. C.B Macpherson, ed. Indianapolis, IN: Hackett.

[40] H. Friedenwald, (1904). *The Declaration of Independence: An Interpretative Analysis*. New York: MacMillan, p. 161.

goes a long way, and, of course, given all the miseries associated with poverty, prosperity is definitely better. Wealth gives better meaning to life here on earth, and rationality prescribes autonomous self-interested actions or behaviors. As a rational being, man must consciously pursue his own happiness. On the contrary, poverty leads to disease, early death and other unnecessary forms of human misery, and no one wishes to be poor. According to Chinua Achebe, good fortune or prosperity is like a juicy piece of meat which the gods put into one's mouth, and no rational person spits it out. Affluence or comfortable life is the goal, which all rational persons everywhere desire and seek.

America was built by puritans who escaped persecution from the old world and made conscious efforts to improve their lives after suffering indignity and inhuman conditions in the old world, including poverty and lack of freedom both, of religion and enterprise. What they were denied in the old world they embraced with passion in the new world. This zealousness for freedom and industry is arguably the main reason why America emerged as the most prosperous and advanced country ever in human history.

Human freedom and economic individualism are the foundation of prosperity; and true freedom is the product of a discerning mind or the intellect. Economic individualism or capitalism is the practical pursuit of economic freedom and industry as prescribed by self-interest seeking reason. It is true that ancient societies exhibited prosperity or affluence; but it was basically the affluence of the ruling class, of kings and emperors, whereas the masses were slaves who simply existed for the pleasures of the oligarchs. Those autocrats decreed what their subject did and how they did it. In all the ancient kingdoms of the past it was clear that general prosperity was never allowed, because the people were never really free. The kings determined what the people did in all aspects of their lives, including what they believed and how they worshiped. In fact, most of the ancient kings made themselves gods and preyed on their peoples.

During the medieval period feudalism held sway, as secular and religious authorities co-operated to promote absolute autocracies. This caesaro-papism[41] kept the people in check intellectually, religiously, politically and even economically. For instance, the Inquisition and other

---

[41] Caesaro-papism is a pejorative term used to describe a political order where religious and state authorities unite against the freedom of the citizens.

official intellectual constraints prevented freedom of belief, thought, action and enterprise, leading to the general stagnation of that era, which is why it was also called the Dark Ages.

Following this era was the Reformation and the rise of Protestantism, especially Calvinism, as espoused by John C. Calvin, which began the freedom of religion and individualism that would set the stage for liberal political economy. With his doctrine of predestination, Calvin put the individual's spiritual and material destiny into his own hands. The Reformation and the Counterreformation marked the dawn of the era of liberalism, enlightenment and renaissance in Europe. The logical outcomes of the renaissance were new freedoms of thought, belief, and enterprise that led to the Industrial Revolution that started in Britain, which was relatively the freest society in Europe at the time.

As America became the new center for liberalism[42], it also quickly replaced Europe as the new center of prosperity. Liberals and freedom seeking Europeans escaping persecution at home migrated to America. Their literal reading of the Biblical promise, that: "God's children can never be poor", became the great incentive for a self-fulfilling prophesy which compelled individual Calvinist Christians, especially American puritans, to work hard and deliberately accumulate capital as a sign of divine benevolence, thus adding a religious dimension to their materialism and wealth exhibitionism. Among the Puritans and early pilgrims in America, the richer one was the more the one claimed to be blessed by God, meaning that the chosen were blessed abundantly. Of course, the lazy and indolent could not naturally claim God's blessing, and, since everyone wanted to be considered blessed, hard work became a moral action. This led to a healthy competition for prosperity and divine blessing, and the economic consequence of this was a very high level of productivity which is always the panacea against poverty.

The new American state was formed as an actualization of a *novus ordo seclorum*, that is, new order for the ages, based on freedom of religion, civil liberties, as well as free enterprise, with two British philosophers, John Locke and Adam Smith providing the framework for the new nation to establish this new order. Locke prescribed the three natural rights: life, liberty and property as the bases for sovereign legitimacy. While Smith established the capitalist or *laissez-faire*

---

[42] Liberalism as used here means freedoms of enterprise and thought, the equivalent of conservatism or limited government, rather than the promotion or big government as used in America today.

economic system as the only way to sustain the freedom of the individual to realize his God-given potential and live the most meaningful and happy life. The United States adopted these two interwoven political and economic philosophies, and that has made all the difference.

CAPITALISM AND AFFLUENCE

The United States adopted Smith's economic principles of capitalism which is driven by the profit motive, the consequence of which is maximum productivity as a result of *laissez-faire* or no government interference in the economy. *Ipso facto*, the capitalist system promotes creativity, inventiveness, innovation and ingenuity. It also promotes equality of opportunities, and glorifies ownership culture, while abhorring idleness and dependency. The United States had already adopted the ownership syndrome within the *Declaration of Independence*, especially by adopting the fact that everyone has the right to life, liberty and the pursuit of happiness. This made Locke and Jefferson on the one hand, and Adam Smith on the other, the intellectual founders of America's political economy, fittingly described as democratic capitalism.

The most common alternatives to capitalism are socialism and communism. But unlike capitalism, which stresses equal opportunity, these encourage equality of results. Socialism and communism reward idleness and encourages dependency by discouraging personal initiatives. They promote public control of means of production. These systems promote consumption rather than production, and eventually lead to decay and poverty rather than prosperity. As a matter of fact, to the extent the United States and European capitalist countries have begun to stray from pure capitalism, their levels of prosperity have also declined relatively. And this is, of course, more so for Europe than the United States, because Europe has also moved further to the left. In short, Europe has become significantly less capitalistic than the United States.

Interestingly, other societies, which have not yet understood or adopted capitalism, have actually remained the bastions of poverty. According to Nobel Prize winning economist, Friedrich von Hayek (1976), non-capitalist systems induce poverty because of their propensity to government intervention and its inherent inefficiency.[43] It is therefore obvious that the adherence to capitalism seems to be the only tested remedy that could cure global poverty, and it makes no sense to shy away from this indisputable fact. Instead, what is needed is a single-minded adoption of capitalism and free enterprise by every nation, with the more experienced economies leading the way and teaching the rest how the system operates. Rather than give them handouts in the form of foreign aid, the advanced capitalist countries should help the less developed ones with reforms and the construction of the necessary political and economic infrastructure so that they can become free enterprise capitalist political economies within the shortest possible time.

Thomas Jefferson *supposedly* declared that government is best that governs the least,[44] and Thomas Paine in the *Common Sense* concurred that government is a necessary evil. In which case, what is evil must either be avoided completely or at best taken with extreme caution. So government intervention in the economy must be minimal at best. Big government is counterintuitive to the promotion of individual autonomy and self-reliance. It inadvertently promotes poverty, because public works do not promote prosperity. Public enterprises provide a false sense of security on the part of individuals because of public ownership of losses and failures. An individual involved in public enterprise does not work with the urgency and efficiency required for survival. Public workers often get away with minimum work. After all, their lives do not really depend on the success of the establishment. They are usually promoted without merit because of the nepotism that is inherent in public institutions. This intrinsic corruption in public enterprises leads to inevitable decay. The only guarantee against the decay in public controlled enterprises is privatization. Therefore, in the 21st century, all existing public corporations must be privatized and governments everywhere must strive to create conducive environment for the private sector to drive their economies.

---

[43] Hayek, Friedrich von. (1976). *The Road to Serfdom*. Chicago: University of Chicago Press.

[44] "The best government is that which governs least", motto of the *United States Magazine, and Democratic Review*, 1837-1859. The motto appears on the title page. The quotation comes from the introductory essay to the first issue of this monthly journal (October issue, 1837). This essay was written by the editor, John Louis O'Sullivan. In 1843 Thoreau published the third essay in this collection. The essay was called *Paradise (To Be) Regained*. "the less government we have, the better" – a similar phrase is also used in Ralph Waldo Emerson's *Politics* (1844), sometimes mistakenly attributed to Thomas Jefferson.

From the foregoing, there is no gainsaying that free enterprise capitalism gave Americans the full advantages of using their natural resources to build large-scale wealth of the magnitude shown by the emergence of tycoons like Andrew Carnegie, John D. Rockefeller, Cornelius Vanderbilt, JP Morgan, and Bill Gates, among numerous others. Capitalism is also the architect of the large middle class extant in America which is the evidence of a generally prosperous society, enjoying some of the world's highest per capita incomes. There is every indication that there is a near consensus that "capitalism is not only the most productive but also the most flexible and adaptable economic system in history, and shows no signs of withering away" (Gamble, 1991).

A cursory look around the world reveals that in societies with less poverty, people are healthier and live longer. Aristotle concurred with this a long time ago, stating that the presence of a large middle class or relative affluence makes a society more stable and happier. This makes it more than just a coincidence that the most affluent and stable societies in the world today are also capitalist. Besides, "the dynamism and vigor of the market has been amply demonstrated by worldwide dominance of Western capitalist states...only these states have come close to achieving the goal of general prosperity."[45] Hence, there seems to be a direct link between affluence and free enterprise capitalism. In short, capitalism can be called the product of that free or autonomous self-interested intellect seeking prosperity through free enterprise.

Scholars and economists have already observed that the shift towards capitalism is bringing prosperity to hitherto poor areas of the world. Professor Jeffrey Sachs (2011, p. 51) acknowledges that extreme poverty is reducing and is optimistic that the world can realistically banish poverty by the year 2025. But why wait for so long when we already know the cure of poverty? It is obvious that most countries want to be like America, so why don't they simply do what America has done? The United States of America is the epitome of capitalist success. Fortunately, the success of America's capitalist political economy is indubitable and constantly staring everyone in the face. It is an experiment which is still attracting freedom and wealth lovers from all over the globe. There is no reason why it should not be the model for all nations seeking emancipation from poverty.

---

[45] Heywood, Andrew. (1994). *Political Ideas and Concepts: An Introduction.* New York: St. Martin's Press.

The United States of America adopted a democratic system of government which permits freedoms of speech, press, religion, assembly and petition as entrenched in the Bill of Rights of the United States Constitution. It also embraced the capitalist free enterprise economic system as the logical extension of the natural rights or inalienable right of its citizens. The combination of these two principles has spurred America's unprecedented prosperity, and made her the envy of the world. Ironically, the advent of cultures that are not in consonance with classical Americanism seems to be compelling the dilution of American capitalism. This is arguably why America is no longer thriving as much as it did in the past. Today the United States seems to be settling for marginal improvements, which though relatively better than everyone else, still falls far short of her hitherto superlative aspirations. This negative acculturation must be checked before it totally destroyed the American genus. The American system must rather be strengthened so that it would readily influence and transform those who come here, rather than allow the system to be undermined by the very people who came to enjoy America.

The American system is humane enough to accommodate the three most vulnerable groups in society without compromising its very nature. These groups are the very young, the very old and the disabled. In fact the very old ought to have already provided for their retirement hitherto. So it is actually about the other two – the very young and the handicapped. Accommodation of these groups cannot be misinterpreted as sustaining indolence and idleness. Society has a moral obligation to do that. But no able bodied person should depend on another for sustenance. Everyone must be at work and in the business of creating wealth and making the world better for himself and his family. The human society is like a colony of ants where every hand is on deck for the survival of the colony. Apparently, the reason this is not happening as it should is because of the intrusion of overbearing governments that create underserved and unending patronage for people who have refused to be productive members of the society.

Capitalism remains the dominant economic paradigm delivering the greatest values and enhancing the true nature of man as a rational co-creator of the universe and provider of good life for mankind here, on earth. It is the most unabashed or non-pretending principle which allows people as individuals to operate at their best using their natural talents and opportunities. Rather than forcing it to succumb to global pressure to dilute its aggressive free enterprise philosophy, the United States should be encouraged and welcomed to transfer her experience to other areas of the world. What everyone must be concerned with should be how to ensure the welfare of the too young, the too old and the too sick or handicapped, and no one else. And this should be a global effort which must be both, political and economic, for the two go *pari passu*.

The United States and her allies must intensify the promotion of the ideals of democratic capitalism around the world, because only stable countries can achieve sustained economic development. According to Nobel laureate economist, Amartya Sen, "the world's worst famines are not caused by crop failure; they are caused by faulty political systems that prevent the market from correcting itself."[46] This is also reiterated by Charles Wheelan[47]. In view of this, there must be a zero tolerance for non-democratic forms of governance. Whatever the political system, legitimacy must be based on the principles of freedom, popular sovereignty, and leadership accountability, complemented by the right to free enterprise. Although the United States is the epitome of successful capitalism, it is not the only one. Others, such as most of the member countries of the Organization for Economic Cooperation and Development (OECD) have also demonstrated the success of capitalism. There are also more recent examples of countries witnessing rapid economic transformations after adopting the free enterprise system. These include: India, Poland and former Eastern European satellite states of the former Soviet Union. These countries started to experience remarkable increase in standard of living once they jettisoned command economies.

The mood of the world was adequately captured by Francis Fukuyama (1992), who proclaimed the end of history as the demise of communism. Consequently, China, the last communist imposter, is currently enjoying unprecedented prosperity and productivity because it has embraced the capitalist system in everything but name. Meanwhile, the rest of the world has all but declared democratic capitalism the *summum bonum* or the ultimate good in the world, as far as economic systems are concerned.

Quite erroneously the Chinese seem to believe they have cheated nature by maintaining a closed political system while embracing the

---

[46] Amartya, Sen. (1999). *Development as Freedom*. New York; Anchor Books
[47] Wheelan, Charles. (2010). *Naked Economics: Undressing the Dismal Science*. New York: W.W. Norton & Company.

market. They claim to have learned from the Russians, who could not control their *perestroika* in the context of *glasnost*. But many economists are certain that the inevitable will happen in China as soon as the children of the rising middle class begin to seek political space and expression. Be that as it may, the Chinese have also validated the ascendency of capitalism because China's pride today is seen more in her recent capitalistic prosperity as the world's biggest creditor nation, rather than by her half a century of communism.

Chinese are excited about overtaking Japan as the world's second largest economy after the United States. The question is why has it taken China, a nation so large, to catch up with small Japan, while still lagging far behind the United States that has only about one fourth of her population? The obvious answer is that China had been operating the wrong economic system. China even undeveloped itself when it adopted the notorious Great Leap Forward policies of the 1970. Obviously, they have now realized that China can only realize its full potential through the capitalist free enterprise system.

Similarly, all the former Soviet satellite states are quietly transforming themselves into prosperous capitalist systems, something they could not do a decade ago if they had not jettisoned Russian-imposed communism. Brazil has taken off as a result of her current market reforms. On the contrary, many previously prosperous states have stalled once they expanded the public sector and stifled the private enterprises. For instance, big government has ruined Zimbabwe. Even France is underperforming because of her socialist tendencies, and the same is true with other European Union countries when compared with the United States. Lester C. Thurow compared the United States and Europe during the era of Bill Clinton when the job creation ratio was twenty-two million to about seventy thousand.[48] Interestingly, most of the twenty-two million American jobs created in that era were created by the private sector, while all of Europe's seventy thousand were in the public sector.

When the Indian Prime Minister Singh took a deliberate decision to implement major economic reform in the early 1990s, few believed the country's economic success could come as quickly as it did. But shortly thereafter, according to Sachs: "To nearly worldwide astonishment, India

---

[48] Thurow, Lester. (2000). *Building wealth: The New Rules for Individuals, Companies, and Nations in a Knowledge-based Economy*. (Audio Book).

became a hub of large-scale service-sector exports in new information technologies."[49]

Even in Africa the little market reforms some countries have recently implemented are showing very positive results. For instance, a study of four African countries by the United Nations Economic Commission for Africa showed that the four countries – Ghana, the Republic of Congo, Rwanda and Tunisia – recorded relatively high growth rates over the last decade or so.[50] In geopolitically strategic African states, such as South Africa, Nigeria, Egypt, Kenya, Ghana, the growth rate is better than in some Organization for Economic Development and Cooperation (OECD) countries. Obviously, these are incontestable indicators that African countries are seriously positioning themselves as serious members of the global capitalist market.

It is clear that the true goal of capitalist development is to move from low to high productivity. Many African countries have bought into this goal and are now complying with the US sponsored African Growth and Opportunities Act (AGOA). Today the agricultural sector is growing everywhere. In Nigeria agriculture is growing at 8% annual rate. In short, things are improving all over the continent. The countries are consciously moving away from their previous rent seekers' economy. But they must fully embrace free market capitalism in order to achieve their full potentials.

According to Sachs, to improve their conditions, the extremely poor countries need six types of capital, namely: human capital as in health, nutrition, and needed skill for each person to be economically productive; business capital, like machinery, facilities, motorized transport used in agriculture, industry and services; infrastructure capital, such as roads, power, water, and sanitation, airports and seaports, and telecommunications systems, that are critical inputs into business productivity; natural capital, by way of arable land, healthy soil, biodiversity, and well-functioning ecosystems that provide the environmental services needed in human society; public institutional capital, like the commercial law, judicial systems, government services and policing that underpin the peaceful and prosperous division of labor; knowledge capital, in the form of scientific and technological know-how

---

[49] Sachs, Jeffrey. (2005). *The End of Poverty: Economic Possibilities of Our Time*. New York: Penguin Book. p.178.
[50] www.uneca.org. Economic report on Africa 2010.

that raises productivity in business output and the promotion of physical and natural capital.[51]

Meanwhile, the perceived inadequacies of capitalism are largely cosmetic, not fundamental to it. They can be said to be weaknesses of operation not per se. For instance, regarding equal opportunities that can easily be ensured by providing a level play field that is devoid of prejudices, and undue advantages to some and not to others. Using the metaphor of a marathon, everyone must begin at the same starting point. This can also be achieved by making early childhood education the most crucial equipment for life. Everyone knows that without equal educational opportunities, there would be no moral grounds to expect fair competitions from everyone in society. But as stated earlier, except in the unusual cases of disability, any healthy individual who is in extreme poverty is certainly either stupid or misguided. Poverty which often comes from irrational living certainly diminishes one's humanity.

Perhaps the only really meaningful criticism that can be leveled against American capitalism is the unpalatable condition of slavery that existed at the beginning, because it undermined the principle of equal opportunity quintessential to capitalism. Fortunately, efforts have been and are still being made since then to perfect the moral order of human equality upon which the country was founded. Giant strides have been made in this regard both, economically and politically. Needless to say, that the significance of America electing Barack Obama – a black man – as president can never be exaggerated. This is what Justice Thurgood Marshall referred to when he accurately stated that the American experiment is constantly improving.

CAPITALISM AND TRADITIONAL AFRICA

If capitalism means the triumph of the private over the public enterprises, Africa is the least capitalist region of the world. Arguably, this is why Africa is also the poorest and least productive region of the world. This was not always the case. Africa's poverty can be said to be the product of colonialism, exacerbated by the disruption of the traditional African mode of production which was inherently capitalistic. Hence, the focus of all who want to cure Africa of poverty must be to entrench capitalist culture thoroughly in that region. All indigenous

---

[51] Ibid. pp. 244-245.

African systems that are already capitalistic must be encouraged, modified and helped to adapt to the modern capitalist system, whereas those that are less so, must be re-educated and re-orientated towards the capitalist culture.

But since another name for capitalism is the 'free market', and in the past, African communities were large open markets, one could say that *perhaps* capitalism began in Africa. Africans practiced capitalism before the advent of European colonialism. They had innate wealth creation mechanisms and attitudes that sustained them over the millennia. The traditional African societies were differentiated wealth holding systems that clearly ensured that individuals were rewarded by their abilities to think and strive. Traditional nobility existed even where there were no traditional monarchies or aristocracies, and the presence of local bourgeoisie was not a strange phenomenon in traditional Africa. It was rather natural. For instance, among the Igbo,[52] who did not have traditional oligarchies, prominence was achieved in any of the following three ways: oratory or intellectual prowess, physical prowess and economic prowess or entrepreneurship.

As already mentioned, in Africa the market was not only free, it was also open. It was open in the sense that transactions were made in open and outdoor settings where the community of buyers and sellers converged to do business by exchanging their goods and services. There were markets in Africa before the coming of Europeans. Ayittey rightly observed that "markets and trading have been part of indigenous African economic heritage centuries before the colonialists stepped foot on the continent. The supposedly backwards chiefs of Africa seldom banned any market trading activities"[53] There were large markets in Timbuktu, Kano, Salaga, Onitsha, to mention but these, and Africans bargained and still bargain for prices in open market.

Even nomadic cattle herdsmen freely drove their animals and sold them to whomsoever they pleased and for whatever bargains they could get, in what was indubitably free enterprise *par excellence*. Craftsmen hawked their wares from one local market to another as dictated by the

---

[52] The Igbo are a notable republican and capitalist national group in Africa inhabiting the South East of Nigeria. They provide the economic engine for free enterprise in the region and beyond.
[53] Ayittey, George. *Traditional African Capitalism*
http:// www.youtube.com/watch?v=_KXDZUdYanM May 11, 2010.

profit motive. Igbo farmers sold their yams or leased them to younger and hardworking sharecroppers as capitalists using ingenious methods to accumulate more wealth.[54] In fact, the market in Onitsha in Igbo land, Eastern Nigeria, was described as the largest market in West Africa.

Furthermore, in Africa, land – the primary means of production – is owned privately. This was similar to what operated during America's frontier period when land was acquired by whoever secured and settled it first. The lineage of that initial owner would then own the land and use it as their heritage. It is owned by the extended family, and it was that extended family unit that operated the land. They kept their proceeds. There was no organized state that could take this away from them. Traditionally, African land was the primary means of wealth production, and although it was family owned, it was usually apportioned annually to individuals who cultivated it to make a living for themselves. The proceeds from one's labor were never taken from him or shared. It remained the exclusive right of the owner. Similarly, in traditional occupations, such as: fishermen, boat-builders, hunters, wine tappers, goldsmiths and blacksmiths, traders, artists, arbitrators, including, of course, farmers, etc., ordinary people owned and disposed their products as they pleased without interference from any one.

In terms of broader economic exchanges, as a matter of fact, within the limits of communications and transportation possibilities, there were very significant free cross-border trade and economic exchanges among the various African nations before they were forced into the artificial political states of today. For instance, Igbo traders did business all over West Africa. Hausas and Fulani freely traded their cattle and exchanged them and other goods for Kolanut throughout the region for centuries before the advent of colonialism.

In view of the fact that capitalism is not alien to Africa, the answer for poverty in modern Africa is to restore the capitalist order that was part of traditional Africa before the advent of European colonialism. In many ways what Africa needs today is the modification of her traditional systems. In Africa, land is held by families and in small portions. The village communities are communal in nature. They are each other's keepers. Since land is the only tangible asset common to all in rural Africa, capitalism must be modified in such a way that it does not strip the people of this critical asset. The only alternative is to bring the

---

[54] Achebe, Chinua. (1958). *Things Fall Apart*. Macmillan Press.

communities together for the aggregation of their limited but critical assets, such as: land, labor and capital. In traditional Africa land was the only tangible asset, and it was held at the micro level by individuals and families or communities. Unwittingly, labor was hardly considered an asset, and liquid capital was nonexistent.

In order to escape the miseries which European farmers and peasants suffered during their agrarian and industrial revolutions, Africa must avoid the enclosure system of Europe, and opt for a new brand of capitalism known as micro-capitalism; and the assumption here is that micro-capitalism is the panacea for global indigence. With minor modifications capitalism can rid Africa of poverty and put her and the rest of the developing world on the path of great prosperity as it did for the United States and other capitalist countries of the world. The following section is a delineation of the principle of micro-capitalism as a blueprint for African capitalism in the 21st century.

MICRO-CAPITALISM – THE PANACEA FOR AFRICA

There is no gainsaying that "what one racial group has done, another racial group can do even better." In this sense, capitalism can liberate Africa the way it did the United States. Indeed it appears to be the only panacea for Africa's economic stagnation. This is on the assumption that a productive population can never be extremely poor, and that most of the world's poor are so because they stay idle for most part of the year. Besides, among the world's poorest places, women only carried out the domestic chores, while engaging in subsistence farming barely sustained families. All the people are never fully engaged in productive ventures. In order to avoid the dissipation of efforts and resources, poor rural communities must come together with all their energies and resources to build wealth together within a system of micro-capitalism.

While seeking the cure for Africa's economic malaise, a Nigerian economic historian, Nnanna Ukegbu (1985), proposed an economic development theory he called 'agrarian revolution without tears'. This system envisages an agrarian development without the difficulties that resulted during similar periods in European economic development. To avoid the miseries which the enclosure system caused Europe, he proposed a uniquely African model known as micro capitalism.[55] His rationale is that in traditional agricultural societies, such as Nigeria and Africa, there can be no economic development without agrarian development, and there can be no true industrial development without agrarian revolution. The challenge is how to co-ordinate these two arms of development in Africa.

First, African capitalism must be predicated on the concept of sustainable development, which is development based primarily on the traditional occupations that sustained the people, and occupations for which there are ready and expandable markets. For instance, the major African food crops must also become Africa's chief cash crops. Sustainable development for the country would therefore be anchored on the mass production of the major African food crop, which would directly lead to food self-sufficiency. Once the staple crop is produced in abundance, the excess would become the impetus for further expansion or industrial initiatives aimed at preserving and exporting the crop and its byproducts to other people and places. The excess agricultural products would become the raw materials for industrial expansion, inevitably leading to improved living standards, which naturally translates into development.

Micro capitalism is the emphasis that autonomous individuals have inherent responsibility to engage in production of goods and services which they can consume or exchange, and acquire skills with which they can engage in such production; it is obvious that, equipped with such skills and muscle, individuals, as in petty farmers, can act in concert to convert their labor into capital and utilize it for maximum economic production.

According to Ukegbu (1985) the principle of micro-capitalism is anchored on the concept of an agrarian revolution without tears, which would constitute the bedrock of what would result in an "Economic Miracle." He introduced the concept of agrarian revolution without tears, after studying the short term difficulties of the enclosure system practiced at the dawn of British capitalism and agro-industrial revolutions. He was particularly worried about how capitalism dispossessed the peasants of their most valuable asset, land. To avoid this misery, and still achieve the goal of capitalist development, he articulates

---

[55] Ukegbu, Basil Nnanna. (1985). *Economic Miracle for Nigeria* 1985-1999: concepts and action programmes.

micro-capitalism in which the same peasants would continue to hold their lands, but bind together in village communities to form huge agricultural cooperatives that would launch them into agro-based industrialization.

To achieve what he considers a lasting remedy against global poverty, there should be systematic plan and action program designed to create world class agrarian and industrial revolution, and induce rapid general economic development in Africa and the developing world. The objectives of this anti-poverty revolution for the twenty-first century have to involve: full-scale agrarian revolution leading to the maximization of agricultural productivity; self-sustaining world-class industrial and financial revolution leading to full and functional employment or self-employment for the citizenry; (both of the above quickened by) a process of educational re-orientation.

I see no reason why African nations could not sufficiently feed themselves, and supply the African and world food markets from their surplus production. The tax revenues of states should quadruple within a short time; as an important by-product of the revolution. Functional illiteracy should be wiped out in the developing world. In short, with the total self-mobilization of the masses for socio-economic development, which the revolution would necessarily involve, virtually new economies would be created in Africa and the rest of the developing world; and the totality of the changes should amount to capitalism-induced economic miracle.

It is becoming increasingly obvious that poverty is in the mind. Many people have defeatist mentality and conclude even before trying that they are meant to be poor or, at best, work for somebody. This is, of course, antithetical to what a successful venture capitalist and economist, our own George Stasen believed as he explained how he instinctively knew from a very young age that he was to become an entrepreneur, creating wealth, rather than just be a job seeker. Obviously, with sufficient mental celerity and focus, anyone can succeed, because poverty and backwardness are clearly socio-economic maladies whose causes are mainly attributable to an inactive and uncreative mind.

Backwardness and low productivity in agriculture and the consequent poverty in purchasing power which it entails, and lower socio-economic and cultural expectations among the great mass of the people makes it impossible for consumer and capital goods and services industries to plan for, or to attain potentially attainable demand-based supply levels and benefits from economies of scale. This position has created a vicious circle of backwards and unproductive agriculture, delaying and stunting industrial growth and general economic and socio-cultural development. Everyone agrees that about 99% of Africa's agricultural land is cultivated or held by so-called 'peasant' micro-farmers.

To incorporate this situation into the proposed African micro-capitalist system, all peasants, or households will continue to own and cultivate their particular farm strip and appropriate the proceeds completely to themselves. Individual farmers and households would pay for the production inputs required for their particular farm plots; and this would be deducted from cash proceeds earned by their own particular products. However, the whole land owned by the community will be treated as if it were owned and farmed by a large capitalist company.

The question that must be asked is: "how will this massive project of agricultural re-organization and development be financed?" The answer is, "through the financial resources which will be generated by organized micro-capitalism." This would then serve as collateral for the purpose of purchasing and using farm machinery, cash loans, crop processing, storage and sale. The surplus value or profit accumulated translates into wealth, which can be reinvested to generate even greater wealth. Agricultural production will be organized to go hand in hand with other areas of human production, in terms of goods and services. This would render the issue of the so-called rural-urban migration totally irrelevant in Africa and the developing world.

In a truly capitalist free enterprise economy the government owes no one a job. Everyone must accept his inherent responsibility to find a way of producing goods and services to satisfy his needs. Productivity or useful economic production must be geared towards supplying ascertainable demands which itself is related to needs' satisfaction. The educational system would also promote self-reliance. People who send their children to school and adults who send themselves, as a matter of critical interest should look at the various areas of human demand and choose those in which they would endeavor to acquire production capabilities. In making their choices they would have to consider the level of actual and potential demand in the particular areas over time.

The primary cause of the present alarming level of unemployment for school leavers is that almost every one of those who went to school, went there to acquire capability for public service employment, especially the purely administrative sub-sector in that service. Yet, the area of human need which the public service should be organized and funded to satisfy, that is, national harmony and cooperation cannot be expected to continue to expand *ad infinitum*. This saturation of the economy with job seekers has resulted in chronic unemployment. Only a functional education can address this anomaly. A good education should result in, at least, a commensurate balance of the numbers job creators and job seekers.

With the current scarcity of employment opportunities across the globe, and especially with people feeling the sharp pinch of over-supply in the public service area, this is the psychological moment to make a radical and positive change in world educational curricula. For capitalism or entrepreneurship to flourish in the twenty-first century, educational systems everywhere, but especially in Africa and the rest of the developing world, must be able to teach productive skills right from grade schools all the way to university, for those who can go so far. It is no longer feasible economically to allow the present situation in Africa, whereby a person can spend eleven years in both, primary and secondary school and yet is in no position to produce any goods or services in demand, which his 'illiterate' mother or father cannot produce. And what is worse, because of his little or no participation in practical training in traditional production techniques, he cannot even produce those goods and services which his "uneducated" parents could. And yet he wants to satisfy his basic needs at a higher level than his parents.

Furthermore, it has to be emphasized that anyone, who is not in a position to produce on his own, the goods and services he can consume or readily sell or exchange for the purpose of satisfying the balance of his needs, is neither autonomous nor viable. Viable here is the same as being adequate. This viability which involves the human capacity to think, and create wealth is primarily the responsibility of an active intellect. When man as a rational being fails to get full utility from his brain, something can be said to be fundamentally wrong with his claim of full humanity. Of course many say that lack of capital is the real constraint. So what about capital?

When we speak of "the means of production" the word "capital" immediately comes to mind. How does one get the capital? A counter question should also immediately arise: "What is *capital*"? To most people, the self-evident answer for "liquid capital" would be "money", whether in the form of gold bullion or in internally convertible currencies, such as the United States dollar, the British sterling, Japanese yen, to mention the most prestigious. In non-convertible currency areas, such as most of Africa and other areas of the developing world, local currencies, such as the Nigerian Naira would be taken to constitute "liquid capital" for local purposes. Fixed capital would consist of buildings and other such durable heavy-cost property, which could be made liquid by sale or lease.

Too many people who are not acquainted with the evolution of modern capitalism, even "undeveloped" land would not be recognized as capital. And for most, if not all social scientist, "labor" could in no way be regarded as "capital". Rather, capital is one of the means required for the employment of labor for profit motivated production. Why don't we look at new settlements, especially in the new worlds, where capitalism had flourished? In all those places the origins of modern capitalism will be traced directly to territorial conquest and the confiscation of land from its original owners or occupiers who were then turned into tenants or serfs. Anything that developed into capital after that was the product of human labor, both, mental and physical. This point will become clearly illustrated to anyone who stops to ponder and ask how much "liquid" or fixed capital the European colonists carried with them to the Americas or Australia for the development of those vast land masses in those great "Frontier" days. Answer: "mostly muscle and machete, digger and pickaxe." Apart from the means of getting there and the food to eat, till cultivated land could yield its own food, the greatest capital asset taken was LABOR resources consisting of mind and muscle.

The idea of Micro Capitalism is therefore based on the basic principle that "labor" is "capital". In a frontier-type and virgin situations as exist in developing countries, where all land is controlled at the micro level and where most of the essential needs of the modern life are imported or are not available, and where demand is not a problem, the individual with muscle and skill or capable of acquiring skill has terrific opportunities awaiting him, if only he can devise a means of employing himself either on his own or in company with others. His trump card is his labor and skill. If he can apply his labor resource, the principles of entrepreneurship-producing, saving and investing – then he is made.

Although the idea of organized Micro Capitalism is original and unique, Ukegbu[56] acknowledged that it did not arise as a result of a purely intellectual investigation or academic exercise. It was rather intuitive. Micro-capitalism permits the achievement of rapid economic development from a base of mass backwardness and poverty, without creating foreign financial domination through perpetual foreign insolvency. For rapid development of the impoverished areas of the world, there is apparently no alternative to organized micro capitalism based on the monetization of labor and its utilization as capital.

The main principle of organized micro capitalism is that people with skill and muscle should be organized to convert their labor into investment capital. They should be encouraged to convert a substantial proportion of their monthly labor value into share-based part ownership of their companies; and they must be trained and organized to take active part in the governance of the enterprise. It would then be impossible for any worker or manger in the company to engage in the colossal fraud that now characterizes government-owned companies. Every share holder would realize at once that the thieving executive or worker is stealing his money, stealing part of the annual dividends, and thus reducing the value of his own shares. There could be no greater check on fraud or inefficiency in these corporations.

A governing policy of these productive projects will be the importation of foreign experts to help design and produce the goods and services locally. It will be the duty of poor countries and their public service to reach a national consensus to forgo the false pleasure derived from the consumption of any goods or services which they cannot produce or hope to be able to produce in foreseeable future. This will constrain them to exert themselves to the utmost in order to gain the capability to produce such goods and services, recalling that Adam Smith had defined the wealth of nation as the capacity to produce goods and services maximally.

What about capital? It is the dearth of capital in developing countries that makes micro capitalism imperative. Since the projects under promotion will be owned jointly (by way of marketable shares) by the workers themselves, they will then have to act as part entrepreneurs by investing such percentage of their labor value as will be calculated and jointly agreed by the group. The balance of the capital can then be

---

[56] Ukegbu, B.N. (1985). Ibid.

borrowed from financial institutions or raised from the general public in the form of debentures or ordinary shares. Even though, of course, the details of these plans cannot be given here, their feasibilities are incontrovertible.

Global agencies that seek to eradicate poverty worldwide should promote new mode of capital formation and make it available to farmers in the newly modernized agro-industrial settlements as already described. New financial institutions ought to be created cooperatively by the participating groups in the agricultural and industrial sectors throughout the developing world, with organizational and promotional assistance through Project Promotion and Management Services. Details of some of the projects, which will require urgent attention, as part of the program for the achievement of the "economic miracle" for the impoverished areas of the world in the shortest possible time, will now be delineated. Micro capitalism will do it even more cheaply and more efficiently in these developing areas with the help of imported foreign experts. Existing public corporations and projects should be sold to the people on purely commercial basis. Government will collect interest and dividends on its investments so far made.

All participants, including ordinary workers, will be required to convert about 50% of the values of their participation into ordinary shares in the company. The balance of the cash requirement will be raised from financial institutions. It is calculated that this project should amortize in a few years and that profit could be very high. Hence, many jobs could be created with little foreign exchange involvement.

Meanwhile, governments around the world must stop deceiving their people with non-productive and consumerist economics. Free enterprise has to be encouraged everywhere. In retrospect, it is now very clear that the bogus policies of nationalization introduced by the post-war Labor Party government in Britain has done a lot of harm to the minds of leaders of many developing countries, especially those who were dependent on British rule. They failed to note the fact that Labor's half-way socialism has been mainly responsible for the decline of Britain's economic position in the world which set in after the Second World War. To a lesser degree the current penchant for socialism or mixed economy everywhere is increasingly diminishing the capacity of the free market or laissez-faire capitalism to replicate the unprecedented level of wealth it produced in the recent past.

CONCLUSION

African countries must imbibe the principles of micro capitalism and agrarian revolution without tears. They can invite this author and other members of the *laissez-faire* fraternity who would have mastered this plan as consultants for the anticipated agro-industrial revolution in their respective countries. It is heart-warming that many African leaders now realize that the past must be incorporated in their countries' revitalization, in an attempt to replicate the phenomenal economic growths experienced by the United States, Europe and Japan. They must also be encouraged by the recent successes in South Korea, the former East European countries, India and Brazil. It is also imperative for African leaders in particular to incorporate and improve on that past by embracing the tenets of micro capitalism as the right policy for the full realization of the desired economic transformation of Africa.[57]

If capitalism is adopted as the guiding principle for global economic development, the twenty-first century could easily be the one in which the dignity of man on this planet would have been fully restored since the indignity of dehumanization orchestrated by mass poverty and its attendant sufferings shall have been addressed. Poverty is demeaning and calls to question the equal dignity of man. The attraction of capitalism also lies in its tendency to spur rational choice in people leading to freedom of action and enterprise. The developing world would be spared the stigma of indignity by adequately addressing the human scourges of poverty and disease.

As capitalism continues to permeate the globe, it becomes imperative for the West, especially the United States to help African countries to entrench capitalist principles, because it is the only sure way to improve the human condition and promote general prosperity. As in all things, what is needed is to promote the African nuances of the phenomenon. Obviously, communism has been discredited because of its own contradiction, which is easily seen in the Orwellian ironies of inequality among the so-called revolutionists once they take charge. In other words, though Marxists assumed that capitalism is evil, they grossly failed to account for why revolutionists immediately inhibited capitalistic tendencies once they replaced the old order.

---

[57] Ukegbu, ibid. (1985).

Over all, it goes without saying that what the former British Prime Minster, Winston Churchill said about democracy and other forms of government is equally true about capitalism and other economic systems. Churchill said that democracy is the worst kind of government except for all the others. Similarly, it is clear that capitalism is the worst economic system except for all the others. As mentioned earlier, capitalism is a non-pretentious system. It is an ally of the strongest and the best with little tolerance for the indolent and invalid, which is why its critics accuse it of being uncaring. But capitalism has also proven itself to be the most generous of all economic systems. For instance, although American capitalism has been maligned by less fortunate countries, global statistics indicate that Americans are the most generous people in terms of humanitarian assistance everywhere in the world.

Obviously, there is no perfect system. Even pretentious alternatives to capitalism, such as socialism and communism, easily betray their own inherent contradictions. They tend to preach one thing and practice the very opposite. For instance, even the leaders of countries that pretend to be socialist or communist almost always deceive their people. They build secret economic security for themselves and their families by stashing huge resources and funds in prosperous capitalist economies of Europe and the United States. They constantly prove George Orwell right by demonstrating that they are better than the very people among whom they preach equality, just like the pigs demonstrated to the other animals in the *Animal Farm* that "all animals are equal but some are more equal than others."[58] Apparently, everyone loves capitalism. Yet some people try to take advantage of the rhetoric of universal equality being preached by alternative "philosophies", to hoodwink their people into allowing them undue privileges.

From the foregoing, we have tried to illustrate that capitalism is the natural process of building wealth, through the use of man's God-given intellect and talents. Capitalism resists the oppression and repression of the human spirit. Capitalism thrives when man is allowed to be himself and fully utilize his faculties and creative genius. It thrives even more when there is also political freedom, under democratic capitalism, which equally entrenches the respect for human rights. Therefore, every effort must be made to liberate the human mind to pursue economic self-actualization. The denial or suppression of political and economic freedoms is the reason for all the inadequacies people exhibit throughout

---

[58] George Orwell. (1946). *The Animal farm* Harcourt Brace and Company

the world, especially in the developing world. Until the human spirit is fully unleashed politically and economically, the inhabitants of this earth will never realize their full potentials. Hopefully, this will be achieved in this twenty-first century.

BIBLIOGRAPHY

Achebe, Chinua. (1958). *Things Fall Apart*. London: Heinemann.

Friedenwald, H. (1904). *The Declaration of Independence: An Interpretation and Analysis* (New York: MacMillan), p. 161.

Gamble, Andrew. (1991). Capitalism. *The Blackwell Encyclopedia of Political Science*. Bagdnor Vernon ed. London: Blackwell publishers.

Friedman, Milton. (1962). *Capitalism and Freedom*. Chicago: University of Chicago Press.

Friedman, Milton. Friedman, Rose. (1980). *Free to Choose*. London: Penguin.

Fukuyama, Francis. (1980). *The End of History and the Last Man*. Glencoe IL: Free Press.

Heywood, Andrew. (1994). *Political Ideas and Concepts: An Introduction*. New York: St. Martin's Press.

Locke, John. (1980, orig. 1690). *Second Treatise of Government*, C. B. Macpherson, ed. Indianapolis, IN: Hackett.

Orwell, George. (1946). *The Animal Farm*. Harcourt Brace and Company.

Rand, Ayn. (1966). *Capitalism: the Unknown Ideal*. New York: New American Library.

Reisman, George. (1998). *Capitalism: A Treatise on Economics*. Ottawa, IL: Jameson books.

Sachs, Jeffrey. (2006). *The End of Poverty: Economic Possibilities for Our Time*. London: Penguin books.

Smith, Adam. (1776). *The Wealth of Nations. Edwin*. Cannan. Ed.,1904. London: Methuen and Co., Ltd.

Smith, Adam. (2008). *The Invisible Hand*. Penguin Books.

Thurow, Lester C. (2000). *Building Wealth: the New Rules for Individual, Companies, and Nations in a Knowledge-Based Economy.* Harper.

Ukegbu, Basil, Nnanna (1985). *Economic Miracle for Nigeria 1985-1999: Concepts and Action Programmes.*

Wallestein, Immanuel. (2004). *World Systems Analysis: An Introduction.* Indiana: Duke University Press.

Wheelan, Charles (2010). *Naked Economics: Undressing the Dismal Science.* New York: W.W. Norton & Company.

CASE STUDY UKRAINE

POLITICAL OVERVIEW

Reevaluating priorities, aspiring to new values, striving for democracy, thirsting for change, – that is how the 21st century commenced in the former Soviet domain, including Ukraine – a large European country with an *overabundance* of all four standard factors of production: land, labor, capital and entrepreneurial ability. It is a vast country which consists of 459 cities, 885 towns and 28,471 villages... and yet today this nation of titanic proportions is experiencing a bitter economic crisis. How did that happen? – Ask the Westerners. I say, ask the citizens of Ukraine, they will provide the inconvenient truth.

It is hard to come by a Ukrainian citizen who does not want to express his or her frustration with the contemporary political and economic issues. People of Ukraine openly talk about their make-shift Constitution, full of legislative and legal mistakes, which was hurriedly and haphazardly put together in 1996. This was one of the major reasons for the political instability and a primary cause of the eventual economic crash. Then there was the 2004 Presidential election and the Constitutional Reform which took place concurrently. They were aimed at fixing legislative problems in the country, providing checks and balances and creating a stable legal environment for economic growth, but it was all in vain. In fact, the infamous 2004 Constitutional Reform dramatically decreased the President's authority and rendered him politically powerless, if not impotent, while increasing the political clout of the Parliament. The West, the politicians and legislators, as well as the people of Ukraine, soon realized that this was a mistake and a catastrophic error, which created political anarchy, and as a result the country spent the past five years watching a most protracted political soap opera, as the infighting between the president, the parliament and the civil servants continued relentlessly. Lawlessness prevailed, the economy was destroyed and at the end the country lost its standing on the international political and economic arena. The effect of this endless internal hostility was especially damaging to the credibility of the Parliament, or, as it is called in Ukraine, the Supreme Council – Verkhovna Rada. Endless fighting between political factions, along with taxing and inexpedient, if not strange and peculiar regulations, as well as foolish mandates, undermined the Parliament and its legitimacy in the eyes of Ukrainian voters. The "People's Chosen Ones"[59], as Parliamentarians (Congressmen) are known in Ukrainian language, lost validity and subsequently lost relevance in the public's view.

Odd as it may sound, in spite of the ongoing political turmoil, the national economy experienced record growth until the fall of 2008. The reason for this is singular, but very simple, – world market prices of raw materials and crude and semi-processed commodities kept rising, and Ukraine had plenty to supply. The price of iron, chemical products, wheat and other grains kept increasing steadily, which also fueled the growth of Ukrainian exports. However, while exports continued to grow, the powerful manufacturing sectors were shrinking. This growth occurred due to the breakup of the Soviet Union and the ensuing free market activity. However, maintaining economic growth requires more than just exporting crude, semi-finished goods and natural resources. Sustainable growth requires intellectual capital and a free market environment. Fortunately, Ukraine has the prerequisites. They have highly educated workers, along with a history of success in manufacturing products, such as machinery and automobiles, along with a substantial presence in the metallurgy and chemical industries. Sustainable success also requires a strong president, a talented cabinet and an effective parliament to support a free market environment by ensuring the rule of law. Unfortunately, in this regard, Ukraine came up short and the country's economy experienced a significant decline.

FRENCH ECONOMIC REVIVAL – A LESSON FOR UKRAINE

World history has numerous examples of nations that have experienced an economic decline as well as a revival, but few are as relevant as the French political crisis of the 1950s which, not unlike the Ukrainian example, resulted in an economic catastrophe. The circumstances were quite similar. The French parliament circumscribed the President's powers and assumed complete political authority; then it degenerated into partisan politics, and party infighting. This caused legislative and executive anarchy which resulted in one of the worst economic disasters in modern European history.

---

[59] In Ukraine the term "Narodni Izbrannik" is applied to a Parliamentarian and means "the people's chosen one" in Ukrainian language.

So, not unlike the current crisis in Ukraine, there was the French political and economic crisis. It happened when the government was ineffective, and the highest echelons of the French public services were permeated with corrupt officials. At that time unemployment was rampant and the nation was experiencing economic agony. But the people of France received a man with keen economic and political sense, a hero of the World War II, General Charles de Gaulle,[60] the founder of the French Fifth Republic who, deeply troubled with his country's political and economic downfall, thus addressed his fellow citizens: "For the past twenty years France has been trying to solve its problems but all in vain, and today, when the country is facing new challenges, let it be known that I am ready to bear the burden of administration of the republic."[61]

In spite of grave and constant opposition from the French Parliament, having popular support on his side, de Gaulle managed to adopt a new constitution which included provisions that gave the president the necessary authority to govern the country effectively without constant interventions from the Parliament, and rather than relying on the hopelessly useless bureaucrats and Parliamentarians, utilizing his own small team of talented reformers, de Gaulle effectively addressed the outstanding economic and political issues within a very short period of time, and put the country on the path to political stability, financial strength and economic growth. This was accomplished through capitalism and capitalism *only*! Shortly France took back its leadership position in Europe. "Ukraine can do the same!" Vice Premier of Ukraine, Sergei Tigipko[62] is trying to inspire the people. Charles de Gaulle would

---

[60] Charles de Gaulle (1890-1970) – a French general and statesman who led the Free French Forces during the World War II. He later founded the French Fifth Republic in 1958 and served as its first President from 1959 to 1969. His illustrious career, encompassing military leadership, politics and economics, commenced during the World War I: in the 1920s and 1930s de Gaulle came to the fore as a proponent of mobile armored divisions, which he considered would become central in modern warfare. During World War II he reached the temporary rank of Brigadier General, leading one of the few successful armored counter-attacks during the 1940 Battle of France, and then briefly served in the French government as France was falling. He escaped to Britain and gave a famous radio address, broadcast by the BBC on June 18, 1940, exhorting the French people to resist Nazi Germany and organized the Free French Forces with exiled French officers in Britain.

[61] The quote is cited from a popular Lomonosov Moscow State University (MGU) textbook widely read in Ukraine and Russia: *Charles De Gaulle*. (1967). MGU.

[62] Serhiy Tihipko is a popular Ukrainian politician and finance specialist. He currently serves as the Vice Prime Minister of Ukraine. He also served as the Minister of Economy and was a presidential candidate in the 2010 elections. Tihipko is widely well-liked by

not have become the president, nor would he have brought the French economy so much success, had he not had concrete plans for action and reform which he openly and earnestly proposed to the French people. As such, he argued: "Is it possible for me to start resolving social and economic issues immediately in our country? Is it possible to accomplish this in an era of science and technology? Is it possible to restore political freedom and improve defense capabilities – so that France, as a state, can once again regain its leadership position in Europe? – There is no time for vacillation! – That is the goal which I must undertake and achieve!"[63] Charles de Gaulle sought no delays and no excuses, neither did he ask for big government. To the contrary, – he created a small team of highly capable, bright, hardworking and highly effective individuals. He planned, he aimed, he worked and he achieved. He theorized as little as possible, and instead he led by giving the people of France greater individual freedom. And with freedom came economic growth, wealth and success.

The Charles de Gaulle era of France is an excellent lesson for Ukraine. History is a good teacher, which no country, no corporation and no individual citizen can afford to ignore. This particular episode of not too distant history is an excellent example of both, the government and the people doing what they do best: first, the government giving its people political and economic freedom and ensuring the rule of law, including the eradication of the long standing corruption, as well as the elimination of costly and useless welfare programs which always tend to increase number of impotent citizens, political slaves and economic parasites; second, the people exercising their freedom and liberty to achieve economic greatness. Ukraine could learn a great deal from this historic example.

---

the people of Ukraine and has vast popular support. His background in finance is as strong as in politics: after the breakup of the USSR and the political power struggles that followed, Tihipko put his political career aside and got involved in banking. He started as a manager in a private bank. Banking and finance were undeveloped industries in the early stages of the former Soviet Union with a lot of potential. It turned out to be a smart move. Tihipko made swift progress and from 1991-1992 he was appointed Deputy Chairman of a small commercial bank, called "Dnipro Bank". From there he became Chairman of the Board of the commercial bank "Pryvat" until 1997, taking the small regional bank to become one of the biggest private banks in Ukraine.

[63] The quote is cited from a popular Lomonosov Moscow State University (MGU) textbook widely read in Ukraine and Russia: *Charles De Gaulle*. (1967). MGU.

EVERY ECONOMY IS UNIQUE

"Ukraine is not Russia!"[64] – the former President of Ukraine, Leonid Kuchma once made a simple statement which summarized his political legacy. The time has come for Ukrainians to look after their own economic interest. One of the most harmful legacies of the Soviet "economic system" was the draining of all natural resources from the fourteen republics in order to support Russia and its despotic rulers in their tyrannical and imperialistic ambitions. Ukrainians know this perfectly well and yet to this date Ukraine keeps exporting enormous amounts of raw materials, unfinished goods and unprocessed commodities below the world market prices to accommodate Russia. But today it is not *just* Russia, – Ukraine has to pay the same tribute to the European Union.[65] People of Ukraine realize that the federal government, as well as local governments, must do more to facilitate a pro-business environment in order to prosper. This is important so that manufacturers and high technology companies are encouraged to process materials before they leave the country. This creates goods with added value which contribute to *overall* economic growth and reduce the practice of exporting cheap raw materials.

---

[64] Leonid Kuchma – the second President of independent Ukraine from 1994 to 2005. Kuchma took office after winning the 1994 presidential election against his rival, then President, Leonid Kravchuk. Kuchma won re-election for another five-year term in 1999.

[65] European Union (EU) – an economic and political union of 27 member states which are located in Europe. The EU traces its origins from the European Coal and Steel Community (ECSC) and the European Economic Community (EEC) formed by six countries in the 1950s. In the intervening years the EU has grown in size by the accession of new member states, and in power by the addition of policy areas to its remit. The Maastricht Treaty established the European Union under its current name in 1993. The last amendment to the constitutional basis of the EU, the Treaty of Lisbon, came into force in 2009. The EU has developed a single market through a standardized system of laws which apply in all member states, including the abolition of passport controls within the Schengen area. It ensures free movement of people, goods, services, and capital, enacts legislation in justice and home affairs, and maintains common policies on trade, agriculture, fisheries and regional development. A monetary union, the Eurozone, was established in 1999 and is currently composed of seventeen member states. The EU operates through a hybrid system of supranational independent institutions and inter-governmentally made decisions negotiated by the member states. Important institutions of the EU include the European Commission, the Council of the European Union, the European Council, the Court of Justice of the European Union, and the European Central Bank. The European Parliament is elected every five years by EU citizens.

CORRUPTION AND ECONOMIC TERRORISM

Solving these problems requires a fresh approach and a new strategy. During the last elections every politician promised to do just that. The newly elected president, Viktor Yanukovych[66] attempted to fix the system, but widespread corruption, international lobbying and political interference halted even the best of intentions and with it all the potential growth.

Corruption is a serious issue in Ukraine. Every citizen is well aware that corruption starts in the delivery room and culminates at the funeral house. Alas, every step of human existence in Ukraine is accompanied with bribery. It has brought economic progress to a standstill, it has undermined the government and it has demoralized the people. But it has made foreign investors, who acquired Ukraine's factories for next to nothing, wealthy. The corruption has also made members of the Ukrainian government wealthy. This unfortunate subversion of free markets has robbed the Ukrainian people.

President Viktor Yanukovych has been trying to eliminate this pestilence and bring economic freedom to Ukraine. He has been successful to a point, as much of his efforts have yielded only short-term results. Corruption has almost destroyed the manufacturing sector and now it threatens the agricultural sector as well. Its roots run deep in this vast nation, but by no means is Ukraine the birthplace of corruption. Much of its current corruption stems from the seventy plus years of Soviet propaganda and dominance. Corruption was also a useful tool of Tsarist Russia. It was effectively applied to "divide and conquer"[67] the countries of Eastern Europe, the Caucasus and Central Asia. But baffled Westerners keep repeating the mantra, what prevents further economic growth in Ukraine? The answer is short and simple, – corruption. Corruption destroys the market the way cancer destroys its host. Poor nations remain poor due to corruption, as at first it only undermines, but eventually it completely destroys the rule of law, the right to private

---

[66] President of Ukraine since February 2010. Yanukovych served as the Governor of Donetsk Oblast from 1997 to 2002. Subsequently he was Prime Minister of Ukraine from November 21, 2002 to December 31, 2004, under President Leonid Kuchma, and he was an unsuccessful candidate in the controversial 2004 presidential election, ultimately losing to Viktor Yushchenko. Yanukovych continued to lead his party, the Party of Regions, after the 2004 election, and he served as Prime Minister for a second time from August 4, 2006 to December 18, 2007 under President Yushchenko. On March 3, 2010, Yanukovych transferred the leadership of the party to Mykola Azarov.

[67] Or "divide and rule".

property and free markets. But some indeed benefit from corruption – dishonest politicians, government bureaucrats, domestic monopolists, and foreign economic terrorists… all of whom try to create conditions *exclusively* favorable to them, and with that deprive a nation of all of its production factors without which neither capitalism nor wealth are possible.

Ukrainian corruption is complex and sophisticated. It is largely approved, if not designed, encouraged and supported, by the West, as well as Russia. By impeding free markets and open competition the corruption undermines Ukrainian economy. Corruption prevents the market from functioning freely and naturally. It delays growth, it inhibits success, and it hinders manufacturing. And without manufacturing Ukraine is forced to sell its natural resources, raw materials, unfinished goods and unprocessed commodities below the world market price to the EU and Russian, as noted previously. It is a truly lose-win-win situation for Ukraine, EU and Russia, and it bears a name, an ugly name of *economic terrorism*! And let it be known to the world that the guilty parties, both, foreign and domestic, have been responsible for the relatively recent starvation, depravation and demoralization of the Ukrainian people.

OUTSET OF INDEPENDENCE

At the breakup of the USSR and the onset of independence the economy of Ukraine was agrarian with a strong manufacturing sector. The manufacturing sector had annual revenue of 224 billion rubles and finished goods were exported to eighty countries worldwide. In 1988 Ukraine's Gross Social Product (GSP)[68] was 222 billion rubles; its National Profit[69] was 100,200,000,000, of which 30% was manufacturing and 53% was provided by agriculture. Before independence almost every state owned Ukrainian manufacturing company was export oriented. Gross revenue of manufactured exports was 3,372 million rubles in 1988. Eastern and Western Europe, as well as South-East Asia, were prime destinations for Ukrainian exports. They were in demand because of their durability and reliability. In addition, every former Soviet republic also bought Ukrainian manufactured goods.

---

[68] Due to centralized planning and Russian exploitation of the fourteen republics, GNP was nonexistent in the Soviet economics; instead they used Gross Social Product.
[69] Net profit from total annual revenue is meant.

A lot has changed since the independence. Old markets were lost due to politics and logistical difficulties, since finished goods now had to cross the newly created borders of the former Soviet states and Eastern Europe. In some cases established suppliers of parts, components and materials were closed. Manufactures which were connected to the former Soviet economy were practically paralyzed. The Soviet command economy and its innate inefficiency proved to be self-destructive. By the end of 1992 manufacturing output decreased by an astounding 35%.

Freedom and Liberty turned out to be expensive treats for the newly independent Ukraine. We know Soviet economists never engaged in calculating GDP, GNP or any other somewhat comprehensive economic indicators, due to political concerns and the need for subterfuge. Published economic data would have exposed not only massive inefficiency, but also the Russian exploitation of the resources of the fourteen oppressed republics. Sound economic data would have also exposed many economic fallacies trumpeted by the central planners and the Soviet politicians. Consequently we cannot accurately assess the true output of the Ukrainian manufacturing sector during that era. However, one thing is clear. The manufacturing sector grew every year from the conclusion of the World War II until 1991. What changed in 1991? Independence brought the loss of established markets and it ushered in an unfamiliar economic environment. Political chaos was accompanied with corruption and economic terrorism from Russia and the West which brought Ukraine's manufacturing to a dismal and lasting standstill. But the newly formed independent nation of Ukraine was determined to succeed. Success would require change.

NATURE OF CAPITALISM

The overhaul of the economy would require: the creation of new political, legislative and judicial systems, a new approach from the government, new fiscal and monetary policy initiatives, and, most important, it would require a new mindset based on capitalist values. Abandoning central planning and converting to market economy is by no means a simple, mechanical, quantitative process. It is a difficult human process that involves a series of changes in the human psyche and adaptation to a new philosophy, – a new outlook on private property, society, citizenship and human relationships. It is a natural positive change with abundant benefits. But sometimes the cure for the disease can be very painful. Vast painful economic and psychological adjustments would be necessary. We believe, and so did the people of Ukraine, that only the market economy can bring prosperity to everyone, not just the chosen few. Economic change alters not only human thought, but also human behavior. Many in the West, as well as the newly liberated former Soviet Republics, were caught up in the euphoria of freedom and liberty, and the end of the dreadful Cold War, but they were not prepared for the hardship that accompanies freedom. They were not ready to be responsible for their own independence: they failed to develop the rational self-interest; they failed to make useful choices; and finally they failed to look for and pursue those opportunities which would have increased their utility. Instead they kept looking towards the government, and the government kept feeding them with suboptimal choices, while keeping the choice cuts for itself. They thought that capitalism was a bed of roses, – an easy and quick way to make money. They were most certainly wrong! – Capitalism is the path to freedom and prosperity, but hard work and dedication are essential. Free market capitalism creates its own checks and balances. It rewards dedication, honesty and hard work, and those who do not adapt, do not benefit. Capitalism is honorable both, for the individual and the society.

Capitalism is no Panacea, neither is it a guarantee for economic success, but examples of free market failure are scarce. No nation with a free market system ever experienced a famine. It must also be mentioned that those rare (alleged) failures of capitalism were due to political corruption, government interference or foreign aggression. Restricting economic freedom always produces poverty, and that axiom fails neither world history nor the tyrannical regimes which sanction them. Some allege that the Great Famine of 1845-1852 was an example of the failure of capitalism. Well, for certain it was a great failure and there was indeed a great famine, yet… capitalism had nothing to do with it. But it had everything to do with dumb legislature, overregulation, corruption and dirty politics, and tyranny and imperialism which must of necessity always follow. In the 17th and the 18th centuries the Irish had been prohibited by the penal laws from owning land, from leasing land; from voting, from holding political office; from living in a corporate town or within 5 miles (8.0 km) of a corporate town, from obtaining an education, from entering a profession, from conducting business and from doing many other things that are necessary in order to succeed and prosper in life. The laws had been somewhat reformed by 1793, and in 1829 Irish Catholics could again sit in parliament following the Act of Emancipation, but it was too late, – the famine was the result of the long-standing economic terrorism against the Irish people, and not *only* the

Irish… the same happened to the Scottish, Welsh, Georgians, Ukrainians… the names of the empires change, but the policies remain the same, – annihilation of the conquered people by economic, as well as political, cultural and other means, – hegemony to starvation, – the British, the Ottomans or the Golden Horde did not much differ from one another… and if anything, by going Westward cruelty only increased.

Economic success, among other things, requires minimal government interference. The government must permit the free market to function freely. It must also try to create a just legal framework to secure the rule of law; and it must endeavor to develop effective tax system. But *that's all*. Both, the law and the taxes must be created in order to accommodate freedom, which is the only basis for successful capitalism, as capitalism requires neither slaves nor masters, but free men. Instead the government often becomes a gigantic factory cranking out roadblocks for freedom and, consequently, for economic success. Data from throughout the world clearly point out that there is a very strong correlation between economic freedom and economic success. Ceteris paribus, less government means more freedom and greater prosperity. The market establishes conditions where the most effective utilization of all production factors, including human talent and natural resources, can take place. Only in merit-based and competitive capitalism do we come across an enlivened and invigorated political entity, – a citizen. Only with political, religious and economic Freedom and Liberty can society produce an energized economic being, ready to create prosperity for himself, and with that *inadvertently* but *surely* benefit his neighbor, his country and humanity at large, – a competitive man. But, as capitalism does not fall from the sky, this Freedom and Liberty must be desired, fought for and valiantly acquired. And that is precisely what was missing in Ukraine. In its place were inaction, lethargy and vacillation, and mistrust toward change and distrust of economic freedom. The core problem was mistrust between the *government* and the *governed*, between the political elite and the people. The government was estranged from Ukrainians and Ukrainians – from the government. Citizens did not place trust in the government. What caused this estrangement? The blame has to fall on the meddling, collusive, coercive and always stifling government and *not* on the people.

It was the government that made countless mistakes during the transition from Soviet politics to freedom and nation building. It is impossible to nurture economic growth without a solid foundation for expedient policy-making and a supportive legislative base. It is impossible to conduct business without the rule of law, as without it neither man's private life, nor his private property would be secured. And that certainly proved to be the case in the newly independent Ukraine. The government failed to provide practical legislation, sound policies for privatization of public property (factories, mills, plants, mines, farmlands, etc.), reduced tariffs to facilitate trade, tax reform that would encourage domestic, as well as foreign investments, and, most important, it was guilty of the failure to inspire and lead the people by example. It wasted the greatest form of capital, – human capital, – because it stole, it plundered, it interfered and it created both, foreign and domestic monopolies throughout its extensive collusive dealings with almost anyone who was willing to pay under the table. That is the capital which usually only a capitalist fully appreciates. The tremendous growth of Japan and South Korea, for example, was not due to abundant natural resources, but to abundant human capital. It must be noted that these problems were not unique to Ukraine. They were ubiquitous throughout every post-Soviet republic. Political stagnation and corruption caused economic problems, and economic failures were followed by social upheaval and political instability. And so a vicious circle of chaos and failure was created and recreated.

It was evident from the start that Ukraine was unprepared to switch from the command economy to the market economy, and that, in spite of great aspirations for freedom, it was unable to embrace economic freedom and fully reap the benefits of capitalism. The nation was not ready for it. Its economy, its educational institutions, its infrastructure, its legislature, its judiciary, its executives, its mind, its psyche, and its morale were not ready for economic freedom. On top of that, educational institutions were failing to retrain new generations. Communist era economics and business professors knew very little about how a free market works, so what could they possibly teach? Universities kept turning out the same brain-washed cadres. They could not produce qualified managers to lead an enterprise in the free economy. With this scenario economic devastation was inevitable. The only reason the Ukrainian economy could sustain itself was the simple fact that Ukraine could still export enormous amounts of agrarian products and raw materials for the world market. So with the currency flow from the exports, economic failures were less severe and therefore less apparent than in other newly independent former Soviet states. This is how a most progressive Ukrainian summarized the state of his country: "Destruction without rebuilding is no revolution; anarchy always takes us to regression and not progression; proper change of one regime with another takes place only when the new plan and the new program are well prepared in advance, as well as new people to serve in the new regime."[70]

INEXPEDIENT LEGISLATURE

It is a universal fact that a sound business structure requires a sound legal structure. In free market societies the law must be just and expedient. It must be designed to support economic growth. Contracts and business documents must be interpreted and enforced in order to attract and maintain enterprise. In capitalist countries the law cannot be static; it becomes dynamic in order to accommodate a constantly changing economic environment. The law must evolve to accommodate the environment and changing technology. It would not be unfair to conclude that economic policy dictates the legislative and legal strategies, as the latter two provide support role for the former. Indeed, in free and unaltered capitalism the rule of law is essential. In a command economy this causation does not exist. In fact, the process takes place in the reverse – it is the legislature which commands every turn and twist of the economy. Such was the case in every totalitarian country (or empire), including the Soviet Union; and such was the case in Ukraine which, alas, inherited many Soviet lunacies, including its backward and subversive legal policy. Instead of being an expedient instrument, the law became an insurmountable stumbling block to freedom, economic growth, and prosperity.

The old economy kept crumbling and the anti-market mindset remained. Names changed and new stumbling blocks were created and quickly enacted. Monopoly, favoritism, cartels, and dissatisfied customers, along with superfluity of rules and regulations, along with endless bureaucracy, were the norm, not the exception. These obstacles virtually eliminated the free market, competition and supply and demand – the cornerstones of capitalism and foundations for long-term economic growth and freedom. In the result, a stagflation after a stagflation followed, finally to climax in a most severe hyperinflation.

The legislature which regulated the conduct of business was put together haphazardly, and, as a result, it was defective from the start. An environment of flawed business laws, erroneous economic policies,

---

[70] Serhiy Tihipko.

constant bickering between the Parliament and the President, utter nihilism in civil and criminal laws, government weakness, along with ceaseless corruption, made civil freedom and liberty unattainable in Ukraine. In addition, corruption was prevalent in the newly established public and government institutions. As Ukraine was undergoing institutional reforms and trying to westernize its establishments, it kept receiving tremendous financial support from Europe and America. These Western funds were easy targets for corruption and, we have many reasons to believe, that from the start they were aimed precisely at encouraging corruption in Ukraine, since this would ensure the free flow of Ukrainian natural resources to the EU and Russian markets. The same was taking place all over the former Soviet Union. Officials from the West were also benefiting from the corruption. This doling out the foreign financial aid benefited many foreigners, as it encouraged Ukraine's international dependence and perpetuated Ukraine's political and economic impotence. In the result, Ukraine had to accommodate foreign influences with its resources. The winners, or I would much rather say *plunderers*, were international organizations, foreign manufacturers and politicians, and large transnational financial institutions; the losers, or rather the *plundered*, were the people of Ukraine.

FROM CORRUPTION TO PLUTOCRACY

Corruption, socially and politically speaking, is a very dangerous occurrence. It not only depletes public finances, but it also aids criminal and anti-economic activities. It creates organized crime and threatens to destabilize a legitimate government and its institutions, including the free marketplace. And as corruption in Ukraine kept growing and flourishing, it created a fertile ground for the creation of Ukrainian Plutocracy.[71] That is rule by super-wealthy, highly unethical individuals, who govern the country and manipulate markets by use of puppet governments, which

---

[71] Plutocracy – fusion of money and government when the unethically enriched super-wealthy manipulate with politics, dictate fiscal, monetary and other economic policies, and thus illegally suppress or completely eliminate competition and monopolize the markets. Plutocrats are usually retired members of the government who through corruption and tyranny gained tremendous wealth. It is a form of money laundering, which itself is the practice of engaging in a series of financial transactions to conceal the ownership, source, control or destination of illegally gained money. Plutocrats reinvest illegally acquired wealth in businesses and through the remaining political capital, as well as by use of the accumulated financial capital, are able to suppress and even eliminate competition, thus creating monopolistic environments to enrich themselves further.

they help to elect, while they remain hidden from the public eye. Plutocrats have their agents and representatives in every branch of government, including the legislative, the executive and the judiciary. They own the press, provide capital, which they acquired unethically, and become the omnipotent power. They are the worldly pantocratic "over-men", to borrow the phrase from the infamous Nietzsche.[72]

The Plutocrats are responsible for maimed capitalism in Ukraine. They are behind the mutilated privatization and flourishing corruption, which is often accompanied by physical intimidation and violence. These perversions have nothing in common with true capitalism, where an individual's industry is valued, hard work pays off and competition is encouraged. We must never confuse capitalism with tyranny. Plutocrats halt economic progress and curb economic liberty, while capitalists produce economic growth and encourage liberty. When it is useful for the Plutocrats, they quell manufacturing in order to eliminate competition and facilitate business for importers, with whom they have criminal associations. Whenever they so desire, modern Plutocrats are able to fix prices on world markets. That said, one can only imagine how easy it must be to fix prices in Ukraine or any other newly independent country.

As we have already explained, Plutocracy feeds on corruption. It eradicates freedom and eliminates competition, and, hence, a true capitalist has no place in such a political state. As industry is driven out, freedom is further suppressed. In such an environment long-term innovation and progress cannot exist, neither can the free competition. That is why it becomes vital for a country to fight corruption. Eradicating it eradicates its toxic side effects, including the Plutocracy.

Hence, we may rightfully conclude that issues relating to corporate governance in Ukraine are primarily linked to large scale monopolization of traditional heavy industries by wealthy, but unethical individuals, who fail to broaden the nation's economic base, and do not provide effective legal protection for investors. Such was the problem and mission before the Ukrainian government and the Ukrainian people in the transitional period from the Soviet era command economy to capitalism.

---

[72] Nietzsche, Friedrich. (1995). *Thus Spoke Zarathustra*. The Modern Library.

SOCIAL MINDSET

Innately people tend to resist change. At least in the short run, change is difficult, painful and fraught with uncertainty, which creates anxiety. But positive change becomes beneficial. Education combined with information is a key to positive economic transformation. A free market is quite logical in the long run. Its irrational tendencies are rare and they are always short-term. Market elements tend to eliminate inconsistencies in a time manner. The key is to allow the market necessary time to do the job. It is true that in the newly independent Ukraine the transition to free markets and competition created numerous short run dislocations. But slowly a new national ideology emerged which encouraged people to be free and financially independent. It ushered in a capitalist mindset – independence. Capitalism brought prosperity to the heart of Western civilization, Europe and America for the past century. The economic success was based on the free market. Post World War II America, France, England and Germany are great examples. Another example is Japan, where, despite scarce natural resources, the Japanese created one of the most successful industrial and high technology economies in the world. Eastern Europe and the former Soviet republics were left behind due to the Russian-imposed failed ideological platform – Communism. Ukrainians, as well as Georgians, Azeris (Azerbaijanis), Estonians, Latvians, Lithuanians and others were enlivened with the desire for economic success, and a desire to achieve independence from their former overlord, the Russian Federation. These healthy nationalist tendencies started to dominate the national policies of the newly independent states from mid-1990s.

A national ideology is a synthesis of a nation's political beliefs. It reflects the people's character, tradition, culture, and history. A national ideology is a complex decision-making mechanism by which a society decides whether to follow this or that political or economic course. The fact that national ideology plays a vital role in international decision-making can be seen in the various political models taking place in Europe and America as we speak.

The failure of Marxism was inevitable. Marxism was never a national ideology or an economic system, but rather the lunacy of an individual who never worked a day in his life and knew nothing about either economics, or the value people all over the world place on freedom and independence. Marxism was destined for failure in the Soviet Union. The USSR was not a country, but a vast despotic empire which combined at least fourteen enslaved nations to serve for the benefit of the tyrannical "mother Russia". The Soviet Union was "the Evil Empire", as Ronald Reagan so frequently and so aptly called it.

A pure laissez-faire never fully blossomed in Western Europe, which has nothing to do with any failure of capitalism, but rather with the culture and ideology of the European nations, and the missed opportunities and failures which followed precisely due to the absence of pure competitive capitalism in there. The mindset of continental Europe was never truly capitalistic. National mindset is frequently behind an economic successes or an economic failure. The question is which mindset, which ideology is most beneficial, which are suboptimal and which are, quite frankly, catastrophically harmful.

No country can progress without a goal or a cohesive ideological orientation – a set of common values. Nationalism is the reflection of people's will and character, and a national ideology is the embodiment of such aims, goals, plans and orientations, without which a nation cannot succeed. Of course having national ideology does not on its own solve economic or political problems or automatically guarantee success. We must consider several issues when evaluating whether or not an ideology is useful and beneficial:

1.   What is its ultimate purpose?

2.   What are the values which it supports?

3.   How reflective is it of the will of the people?

4.   Is it a result of a consensus – supported by the majority, as well as the minorities?

5.   Does it reflect only the present interests or is it also aimed at achieving long-term interests.

6.   How does it fit in the global scale?

NATIONALISM – PANACEA OR POISON?

Switzerland and the United States are great examples, where a healthy form of nationalism economically benefited not only them, but the entire world. Not infrequently their international economic policies made their foes into their friends and trading partners. The Swiss who were once involved in almost every major conflict in Europe as mercenaries, now enjoy commerce and prosperity with Europe and the rest of the world, so much so that Switzerland did not mind dealing even with the Soviet Union, – the political enemy of Europe and the enemy of freedom and liberty everywhere.

Unhealthy national idealism, on the other hand, if such a thing may be called idealism, can create global separatism and ethnic hegemony, as well as destabilize social, national and even international unity and threaten freedom, peace and economic prosperity everywhere. Such was clearly the case with Russia where adherents to the communist ideology slaughtered their fellow citizens and then moved on to massacre people from the Baltic countries, the Caucasus, Central Asia, the Middle East and even Southeast Asia; but beyond that, for seventy years it kept destroying its own economy, as well as the economies of the subjected countries. This is clearly reflective of the communist lunacy as an ideology.

A national ideology should not become an instrument of a country's isolation from the rest of the world. To the contrary, it must be used for strengthening international ties and building multinational partnerships. It is a well-known fact that in modern Western Europe swelling nationalist ideologies, whether expressed in capitalism or socialism, or in economic or political policies, do not rest in the extremes of the game theory and therefore never entail aggression against other countries. Western Europeans have tried to create win-win conditions for the European Union states, and sometimes for the rest of their economic and political partners in the world. In this modern age of technology it has become exceedingly easy to develop and spread destructive national sentiments which sooner or later translate into national policies. Aptitude of modern governments ultimately must be measured by their ability to channel national ideologies in healthy and globally beneficial directions. Truly able governments manage to promote national interests, and at the same time adapt to the global environment, which results in the fact that they are able to retain their identity and embrace international partnerships. Success lies in such balanced economic and political policies. However, people's mindset must change before such governments are elected and such globally beneficial policies come to fruition.

The onset of capitalism was severe for Ukraine. Businesses grew considerably and economic activity increased, but not all Ukrainians were willing to adapt to the change and the fast pace of the free market economy. Corrupt capitalism, the "Yellow Devil", as the current Vice Premier Minister[73] once called it, and not without good reasons, has a tendency to transform people from human beings into a cheap labor source. Pseudo-capitalism sets monetary value as an overlord and tramples education, spirituality and patriotism. When capital is the only value it is no longer capitalism, but *sheer* madness. Such pseudo-capitalism is created not through industry and competition, but through corruption and plunder; and Ukraine was never short of these; and hence the madness and trampling of intangible values was present everywhere.

Economic policies, or any policy for that matter, must obtain the final rite of passage and the seal of approval in politics; and in the result whether or not these policies and ideologies are channeled in the right direction rests with the government. The Ukrainian government has made many cardinal mistakes. Instead of promoting freedom, merit-based success and competition, it became a policy maker supporting the rich, creating monopolistic powers, and draining the country of its natural resources and raw materials on daily basis; accommodating its Plutocrats while ignoring outcries of its own citizens. If one cannot call the policies of the eighteenth century British Empire capitalism, then we cannot possibly call fiscal mismanagement and economic chaos of Ukraine capitalism either. The government bitterly failed to conduct thorough reforms to transform the country from the Soviet command economy to a market economy – no failure of capitalism, but a failure of the government! Failure, as well as success, comes gradually. The economic breakdown was also ushered in step by step in Ukraine:

1.   Privatization was accompanied with corruption;

2.   Tax reform was never completed;

3.   Trade regulations were never implemented;

4.   Social services were not restructured.

Failure to reform social services endangered the society at large. Ukraine was neither a welfare state, nor a capitalist country. It was

---

[73] Serhiy Tihipko is meant.

something in-between, something most unnatural and repulsive. The results were vividly visible and ubiquitous: mass closings of public schools, thousands of school age children left roaming city streets, closed down hospitals which caused a dramatic increase in mortality rates, the elderly left homeless and without geriatric care, and there was an absence of basic necessities, such as electricity. The government would neither sell off the public property, nor would it continue supporting the institutions it housed. The situation was truly grim and yet the government kept stubbornly pursuing the same old policies, and persistently blaming its neglect and failures on capitalism and competition. We know that the nature of economic freedom is not to promote competition over a loaf of bread among children and the elderly, but such was how the government viewed or rather wanted to view and portray the new economic ideology, which, when practiced truly and properly, and, most important, freely and naturally, never failed to bring not only a loaf of bread, but genuine and lasting prosperity. However, big intrusive governments, on the other hand, always bring corruption, poverty and misery, along with sweet talk and powerful rhetoric to castigate business and industry – the very enterprises which fight poverty.

Due to Government misinformation many Ukrainians started to develop, if not resentment, at least skepticism with regard to capitalism. It seemed that no one understood the essence of true competitive capitalism. That is not surprising, – Ukrainians needed to understand freedom and liberty and the essence of democracy before they ventured into comprehending and practicing capitalism. What is democracy? Let us go beyond the immediate presence of America and Europe, and delve into its past and original history.

CAPITALISM AND DEMOCRACY: FROM ATHENS TO UKRAINE

There are many countries where democracy is still an obscure phrase. The Chinese people, for example, never really had a notion of democracy. The word itself was imported to China by Christian missionaries in the 19th century. Until recently the Chinese national mindset was strictly socialistic, – community before individuality, and common goals, as determined by the learned, the elite or the elderly, before freedom and liberty. The unique quality of modern Chinese political and economic development is that today's democratic aspirations in China were brought on by relative economic freedom, and not the other way around. The desire to be financially successful shifted China from the Soviet style command economy to limited capitalism, and it is precisely capitalism that has inspired the Chinese people, which shall one day bring democracy and political freedom to that nation.

Russia, on the other hand, never experienced democracy: Russ Vikings had no regard for human life or human liberties, the Russian Empire trampled on human rights and civil liberties from the Middle Ages, and the Communist Party from its very inception brought this disregard to a new zenith. The closest Russia ever came to democracy was during Peter the Great, when individuals were promoted and achieved success based on merit and not lineage, or the accumulated wealth previously acquired by hook or crook. The fact that this was the golden age of the Russian economy, as well as political, cultural and educational life, is no coincidence and must be properly noted. Peter the Great's respect of individual liberties and his rule based on meritocracy resulted in economic, political and even military success never before seen in Russia. Although that properly cannot be called *Russian* success, since Peter the Great himself was part Georgian and part German, and his mindset was completely Iberian-Germanic, *not* Russian, and with a few exceptions, so were the philosophical, as well as anthropological, backgrounds of the successful military and business leaders on his team of progressive thinkers. They were men of action, – they were of Georgian or German noble descent.[74] During the past two centuries, the only lasting democracy that existed in Russia is the one which to date is still confined to its academic settings, especially among the intelligentsia of St. Petersburg, and oddly enough for Westerners, not so much in

---

[74] Peter the Great was an illegitimate son of the Georgian Prince Nikoloz Batonishvili and the wife of the Tsar (Emperor of Russia) Alexei II, Nataliya Naryshkina. This Batonishvili is known in Russian annals under the name Nikoloz and in Georgian history under his proper, indigenous name Erekle I, and was the deposed King of the Georgian Kingdoms of Kartli and Kakheti. This many Russian historians deny, but many – admit. History itself is clear about it and offers many facts to substantiate the story. For example, Peter's half-sister, Sophia openly publicized this fact, first made it into a scandal and even tried to get Peter the Great killed by the Streltsy – the elite units of the Russian guardsmen in the 16th-18th centuries, armed with firearms. Streltsy were enraged when they found out that the Emperor of Russia was not Russian at all, but Georgian, and that too of the Georgian Royal Family. They tried to assassinate Peter outside of Moscow. Peter narrowly escaped the assassination. Picture is worth a thousand words: dark and wavy haired Peter the great with the Roman nose, large and bright eyes, curled up mustache, broad forehead, powerful jaws and the chin, and the prominent chick bones, – such a face could never be found among Russians who are of Viking descent and have a very light and subtle complexion. Peter's features are typical only to the ethnic Iberians.

Moscow. But nothing resembling democracy was ever put in practice in Russia, with that one often overlooked exception duly noted above.

The examples of China and Russia alone prove that democracy is not a universal political phenomenon or objective. One could easily argue (and prove) that freedom is indeed embedded in every human being, but alas, it cannot be said that social freedom and democracy are inherently present in every nation. We can trace nations, some extinct and some still present, where democracy and economic freedom have a long standing history, tradition and rich legacy.

One of the best documented examples of an ancient democracy takes place in Athens, Greece in the 5th century BC, where the basis of democracy and economic freedom was composed by Solon, the legendary Athenian statesman, lawmaker and poet. We must note that even though Solon authored the reform, it was not fully implemented in the archaic Athens, and was utilized in later centuries to build the foundation for the Athenian democracy. The sequence is of utmost importance, – Solon's legislative reform implemented almost two centuries later ushered in democracy to Athenians and with that came economic freedom and prosperity. And the subsequent decline of Athens was due, *of course*, to corruption. The economic life cycle was complete. Foreign invasions aside, it is always corruption that ends freedom, and the end of freedom ends prosperity.

Solon's transformation of Athens to democracy commenced with a series of economic and political reforms. First were his tax reform and tax amnesty, when Solon temporarily freed the struggling families and new businesses from taxes. This financial relief encouraged entrepreneurship among the Athenians. This was no small step and had major positive implications, – lower classes did not have to pay back-taxes to the Eupatrids,[75] which meant that no citizen would be sold into slavery due to the old or new back taxes. The news of the amnesty spread rapidly and former citizens of Athens, who owed back-taxes and had run away in fear of slavery, started to re-emigrate back to the city. This injected tremendous human capital into the city's economy and created sensational vivacity in all areas of economic activity. Developing nations today could learn valuable lessons from this example, and that includes modern Greece, as well as the US.

---

[75] Eupatridae – the ancient nobility of the Greek region of Attica (the historical region containing Athens).

The Second reform was meritocracy, – Solon abolished distinction by nobility and supported both, economic and merit-based timocracy, – a society where people of merit and honor, as well as financial success, were valued and elected to the government. Due to this reform the very structure of the society changed. People were no longer divided into nobility, artisans and farmers, but instead they were classed according to their economic and non-economic (education, valor, warfare, etc.) accomplishments. This division included the following new classes:

1. Pentacosiomedimnoi – valued at 500 medimnoi of cereals annually and eligible to serve as Strategoi (Generals);

2. Hippeis or Triacosiomedimnoi – valued at 300 medimnoi production annually and eligible to serve as Knights in the cavalry;

3. Zeugitai – valued at 200 medimnoi and eligible to serve as Hoplite (infantry);

4. Thetes – valued at 199 medimnoi annually or less and eligible to serve as auxiliary forces or as rowers in the Navy.

Solon gave autonomy to each geopolitical district and each branch of the government. He only presided over Areopagus.[76] Solon created universal measurement and monetary systems, and gave greater freedom to individual citizens. For example, instead of imposing public education, he allowed parents to choose education for their children, as long as the level of education met minimum standards of Athenian education. He created legislation for punishing almost all counterproductive activities, including the use of imprecation and profanity.

---

[76] Areopagus – in pre-classical times (before the 5th century BC), the Areopagus was the council of elders of the city of Athens, similar to the Roman Senate. Like the Senate, its membership was restricted to those who had held high public office, in this case that of Archon. In 594 BC, the Areopagus agreed to hand over its functions to Solon for reform. He instituted democratic reforms, reconstituted its membership and returned control to the organization. Now, the history goes beyond that: Areopagus or Areios Pagos is the "Rock of Ares", north-west of the Acropolis, which in classical times functioned as the high Court of Appeal for criminal and civil cases in Athens. Ares was supposed to have been tried here by the gods for the murder of Poseidon's son Alirrothios – a typical example of an aetiological myth.

Solon's economic reforms need to be understood in the context of a primitive, subsistence economy that prevailed, both, before and after his time. Opportunities for international trade were minimal. It has been estimated that even in the Roman era goods rose 40% in value for every 100 miles they were carried over land, but only 1.3% for the same distance they were carried by ship, and yet there is no evidence that Athens possessed any merchant ships until around 525 BC. Until then, the narrow warship doubled as a cargo vessel. Athens, like other Greek city states in the 7th century BC, was faced with increasing population pressures and by about 525 BC it was able to feed itself only in "good years".

Solon's reforms took place at a crucial economic transitioning period for Athens, when the rural economy increasingly required the support of the nascent commercial sector. The following economic reforms are credited to Solon:

1. Foreign tradesmen were encouraged to settle in Athens;

2. Cultivation of olives was encouraged and so were its exports;

3. Exports of all other produce was prohibited to avoid shortages;

4. Revision of weights and measures facilitated trade;

5. Production and exports of Athenian Black-figure Pottery were encouraged through various tax incentives.

Athenian democracy is considered a shining example of political and economic democracies. It must be noted that the Athenian success story started with legislation, and then legislative reforms were aimed simultaneously at political and economic changes which brought progress and prosperity to the city state. The Athenian example proves that a greater degree of economic liberty brings more political freedom and vice versa, and that unhindered competition results in wealth and prosperity not only for the immediately enriched individuals and businessmen, but for the society and the nation at large.

UKRAINE'S ECONOMY: BIG PICTURE

Something was missing in Ukraine. Haphazard and corrupted laws and regulations produced perverted forms of political and economic policies, and, hence, pseudo forms of both, democracy and capitalism. If not for the lack of legislation, Ukraine's economic health, even during the Soviet era, was healthy enough to overcome difficulties and transition smoothly to the free market system. Let us discuss Ukraine's economy from a historical perspective:

Ukraine's economy was the second largest in the Soviet Union throughout the 1980s. It was an industrial, as well as an agricultural economy. With the collapse of the Soviet system, the country moved from a planned economy to a market economy. The transition, which was difficult for the population, produced widespread poverty. The economy contracted severely following the Soviet collapse. Day to day life for the average citizen was a struggle. Rural peasants survived by growing their own food; frequently working two or more jobs. In many rural areas the economy reverted to mediaeval bartering. Country folks were buying basic necessities through this newly hatched barter economy, but still they were deprived of essentials, such as electricity and running water. The elderly were often denied their pension benefits on a temporary or permanent basis. Schools were closing and generations were denied basic education. This was not the fault of the market system, but the residual failure of socialism and the ensuing corruption and inefficiency. The government liberalized most prices to combat widespread shortages, which was modestly successful. But it was not a market solution. At the same time, the government continued to subsidize state-run industries and agriculture. The loose monetary policies of the early 1990s resulted in inflation and then in hyperinflation. Ukraine holds the modern world inflation record for one calendar year. The year was 1993. Of course, those living on fixed incomes suffered the most. Teachers, medical workers, retirees and public servants were driven to starvation. In 1996 a new currency, the Hryvnia was introduced and prices began to stabilize.

Structural reforms were failing bitterly. The worst failure was Ukraine's privatization reform. The Ukrainian government and the Western press kept placing the blame on Ukrainian people. They blamed the people for their lack of understanding of basic economic concepts, international investment and local privatization. As reform stalled, a large number of the state owned enterprises had to be exempt from the process.

In reality, not the people, but a most unnatural force was hindering the privatization in Ukraine, – government corruption was rampant and Western investors kept encouraging it. They were successful at acquiring industrial and agrarian capital for next to nothing, – factories, mills, automotive plants, as well as large parcels of land were sold from behind closed doors. National capital was taken right under the noses of the Ukrainian people. Seeing that, the public started to oppose privatization altogether, and the government infused the notion that capitalism was injurious and destructive.

At some point history shall set the facts straight and vindicate the people of Ukraine, as well as capitalism. Human nature inherently seeks freedom above all else and that includes economic freedom. The great majority of the Ukrainian people yearned for greater economic freedom and capitalism, but the backroom dealings between some unethical Western businessmen, Ukrainian Plutocrats and corrupt Ukrainian government officials had left a very bad taste in the mouths of the Ukrainian people, metaphorically, as well as literally. People were starving while Ukrainian Plutocrats (who should not be called *businessmen* under any circumstance) and Western investors (who do not deserve the name businessmen *either*!) were reaping monopolistic profits. And once again, we may quite freely and rightfully conclude that corporate malfeasance was due to large scale monopolization of heavy industries by ethically challenged autocrats, who failed to protect legitimate investors and their investments, – and in that regard we mean the physical protection of the competitive and ethical investors, and their capital.

By 1999 the GDP had fallen to about 40% of the 1991 level. It started to recover quite gradually and by 2006 reached the pre-independence level of 1991. But that was not the result of sound economic policies. To the contrary! That was a short-term masking of Ukraine's long-term problems. In early 2000 the economy started to show strong gradual growth of 5% annually, because export-based growth reached 10%. An increase in the exports of raw materials, as mentioned previously, offset and disguised the failures. Official statistics in Europe, as well as in Ukraine, show that Ukraine's industrial production officially achieved a 10% annual growth rate. But the data is misleading nevertheless. That 10% did not contain a single share of manufacturing. In fact, as "industrial production experienced 10% annual growth", manufacturing kept declining. There was no data to show the decrease, but the data for the year 2008 would make it all quite evident.

In 2008 Ukraine was hit with another economic crisis. In November 2008 the International Monetary Fund readily approved a stand-by loan of US $16.5 billion. *Coincidence*? We do not think so. Monetary drainage of natural resources suited the European and Russian economies, as Ukraine's manufacturing sector kept crumbling. America and Asia never directly benefited, but neither did they object to the looting and plundering. Let's examine some statistical information to this effect:

Ukraine's 2007 GDP (PPP), as calculated by the CIA, ranked 29th in the world and was estimated at US $359.9 billion. Its GDP per capita in 2008 according to the CIA was US $7,800 (in PPP terms), which ranked 83rd in the world. Nominal GDP (in U.S. dollars, calculated at market exchange rate) was US $198 billion, ranked 41st in the world. By July 2008 the average nominal salary in Ukraine reached 1,930 Hryvnias per month. Despite remaining lower than neighboring central European countries, the salary income growth in 2008 stood at 36.8 %. According to the United Nations Development Programme (UNDP) 4.9% of the Ukrainian population lived under 2 US dollars a day in 2003 and 19.5% of the population lived below the national poverty line that same year. Are these indicators showing an *unexpected* bubble and bust cycle? We do not think so. The evidence was there right from the start; economic growth was based solely on the export of raw materials amidst a decline in manufacturing, increasing corruption, growing Plutocracy, political power struggles, and the ubiquitous presence of Western investors with shady reputations, all of which caused immeasurable harm. One thing is certain, the corruption and corrupt practices were not the result of a market failure. To the contrary – they were the results of the socialist "business" as usual, – popular *socialist* egalitarianism of the European Union, brotherly *communist* love of the Russian Federation, a most inexpedient Ukrainian government and undue government intervention. In fact, had the market been allowed to function without government interference, dictate of various international organizations, the killing egalitarianism of the EU, big-brother-mentoring of Russia, and intimidation from the Plutocrats, Ukraine would have flourished in all likelihood.

UKRAINE'S HEAVY INDUSTRY BASE

Ukraine has a substantial heavy industry sector, in conjunction with one of the largest metallurgy productions in Europe. Ukraine is also well known for its production of high technology goods, the aircraft and automobile industries, such as the Antonov aircraft, and various private and commercial vehicles. Widely recognized Ukrainian brands include: ZAZ, KrAZ, Antonov, Naftogaz Ukrainy, PrivatBank, Roshen, Yuzhmash, Nemiroff, Motor Sich, Khortytsa, Kyivstar and Aerosvit. Rapidly growing sectors also include information technology which exceeded all other Central and Eastern European countries in 2007, growing by 40 %.

Ukraine has a longstanding tradition in automotive and aircraft manufacturing. This part of its heavy industrial base was flourishing during the Soviet era, but since the collapse of the USSR it has remained largely underdeveloped. Many Ukrainians, as well as some Western analysts, believe that these sectors house tremendous potential for sustainable economic growth and long-term success. Let us explore some of these companies:

ZAZ

ZAZ or Zaporizhia Automobile Building Plant is the largest automobile manufacturer in Ukraine, based in the south-eastern city of Zaporizhia. It was formerly known as AvtoZAZ. In the first half of 2008 ZAZ manufactured 153,407 cars and commercial vehicles, a 29% increase from the same period in 2007. The company was initially a state works Kommunar, producing combine harvesters. In November 1958 the Soviet government decided to change its profile and started production of small popular cars, changing the name to ZAZ – Zaporizhia Automobile Building Plant – in order to reflect the new profile. The first car, designed in Moskvitch factory, was ZAZ-965 Zaporozhets and entered production in 1960. From 1975 to 2002 the factory was a part of AvtoZAZ holding, which was transformed into a joint-stock company in the 1990s. ZAZ products were never held in high esteem by the Soviet population. Although ZAZ did achieve its original mission, – creating a "people's car", similar to what Volkswagen's[77] original did in Europe.

---

[77] Volkswagen means "people's car" in German.

In 1998 AvtoZAZ-Daewoo, a joint venture with Daewoo Motors was formed. At that point ZAZ was assigned to the new company as a 50% shareholder on behalf of AvtoZAZ. Daewoo Motors made a large investment and established the production of its own models, while keeping and modernizing the native ZAZ brand. Complete Knock Down (CKD)[78] kits of Daewoo Lanos started assembling the same year; at the same time, CKD assembly of a number of older VAZ models got started. Following the bankruptcy of Daewoo Motors in 2001, UkrAVTO corporation bought out AvtoZAZ holding in 2002. All of the AvtoZAZ manufacturing facilities (most notably, MeMZ and Illichivsk assembling plant) were reincorporated into ZAZ. The company even adopted a new logo. The Daewoo part in the joint venture was bought out by Swiss venture Hirsch & CIE in 2003.

Starting in the early 2000s ZAZ's Illichevsk facility (Illichivsk Automobile Parts Plant) performed a Complete Knock Down (CKD) assembly of popular models for a number of American, European and Asian automobile brands: Chevrolet Aveo, Chevrolet Evanda, Chevrolet Nubira, Chrysler 300C, Daewoo Lanos, Daewoo Sens, Kia Sportage, Kia Lada 21093, Lada 21099, Opel Astra, Opel Vectra, Mercedes-Benz E-Class and Mercedes-Benz C-Class. The Illichivsk facility is currently used for CKD-kit assembly of Chevrolet Aveo and Chevrolet Lacetti. An adapted version of the Lanos with a MeMZ engine, Daewoo Sens, has been in production since 2002. The end of 2004 saw the beginning of full-scale production of completely domestic ZAZ Lanos T150, now that CKD kits of Lanos are no longer supplied. UkrAVTO has plans to transfer its transmission plant from the assets of FSO car factory to the ZAZ. It is also considering engine facilities of former Daewoo Motors subsidiary in India.

LuAZ

LuAZ is a Ukrainian automobile manufacturer located in the city of Lutsk. It manufactures legendary four-wheel drive super-rugged off-road sport utility vehicles for both, civilian and military uses. LuAZ off-road vehicles have always been sturdy, simple and low maintenance, although a bit outdated. The company is now a part of the Bogdan group, which also controls bus manufacturing facilities in Cherkasy. In the former

---

[78] CKD kit – a kit containing the parts needed to assemble a product. The parts are typically manufactured in one country or region, and then exported to another country or region for the final assembly.

Soviet republics to date, many consider LuAZ the best off-road vehicle for the price. It is odd, but its appearance to date resembles G-Class Mercedes-Benz and its capability to navigate in a rough terrain is not at all behind its German rival, although its interior and comfort were and are still based on Soviet standards, which is no standard at all. In 2005 LuAZ commenced assembly of Hyundai and Kia cars from kits. A major expansion program is planned, which will see construction of a new car manufacturing facility in the city of Cherkasy, including a new paint shop with planned annual assembly of around 60,000 Ladas and 60,000 Hyundais and Kias starting 2007. Passenger car production will be transferred from Lutsk to Cherkasy, while bus production will move to Lutsk.

Antonov

Antonov Aeronautical Scientist-Technical Complex (Antonov ASTC), formerly the Antonov Design Bureau, is a Ukrainian aircraft manufacturing and services company with particular expertise in the field of very large aircraft construction. Antonov ASTC is a state-owned commercial company with headquarters in Kiev. The company is named after Oleg Antonov, its founder and the head designer of An-2, An-24, An-22 and other legendary planes well known not only in Ukraine, but around the world.

The Antonov company lacks facilities for full construction of some aircraft, which is the result of a Soviet industrial strategy that split its military production between different regions of the USSR. Soviets claimed that this distribution philosophy minimized potential production loss in case of war. In reality it was designed to make the fourteen *oppressed* countries economically interdependent and this way force them to think twice about the economic consequences of secession from the USSR; and with this aggressive form of economic terrorism, it forced them to maintain the unholy union with the Soviet Union, i.e. Russia. Antonov airplanes were often constructed by aerospace companies in Kharkiv (Ukraine), Novosibirsk (Russia), and Tashkent (Uzbekistan).

Antonov's airplanes (design office prefix An) range from the rugged An-2 biplane (which itself is comparatively large for a biplane) through the An-28 reconnaissance aircraft to the massive An-124 Ruslan and An-225 Mriya strategic airlifters, the latter being the world's heaviest aircraft with only one currently in service. Although less famous, the An-24, An-

26, An-30 and An-32 family of twin turboprop, high winged, passenger/cargo/troop transport aircrafts are important for domestic short-haul air services, particularly in parts of the world once led by communist governments. The An-72 and An-74 series of small jetliners are slowly replacing that fleet, and a larger An-70 freighter is under certification. The Antonov An-148 is a new short-haul airliner of twin-turbofan configuration, which is awaiting Western certification. Over 150 aircraft have been ordered since 2007 by Russian and former East-bloc operators, plus Cuba. A stretched version is under development, the An-158 (from 60 to 100 passengers).

IDENTIFYING THE PROBLEMS

Let us recapitulate what we have observed about free market capitalism and its potential in Ukraine:

1. From historical, theoretical and practical perspectives free market capitalism is the only economic system which values freedom and provides opportunities to achieve the long-term individual and national prosperity. Price and competition, which are the two cardinal market forces, encourage both, freedom and prosperity.

2. Deviated capitalism is *not* capitalism. All undue government intervention is interference. Such interference with natural elements of capitalism can be disastrous, and may cause economic, as well as political catastrophes.

3. Capitalism is not a free ride. Its nature must be thoroughly observed and studied, and its fruits must be cultivated through hard work and dedication.

4. Capitalism is by no means perfect. Economic perfection does not and cannot exist. In a capitalist system some will be left behind, some will never achieve economic prosperity, but that will be a function of their decision-making, and not the result of a government mandate.

5. Capitalism provides economic freedom, which leads to political freedom. Freedom, civil liberties and free markets are mutually interdependent. The government and the people of China are

beginning to realize that freedom becomes tenable when markets are allowed to function freely.

6. Capitalism is not for simpletons or the languid. Capitalism does not mean exploiting a nation's natural resources by exporting them to foreign markets below the world market price. That is a sub-optimal outcome due to collusion, and not to a market based function. Capitalism is for people who exhibit talent, ingenuity and industry, who are also of high moral character. By appealing to the best and the brightest economic outcomes are maximized and all of society benefits.

Let us now examine what we have learned about Ukraine, its most developments, its government, its corporate culture and, most important, the people of Ukraine.

1. Ukraine, its economy, its politics, its culture and its people are unique. Ukrainians are *not* Russians.

2. Ukraine, like many former Soviet States in transition to a free market system, suffers from widespread corruption, which is pervasive through all aspects of life and every stratum of the society.

3. Years of corruption have created Ukrainian Plutocracy, – the arch enemy of freedom and capitalism, and *the* nemesis of the Ukrainian people.

4. Ukraine's government, due to the absence of true democracy and free markets, failed to provide effective political leadership, conduct legislative and equitable tax reforms, which led to widespread and pervasive economic failures.

5. The fraudulent Ukrainian privatization policy, carried out by corrupt politicians, and criminal foreign and domestic coconspirators, irreparably harmed the economic base of Ukraine and robbed the Ukrainian people of their birthright.

6. Legislative leaders of Ukraine, political executives and their cabinet members are rendered powerless and ineffective due to the powerful Parliament and its Parliamentarians.

7. Ukraine has been exposed to economic terrorism of Russia and the EU, which has exacerbated the nation's economic and political problems.

8. Ukraine is a nation of substantial potential which also has the capability of becoming a heavy industry superpower. Aside from economic resources, the nation has vast intellectual capital supported by a large, highly productive, and educated workforce, especially trained in polytechnic fields.

9. Ukraine has a core political resource – many in the current, as well as in the previous administrations are honest, hard-working and well-educated leaders who enjoy popular support from the people. Several key government executives, their cabinet members, and business tycoons, such as the former Minister of Economy and the current Vice Prime Minister, Serhiy Tihipko, are trusted, well-respected and well-liked by the public. They also have bi-partisan support in the Parliament. But most important, they understand the importance of freedom, liberty, competition, democracy and hard work.

SOLUTION(S)?

Ukraine must sell natural resources and raw materials to the highest bidder and adhere to the market, not to political directives. Markets beyond Russia and the EU member countries should be actively explored. When market forces are ignored profit is suboptimal, resource allocation is distorted and chaos ensues.

1. For every Euro received from the inefficient exports of raw materials, there is a loss of value to non-competitive buyers which could have been earned from producing finished goods for export at world market prices.

2. Collusive exports of precious raw materials and manufacturing finished goods are mutually exclusive events in Ukraine. Natural resources are disproportionately exported, and Ukrainian manufacturers are deprived of the raw materials required for manufacturing, even though, at least for now, *they* are the highest bidders.

3.   The social costs of the collusive exports of raw materials are great. A highly educated and experienced workforce is suffering from massive underemployment.

4.   The underutilization of talented workers reinforces a culture of underachievement which is economically destructive.

5.   If skilled workers and knowledge workers do not have satisfactory employment, Ukraine will lose its most precious resource – its intellectual capital and skilled workforce. They will, of necessity, emigrate to the EU, the United States, and other parts of the world. This will further erode the Ukrainian economy.

Ukraine's manufacturing industry would benefit from restructuring. Ukraine's neighbor, the Russian Federation, for once could serve as a good example. By 1992 the majority of Moscow's heavy industry base was engaged in manufacturing goods for military application. More than a billion people were employed in this sector. As the Soviet legacy kept collapsing and economic partnerships with the West and the US started to develop, Russian manufacturers carefully employed key features of capitalism and switched from *making guns to making butter*, to coin a famous economic truism. Resources are limited and the production of one good limits the production of another. If a nation devotes all of its resources to armaments, it cannot produce butter. It is this analogy that ended the cold war. Ronald Regan clearly understood that the Soviet Union could not afford to provide a counter mechanism to the Strategic Defense Initiative Organization of March 1983-1984, better known as the Star Wars. As to whether Regan was bluffing, we will never be sure, but the world is better off from this lesson in economics.

It was precisely during the Presidential visit of George Bush Sr. to Moscow, when a Moscow based manufacturer of bomber aircraft started to produce bicycles instead of military aircraft, – first such case in Russian history. At the XXVII Congress of the Soviet Communist Party the General Secretary of the Communist Party of the USSR, Mikhail Gorbachev[79] categorically emphasized that the "1917 Red October

---

[79] Mikhail Gorbachev – former Soviet statesman, having served as the General Secretary of the Communist Party of the Soviet Union from 1985 until 1991, and as the last head of state of the USSR. He served from 1988 until the collapse of the USSR in 1991. Gorbachev initiated the two radical reforms: 1. Perestroika – meaning, "reconstruction"

Revolution[80] was a mistake and the seventy years of marching in the Soviet shoes was marching in a wrong direction." He was perfectly right and the lesson for Ukrainians must be that the rudiments of the Soviet era thinking, business practices, legislature, etc. must be abandoned at once, and once and for all.

Among the key factors that negatively affect the ability of manufacturing and other businesses in Ukraine to earn an acceptable rate of return on their investment are the legal and bureaucratic hurdles which have gone unchecked. Nations that experience consistent economic health have minimal hurdles for business formation and low corporate tax rates. As of this date – 2011 – *even the United States* is losing its competitive edge due to the policies of the Obama administration.

In Ukraine the old Soviet mentality must be eradicated, – taxes cannot pinch the lifeline out of entrepreneurs, and laws that interfere with or hinder business operations must also be abrogated. A new tax structure and business friendly legal framework must be designed to stimulate, not prevent, future economic growth of the nation.

Privatization must be a simple and transparent process. Information must be made public in order to prevent further backroom dealings and corruption. This is an inexpensive solution for decreasing corruption from within, as well as without.

Constitutional change is long overdue in Ukraine. The Parliament must restrict its activity to positive legislative efforts and leave execution to the President and the cabinet members. Even most moral Parliamentary institutions are ineffective in decision-making. It is the nature of government, since government is run by legislators. The

---

in Russian, was the reform which was aimed at economic policy changes in order to overcome economic stagnation by creating a dependable and effective mechanism for accelerating economic and social progress. 2. Glasnost – meaning "openness" in Russian, was the reform aimed at increasing civil rights and liberties.

[80] October Revolution – also known as Red October or the Bolshevik Revolution, was a political revolution and a part of the Russian Revolution of 1917. It took place with an armed insurrection in Petrograd, traditionally dated to October 25, 1917 Old Style Julian Calendar (O.S.), which corresponds with November 7, 1917 New Style (N.S.) Gregorian Calendar. The October Revolution in Petrograd (St. Petersburg) overthrew the Russian Provisional Government and gave the power to the local soviets dominated by Bolsheviks. As the revolution was not universally recognized outside of Petrograd, it was followed with the struggles of the Russian Civil War (1917-1922) and the creation of the Soviet Union in 1922.

President and his ministers must have the necessary power to act quickly in matters regarding trade and economy, while keeping in mind that ultimately it is the free market, and not the government, that creates and shall create prosperity. Government cannot create wealth, it can only confiscate it. This will also eliminate the plague of economic terrorism, which shall help Ukraine to deal with the Russian Federation, the European Union and even the US.

Talented, ethical citizens must be recruited and trained as government officials. Serhiy Tihipko and other enlightened politicians, who have a lifetime of experience in business, banking and finance, are the future of Ukraine, and not the former Soviet bureaucrats.

CONCLUSION

The problems of Ukraine need simple, basic solutions, and a bit of legislative, political and economic reshuffling, accompanied with some *common sense*. The situation is a little grim, but only in the short-run. If the market is allowed to function freely and Ukraine's government is able to provide the rule of law, economic success of Ukraine is inevitable. In fact, Ukraine is a perfect case of Pareto Efficiency, – it has sufficient resources and overabundance of four cardinal production factors: land, labor, capital and entrepreneurial ability, – but they must be used effectively in order to create multiple positive and, most important, economically optimal outcomes. Everyone who is honest, keen and hardworking will benefit, – just let the free market pick the winners and losers. Almost overnight plutocrats will be replaced with capitalists: that rare breed of men and women who are highly motivated, intelligent, and competitive and know the true value of capital and how to deploy it.

After all, what is capitalism? Is it idolizing money? Hording wealth? Greed? Or perhaps Scrooging and Skinflinting? Not at all! Capital must be used and employed properly. That is precisely what a *true capitalist* knows better than anyone else; for capitalism is *nothing* more than knowing how to apply capital in the most efficient manner, so that entrepreneurs and the people may benefit.

We hope that the current Ukrainian government, which has already taken some necessary steps towards progress, takes a more earnest look at the free market system and the benefits that can be derived from Adam Smith's "invisible hand". Ukraine must encourage its people to grow and once and for all quell borrowing from the World Bank and the IMF,[81] – a dangerous tendency which, if continued, will surely ruin Ukraine, as well as Georgia. "Think what you do when you run in debt: you give another Power over your Liberty",[82] Benjamin Franklin taught the Americans once, and I, personally, never forgot the lesson. I also never forgot what I learned from my father in concise Georgian: "Rather go to bed supperless, than rise in debt".[83] Later on I discovered that Benjamin Franklin too, and many New Englanders before or after him, preached and rigorously practiced this very same and very true dictum.

Remember: a capitalist is compelled by his nature to deploy his capital in the most efficient manner possible, in order to increase his wealth and, as a result, all of mankind benefits.

To use an old New England proverb, "It is hard for an empty Sack to stand upright".[84] Ukrainian people need no New Englander to remind them that an empty sack could be filled by only one method – hard work.

---

[81] The International Monetary Fund (IMF) is the intergovernmental organization that oversees the global financial system by following the "macroeconomic" policies of its member countries, in particular those with an impact on exchange rate and the balance of payments. It is an organization formed with a stated objective of stabilizing international exchange rates and facilitating development through the enforcement of liberalizing economic policies on other countries as a condition for loans, restructuring or aid. It also offers loans with varying levels of conditionality, mainly to poorer countries. Its headquarters are in Washington, D.C.. The IMF's exceedingly high influence in world affairs and development has drawn heavy criticism from many sources.

[82] Franklin, Benjamin. (2006). *The Way to Wealth and Other Writings on Finance.* Sterling Publishing Co., Inc.

[83] An old Georgian proverb, which was also a popular maxim among the New Englanders. Benjamin Franklin mentions it in his book, *Borrowing.* See: Franklin, Benjamin. (2006). *The Way to Wealth and Other Writings on Finance.* Sterling Publishing Co., Inc.

[84] Franklin, Benjamin. (1980). *Poor Richard's Almanac.* Peter Pauper Press.

BIBLIOGRAPHY

Aslund, Anders. (2009). *How Ukraine Became a Market Economy and Democracy*. Peterson Institute for International Economics.

Bilaniuk, Laada. (2006). *Contested Tongues: Language Politics and Cultural Correction in Ukraine*. Cornell University Press.

Charles De Gaulle. (1967). MGU

Franklin, Benjamin. (1980). *Poor Richard's Almanac*. Peter Pauper Press.

Franklin, Benjamin. (2006). *The Way to Wealth and Other Writings on Finance*. Sterling Publishing Co., Inc.

Nietzsche, Friedrich. (1995). *Thus Spoke Zarathustra*. The Modern Library.

Wilson, Andrew. (2006). *Ukraine's Orange Revolution*. Yale University Press.

Wolczuk, Kataryna. (2002). *The Moulding of Ukraine: The Constitutional Politics and State Formation*. Central European University Press.

Yekelchyk, Serhy. (2007). *Ukraine: Birth of a Modern Nation*. Oxford University Press, USA.

ECONOMIC PHILOSOPHY AND GEORGIA

PREMISE AND PREFACE

The thesis will be based on deductive logic and subsequent inferences, as I firmly believe that the complexity of human behavior makes mathematical modeling of an evolving, dynamic and developing market largely an inadequate endeavor. This thesis will contain no empirical analysis. Instead it will offer logical explanations of human behavior, – after all, it is a human being, and not a mere number, that *is* the market. In light of the foregoing, I would advise the reader, who nevertheless insists on empirical calculations, to use an abacus as a footstool while reading this book, – that shall do the science, as well as the practice of economics as much good as all the mathematical modeling hitherto.

I decided not to defend the Austrian School[85] in this thesis. Its verities are so indisputable, its principles are so sound and its wisdom is so transparent that, I strongly believe, my apology would be most unnecessary and redundant. I also know that, even with the best of my efforts, I could not make any man, blinded with a mathematician's trade, see the essence and beauty of the real science of economics.

Logical explanations deduced from philosophical discourses will be supported with historical precedents taken from different parts of the world. The purpose of this method is to offer universal analyses by

---

[85] The Austrian School – an orthodox school of economic thought that emphasizes the natural, spontaneous organizing power of the price. Its name derives from the identity of its founders and early supporters, who were citizens of the old Austrian Habsburg Empire, including Carl Menger, Eugen von Böhm-Bawerk, Ludwig von Mises, and Friedrich Hayek. Currently adherents of the Austrian School can come from any part of the world, but they are often referred to simply as Austrian economists and their work as Austrian economics. Austrian School principles are based on strict adherence to methodological individualism – analyzing human action exclusively from the perspective of an individual agent. Austrian economists also argue that mathematical models and statistics are an unreliable means of analyzing and testing economic theory, and advocate deriving economic theory logically from basic principles of human action, a method they term "praxeology". Additionally, whereas experimental research and natural experiments are often used in pseudo economics, Austrian economists contend that testability in economics is virtually impossible since it relies on human actors who cannot be placed in a lab setting without altering their would-be actions. Austrian School economists hold that the complexity of human behavior makes mathematical modeling of an evolving market extremely difficult. They advocate a *laissez faire* approach to the economy.

transcending time and space, and to avoid confining my, as well as your scholarly endeavors to today's fleeting economic realities or to a single nation. I was also compelled to include some parts of Georgian history in order to educate the world about this small, but culturally most advanced and brave ancient Christian nation. I did not use peacock language. If at times history seems to be too bitter to the pallet of some readers, I would advise them to do away with history and pick up a book of fairytales. Although I recognize that not all men have an ability to digest the grit and roughage of the most natural fiber, I make no apologies for the truth, no matter how sharp its taste and how indigestible its substance. I am sure such endeavors on my part will not go unnoticed among my supporters, but especially among my critics. I shall wholeheartedly tolerate opinions of both.

I hope these premises are not seen by the reader as radical hypotheses or as dangerous assumptions on my part.

RECONCILING INDEPENDENCE WITH INTERDEPENDENCE

The principal objective of a state should be to maximize freedom of its citizens. Then it only follows that the optimal decision in governing a state is the one which brings the state and its citizens closest to this original goal. The fundamental law of economics dictates that "we live in a world of limited resources". Whether or not we are sober-minded enough to accept the science of economics or its most essential axiom, the nature itself shall unequivocally demonstrate that scarcity of resources bears a significant influence on our freedom. Alas, with this universal limitation comes universal interdependence.

Interdependence is a sheer and unavoidable necessity for every single human being: as I do not bake, I depend on others to bake my daily bread, literally speaking; as others, who do not write, depend on me to produce a useful book. From historical standpoint, this is a fact. It is also an unavoidable fact that such interdependence requires a significant compromise, – sacrificing parts of individual liberties and curbing personal freedom in order, if not to concord, at least to coordinate my life with the life of the baker. The weight of this abstract argument perhaps can be best demonstrated by the same practical example of a baker and a writer: I temporarily surrender my money, as well as my preferences for the bread-baking, to the baker, just as the baker surrenders his money and his preferences for the book-writing to me. The matter gets even more complicated when we approach such vital, but common and unavoidable issues for all members of the society, as the national defense, law and trade.

There is no avoiding the need for some paternalism either, – we cannot possibly leave vital national decisions to the mere vote of majority in this world of universal ignorance, madness, danger and duplicity. As one of the greatest economists of the 20th century, Milton Friedman eloquently puts it, "Paternalism is inescapable for those whom we designate as not responsible."[86] But who is to tell that the designations are just and correct? And besides, who is to say that we are those wise and judicious arbiters whose opinions and designations the society must blindly follow?

The fact that the social nature of men is such that both elements, independence and interdependence, must exist in order for us to perpetuate our individual, as well as common lives, brings us to a challenging, but a necessary undertaking. We, as free men, have a difficult task to reconcile our individual freedom, i.e. natural independence with expedient interdependence. Today's anarchist ignores the sheer necessity for interdependence, while today's "liberal" does even worse by ignoring the reality of human nature, – the fact that a human being is firstly and mostly an independent and freedom-aspiring creature. Ignoring the need for coordination of these two *seemingly* opposing aspects of human existence will cure none of the underlying difficulties and shall make adjustment to them only more painful. And yet history proves that, to some degree, this universal interdependence for all human beings, let alone for fellow citizens, is reconcilable with independence, and this sometimes can be at least expedient, and quite often even beneficial.

In light of the foregoing, two questions naturally arise: one, how do we reconcile the necessary interdependence with our God-given freedom and liberty? Two, how can we make this unavoidable interdependence beneficial? Below I will endeavor to analyze the issue of the social interdependence and the subsequent individual agency from a historical perspective, and answer the above-noted two cardinal questions.

---

[86] Friedman, Milton. (2002). *Capitalism and Freedom*. The University of Chicago Press.

I am not the first to inquire into this issue. Ancient "civilizations"[87] pondered on it and they all, without an exception, came up with commanding *resolutions*, although very few nations managed to come up with natural and, therefore, viable *solutions*. And that seems to be the problem and the widely debated issue of our times as well. Let's take a quick glance at history:

Ancient Sumerians, Babylonians, Hittites, Persians and Egyptians pursued a strange path of "resolutions", – sometimes willingly and sometimes grudgingly they all resolved on transferring their God-given freedom to the agent of the state, – the government. The government, on the other hand, always resolved on usurping, extending, expanding and increasing this temporarily vested power. These broadened and perpetuated powers gave governments the means by which they could coerce the nations and extort from the very people who rendered them powerful by placing their common trust in them in the first place. In the result, throughout history, these ancient Sumerians, Babylonians, Hittites, Persians and Egyptians spiraled down the path of self-destruction. They lost every bit of their individuality, individually speaking, and, in an aggregate sense, they lost their ethnos, ethos and national identity.

Such an outcome was inevitable, – a tyrannical monarchy (or a tyrannical democracy, for that matter) which degrades its citizens for generations shall inadvertently annihilate human spirit both, in individual citizens, as well as in the ruling class. Perpetual slavery degrades the enslaved men and morally destroys them; while perpetual sin of imposing slavery on the fellow men degrades the tyrant and morally destroys him as well. *That's* why there is no room for a man, for a citizen, for a human being in any empire. *That's* why empires are not comprised of men, but of mere brutes, – tyrants and slaves. And *that's* why empires self-destruct, dissolve and vanish. Freedom, and near immortality – nationality – which naturally comes with it, is an exclusive quality of a nation, *not* an empire.

A nation is formed only when people are wise enough to regard an individual as the basis of their country, and freedom – as the most essential element of life.

---

[87] Empires are meant.

As Homer put it, "Born a slave, what need have you of speech or thought?"[88]

Iberians and Colchis, Scotts, Welsh and Irish, on the other hand, placing the greatest value on their individual freedom and liberty, historically rendered very limited powers to the state; and the state itself, geopolitically speaking even in the most dangerous of times, tried to defend and retain freedom and liberty of the cumulative self, and with that the freedom and liberty of its individual citizens. Granted, this freedom and liberty came at a huge cost, but in the long run these civilizations survived and so did their love of freedom: in spite of the most adverse geopolitical circumstances, the descendants of the ancient Iberians and Colchis – all of Georgians, including Mushkis (Iberians), the Laz people and Megrelians, as well as Chechen, Ingush, Circassian (Cherkess) nations, who stem from the same common Iberian anthropological root, and besides them Cappadocians, – the proto-Iberian people[89] who have made a most significant impact on Christian culture, theology and philosophy, – all of these people retained their freedom and liberty, and with that their unique identity. The same accomplishment and accolade applies to the Scotts, the Welsh and the Irish.

Now, I don't know what label would a citizen of any other country place on the story of the people of the practical, if not heroic, freedom-loving nations described above, but I know for sure that to a citizen of the United States, to an American whose ancestor fought at Lexington and Concord, to the descendant of the martyr who bravely and uncompromisingly hung on the gallows of Harper's Ferry in order to defend honor of all Americans and their right of universal freedom,[90] to the sons and daughters of Thoreau, this must mean only one thing, – success. This success was a function of limited agency, – unlike the citizens of their contemporary empires, proto-Georgian, Scottish, Welsh and Irish people viewed the government only as a sheer necessity to attain expediency, not as a demigod or a Lord. The government had only one function: to act as a *necessary* common agent for its citizens *only when necessary*. As it has been already mentioned, this success came at a great cost, – many citizens spilled their blood and sacrificed their lives to defend these individual freedoms either from the frequently invading

---

[88] Homer. *Odyssey. Book IV.*
[89] Proto-Iberian people – ancient Japhetic people are meant, including Pelasgians, Mushkis or also known as Iberians, and Cappadocians.
[90] John Brown is meant.

external forces, or from the native government when, on rare occasions, it became too big, overbearing and threatened the freedom of its citizens.

The above-described historical perspective provides a clear answer to the first cardinal question: how do we reconcile the necessary interdependence with our God-given freedom and liberty? And the answer is simple: through a most limited surrender of our individual freedoms to an agency of *any* kind, especially the government.

DEMOCRACY – MERELY A TOOL

Our conclusion of the previous chapter brings up another widely debated question, which bears some significance to capitalism. It is the question which in the 20th and the 21st centuries almost no one seems to have the intellectual capacity to solve, or sheer guts to voice, – does it matter which *political* form of government people have? It is necessary to emphasize the word "*political*", to differentiate it from economic modes, such as capitalism, socialism, etc. This issue offers, for our modern, but by no means intellectually advanced society, rather a radical, but a simple and truthful fact, – it is irrelevant what form of representative government people have, as long as it is a good government, i.e. the government which acts as the representative agent of its citizens, and not as its Lord, and endeavors to maximize individual freedoms of the citizens by coordinating their interests and subsequent economic and political activities by means of maintaining the rule of law, in order, besides freedom, to achieve economic prosperity. Case in point: a democratic government comprised of despotic individuals can be just as tyrannical as a single despot, i.e. a tyrannical royalty. The same can be said about aristocracy, oligarchy, royalty and other modes of governing. The evidence is overwhelming to compel us to conclude that it is not the *quantity* or the method of appointment of the people's agents that makes the government good or bad, but that is determined rather by the *quality* and subsequent designs and actions of these agents. Let's look at historical evidence which shall demonstrate conclusively that a good government is always the function of the quality of its members, and not of quantity, pretty much just like a quality pizza is always a function of the quality ingredients.

It is a common belief among modern day Westerners that democracy cannot be an instrument of evil. It has become a religious conviction, philosophical truism and precisely calculated axiom that democracy commits no evil, or that if you have democracy with its majority, and by that I mean a mere multitude, an accidental preponderance, a deceived mass, and not the *essential* majority, you are automatically just, free and prosperous. How odd is this notion, especially when it is voiced in a freedom-loving country, such as the United States! In the country where resourceful, bright and industrious citizens always came up with many ways to skin the cat, meaning, to achieve freedom and prosperity. In the country where results matter and theoretical hodge-podge historically always takes a back seat. Don't get me wrong, democracy is a wonderful form of government, but only as long as it aims at freedom and prosperity of its electorate. Our ultimate goal is not democracy, but rather, first, freedom and, then, prosperity, and democracy is a mere instrument, or rather one of many instruments, at our disposal to help us achieve this ultimate objective, – freedom and, with that, inevitable prosperity. The same simple, and yet universally overlooked truth was expressed by the great Joseph Schumpeter: "Democracy is a political method, that is to say, a certain type of institutional arrangement for arriving at political – legislative and administrative – decisions and hence incapable of being an end in itself."[91]

Democracy can also give a false impression of freedom. It simulates essential freedom by giving people political freedom of choice which is almost always non-essential, – when was the last time an issue of national, not to say of universal, importance decided by vote in the United States? The mere fact of somewhat free elections and the ability to vote is by no means freedom. As one of the greatest economists and philosophers of the 20th century, Friedrich Hayek put it: "Perhaps the fact that we have seen millions voting themselves into complete dependence on a tyrant has made our generation understand that to choose one's government is not necessarily to secure freedom."[92]

Another cardinal defect of democracy is, as Aristotle describes in his *Politics*, the fact that "Democrats say that justice is that to which the majority agree."[93] And so it comes about that justice in a democratic society is anchored not on *truth*, but on an *opinion*, and an old and outdated one at that, meaning *the constitution*; and, in the result, defending justice in such a society does not require being *truthful*; what it

[91] Schumpeter, Joseph. (1962). *Capitalism, Socialism and Democracy*. New York: Harper & Row.
[92] Hayek, F. A. (2011). *The Constitution of Liberty*. The University of Chicago Press.
[93] Aristotle. (2000). *Politics*. Dover Publications, Inc.

requires is merely being *consistent*. I heard a true defender of genuine justice once say, "No man sent me here; it was my own prompting and that of my Maker."[94] Instead of thanking him profoundly, this *man* was sent to the gallows, as *apparently* his actions were not quite *constitutional*.

I believe that we are yet to declare our independence.

Democracy also has a strong tendency to pave the way to one of the gravest injustices mankind is capable of perpetrating, – communism. To refer to Aristotle once again, "if justice is the will of the majority, as I was before saying, they will unjustly confiscate the property of the wealthy."[95] Graduated and highly progressive taxes in America are the living proof of that immoral sentiment. It is on these grounds that a few propagandists, by preaching usefulness of false equality, convince the mediocre majority to redistribute the income, – to rob the talented and fortunate in order *supposedly* to bestow it onto the unfortunate mob. What the people-turned-masses do not know is that, one, in the process the socialist propagandist creates a nice spread for himself and his communist comrades; and two, he will not pay the funds in a lump sum, but rather he shall try to draw it out in a terminating stream of fixed payments in the longest possible period, also known as welfare checks, and what I call *tramp annuities*, in order to perpetuate the dependency he has already devised.

If Schumpeter's, Hayek's and Aristotle's arguments do not seem to be persuasive enough, I will use three prominent and unambiguously dramatic historical examples to dispel this myth about democracy being the ultimate moral goal of mankind. The first example is from the cradle of democracy, ancient Greece. In 399 BC Athens was a flourishing democracy, and, without a doubt, with more democratic institutions and political elements than even the 21st century United States, and yet it managed to condemn and murder its greatest citizen, Socrates. The second example is of Christ. God of Christianity was publically

---

[94] *Brown's Interview with Mason, Vallandigham, and Others*, as reported in Franklin Benjamin Sanborn's hagiographic book, *The Life and Letters of John Brown: Liberator of Kansas, and Martyr of Virginia*. Henry David Thoreau also quotes the same passage in his moving essay, *A Plea for Captain John Brown*. See: Thoreau, H. D., Sanborn, F. B., Lazarashvili, Z. K. (2011). *American Heroes: Thoreau and Brown*. Georgian International University Press. Also see: Sanborn, Franklin, Benjamin. (2010). *The Life and Letters of John Brown: Liberator of Kansas, and Martyr of Virginia*. Nabu Press.
[95] Aristotle. (2000). *Politics*. Dover Publications, Inc.

condemned and crucified not by an order issued by the elite, although the imperial elite had indeed conspired against him, but by the democratic process of voting, when people, the majority decided to vote for the release of a thief, murderer and a terrorist of his day, named Barabbas, instead of voting for Christ. The third example is from our neck of the woods, the 19th century United States of America. In 1859 the United States was already claiming the title of the champion of freedom, and yet on December 2 of that year it publicly, and I would say even proudly, murdered its best and brightest citizen – John Brown.

In all three cases, whether in Athens, Jerusalem or the United States, public murders of the best and the brightest were the functions of democracy. Franklin Benjamin Sanborn, the most prominent American hagiographer, historian and journalist, duly noted the undeniable similarities between the three murders: "In this respect he [John Brown] resembled Socrates, whose position in the world's history is yet fairly established; and the parallel runs even closer." Sanborn continues: "There is an example even higher than that of Socrates, which history will not fail to hold up, – that Person of whom his slayers said: 'He saved others; himself he cannot save.'"[96]

But why did it happen that the accidental and transiently powerful majority so violently endeavored and succeeded in the public murders of their contemporary good men? Or as Henry David Thoreau would say, "Why does it always crucify Christ, and excommunicate Copernicus..."[97] – Indeed why? – Because it is very difficult for the majority, that is the immoral, lazy, cowardly and untalented to face its own deficiency. Immorality, laziness and inability of such "men" only come to light, when a highly moral, able and talented man is born among them. Following this logic, I must conclude that the same rule applies to economy: when an honest, talented, hardworking and industrious man – a capitalist – is born in our midst, the dishonest, the dumb, the lazy, the gutless and the stagnant always vote to condemn him.

But the times have changed. Back in the day the penalty was death. Today the penalty is the disproportionate, biased, unfairly discriminating graduated taxation, licensure, regulations, and the list goes on. The same

---

[96] Excerpts from the chapter *The Death and Character of John Brown*, from Franklin Benjamin Sanborn's hagiographic book. Sanborn, Franklin, Benjamin. (2010). *The Life and Letters of John Brown: Liberator of Kansas, and Martyr of Virginia*. Nabu Press.

[97] Thoreau, H. D., Sanborn, F. B., Lazarashvili, Z. K. (2011). *American Heroes: Thoreau and Brown*. Georgian International University Press.

mediocre men who voted to condemn Socrates to death are now voting to condemn an industrious entrepreneur with economic instruments of torture and sometimes even with political devices. They both constituted the majority of their "respected" time and space, – the era and the state. It is that ninety five per cent which has voted for the punitive taxes on the other five per cent at the dusk of the 20th and the dawn of the 21st centuries. But I am not after that misguided majority in this thesis or in real life. I am after the members of that evil minority, the Barabbas, the Pharisees, the Herodians and the Pilates,[98] the Meletuses, the Anytuses and the Lycons,[99] and the Masons, the Vallandighams and the Stuarts,[100] that are now persecuting all able and talented men who are trying to earn their share of wealth by their merit, and not by the conspiracy, collusion and fraud which these above-mentioned despots condone and encourage.

If it was purity and wisdom of the God Christ, Socrates and John Brown, which back then made the Jewish, the Athenian and the Southern people look foolish, today it is the able capitalist who is making the entire American society, but especially its "elite" – the demagogue incubated and hatched in a "liberal" "college", now cooped up in a government office, in the same decadent "academia", in an international organization or a Washington think tank... look utterly unwise, if not, quite frankly, just silly and stupid. The "men" who in the past were crucifying the spiritually successful out of envy, are now jealous of today's financially successful. It gets even worse. I am afraid that the situation in some respect is more critical now than before. You see, the jealous and murdering idiot of the past could not obtain a piece of, for example, Socrates' success, as spiritual success is metaphysical (it would be utterly wrong to say *intangible*), while success of today's capitalist is of physical nature, so it *can* be taken away or rather *taxed* away, – Soviet socialists' preferred method of robbery of the successful was to take it away by force; our "Democratic" robber, on the other hand, prefers to tax it away by the force of law and regulation. And you see, once again, political mode is unessential, – the only difference between the Soviet OBXSS[101] and our IRS was in the method of auditing, but the aim (or rather the design) and the end result of both was the same, – robbery of the successful citizens.

---

[98] Eponyms for the prosecutors of Christ
[99] Eponyms for the prosecutors of Socrates
[100] Eponyms for the prosecutors of John Brown
[101] The Department for Fighting with Larceny of Socialist Property, formed in the Soviet Union as a police department of law enforcement part of the NKVD (People's Commission for Internal Affairs).

In order to dispel all myths regarding the importance of political forms of government, I would like to offer you examples on other historically common political modes, such as aristocracy and royalty. With regard to aristocracy: even though in Cicero's time Rome was officially the Roman *Republic*, it was still the Roman *Empire*. Moreover, in the 1st century BC the Roman Empire was ruled by learned aristocrats. Yet in 70 BC it managed to produce a villain, such as Gaius Verres, the former governor of Sicily. And yet it was this same aristocracy that at the very same time had produced young Cicero, who with his zestful speech and relentless effort managed to vanquish the band of parasites, – Verres and his supporters.[102] With regard to royalty: Herod the "Great" who attempted to destroy the Hebrew nation spiritually, intellectually, politically and eventually even economically, was the result of none other but royalty, and, to the contrast, so had been the greatest leaders of the Jewish nation, the great King David and King Solomon, and the greatest leaders of Georgian nation, the great King Davit the Builder and King (Queen) Tamar, – the likes of which are seldom found throughout world history. These are not merely, to use an economist's jargon, statistical anomalies. History is fairly consistent in demonstrating that such diverse results arise in the most diverse political environments.

The evidence overwhelmingly supports the fact that relatively it is of little consequence what form of government people have, as long as it is a small (meaning, not undue in size), practical, efficient and beneficial government which aims at fulfilling its duty as the people's agent with this simple goal in mind, – to maximize freedom and prosperity of its "shareholders" and nothing more. On the other hand, the same indifference cannot be exercised when choosing an *economic* course for a nation, – socialism, interventionism, communism, at best, result in economic stagnation, i.e. poverty, and, at worst, become monstrosities that suck the life breath of the very people they are designed to serve, while capitalism always, and without a single exception, provides long-term prosperity, as well as political freedom for its participants. And with that it becomes clear that capitalism, not democracy, as some may have us believe, is the real champion of freedom and liberty in this modern, sophisticated and ever so globalizing political world.

Even though today the same old problem of defending our individual liberties exists, methods required for a successful defense have

---

[102] Cicero. (2009). *Political Speeches*. Oxford University Press, USA.

changed, – economics, not politics is today's sword with which our individual liberties must be enhanced, – I would refrain from using the words "preserved" or "conserved" or even "defended", as in my mind they are often associated with the elements of phobia, conspiracy and stagnation. In today's sophisticated global enterprise, it is economic freedom which serves as the primary necessary condition for political freedom for a nation. And unless, in the most timely manner, people commence to place an increased emphasis on our economics, just like a blindfolded beast, our politics, left to its own devices, will vanquish our entire state, and with that our very existence as free men of a freedom-loving nation. To paraphrase the most learned statesman, Ilia Chavchavadze, canonized by the Georgian Apostolic Autocephalous Orthodox Church in 1987 as St. Ilia the Righteous, who, among other things, was an expert financier and a visionary economist, *if we desire freedom, swords must be put aside and abacuses must be picked up and fully mastered.* And with that this great Georgian visionary of the 19th century, fully realizing natural and, therefore, nearly perpetual power of economic forces, predicted that in the 21st century economic freedom would pave the way for political freedom, and not the other way around.

This economic freedom is called capitalism, – free, open, unbiased and competitive capitalism. It ensures nothing! It guarantees nothing! It gifts nothing! It praises nothing! It boasts of nothing! But it provides the only reliable and, at the same time, honorable path to mutual freedom and mutual, but by no means equal, prosperity for every participant. And that delivers a clear answer to the second cardinal question: how can we make this unavoidable interdependence beneficial? And the simple answer is: economic freedom, i.e. capitalism, will inadvertently result in the greatest political freedom both, for individual citizens, as well as for the entire state, as a whole.

WARNING: YESTERDAY'S COMMUNIST – TODAY'S "LIBERAL"

Globally we have introduced enterprises which are intermediaries between individuals and their God-given right, – freedom. These enterprises after a short while, if not from the very beginning, seem to usurp the same individual freedoms they are designed to protect. They also euphemize their iniquitous activity and appropriate to themselves such honorable names as "liberals", "democrats" and "humanitarians". The great economist and political scientist of the 20th century, Joseph

Schumpeter once noted that, "as a supreme, if unintended, compliment, the enemies of the system of private enterprise have thought it wise to appropriate its label".[103] We must discern the falsehoods behind honorably sounding labels, such as "liberals", "democrats" and "humanitarians". They have been stolen by thieves and plunderers, and we must take back their ownership once and for all. The reasons are clear and fairly simple: I see no liberal love of fellow human beings in nationally imposed stagnation, unnecessary and artificial poverty that is; I perceive no democratic process in perpetual welfare and the subsequent economic slavery; I discern no humaneness in diminishing an individual to a statistical unit, and, certainly, I cannot possibly call such paternalists *humanitarians*, who fail to recognize uniqueness of an exceptional individual, his talent and the fruits of his labor, and by overtaxing throw him into a statistical chart as a mere number or a unit, instead of giving him a chance to enjoy the fair compensation which the market had allocated to him according to the merits of his work in supplying the services and goods demanded. Forgive me the dullness of my perception, as I fail to observe intelligence, let alone benevolence, in the designs and actions of the modern-day "egalitarians" and "democrats" and "liberals", and I see nothing but cunning and common crockery aimed at manipulating the nations, and even the entire mankind, in order to perpetuate people's dependence on this gargantuan "beneficent" monstrosity, – the oversized government.

Communism and socialism, sometimes openly, and more often covertly, disguised under the names of a modern "Democrat", "Liberal", Social "Democrat", Labor "Movement", or "Public" Ownership have been attacking the lives of freedom-loving nations and its citizens from pole to pole. Nowadays this repulsive ideological sickness seems to penetrate, historically speaking, even the most freedom-loving countries, such as the United States and Georgia. And unless the people recognize the danger of the universal dependence, and nationally produce the shift in economic policy, marked by reduced reliance on centralized plans and programs, our freedom, our liberty, our American and Georgian way of life, and, shortly after, our very identities – and statehoods too – *shall* be lost. A socialist makes no distinction between sacrificing one's individual sovereignty to a state, and selling the sovereignty of the state to another state or to an ecumenical international organization.

---

[103] Schumpeter. (1954). *History of Economic Analysis*. Oxford University Press.

But why did people lose their economic and political liberties in the 21st century so easily and ever so willingly? The only proximate explanation I may offer in this regard is the old truism, that "absolute power corrupts absolutely",[104] and that the institutions in which people had originally placed their common trust, in the best cases became anthropomorphic Golems[105] and self-abortive Homunculi,[106] and, in the worst case, Frankenstein monsters devouring one citizen's liberty after another. The Soviet Union, China and most of Africa serve as excellent examples of recent history, while today's Russian Federation, Nicaragua and Venezuela are the dismal live cases unfolding in front of our very eyes.

But why did people place their trust in such monstrosities in the first place? The answer, yet again, is simple, – the monster, and an old monster at that too, used a disguise and wrapped its old wolf-face in a sheepskin (yes, the pun intended),[107] and offered its poisonous ideology with a touch of sugar. *That's all*! Unless people start to recognize that allegedly new is nothing, but an abominable and abortive reject of the previous two centuries, and that too in a rickety camouflage, they will be deceived and enslaved in a communist welfare state by our modern-day "liberals" for-EVER.

Even when people are able to recognize the truth, a momentary gratification that may be enjoyed immediately, often overrules their reason, compels them to abandon their long-term happiness and forces them to pursue those harmful delicacies which are gratifying today, only to become poisonous realities of tomorrow. Most people have dulled their reason to the point that they no longer possess the basic intellectual endowments, such as willpower, courage, prudence and foresight required for a *purposeful* behavior. Such beings become impatient and somewhat neurotic, as their immediate self-interest keeps eroding their long-term self-interest. Instead of embracing logic and their natural propensity to think, they become overwhelmed with desires and

---

[104] The proverb comes from a letter written in 1887 by the English historian, Lord Acton: "Power tends to corrupt, and absolute power corrupts absolutely."

[105] Golem – in Jewish folklore an animated anthropomorphic being, created entirely from inanimate matter.

[106] Homunculus – a term generally used in various fields of study to refer to any representation of a human being. Historically it referred specifically to the concept of a miniature, though fully formed, human body, for example, in the studies of alchemy and preformationism.

[107] "Sheepskin" as a sheep's skin, and as a diploma of a "liberal" college, with all due honors and privileges, i.e. brainwashing and impotence.

fantasies. They demand constantly, but rarely supply anything in return. They consume a lot, but produce very little. Although such people cannot properly be called consumers, as "consumers are *purposeful* in deciding what goods and services to buy."[108] That *purpose* no longer exists in them. The government too goes out of its way to cater to them. Government-sponsored academics have gone as far as to invent new, untested and *experimental* sciences, such as Keynesian macroeconomics, in order to justify the need for such an irrational behavior with the so called aggregate demand, – as if people were mere lab rats with a sole purpose to benefit *their* experiment. I have seen some effort made to disprove such "academics" and their mock-science. Most recently I have witnessed resurgence of the supply-side economics, – a movement among the true economists which emphasizes importance of the supply, rather than the hedonistic adherence to the demand. It argues that economic growth can be most effectively created by lowering barriers for people to produce (supply) goods and services. But the problem is that nowadays *people* enjoy being handicapped, – they are fond of their government-supplied free wheelchair. They love their free lunches, as well as their "public" libraries, "social" security, "National" "Public" Radio, and I am sure they will fall in love with "their" "universal" healthcare as well. But nothing is free, and the socialist government is the first to remind you of that – before they deliver their promised "public" paradise – the wheelchair, the lunches, the radios, the pension plans, the libraries and the healthcare – you must pay up. This payment differs from the market price in a way that it requires not a set payment, but a full confiscation of your property rights, as well as freedom. It demands most of your past, present and future earnings. And the only difference between the American socialist and his Russian or German counterparts is that our socialist will put you on a payment plan, while Russian Communists and German Nazis would have demanded the payment upfront by confiscating everything you owned on the spot. Such is the state of American people today, and has been for quite some time. And to this dismal fact I feel bound to call the attention of my fellow citizens.

Most people have no willpower to make the necessary provisional sacrifices required for a free and independent life. They have become ever so risk averse that they refuse freedom since it entails responsibility and risk. They no longer want to be responsible for their own destiny. They surrender their able bodies, their minds and their souls to the

---

[108] McConnell, C. R., Brue. S. L., Flynn. S. M. (2009). *Microeconomics*. McGraw-Hill.

government in exchange for the rickety wheelchair of socialism. Labor, mental and physical, invokes pain, and man being naturally inclined to avoid it, provided all socialist tyrants with a powerful opportunity to promise a bargain: in exchange for eliminating pain, mankind would surrender its birthright – its God-given freedom.

Creators of such anthropological, as well as political-economic monstrosities always seem to have well-formulated plans and objectives, and these plans and objectives always *seem* to be noble, beneficent and humanitarian, but the end result of their "great enterprise" and work of social "science", without a single exception, is always a gloomy, dismal and morose hodge-podge: FHA, FCC, SSA...[109] The fact that they are acronyms already indicates that they are indeed counterfeits of truth and mere hodge-podges of evil intended to deceive the gullible and the ignorant. Don't believe me? Ask any former citizen of the Soviet Union. Ask the majority. Ask the minority. Ask the essential mean. The Soviets had plans and stated objectives, sometimes annual and sometimes Five-Year[110] goals. In fact, may I remind you, that their grand enterprise was called "*planned* economy"? And they too peculiarly resorted to the use

---

[109] The Federal Housing Administration (F.H.A.) – a U.S. government agency created as part of the National Housing Act of 1934. The goals of this organization are to improve housing standards and conditions, provide an adequate home financing system through insurance of mortgage loans, and to stabilize the mortgage market. The Federal Communications Commission (F.C.C.) – an independent agency of the U.S. government. The FCC works towards six goals in the areas of broadband, competition, the spectrum, the media, public safety and homeland security, and modernizing the FCC. The FCC was established by the Communications Act of 1934 as the successor to the Federal Radio Commission and is charged with regulating all non-federal government use of the radio spectrum (including radio and TV broadcasting), and all interstate telecommunications (wire, satellite and cable), as well as all international communications that originate or terminate in the U.S. The Social Security Administration (S.S.A.) – an independent agency of the U.S. federal government that administers Social Security, a social insurance program consisting of retirement, disability, and survivors' benefits. To qualify for these benefits most American workers pay Social Security taxes on their earnings; future benefits are based on the employees' contributions. The SSA was established by a law currently codified at 42 U.S.C. § 901.

[110] The Five-Year Plans for the "National" Economy of the Soviet Union were a series of nation-wide centralized exercises in rapid economic development in the Soviet Union. The plans were developed by the State Planning Committee, more commonly known as Gosplan, based on the Theory of Productive Forces that was part of the general guidelines of the Communist Party for economic development. Fulfilling the plan became the watchword of Soviet bureaucracy. The same method of planning was also adopted by most other communist states, including the People's Republic of China. In addition, several capitalist states have emulated the concept of central planning, though in the context of a market economy, by setting integrated economic goals for a finite period of time.

of acronyms and euphemisms in order to disguise the real evil embedded in their programs and to keep the people in a state of ignorance as long as possible.

Covert socialists have deceived American citizens for too long! The great countries, where an individual exercises his or her God-given freedom, where he or she can speak, think and earn the daily bread as long and as much as he or she desires freely and liberally, were built neither by acronyms, nor euphemisms, but by hard work on the free market platform, where all are *naturally* rendered equal rights, if not equal opportunities, and all have a chance to achieve greatness through competitive exchange of goods and services. And that is something no government can do, but it can be achieved only via the natural method, – freedom, which the free market always renders.

Most socialist, i.e. tyrannical devices are based on plain falsehoods. But their most powerful ideological weapons are not mere untruths, but rather sound fictions which have *internal logical consistency*. It is this internal logical consistency that is present in their macroeconomics, redistribution of income, equality and the universal healthcare. People who are shortsighted and impatient do not take necessary time and effort to weigh *universal healthcare* against *universal truth*, as the socialist fiction *seems* to make sense. What people forget is that *seeming* and *being* are often two radically opposing notions with many radically opposite results. I am bound to remind them that many lunatics, plunderers and murderers also have internal logical consistency on their side, but *never* the truth.

OUTLINE OF THE THESIS

This thesis is not intended to produce any incendiary effect either in academic or political circles, whether in the United States or Georgia, or anywhere else, as a matter of fact. Neither does it carry any surreptitious political or even partisan agenda. It rather openly and unambiguously serves the one and only useful objective – the truth, – in order to benefit Georgian and American nations, their citizens and, oddly, although surely, enough, their governments. I hope no one accuses us of tautology if we repeat the familiar formula as our scholastic creed of a sort and basic premise to this essay, – *we believe that only the truth shall set us free.*[111] And considering the fact that it is *freedom* to which we all aspire, seeking the truth cannot be such a bad thing after all.

Furthermore, as indicated elsewhere, I will endeavor to the best of my ability to avoid using examples of failures of Georgian and American governments, as well as institutions, as due to geopolitical sensitivities and, quite frankly, constant threats which these two nations face, I refuse to do any harm to their reputation, lest the enemy perceives these as their weaknesses and tries to aim at their Achilles' Heel. Due to my immense love of both nations, I will attempt to seek the truth gently and speak it subtly, although there may be instances when the truth itself demands a sterner approach and a sharper language, in which case I shall accommodate it in order to preserve my integrity and my goal. As the great Thomas Sowell put it, "When you want to help people, you tell them the truth. When you want to help yourself, you tell them what they want to hear."[112]

In light of the foregoing, the thesis has the following objectives:

1. To unveil multifaceted forms of economic serfdom, and to show correlations between economic serfdom and political slavery, on one the hand, and, on the other hand, between economic freedom, i.e. capitalism, and political freedom.

2. I will discuss these issues in general terms, and also relative to the country of Georgia and the United States, and I will draw parallels between the two freedom-loving nations. I will also demonstrate the monstrous end-result of the socialist doctrine, – slavery and poverty, – in contrast to the two staple products of capitalism, – freedom and prosperity.

3. In the proceeding chapters I will discuss political freedom as the function of capitalism, the role of capitalism in government, education, national security and economic welfare, the function of a competitive corporation and benefits of natural, i.e. competitive monopoly, and the notion of capitalism in Orthodox Christianity.

---

[111] Paraphrasing, John 8:32: "And ye shall know the truth, and the truth shall set you free."

[112] Sowell, Thomas. (1999). *Barbarians Inside the Gates*. Hoover Institution Press.

HISTORY GEORGIA

It was Rome's greatest statesman and philosopher, Cicero, who so eloquently postulated the following idea in his *Republic*: "…for there is a type of unjust slavery when people who *could* be their own masters are subject to someone else; but in the case of those who are fit only to be slaves, no injustice is done."[113] And then it was the famous economist Thomas Sowell, an American champion of economic freedom and liberty, who stated: "If the battle for civilization comes down to the wimps versus the barbarians, the barbarians are going to win."[114] Cicero was right; and so was Sowell. Although, Cicero's truth was universal, while Sowell's… I would say, was a statistically and, hence, generally correct statement. The reason for this distinction is simple: Sowell's knowledge is limited to histories of a small number of nations, almost all of whom were indeed either wimps or barbarians, i.e. serfs or aggressors, peasants or robbers, plunderers or the plundered, and, in the result, so is the scope and the conclusion of his observation. He was examining only a limited area, geographically and historically speaking, and did not take into account the cumulative heritage of mankind, which includes at least a few nations who never belonged either to barbarians or wimps. So only in this limited sense, Sowell's conjecture that possibility there could be the ultimate battle between these two types of "men", and his speculation with regard to its outcome were true. But we must know that the ultimate battle of civilizations will not come down to wimps and barbarians, but rather it will be the battle between the truthful and the false, that is the truthful who are *brave*, and the false who are merely *brutish*. As the saying goes, *Cowards prove their courage by their ferocity*. Allow me to explain further by specifically using Georgia as an example:

We, the Georgians are a great nation, and it ill behooves us to be either barbarians or wimps. It certainly does not befit us to be slaves. Our ancestors neither did such monstrous things as barbarians – enslaving other nations, nor did they submit to serfdom of any kind, like wimps. I can say verily and somewhat proudly that, historically speaking, it is impossible to come up with a *single* instance when the Georgian nation, or even a minutely significant part of it, on the one hand, either submitted to serfdom like wimps, or, on the other hand, itself became an aggressor, i.e. a plundering barbarian.

---

[113] Cicero. (2009). *The Republic and the Laws*. Oxford University Press, USA.
[114] Sowell, Thomas. (2006). *Ever Wonder Why?* Hoover Institution Press.

Georgians are an ancient people who have created a most unique and one of the most ancient civilizations in the world. Georgia is beautiful, sheltered in the skyscraping peaks of the Caucasus Mountains from North and South, with its entire topography anticlimaxing in the emerald shores of the Black Sea in the West. Also, I could effortlessly substantiate how handsome Georgian people are by quoting the father of modern anthropology, Johann Friedrich Blumenbach,[115] or cite Assyrian, Greek, Roman, Persian and German historians or philosophers, – from as far back as Herodotus and Strabo, – easily to authenticate the fact that this is a country with ancient culture characterized with high regard to literature, philosophy and different forms of art, including the art of war, but this book is neither a panegyric to Georgia, nor is it an apology for Georgian people, brave and educated as they are. There are people who are fairly good at doing precisely that, – praising in an extolling manner. I, on the other hand, intend to give you only those facts about Georgia and Georgians, which are relevant to decision making ability necessary for achieving freedom and prosperity via capitalism.

Georgia was the first country to accept Christianity as the official state religion,[116] and throughout history remained the defender of the

---

[115] Johann Friedrich Blumenbach (1752-1840) - a German physician, physiologist and anthropologist, one of the first to explore the study of mankind as an aspect of natural history, whose teachings in comparative anatomy were applied to classification of what he called human races, of which he determined five. Blumenbach was the first to use the term "Caucasian" or "Georgian" to designate the race of European people, as he correctly believed, that the indigenous Europeans were Georgians, and not the Indo-European people who settled in Europe only in later period, such as, for example, Greeks. Blumenbach writes about the Caucasian race: "Caucasian variety – I have taken the name of this variety from Mount Caucasus, both because its neighborhood, and especially its southern slope, produces the most beautiful race of men, I mean the Georgian; and because all physiological reasons converge to this, that in that region, if anywhere, it seems we ought with the greatest probability to place the autochthones (birth place) of mankind." His theory was fully substantiated by the anthropological findings in the second half of the 20th century, and the theory is now accepted as an axiomatic theory if not by the public, at least by scholars of anthropology.

[116] Armenian claim of being first to accept Christianity as the state religion, if not the *entire* Armenian "historiography", is a *sheer* fabrication of history. Please see: Thompson, Robert W. (1996). *Rewriting Caucasian History: The Medieval Armenian Adaptation of the Georgian Chronicles: The Original Georgian Texts and the Armenian Adaptation.* Oxford Oriental Monographs. Oxford University Press. The chronicles deal with the history of Georgia from its mythical origins to the time of their composition, and are of particular interest to historians, for they show the way that the ancient chronicles were then altered and falsified by the "pioneering" Armenian "experts" of "historiography" in a pro-Armenian manner. This falsification is by no means an isolated incident, – to this date, falsification of history is the central element of both, the Armenian "culture" and the official Armenian state policy.

creed in the Caucasus, as well as in Anatolia. To this date people of Georgia show unprecedented devotion to Orthodox Christianity, philosophy, Christology and theology. This is important because Orthodox Christianity, historically speaking, always fostered and encouraged freedom, as well as pursuit of truth, including in sciences, philosophy and even economics. As a matter of fact, the concept of Oikonomia – economy – is *native* to the Orthodox Church, which was studied under two branches of theology, Divine Economy and Ecclesiastical Economy.

Georgia is the nation with its own alphabet, its own language (which is a language group on its own with absolutely no relation to Indo-European group of languages), prose, poetry, literature, and even folklore and cuisine. Georgia has had the highest literacy level in the world for several decades. Georgians are the only indigenous southern European people who managed to defend and retain their statehood in spite of the Indo-European (Greek, Scythian, Sumerian, Armenian), Arab and Asian (Persian, Mongol, Khwarazmid and Turkic) invasions, all of which forever changed political, cultural and anthropological landscape of Europe. Before Greeks appeared in Europe, proto-Georgian people of Iberians (also known as Mushkis or Moschoi or Kartvelians), Colchis (also known as Laz or Megrelians), Cappadocians, Etruscans, Trojans, Amazons, Albanians (meaning Caucasian Albanians), Chechens, Ingush, Cherkess, etc. were the indigenous population of southern Europe. While some of these indigenous people ceased to exist (for example: Etruscans, Trojans, Amazons and Caucasian Albanians), and some exist, but are deprived of statehood (for example: Chechen, Ingush, Cherkess and Cappadocian people), Georgians still live freely. How did that happen? – The Iberians absorbed Colchis, established a Georgian (also known as Kartvelian) state, and successfully defended the statehood now for almost three millennia. By spilling blood in defense and with the wholehearted devotion to Orthodox Christianity the nation has retained its ethnos and ethos, and survived both, anthropologically, as well as culturally.

The Battle of Didgori – August 12, 1121 – King Davit IV with his Army of 40,000 Georgians, 15,000 Kipchaks, 500 Alans and 100 Frankish Crusaders defeats one of the biggest and fiercest Mohammedan coalitions comprised of 850,000 gangsters, assembled by Sultan Mahmud II of Baghdad, the ruler of what is today Iraq and Persia, for a specific expedition to annihilate Georgia and with it Christianity in the

Caucasus, Anatolia and the Middle East. 55,600 freedom-fighters defeat the 850,000 thugs – *overwhelmingly*!

Odds were great back then, but they are greater still. The old Battle of Didgori was won by sword, foresight and prayer. The new Battle of Didgori, taking place daily in the lives of all freedom-loving men regardless of nationality, must be won by utilizing all of the old devices, in conjunction with the new and the most powerful weapon ever invented – capitalism. Back then the thugs could have easily robbed you of your sword, but today, as Epictetus predicted it, "No one is robbed of his own free will."[117] And with this most essential capital – our free will – *today* we must win the *ultimate* Didgori.

SOCIALISM: AN EFFECTIVE INSTRUMENT FOR SERFDOM

Warlike Georgians managed to retain statehood until the Soviet Union. But how did it happen that the essential majority of such a brave nation, which had effectively withstood invasions from other historical aggressors for millennia, was at least substantially, if not effectively, subdued during the 70 years of the Soviet era? Besides the sheer military size of the enemy, the Russian Federation that is, and constant persecutions, the gulags and the Siberian repressions, not to mention the occasional, but by no means sporadic, massacres, there was one other factor which contributed to the success of the Russian tyranny in Georgia, and that is the destruction of the capitalist system native to this ancient country. Annihilation of economic freedom, by interchangeably imposing sometimes communist and sometimes socialist economic mandates, which resulted in economic serfdom, in turn, over the years, translated in "natural" dependence and conformity. By extinguishing the remote possibility of both, owning private property and building private enterprise, Russia managed to destroy Georgian economy, and, more important, it extinguished desire among Georgians to be economically self-reliant. And as we know, without zest, oomph, vigor and guts to be self-reliant, economic strength is never realized, and without some economic strength, even the best of armies, heroes and patriots become powerless.

The above-example alone should suffice as the proof for the universal fact that only through capitalism could people sustain and

---

[117] Epictetus. *Discourses. Book III.*

effectively defend their political freedom. If the Russian imperialists regarded capitalism as a potent enough force to destroy their iron-clad empire, why can't we, the freedom-loving people of Georgia and the United States realize the power of capitalism, and understand that socialism and communism are only sugarcoated instruments to produce poverty, welfare, dependence on the state, and, in the result, a perpetual political serfdom?

Correlation between economic and political slavery is irrefutable. As Greek, Roman, Persian, Egyptian, Russian, German historiographies evidence bravery of Georgian men and women, as well as their devotion to freedom, and as I too personally have never come across either a more freedom-loving or more war-like nation as Georgians, I must admit that the evidence is conclusive, – economic paralysis rendered through systematic injections of socialism and communism will logically result, first, in political submission, and, then, in complete slavery. If that happened to such an unconquerable and extremely hard-to-rule Georgians, it can happen to everyone. But we must underscore one clear difference between the current socialist tendencies and sentiments in modern Georgia and the United States, on one hand, and the 1921 Georgia, fraught with the tyranny of the invading Soviet Russian empire on the other: Georgians in 1921 were given these injections of communism and socialism forcibly, at gunpoint; while today's Americans, and to a lesser extent Georgians, are taking these foreign injections at will. I hope that both freedom-loving nations make the right decision, and choose freedom, even if it is laden with dangers, risks and a certain degree of uncertainties, i.e. all the natural serendipities which make up the fabric of *free* life, over a welfare state of socialist slavery, even if it offers a secured bowl of daily pottage. Yes, the *uncertainty*! That healthy grit, bitter herb and tart fiber, which makes men humble, inclined to learning, hardworking, full of ingenuity and desire to obtain something eternal and lasting, along with some things fleeting, in this life. One of the most learned and talented men I ever came across in the depths of a library, French theologian and physicist, Blaise Pascal, the man most enlightened both, in physical and metaphysical sciences, wrote in his *Thoughts* (also known as *Pensees* in French):

"God wants to motivate the will more than the mind. Complete clarity would be of more use to the mind and would not help the will.

Humble their Pride."[118]

Capitalism, being the most natural of economic modes (and, I believe, because of its being natural, most akin to God's will as well), has the element of uncertainty in its very core and with this small, but an important element it indeed motivates the will to acquire prosperity. And yet today we – the people – are shifting away from the natural freedom and prosperity in order to scoot closer to poor mediocrity and centralized controls, which are precursors to inhuman peace and ruthless security.

One of the greatest of the 20th century economists and philosophers, Friedrich Hayek also feared that the chronic "advancement" towards centralized control of economic activity, whether in a country or an empire, would without a doubt prove to be *The Road to Serfdom*. Hayek also wisely predicted that, first, for the achievement and, then, for the perpetuation of such a sinister goal, the modern imperialist would use two devices, – promise of material equality and simulated emergencies, – as the pretext to usher the entire nations into this willful and enduring form of serfdom. Here is what this truly learned and farsighted man has to say about the promise of equality, i.e. the first tool used in the implementation of the socialist serfdom: "A claim for equality of material position can be met only by a government with totalitarian powers."[119] And then he eloquently explains the second method, which I would call the invention of a perpetual boogieman: "'Emergencies have always been the pretext on which the safeguards of individual liberty have been eroded."[120] I think these two statements are all-encompassing and quite self-explanatory to require further elaboration.

I had decided to conclude this chapter with the preceding paragraph, but then I recalled something I read in Cicero's *Republic* long time ago: "where the Nile comes hurtling down from the mountain peaks at a place called Catadoupa, the local inhabitants have lost their sense of hearing because of the loudness of the roar..."[121] And it dawned on me that man, constantly subjected to the socialist propaganda, engulfed with falsehood and untruth, could have his hearing so dulled and his mind's eye so muffled that he may not hear or see the obvious, – that the claim of the

[118] Pascal, Blaise. (1999). *Pensees and Other Writings*. Oxford University Press.
[119] Hayek, Friedrich, A. (1976). *Law, Legislation and Liberty. Volume 2. The Mirage of Social Justice*. The University of Chicago Press.
[120] Hayek, Friedrich, A. (1976). *Law, Legislation and Liberty. Volume 3. The Mirage of Social Justice*. The University of Chicago Press.
[121] Cicero. (2009). *The Republic and the Laws*. Oxford University Press, USA.

socialist equality is an effective form of slavery, and no equality at all. And so I was compelled to carry on.

Equality is what nature bestows: we inherit talent (both, metaphysical and physical) and wealth. That is the equality of nature. Socialists believe that they can improve on that most natural equality by forcing the fortunate to give up both, talent and wealth. Wealth is confiscated surgically, – by force (as in the U.S.S.R.) or by taxation (as in the U.S.). Talent is confiscated by use of a more sophisticated method, – de-incentivizing success which is the function of talent and hard work. Socialists call it *redistribution of income*, I call it *plunder*! The worst of all, socialists, under the pretext of justice, do this with the long-reaching arm of the law. I believe that the laws enacted by socialists are not laws or decrees defending justice, but they are rather lawful injustices. To quote Cicero once again: "And what about the many harmful and pernicious decrees passed in human societies, – decrees which have as little in common with the laws and justice as the agreements and decrees consented among the mob of criminals? If ignorant men prescribed a lethal poison to a patient, surely, such a prescription could not possibly be called a medical treatment. Law of just any kind would not be embraced in a good community, even if the majority of people, in spite of its harmful character, have accepted it. Hence the law means making a distinction between the just and unjust, and it is created in accordance with that most ancient and most important of all things – the nature. It is precisely by nature that human laws are guided in punishing the evil and protecting the good."[122]

It was the great Frederic Bastiat who for the first time unveiled for many Europeans the unlawfulness of the modern law and the injustice of the modern justice system, – all of which exist in a *demoncracy*.[123] As he noted, it is the law that "has placed the collective force in the service of those who wish to traffic, without risk and without scruple, in the persons, the liberty, and the property of others; it has converted plunder into a right, that it may protect it, and lawful defense into a crime, that it

---

[122] Cicero. (2009). *The Republic and the Laws*. Oxford University Press, USA.

[123] Demoncracy – a tyrannical (almost Demonic) democracy: a distorted form of democracy where an accidental majority elects a corrupt government. Demoncracy is based on satisfying sentiments of this accidental majority and the dictate of the corrupt few running the government and the unnatural monopolies created not by the market, but precisely by such a corrupt and collusive government. Etymology of the term stems from a word play on *Demon* and *democracy*.

may punish it."[124] As time goes by, I notice that the law is less and less confined to its proper sphere, and more and more it becomes a most *unnatural* invisible hand intruding on our freedom and our liberty. This almost Demonic invisible hand is diametrically opposite of and utterly different from that most *natural* and *beneficial* invisible hand described by the great Adam Smith in *The Wealth of Nations*.[125] As this book went to print the Congress of the United States passed the law which insists that pizza is a vegetable. And perhaps not immediately, but in a not too distant future, American people will perceive this law as an axiomatic truism. Furthermore, they will assert that it is not only a scientific, but a historical fact that pizza is indeed a vegetable. They may also state that it is their constitutional right to perceive things this way. I am afraid that as much as the government has failed in turning pizza into a tomato, it has succeeded in turning an American citizen into a potato.[126] That same government has been steadily converting the law into an instrument of plunder and injustice. Now it is after our most precious private property – our brains!

I am afraid our socialist is no egalitarian, for he tries to redistribute assets, which have already been most properly and justly distributed by nature (and ultimately by God), according to his fancy. No wonder communism and atheism always go hand in hand. In that light, I see communist "success" throughout the ages: Bonnie and Clyde, George "Baby Face" Nelson and George "Machine Gun" Kelly,[127] – they too were communists of a sort, as they could not bear either inherited or merit-based success of others, and engaged in the business of redistributing income. But they are small fishes[128] compared to other precedents history has to offer: Joseph Stalin started his career as a bank robber too and then moved on to robbing entire free nations, including Georgia. And if you dig deep enough, you will find that all the great tyrants, regardless of their origin, pursued similar career paths of "redistribution of income" from the free, talented and successful to the licentious, brutish and poor. Seneca[129] in his Epistle IX: 6 quotes

---

[124] Bastiat, Frederic. (2010). *The Law*. Tribeca Books.
[125] Smith, Adam. (1991, original 1776). *The Wealth of Nations*. Everymans Library.
[126] Haven't you seen a couch potato?
[127] They were Depression-era outlaws.
[128] Being a New Englander by adoption, in plural I use the term "fishes" instead of "fish".
[129] Seneca the Younger (4 BC-65 AD) – a Roman Stoic philosopher, statesman, dramatist, and in one work humorist, of the Silver Age of Latin literature. He was tutor and later advisor to Emperor Nero. He was later forced to commit suicide for complicity in the Pisonian conspiracy to assassinate this last of the Julio-Claudian emperors;

Hecato's[130] words: "If you want to be loved, love." – I'd remind the "kindhearted" and always "well-intending" socialist egalitarian, that the sentence ends with *love* and not with *rob*.

Our socialist wants to ensure not only real equality, but *equality of results*. As he endeavors to improve on that equality which God through nature has already bestowed on men, it turns out that our "learned" and always "wise" socialist is paternalistic not only toward his fellow citizens, but also toward the *nature*. He wants to control nature and substitute its outcomes with his engineering. But he is more than that! More than just a simpleminded and impulsive control freak. He is a cheat, and that most unnatural of all equalities, socialist equality he has been trumpeting is nothing more than a blueprint for *mutual cheating*. Talent bestowed by God and hard work rendered by man, when linked in a free environment that is secured with the rule of law, produce unequal and diverse results. They are unacceptable to the dull pallet of the cheating comrade. And when you see the socialist with his promise of equality and his heavy-handed cookie cutter going after these outstanding effects, – wealth, prosperity, affluence, innovation, wisdom, philosophy, science, superior craftsmanship, unmatched morality, strong principles, even good looks, – remember that ultimately he is going after their cause, – God and man! He hates creativity. He detests uniqueness. He despises diversity. He loves *grandeur*, but loathes *greatness* and the source of all greatness, and so it comes about that the socialist *truly* abhors God and man alike, as God and man are the only entities who do not accommodate his fancy, his design and his wish. As a great Danish Christian philosopher, Soren Kierkegaard wrote, "…only the wish pains, while the Eternal cures."[131] In this case, markets, natural equality and competition represent the *eternal* (i.e. natural), and the socialist fancy for false equality, his social engineering and his madcap mandates represent the *painful wish*. I would like to rid him of this pain.

---

however, he may have been innocent. His father was Seneca the Elder and his older brother was Gallio.

[130] Hecato of Rhodes – flourished in 100 BC. Hecato was a native of Rhodes, and a disciple of Panaetius, but nothing else is known of his life. It is clear that he was eminent amongst the Stoics of the period. He was a voluminous writer, but nothing remains. Diogenes Laertius mentions six treatises written by Hecato. In addition, Cicero tells us that Hecato wrote a work on *On Duties*, (Latin: *De Officiis*) dedicated to Quintus Tubero. Hecato is also frequently mentioned by Seneca in his treatise *De Beneficiis*. Please see: Cicero. (2008). *On Obligations*. Oxford University Press, USA.

[131] Kierkegaard, Soren. (1956). *Purity of Heart: Is to Will One Thing*. HarperOne.

A most keen and farsighted son of Scotland, Arthur Conan Doyle once wisely noted: "When one tries to rise above nature, he is liable to fall below it. The highest type of man may revert to the animal if he leaves the straight road of destiny."[132] And I would add, what is that *nature* but our God-given disposition, and what is that *destiny* but God's will? So then we *must* ask: what is that "redistribution of income", time after time promoted and trumpeted by all socialists, but an impudent attempt by pompous men, who are wise only in their own conceit, to rise above *nature*, to rise above *God*, to rise above their fellow *men*!

In his remarkable work of moral and secular philosophy, *De Officiis* or *On Duties*, among other hypothetical queries of Hecato, the II-I century BC stoic philosopher, Cicero cites this famous question, – if a fool should snatch a plank from a shipwreck, should a wise man wrestle it from him if he is able?[133] Many good men have answered this question conclusively, and they all clearly stated in their writings, as well as throughout their exemplary lives by their highly moral conduct, that the only answer shall be and is "No!" Cicero time after time states the same in his book.[134] Now, imagine not a wise man, but a devious crook and a good man contesting tenure of all planks. The crook, in the *name* (and not in deed) of charity and helping fools, – i.e. poor due to bone idleness, – and naturally poor, – i.e. poor due to old age, disability or temporarily poor by birth, – appropriates all the planks in the world to himself. That crook, that criminal element, that most insolent, violent and atheist "over-man" (as Nietzsche called his favorite race of men-turned-brutes)[135] is our socialist! Beware of him!

What distinguishes a brute from a man, if not the lack of sanity which resides only in spirit and therefore has no place in an animal? In that light, I would argue that any man turned brute is no longer sane, but a madman, and that's *precisely* what all communists and socialists are. More violent madness produces communists and Nazis (National Socialists), while less violently disposed lunacy produces socialism. In their madness they hallucinate and acquire bizarre and outlandish visions, ideas, imaginations, and then they try to carry them out in

---

[132] Doyle, Arthur, Conan. (2004). *The Complete Sherlock Holmes*. Barnes & Noble Classics.

[133] Cicero. (2008). *On Obligations*. Oxford University Press, USA.

[134] A certain coincidence is worth mentioning: this work of Cicero's, where in the last part, Book III, he discusses the moral questions raised by Hecato, is titled *De Officiis*, and so is the work of Hecato from which these questions originally derive.

[135] Nietzsche, Friedrich. (1995). *Thus Spoke Zarathustra*. The Modern Library.

reality. Socialists do it with propaganda, communists (and Nazis) do it with force, especially when human society protests. They did all that in the Soviet Union. Imagine having such a *madman* as a *compulsory* big brother! – A lunatic paternalist who thinks he knows better than God, better than nature and, *certainly*, better than his fellow men! As Plato tells us through the mouth of Theatetus, "Really, I cannot undertake to deny that madmen and dreamers believe what is false, when madmen imagine they are gods or dreamers think they have wings and are flying in their sleep."[136] For now we are faced with such hallucinating dreamers – the socialists, – but if we don't disprove them at once, soon more violent madmen – hordes of communists – shall follow.

What has socialism achieved so far? By discouraging personal initiatives it has rewarded idleness and encouraged dependency. It has promoted consumption rather than production. It has brought poverty to nations, regions and even entire continents, and in exchange it has taken away freedom and prosperity. All of that can be forgiven, but it has done something much worse, – socialism has made perfectly good men economically impotent, and it has left perfectly fine nations economically paralyzed. This I must explain in some detail:

By eliminating private ownership, by usurping private property and by creating government enterprises, the socialist became *the* employer. Individual citizens had no other choice but to work for him. Having no incentives, an individual involved in a "public" enterprise did not work with the urgency and efficiency required for survival. Public workers often got away with minimum work. After all, their lives did not depend on the success of the establishment. As incentives did not exist, men were deprived of innovation, creativity and authorship. Our socialist did not mind that. In the result many, but not all, learned men unlearned their lore, forgot their talents, their crafts, their industries; they dulled their abilities and blunted their competences. Men lost their survival skills because their immediate reality stopped corresponding with the natural economic realities, thanks to the deliberate efforts of our socialist. That's what happened in Georgia, Estonia, Latvia, Lithuania… and worse: new generations born into that dismal communist regime had nothing to unlearn, – unlike their fathers, they never participated in practical training of capitalism, they never invented, never invested, never risked, and they rarely competed in business or industry. Because of this they

---

[136] Plato. (2005). *The Collected Dialogues of Plato: Including the Letters (Bollingen Series LXXI)*. Princeton University Press.

also lacked common sense. After the breakup of the Soviet Union the newly independent nations naturally reverted back to capitalism, only to discover that at the markets an educated communist son could not do that which his uneducated grandparents and parents could, and that is *to compete*. Georgians worked hard to restore competitive capitalist elements that were important parts of traditional Georgian way of life before the rude advent of the Russian communist imperialism. Little by little people relearned what they had forgotten – skills, trades, risk and competition. They learned how to demand more not from the government, but from themselves. And as "the law of demand is consistent with common sense",[137] with that healthy demand they also developed common sense, – that vital knowledge necessary for success which, it seems to me, a great majority of our university professors do not possess and, therefore, cannot teach.

Today a new horde of socialists threatens to destroy both, Georgia and America. These are more sophisticated and better educated propagandists than their Russian counterparts. They are born, raised and bred among us in the best "liberal" colleges of America. They work either for Washington or a Washington-based international organization. They "*aid*" Georgia. They "*welfare*" America.[138] They create perpetual dependencies, promote consumerism and encourage mediocrity. If we do not count a choice between a pink slime[139] double cheeseburger and a hot dog, they have successfully eliminated freedom of choice in America, and are trying their best to do the same in Georgia. If their "egalitarianism" continues, within a generation Georgians and Americans will find themselves economically paralyzed, – with their skill gone and their competitive nature forever dulled. I am fully aware that the aid is temporarily gratifying, and that cessation of the aid will cause pain, but continuing it shall cause death. In case of America, it will be economic death only. In case of Georgia, the demise will be a complete *transmoral* infarction,[140] destroying every aspect of Georgian

---

[137] McConnell, C. R., Brue. S. L., Flynn. S. M. (2009). *Microeconomics*. McGraw-Hill.

[138] To welfare – to plunder by compelling the plundered to surrender willingly their greatest capital – freedom, with all of its present and future proceeds to the plunderer in exchange of secure, but substandard (or rather subsistence) living. This is a new verb created by the author of this article. Its inception was long overdue, as the act which this verb describes has been a common practice in Europe now for a century, and in the U.S. since F.D.R.

[139] A derogatory term that refers to ammoniated boneless lean beef trimmings or similar products, which are considered "unfit for human consumption" until the ammonia has been added.

[140] A word play on *transmural* infarction.

life, economic and noneconomic. It is common knowledge that every poor nation receiving such "aid" has abundance of two things: Swiss bank accounts for its few, and starch-based diets for its many citizens. Inflated tuition, housing market, healthcare and, lately, even food prices are the results of such egalitarian "programmes"[141] and "projects", which bring easy money and threaten to destroy competitive nature of Georgian people, their unique culture and extraordinary ability for self-reliance and self-governance. In light of the foregoing, I advise Georgians to reject "international" "aid". Georgia, unlike Greece, has no islands to sell when the easy money and the accompanying temporary gratification run out and then, not merely an economic crisis, but a catastrophe will hit them in the face:

> The good is one thing, the gratifying is quite another;
> their goals are different, both bind a man.
> Good things await him who picks the good;
> by choosing the gratifying, one misses one's goal.

> Both the good and the gratifying
> present themselves to a man;
> The wise assess them, note their difference;
> and choose the good over the gratifying;
> But the fool chooses the gratifying
> rather than what is beneficial.[142]

DIVIDE ET IMPERA

"Divide Et Impera" is a Latin saying which in English translates as "Divide and Rule". It refers to an ancient policy, used by such tyrants as the Caesar and Napoleon, Shah Abbas the first of Iran and the heads of the Russian empire (both, Tsarist and modern), and everyone in-between, in order to sink their native, as well as conquered people into perpetual serfdom. It is a combination of political, military and economic strategies aimed at gaining and maintaining power by breaking up people in order to deter a possibility of larger concentrations of power. The ensuing result is that the divided people individually have less power than the one implementing the strategy, – the oppressor. The use of this technique is meant to empower a dictator (or a group of dictators) to control subjects,

---

[141] Peculiar spelling of the word is no coincidence.
[142] Olivelle, Patrick (translator). (2008). *Upanisads*. Oxford University Press, USA.

populations, or factions of different interests, who collectively might be able to oppose his rule.

Niccolo Machiavelli identifies a similar application to military strategy, advising in Book VI of *The Art of War* (*Dell'arte della Guerra*), that a Captain should endeavor with every art to divide the forces of the enemy, either by making him suspicious of his men in whom he trusted, or by giving him cause that he has to separate his forces, and, because of this, become weaker.[143]

In the 19th and 20th centuries the strategy fast evolved and developed into a highly effective, micro-social and, I would say, cellular science for a relatively amenable implementation of serfdom en masse. Allow me to explain:

History is full of examples when it is either difficult, or financially burdening, or even quite impossible for a despot to procure by sheer force his tyrannical rule over certain foreign nations or certain people within his native nation. Before the 19th century a despot would try to conduct a social surgery, – to disassociate the targeted people from their legitimate (truly beneficent) sovereign, or to disassociate the sovereign from the elite, or to disassociate one ethnic people of a given nation from another, – the old versions of divide and rule. Essentially what the old despot was doing is that he was isolating people with common interest from one another, much like what the English did to the people of Scotland for centuries, and what Russians in vain tried to do among the indigenous nations of the Caucasus.

But soon the question arouse among the professors of Moriarty creed of the day, – Marx, Engels, Lenin and the like Sophists, – would it not be better if we manage to disassociate willingly the targeted individual not merely from the state, the beneficent sovereign or his fellow men, but rather from his very self, – his God-given nature, – freedom? After much trial and error they found the way to accomplish just that. Like all good Pharisees and hypocrites, they too adhered to the rule of thumb of sugarcoating evil, and decided to euphemize the new-style divide and rule policy by calling its milder version "socialism" and its more "beneficent" margin "communism".

---

[143] Machiavelli, Niccolo. (2001). *The Art of War*. Da Capo Press.

In every case through history socialism and communism have two initial goals: they must take away from the people, first, the right to private property and, second, natural propensity for merit. The latter is done by establishing flat remuneration regardless of value. The former is done by promoting "public" enterprise. Without property people are rendered economically paralyzed, and without merit-based compensation people are left demoralized. Let's discuss abolishing merit and establishing flat wages more in depth: for one, Leonardo da Vinci and a dimwit who just dropped out of a trade school are being paid equally. In another example, a talented athlete and a fatso, who can hardly make a step, are both slouching at the track, as at the end of the race they both get the first prize, and, by the way, the first prize is always something utterly dull. Now, the dimwit is happy, and, definitely, so is the fatso, but both, Leonardo and the athlete are suicidal. Why? Because they know they are penalized for their talent and ability, – the fatso and the dimwit seem smarter, as they are accomplishing the same result as da Vinci and the athlete with less effort. But eventually both, da Vinci and the athlete grudgingly accept the prize of the day, – the identical, undifferentiated and ubiquitous first prize (the same that the fatso and the dimwit have been taking for a long time). Pretty soon they all start taking it willingly and, soon after, even happily. Mission accomplished, – by taking morsels off the hand of the tyrant, people dissociate themselves from two cardinal elements of economic freedom, – merit and competition, and at last disregard political freedom as well. The social micro-engineering project at the cellular level affected the very core and essential fibers of the individual and divided him from his own self, his nature, his God-given freedom. Instead of earning a fortune, he is receiving a pittance. One of his most important brain cells – the one which connects man with his natural independence – has been effectively destroyed.

I believe that, irrespective of our political associations or philosophical views, at least in theory, if not in deed, we shall all unanimously and without much ado agree that freedom is an essential part of a human being. We may go as far as to concur that freedom is the very essence of a human being. Then it only follows that anything that perpetually hinders freedom is deadly and, therefore, bad; and conversely, – anything that perpetually supports freedom is vital and, therefore, good. We saw that socialism and communism, as they take away the right to own property and eliminate incentives, create a welfare case out of a citizen, who, in turn, grudgingly accepts the *immediate* (artificial) reality and forgets about the *universal* (natural) reality, – his own nature and freedom which is at its core. This eventually results in conformism and, finally, in perfect serfdom. The man estranged from his freedom becomes an animal, a beast, a mindless zombie who is no longer capable of taking risks, planning ahead, working hard, using his talent, – and in a sense, he is no longer capable of anything which is essential to life, that is to the life of a free man. So, by means of abolishing incentives and property rights, and the subsequent introduction of welfare, a man dwindles into an odd fellow, called a slave, and a nation – into a mass of conformists, called serfs.

Ilia Chavchavadze knew that the battles of freedom in subsequent centuries would be won not by sword, but by sound economics. He often stated that Georgians must now pick up and learn how to use an abacus, instead of the usual sword and shield. In fact, this most learned and talented man, the likes of which are scarcely found in the entire history of humanity, once introduced to finance and economics, picked up the abacus and never went back to the pen, – after establishing the first bank of Georgia and a few other large capitalist enterprises, he never went back to poetry, and rarely got engaged in prose, history, law or even philosophy. He did not write a single poem after that point. This fact is hardly an accident. And in light of the foregoing, I here end my discussion of this topic, and move on to another chapter, in order to keep my writing brief and my actual work, which awaits me after I am done with this manuscript, vast.

USEFUL MONOPOLY

One of the claims socialist ideologists frequently, but quite obliviously, use against capitalism is the argument of monopoly. They state that the existence of monopoly clearly demonstrates imperfection of the market and the failure of the "invisible hand". In light of the foregoing dangerous, but by no means truthful propaganda, I must admit that I find it all the more necessary to move away from typical theorizing expected from a typical economist and delve right into the essence of monopoly. For this reason you will not read the conventional and, quite frankly, somewhat redundant theorems and basic formulations on monopoly, oligopoly, duopoly, etc., found just as frequently in a standard undergraduate microeconomics textbook, as in any MBA book on managerial economics, even though today's economists, or rather mathematicians turned economists, do not like to admit that in essence these two textbooks are essentially the same. Such talentless academics have limited the science of economics and made it into a finite discipline of repeating the fundamental theorems. The only new additions to microeconomics textbooks are the so called progressive hypotheses (such as normative economics) and flawed empirical analyses. They have failed to advance microeconomics beyond the size of a single textbook. All of this considered, I am compelled to abandon standard textbook language and to look at monopoly from a different angle. Even on the surface, it is clear that saying something in defense of the market and certain forms of monopoly seems all the more necessary, if we consider the fact that with their false arguments today's socialists increase the danger of the scope of government expanding to the activities that in a free society must be left unregulated, as they are best regulated by natural forces of the market.

Contrary to the common belief, monopoly is rarely created by the free market. Moreover, it is well-documented that monopoly is quite frequently the result of government support, overregulation, intervention or collusive (and *illegal*) agreements between the government and the private enterprise, the latter often, if not always, with direct ties to the government. This sort of monopoly heretofore shall be referred to as *"unnatural monopoly"*. The weight of this abstract argument perhaps can be best demonstrated by some practical examples: Georgians often complain about the ubiquitous monopoly permeating almost every major segment of business, including construction, telecommunication, transportation, education, tourism, alcohol, and food industries. By false default people immediately tend to blame capitalism for creation of these monopolies. Let us explore how and why this happens.

Because Georgia is a democracy, and capitalism nowadays frequently exists during such a democracy, Georgians start to associate these unnatural monopolies with capitalism, instead of the widespread clannish corruption and the remnant elements of socialism, which oddly enough also could be, and indeed are, associated with and present in a democracy. In fact, biased support, unnecessary and quite often unconstitutional intervention in the free market, and collusive agreements between members of the government and people related to these members, first, originate and, then, perpetuate such monopolies. Things get even worse for capitalism, as the United States knowingly and willingly quite often turns the blind eye to such questionable dealings of senior members of the Georgian government. Not only Georgians, but people around the world, associate the U.S. with democracy and capitalism, and when they see such collusive dealings of Tbilisi are openly condoned by Washington, they think that the corruption and the subsequent unnatural monopolies are related to or caused by capitalism.

The truth of the matter is that capitalism does not correlate with corruption or the subsequent unnatural monopoly. Capitalism sometimes coincides with democracy, and democracy sometimes coincides with corruption, which, in turn, is always accompanied with unnatural monopolization of the markets. And in this long and drawn-out chain reaction of coincidences, causations and correlations, with a bit of added encouragement and propaganda coming from today's covert communists, i.e. "liberals", capitalism, which is the true beacon of freedom in the modern world, is unfairly associated with the government corruption. In the result capitalism is blamed by the essential majority, and gets the labels of monopoly and corruption stuck all over it.

I challenge both, people of Georgia and the goading socialists to show me a single case of monopoly in the entire history of the Georgian nation which did not start with an undue government intervention, overregulation, support or collusive agreements between the politicians and their relatives-turned-"businessmen". If they trace histories of the present monopolies in Georgia, not in history books, but rather in their immediate memory, they will find that the original founder, if not the present CEO, of each of the current monopolistic companies in Georgia is a retired member of one political regime or the other.[144]

Now let's discuss, what I would call, *natural* monopolies. A natural monopoly is a condition on the cost-technology of an industry, whereby it is most efficient for production to be concentrated in a single form. In some cases, this gives the largest supplier in an industry, often (but not always) the first supplier in a market, an overwhelming cost advantage over other actual and potential competitors. This sometimes tends to be the case in industries where capital costs predominate, creating economies of scale that are large in relation to the size of the market, and, hence, high barriers to entry, for example, public utilities, such as water services and electricity. It is very expensive to build transmission networks (water and gas pipelines, electricity and telephone lines); therefore, it is unlikely that a potential competitor would be willing to make the capital investment needed even to enter the monopolist's market. Monopoly which takes place in the industries that have high barriers of entry is created due to natural limitations of resources. So it is

---

[144] Use of article "the" is no coincidence.

in fact a *natural* monopoly, but I would like to differentiate it farther from other forms of natural monopoly by calling it *technical* monopoly, as it is a direct result of technical factors that are economically limiting. I will use the term *natural monopoly* with the monopoly created when a firm beats all other competitors and achieves monopolistic position in the market due to its competitive success and not because of vast limitations in natural resources.

So far economists have suggested only three alternatives for dealing with natural monopoly, meaning when, in spite of market elements, which naturally tend to demonopolize, either an economic environment or technical conditions make a monopoly the natural outcome of the competitive market forces: public monopoly, public regulation and private monopoly. They are all flawed, but private monopoly, statistically speaking, proves to be less harmful than public regulation, and public regulation tends to be less harmful than public monopoly. Public monopoly is the worst of the three evils. First, because it is a deceiving euphemism, – the word "public" is quite unjustly used here, the term *government monopoly* would be much more appropriate. Second, the government monopoly means that the government's power is expanded to the point that it not only oversees, i.e. regulates the market activity, but rather runs it, i.e. actively manages it and participates in it, – the government becomes *the* administrator of an important market element, if not the entire market. This could be not only harmful, but also disastrous. Such was clearly the case when F. D. Roosevelt created the Frankenstein economic monster, called the Tennessee Valley Authority (TVA), which destroyed lives of many competitive men and quite a few sound private enterprises.

Public, i.e. government regulation is better than government administration, but it is still ineffective, inefficient and opens numerous opportunities for corruption and collusive business practices. Government regulation has a tendency to become overregulation. Even those American regulatory institutions which were originally quite useful are now useless and, most important, taxing.

Private monopoly is not a pleasant cakewalk either, – an exceedingly large corporation can set prices singlehandedly. But such a monopolistic corporation is still considerably smaller, and therefore less powerful, than the government. And I would rather have a small tyrant dictate to me than a big one. Economists have failed to come up with alternative solutions, but *we* shall *not*. In the remainder of this section I will discuss two reliable and simple solutions for dissolving the monopolistic market back to its natural, competitive state by two natural, i.e. competitive forces.

So the market is imperfect, at least technically speaking. But this does not automatically constitute that it is inadequate. And certainly it does not mean that it is adequate for the government to intervene (or I would rather say *interfere*). Let's start with the government intervention. Does anyone honestly think that the governments are comprised of more talented people than the private sector? There is more money in private enterprise than in government, – honest money that is, – so exceptionally moral and talented would be more inclined to find employment in private sector, while less moral and less talented would be more inclined to seek employment in our government. While this is not true in every case, it is true most of the time. Furthermore, show me a government bureaucrat who can do as much as a retail general manager and is able to run a high-volume American store. Show me a public servant who can initiate and conclude a single trade on Wall Street. I am willing to stake my life and my reputation that a vast majority of civil servants of *any* country would fail at both challenges. And under these considerations, today's covert socialist – the loud-mouth "liberal" – keeps insisting that we must turn over the monopolized market to this largely (but not thoroughly) incapable herd of always indifferent and often immoral people who, I admit, are well-experienced at being managed, but know nothing about managing an independent entity, a free economic enterprise – whether animate or inanimate – human or physical. I am afraid that, at least in this case, the cure would be worse than the disease. Most capable men and women naturally belong in the private sector and if they cannot improve, well, then neither can the government.

Now, let's discuss market imperfections. As stated above, the fact that the market, at least technically speaking, is imperfect, and allowed natural or technical monopolies to be created, does not automatically constitute that it is also inefficient in the long-run, and, therefore, inadequate. Today, perhaps more than ever, two cardinal factors will make most of monopolies short-lived:

1. Modern telecommunication and transportation infrastructure which, for the first time, has truly globalized the world;

2. Modern technology which constantly offers alternative products and services.

Let's discuss them one at a time. First, modern transportation infrastructure is such that, for the first time, it has globalized the world by making almost every commodity and every service mobile, which, in turn, created an unlimited and almost invisible Silk Road with almost endless possibilities for global trade. If we are facing a form of natural or even most forms of technical monopoly at home, all we have to do is lift the unnecessary trade barriers and let the foreign competition diversify our market until the national company gets a rude awakening and, through the power of competitive capitalism, is "courteously" reminded that the customer must be treated right and prices must be lowered. An influential English-Portuguese political economist, David Ricardo realized this back in the 19th century. He writes: "If we were left to ourselves, unfettered by legislative enactments, we should gradually withdraw our capital from the cultivation of such lands, and import the produce which is at present raised upon them."[145] Ricardo is perfectly correct, – laissez-faire approach which would lift all the unnecessary trade restrictions, considering today's advanced transportation infrastructure, will bring so much competition and such an abundance of competitively priced products and services into our native market that our compatriot monopolist shall indeed have a rude awakening. And the American consumers shall benefit.

Modern telecommunication in various service industries has already achieved that which modern transportation is yet to realize once trade restrictions are lifted. Not to say that telecommunication is free of regulation, but it is considerably less restricted than trade, and for that reason it has transformed, for example, the IT service industry into a globally competitive marketplace.

Modern technology, which constantly offers alternative products, is another cardinal reason why most forms of technical and all forms of natural monopolies will be short lived in today's world. It requires nothing more than knowledge of basic economics and/or a bit of common sense to know that entrepreneurs' decision about what goods to produce, how they should be produced, and for whom they should be produced are essentially market oriented. That is, firms choose to produce certain goods and services because, given the demand for these products and the cost of using scarce resources, they can earn sufficient profit to justify their particular use of these resources. Moreover, they

---

[145] Ricardo, David. (2010). *The Works of David Ricardo*. General Books LLC.

combine their scarce resources to produce maximum output in the least costly way. Finally, they supply these goods and services to those segments of the population expected to provide the most material reward for their efforts. Now, all this is relevant to technical and natural monopoly as the insatiable drive for economic success, present in a single entrepreneur or a corporation comprised of such entrepreneurial individuals, combined with today's diverse and advanced technological advancements, shall constantly come up with alternative products either by alternative use of the same technology which the monopolist uses, or by using an altogether alternative technology. This is possible not only in a private enterprise, but also in the government sector when the government, for a change, does the right thing and takes on a project which the market cannot handle at all or its handling is suboptimal. Case in point: when the U.S. government decided to develop the Dwight D. Eisenhower National System of Interstate and Defense Highways, more commonly known as American Interstate Highway System, through the Federal-Aid Highway Act of 1956, road infrastructure grew to such an extent that it became a direct competitor to the railroad system, previously held as the unchallenged monopoly in the country. As a result, millions of Americans became self-employed truck drivers (a most honorable employment in my mind), and American people started to receive the goods quicker and at lower cost. What the government did back then, technology can do it now, – modern technology constantly helps us to invent alternative or substitute products and services. Remember what happened with the iPhones? – Potential for profit-making was so high that they inadvertently produced *global* competition, – high technology firms from Korea to Germany and from Japan to China started to produce substitute products. And the American consumer benefited.

During competitive capitalism monopoly may still develop, but it will be a natural monopoly. Such monopoly arises on competitive grounds, which is perfectly acceptable to me. The reason is quite simple, – when such a monopolist starts to underperform, he shall lose his monopoly on the same competitive grounds. Supply and demand are wise (I would not say *blind*) and effective forces which do not discriminate against any nationality, color, creed, age or even size of any individual or a corporation. It is the government who does all that.

Some argue that the size of a large corporation should be of utmost concern, as it may have dangerous neighborhood effects. I must admit that this fear is justified to a point, – larger the organization, more power it wields, and more massive and encompassing its actions could be. But on the same ground, how can we justify either the government or its intervention? Have you seen anything more massive than our government? Even a minor negative step of this colossal squid, whose tentacles furiously try to grasp every sphere of human existence, always carries not just a neighborhood, but rather national, or even transnational, or global effects. A corporation, in comparison to a government, is merely a frail Thumbelina. So the "size" argument can never stand, as long as the government is larger than the corporation.

Moreover, why does size bring up such a negative connotation among the majority? How can an enterprise, which in fact started as a Ma and Pa shop at the corner of a small side street in Southwest Philadelphia, having grown fair and square, and during this growth employed many of our neighbors, be the subject of despise? I shall treat size of an enterprise elsewhere in proceeding chapters, but, as of right now, I cannot help but believe that people who loath success, whether it is an individual or a group achievement, are incapable of success themselves and, therefore, become envious, while the fact that someone else has succeeded and has achieved a considerable size is music to the man's ears who himself desires and strives for success. Someone else's success brings hope to the aspiring others, – if I know that Joe, who grew up in Southwest Philly, two blocks from me, became a success by doing something thoroughly good, I too, who grew up in Southwest Philadelphia, do good and desire to work, should have some hope of becoming successful.

Now, there are some who condemn natural monopoly on the grounds that they are against big businesses in general. Their claim rests on a single far-fetched conjecture that a large enterprise cannot contain honest men. Henry David Thoreau, who to me is one of the most honest, moral and learned man this country ever saw, and who also happened to be more removed from all corporate affiliations than anyone else I know, recognized the natural fact that "a corporation of conscientious men is a corporation with a conscience",[146] and at least in my mind, put an end to this argument both, with this statement and with his exemplary life. There is as much naturalism in this economic statement, as it is in his writings on Walden Pond, Concord and Merrimack rivers and the Maine woods. In fact, people who condemn economic realities of a free market,

---

[146] Thoreau, H. D., Sanborn, F. B., Lazarashvili, Z. K. (2011). *American Heroes: Thoreau and Brown*. Georgian International University Press.

almost always tend forcibly to ignore economic realities of the nature, – ubiquitously present throughout its every stratum and every sphere. The nature economizes when it goes through foliage, when a flower withers, an ocean swells or an eagle devours a groundhog, but it does not mean that Uncle Sam *must* come running to interfere with its natural ways. Supply and demand, evaluation and devaluation, the haves and the have-nots are just as much a part of the nature as growth, carnage, death and birth, which daily take place in its flora and fauna. As the last of the Five Good Emperors of Rome, Marcus Aurelius put it, "Don't fear death, but give it a friendly greeting. Nature sends it along with everything else. ...our dissolution is just one of life's natural processes." And then he concluded: "As you now wait for the unborn child to burst from your wife's womb, so should you anticipate the moment when your soul will slip from its shell."[147] If nature, expressed in the market and its competitive elements, managed to create a large corporation and with it natural monopoly, believe me, it also has the necessary power to destroy it once such a monopolistic corporation loses its competitive edge and becomes redundant. "Dear" government, stand aside and let the *market* complete the cycle of the creative destruction. After all, it was the market that allowed this natural growth, so let *it* sanction the natural death as well, as it knows best when such a demise is due and most appropriate.

My still somewhat dear, but surely ignorant socialist, once again I would like to use the opportunity and in this conclusive part of the chapter remind you of the following: it was also nature who crafted a titanic elephant and a miniscule ant, and everything in-between, but just because an elephant does not conform to your standards of mediocrity, i.e. the non-existent and, therefore, false equality, which you always fancy for the people (but *never* for yourself), does not give you the right to step in and eradicate all the elephants and all the ants. Remember that a proud elephant or a timid ant shall never be made into a perfect-size conformist jackal which you always so diligently try to engineer. In fact, you do not and never shall have adequate power to do that, in spite of the minions, which today are blindly harnessed in your bureaucratic, taxing and policing machinery, – big and meddling government. Next time, when you see a stork devour a goldfish, please do not call 911, or the FCC when a wolf howls not quite to the right note, or the FHA when a rabbit fails to dig a burrow on the first try, – let nature take its course. The stork, the goldfish, the wolf and the rabbit are *always* better off without calling the lion for mediation. And as much as I would like to

---

[147] Aurelius, Marcus. (2002). *The Emperor's Handbook*. Scribner.

extend the same logical deduction and state that the humanity is always better off without you, my dear socialist, I realize that this would be a wrong thing to do, as it was nature which ordained your birth, and for that reason, and for that reason only, I must tolerate you, but… not your flawed theories or your despicable actions.

HIGHER EDUCATION: LAISSEZ-FAIRE

Education is yet another area which can be effectively regulated by the free market, but all over the world people seem to be under a false impression that market elements, as well as natural market forces are *completely* ineffective. People mistakenly believe that if the market is blatantly truthful in its allocation of funds needed for education, it is also inapt; and if it is inapt, the government must finance; and if the government must finance, it must also administer.

This troubling circumstance, incongruous both, with the immediate realities and with historical, i.e. universal truth, is yet another proof that people have been put through the laud propaganda machine of systematic brainwashing, which belongs to the same old socialist tyrant, who back in the day was called a communist, but now goes by the name of a modern "liberal". I shall explain what I meant by the *immediate realities*: given a simple choice, where would people, or the socialist himself for that matter, send their children to study economics, the University of Chicago or a state university with an open admissions policy? The overwhelming vote would be for Chicago, – one of *many* private institutions of higher education which naturally achieves academic excellence.

Now I shall explain what I meant by the *historical*, i.e. *universal truth*. Historically speaking, all great enterprises, including centers of education and enlightenment, are self-sustaining, – as Thoreau once said, "The poet, for instance, must sustain his body by his poetry, as a steam planing-mill feeds its boilers with the shavings it makes…"[148] And then he continues: "Merely to come into the world the heir of a fortune is not to be born, but to be still-born, rather. To be supported by the charity of friends, or a government pension, — provided you continue to breathe, — by whatever fine synonyms you describe these relations, is to go into

---

[148] Thoreau, H. D., Sanborn, F. B., Lazarashvili, Z. K. (2011). *American Heroes: Thoreau and Brown*. Georgian International University Press.

the almshouse."[149] Thoreau was perfectly correct, and the essence of his truth can be substantiated not only with history of the United States, but also with the constant background theme of Georgian history:

Historic academies of Georgia, including the Fazisi Academy, which arguably is the oldest continuously functioning institution of higher education in the world, where, among other noted men, Plato's son was educated, Ikalto Academy, Gelati Academy, Tbilisi State University, etc. were all self-sustaining private enterprises. The Tao-Klarjeti[150] monasteries of the 11th-13th centuries, famed for being the cradle of culture and philosophy of not only Georgia, but the entire Orthodox Christian world, were also self-supporting. They had benefactors, but no Sovereign or a mob of sovereigns (the big elitist governments) administered them or interfered with their philosophic pursuits or enrollment policies. The same applies to every great and longstanding and, therefore, historic Georgian institution of learning both, in and outside of Georgia. Georgian theology schools, such as Petritsoni in Bulgaria,[151] Monastery of the Cross[152] built in the 11th

---

[149] Thoreau, H. D., Sanborn, F. B., Lazarashvili, Z. K. (2011). *American Heroes: Thoreau and Brown.* Georgian International University Press.

[150] Tao-Klarjeti, also known as Meskheti – the term conventionally used in modern history writings to describe the historic south-western Georgian principalities, the cradle of both, pre-Christian and Christian Iberian civilizations, now forming part of north-eastern Turkey and divided among the provinces of Erzurum, Artvin, Ardahan and Kars. Historically the area comprised of the following provinces: West of the Arsiani Mountains were Tao, Klarjeti and Shavsheti, to the east lay Samtskhe, Erusheti, Javakheti, Artaani and Kola. The landscape is characterized by mountains and the river-systems of the Chorokhi and the Mtkvari. Tao-Klarjeti's geographical position between the great Empires of the East and the West, and the fact that one branch of the Silk Road ran through its territory, meant that it was subject to a constant stream of diverging influences. Tao-Klarjeti was ruled by the Bagrationi dynasty, the royal family of Georgia which actually descended from that region, and, hence, the region played the *most* crucial role in the unification of the Georgian principalities into a single feudal state in 1008. Alongside the magnificent nature, the architectural monuments of Tao-Klarjeti – Georgian Orthodox churches, monasteries, bridges and castles – function as tourist attractions today, but many monuments are endangered, since nothing is done for their preservation. There have been also cases of deliberate destruction by Turks, for instance, in Opiza, Bana and Tbeti. Armenians, on the other hand, have been long engaged in cultural and historical terrorism, – erasing Georgian frescos and Georgian inscriptions on the ancient churches and inscribing graffiti in their native tongue in order to usurp cultural heritage of this not only important, but vital region for Georgian nation, from which Georgian language, alphabet, Christianity, royal dynasty, monastic culture, literature, theology and philosophy take origin *and* sustenance – the cradle and alma mater of Georgian civilization.

[151] Petritsoni Monastery – an important monument of Christian architecture and one of the largest and oldest Eastern Orthodox monasteries in Eastern Europe located in

century by the Georgian King Bagrat IV in Jerusalem, located below the Israel Museum and the Knesset (the Parliament of Israel), as well as its predecessor institution established by the Georgian King Mirian III of Iberia (his official title) in the 4th century AD, the Holy Monastery of Iviron[153] (i.e. the Holy Monastery of Iberians) at Mount Athos in Greece

---

Bulgaria. The monastery is known and appreciated for the unique combination of Georgian, Byzantine and Bulgarian cultures, united by the common faith. The monastery was founded as an Iberian Orthodox monastery in 1083 by Prince Grigol the son of Bakuriani (also known in Greek as Gregory Pakourianos), a prominent Georgian statesman and military commander in the Byzantine service. The Cathedral Church of the Virgin Mary (dating from 1604) is the place where a valuable icon of the Virgin Mary Eleusa is kept, which was brought from Georgia in 1310. The icon is wonder-working, attracting many pilgrims. The monastery was known as a cradle of Christian and Neo-Platonist philosophies. The school was led in the 11th and 12th centuries by Ioane Petritsi, who was a Georgian Neoplatonic philosopher, best known for his translations of Proclus, along with an extensive commentary. A silver-gilded cross rising from the dome of the church bears the inscription in Georgian: "Always win!"

[152] Monastery of the Cross – a monastery near the Nayot neighborhood of Jerusalem, Israel. It is located in the Valley of the Cross, below the Israel Museum and the Knesset. The monastery was built in the 11th century, during the reign of King Bagrat IV of Georgia by the Georgian Giorgi-Prokhore of Shavsheti. It is believed that the site was originally consecrated in the 4th century under the instruction of the Roman emperor Constantine the Great, who later gave the site to the Georgian King Mirian III of Iberia. Legend has it that the monastery was erected on the burial spot of Adam's head from which grew the tree that gave its wood to the cross on which Christ was crucified.

[153] Holy Monastery of Iviron – an Eastern Orthodox monastery at the monastic state of Mount Athos in Greece. The monastery was built under the supervision of Ioane (Ioannes in Greek) the Iberian and Tornike (Tornikios in Greek) between 980-983 AD and housed Iberian clergy and priests. The monastery ranks third in the hierarchy of the Athonite monasteries. The library of Iviron monastery contains 2,000 manuscripts, 15 liturgical scrolls, and 20,000 books, most of which are in Georgian, Greek, Hebrew and Latin. The name Iviron originated from the ancient Georgian Kingdom of Iberia (Iveria) where the master architect of the monastery Ioannes was from. The monastery has the relics of more canonized saints than any other on Mount Athos. The Panagia Portaitissa, the famous 9th century icon, is also located at Iviron. The monastery was once the leading school of Christian and Neo-Platonist philosophies and theology in the world. Among its prominent scholars was Euthymius the Athonite – a renowned Georgian philosopher and scholar, also known as Eufimius the Abasgian or St. Euthymius the Georgian. Fluent in Georgian, Greek and other languages, he translated many religious treatises and philosophical works. Among his major works was the translation of *Sibrdzne Balavarisa* (*Wisdom of Balahvari*) – a Christianized version of episodes from the life of Gautama Buddha that became very popular in Medieval Europe as the story of Barlaam and Josaphat. Another famous scholar of the school was Giorgi Mtatsmindeli (George the Hagiorite in Greek) (1009-1065) – a Georgian monk, religious writer, and translator, who spearheaded the activities of Georgian monastic communities in the Byzantine Empire. One of the most influential Christian churchmen of medieval Georgia, George acted as an arbitrator and facilitator of cross-cultural engagement between his native country and the Byzantine Empire. He featured prominently during the Great Schism between the Eastern

built and established under Ioane (Ioannes in Greek) the Iberian and Tornike (Tornikos in Greek) in 980-983, – they were all private enterprises independently run by those illustrious Georgian people who, as free men, and not as serfs or agents of government, were willingly involved in their administration. The fact that freedom was affixed the highest value in Georgian culture is clearly demonstrated in the laissez-faire, self-sustaining and self-governing way these ancient centers of liberal education were run and maintained. For a detailed account see Appendix B at the end of the book.

It was explained in some detail in previous sections that the invention of a perpetual boogieman simulates emergencies. This becomes the pretext for government intervention which, in turn, allows eroding of all safeguards of an individual's liberty. It was this way that the socialists successfully rescinded the fundamental moral law which states in the very depth of human heart, that God-given freedom is indeed man's life, and anything other than freedom is death. They were also able to uproot the canon law from man's conscience, which states from the time immemorial that *a man must earn his daily bread by the sweat of his brow.*[154] – Meaning, a man must be *responsible* for his freedom and independence. The seventy years of the Russian rule did this in Georgia, – the nation which was fully devoted to economic freedom even at most seemingly incongruous venues by today's standards, such as the administration of a church, a monastery or an institution of higher learning – an academia. Soviet socialists were frequently successful in forcing their flawed ideology, but, even at gunpoint, during the entire seventy years of the Soviet tyranny they could never repeal the most elementary of economic laws, that a sufficiently high price will result in production of supply. The ensuing argument for improving education by essentially eliminating almost all government intervention will rest precisely on this elementary economic argument, which is so akin to human nature that it proved to be durable and enduring even in the times of the universal socialist attack, as demonstrated by a huge underground economy which existed in Georgia for the entire duration of Russia's communist rule. Let's delve right into it:

---

and Western Christendom, being one of the few Eastern churchmen who defended the separated Western brethren.

[154] Genesis 3:19. Paraphrasing: "By the sweat of your brow, you will produce food to eat until you return to the ground, because you were taken from it. You are dust, and you will return to dust."

In order to put an end to perpetuating *adverse* inequalities, to help shape good citizens with distinctly Georgian common values, we need not mere schooling, but education; and for education we need to make capital more widely and more directly available not to government units, but to *deserving* students. But how can the state fairly and expertly determine who is and who is not *deserving*, meaning *eligible*? Besides, how could a state come up with such capital so expediently? – Surely, simply printing money, even if it is out of thin air, would not suffice, although all governments can do just that, and most of them indeed do it, not knowing that by such a gullible act they devalue labor output of their own nation, as well as currency which is reflective of this common labor, and, in the result, they only achieve perpetuating poverty and serfdom, and nothing more.

As George Santayana once noted, "A child educated only at school is an uneducated child."[155] Alas, activities of most governments are mostly concentrated on schooling, and, I believe, if not the education I received from my family, strictly left to school or to my own devices, I too would've turned out to be not a free man, but a government bureaucrat on either side of the Atlantic. In fact, more dictatorial the governments, more they tend to ignore education and concern themselves with schooling, that is – ushering people indiscriminately into some sort of a common edifice where highly censored lectures are held, just like you would expect an ignorant, but a roughneck and somewhat cunning shepherd to usher his sheep into a long slaughterhouse. That was certainly more prevalent in the Soviet Union than anywhere else. In fact, a Soviet school actually resembled a slaughter house with its outward appearance, not to speak of its essence embedded in the inward decor of that building. I still vaguely, but nevertheless quite bitterly remember the law enforcement agent of the city police, assigned to my neighborhood, scouring a block after block in the 12th Micro Region[156] of Rustavi City, Georgia, in an effort to catch young men in their late teens, who were skipping high school, and send them back to the cookie cutter Rustavi City School No23, which had a great knack for uniformity and offered its uniform intellectual diet most indiscriminately and free of charge to everyone. The problem was not everyone enjoyed the Soviet academic diet, – didn't matter how enlightening or how cheap it was.

---

[155] Santayana, George. Cardiff, Ira. (1964). *The Wisdom of George Santayana: Atoms of Thought*. Citadel Press.
[156] Micro Region – a city district in Soviet cities built after early 1980s.

Humoring socialism with a bit of added sarcasm aside, capitalism has a problem, – gifting the capital is *not* an option: besides the fact that funds are scarce, it ushers issues of inevitable corruption, prejudice and nepotism if the government decides to finance education with or without administering it. Also, given the nature of a student loan, it is my firm belief that lending the capital is also out of question. I do not intend to address the issue of student loans in this thesis, but I will only mention that my belief stems from the fact that such loans are most unsecure, incongruous to capitalism and very risky.

Furthermore, whether in the case of a student loan or direct government financing, we must consider that students have diverse needs within the broad field of education, which may not necessarily agree with our preferences. If I am a taxpayer and, based on a government mandate, as well as on some morally compelling circumstances, I am to contribute to the government expenditure in order to finance someone else's education, I want to make sure that it is indeed education that I am financing and not the college sports, cheerleading, basket weaving or the study of the pseudo-philosophical, i.e. Sophist doctrine of hedonism, all of which, we must all admit, goes on in today's establishments of higher education, especially in the United States. On the other hand, what *I* consider education, may not necessarily suit the needs of a particularly talented student, – to most taxpayers the science of hydrodynamics may be an unknown and, therefore, an unimportant pursuit, but it does not mean that it is not important to a particularly gifted student. The same applies to philosophy, economics, exegesis and many other most essential academic subjects. In light of the foregoing, my gut instincts tell me that "something is rotten in the state of Denmark"[157] whenever I see a student loan being offered in this country or elsewhere. I am inclined to think that student loans are the production of the same unnatural forces, which, under the pretext of socialist equality (nonexistent in nature), in a brutish way endeavor to interfere with free market forces and to engineer the society of Frankenstein monsters. One thing I know about the free market is that it does not reward those activities which are not economically viable. And I also know that a student loan on its own is not economically viable. That's all.

Years ago when I strove to rise above the poverty of my initial state, I applied for my first job in capital markets by writing a letter to a Wall

---

[157] Shakespeare, William. (2005). *The Yale Shakespeare: Complete Works*. Barnes & Noble.

Street executive, which culminated with this concise, but all-encompassing sentence: "I have *ability*, all I need is an *opportunity*". It is a fact that people are born with the "haves" and the "have-nots". This rule of nature applies to talent, just as much as it applies to wealth, and it is precisely this rule of nature that our "democrat" would like surgically to uproot – to lobotomize. So it happens, and not infrequently, that a young fellow is endowed with talent (which has been developed in ability), but he has no wealth necessary for further advancing or applying this ability through education. And that is one of the very few cases when, I believe, at least theoretically, that possibly it *could* be justified for the government to step in to correct the imperfection of the market, market elements and its institutions, if, and *only if* it can be conclusively demonstrated that the market fails *completely*. But, even during the most expedient circumstances, this has to be done in a way that entails the least degree of artificiality and the most degree of the natural economic element – competition. Governments throughout the world and throughout history have attempted to do just that, but they all failed miserably. The failure is evident in the fact that to this day I am still unable to discover a single country with a comprehensive system of higher education which does not penalize its taxpayers.

I often reread a thought-provoking novel *Michael Torey* by a fine, but nowadays quite long-forgotten New England novelist and philosopher, my Mentor, Janet Mathewson, who on moral grounds once refused to complete her doctoral studies at Yale.[158] Its opening paragraph commences with these words: "There were the rich and the poor, the haves and the have-nots in the world, Michael Torey reflected as he sat in New York's Yale club nervously waiting for his appointment with the great Channing Redfield." Then she continues: "Confidence surrounded the rich like the air they breathed, the shadows that clung to them, and either you had that aura of money or you didn't." And finally, unlike a wimp, an economic impotent of our day – a covert socialist, the great Yankee novelist crowns her philosophic, yet highly practical opening paragraph with oomph, zest, vigor and gusto so ubiquitously present in the character of all true New Englanders: "But what could you do to acquire it?"[159] Now, to use an American cliché, *that is indeed the million*

---

[158] Janet Mathewson (1914-2002) – a prominent New England novelist, poet and philosopher, author of *Michael Torey* and *A Matter of Pride*; daughter of Champion Mathewson, the founder of the first metallurgy laboratory and the department of metallurgy at Yale University.

[159] Mathewson, Janet. (1962). *Michael Torey*. Garden City, New York: Doubleday & Company, Inc.

dollar question! At the end of the book the author answers this question quite clearly through the life of the book's main character, Michael Torey (whose persona was based on a true life story of a young Southern man, who was dirt-poor, but had brains of a genius and work ethic of a Spartan, and whose name at least for the time being shall remain anonymous) – you must work *cleverly* and *relentlessly*.

Usually we have two forms of government intervention in the field of university education: one, countries who have exercised complete control in the field of higher education by actually administering universities. The end result of that is a cookie-cutter system full of bureaucratic hurdles, academic stagnation, deficit of intellectual originality, and lack in advancement of scholarly thought; two, countries which exercise a more moderate control by ensuring standards of the institutions through certain government supervisory commissions, and by directly financing education through government expenditure and subsidizing the private lending sector.

As the great economist, Thomas Sowell said, "each new generation born is in effect an invasion of civilization by little barbarians, who must be civilized before it is too late."[160] I do not want to be overrun by barbarians, *especially* of my own descent, so I wholeheartedly agree with Sowell, – they must be civilized. Furthermore, I propose we do this quickly, but, at the same time, most naturally, in order to end up with the most natural results. That considered, before introducing artificial fillers (i.e. government mandate, social engineering, "public" administration and "public" financing) into our social ratatouille,[161] let's try to work strictly with those natural ingredients that the free market has to offer.

Legend has it that glowering over the entrance to Plato's Academy was the motto, "Let none ignorant of geometry enter here." Men versed in philosophy would agree that most of the great wisdom is deep, mystical and symbolic, and cannot be taken only literally, including these words of Plato, who himself was a great mystic of antiquity. We must seek the meaning of this inscription not only in its *letter*, but also in its hidden *spirit*. Geometry was the physical science of the day with which one could earn a very good living. This considered, the motto conveyed an important message: let no one, who does not have a trade, enter the realm of philosophy, which is concerned with the world beyond physical,

---

[160] Sowell, Tomas. (2007). *A Conflict of Visions*. Basic Books.
[161] Ratatouille is a popular dish in all Mediterranean cuisines, including Georgian. It was popularized by the French, but its origins are not French.

i.e. let no one, who has not learnt the corporeal sciences, endeavor undertaking the spiritual science – philosophy.

The same idea is reinforced by Philo of Alexandria, a brilliant Hebrew philosopher primarily occupied with the esoteric and highly symbolic branches of philosophy, called exegesis and hermeneutics. Philo argues that the Old Testament story of Abraham must be read metaphorically, as the story about a man who set out on an Odyssey: Sarah was the first wife of Abraham and the mother of Isaac, the second son of Abraham. Her name was originally Sarai. According to *Genesis* 17:15, God changed her name to Sarah, as part of a covenant, after Hagar bore Abraham his first son, Ishmael. Hagar was a handmaiden of Sarai. The name Hagar means "a stranger" in Hebrew. The name Sarah means "a princess" or "a lady". Philo argues that the author of the Book used the names metaphorically to describe that Abraham, symbolizing a young man journeying through life, first obtained benefits through Hagar, symbolizing a trade, physical sciences, or as Philo calls them *encyclical* sciences, with which a man can bodily sustain himself. Only after that did God grant Abraham an opportunity to get to know Sarah intimately, and subsequently to reap the benefits from her, symbolizing philosophy, – the knowledge concerned with the things beyond physical existence (meaning moral, spiritual, metaphysical, etc.), declaring that philosophy is most essential to man. At the end Sarah indeed, and not merely in name, became the *lady* and the influencer of this man's mind, while Hagar indeed, and not merely in name, became a *stranger* and a *handmaiden*. Only after these life-altering changes had transpired, did the God rename this great man from Abram to Abraham, which means "the father of multitude" in the old Hebrew. Timing of the transformation of the name *Sarai* to *Sarah* is also by no means random.[162]

I do not want you to think that what I am about to say is either lunacy or a too grand an endeavor, – I envision these examples of Michael Torey, Plato's Academy and Philo's exegesis on Abraham to be ideal models of successful education and the most wise instructions on obtaining education for brilliant, but poor students. The model is a two-step process, – acquire a trade with which you may procure means for subsistence, and then, and *only then*, move onto enlightenment, i.e. education. Today's diverse economic environment offers an array of employment opportunities to American students (I will speak of the Georgian market soon after), and by that I do not mean the retail and the

---

[162] Philo of Alexandria. (2005). *The Works of Philo*. Hendrickson Publishers.

restaurant world which pays minimum wages and offers no benefits, which for some strange reasons seem to be the only employments American students endeavor today. I speak of the long-forgotten fields which, only a century ago, were considered as suitable trades for a young man or a woman trying to save up for college, but today are left to immigrants. Now, this is not in any way an anti-immigration argument, – I do not want the critics even to venture down this path. My argument is simple, – if there are trades which support immigrant families, they can also employ young Americans who desire to work, to save and to pay for their education, – anything from landscaping to caregiving to mushroom farming or truck-driving. In Georgia professions of a hotel manager, construction worker, car mechanic, cook, truck driver or a laborer are just a few to name.

There is an important element in this model which no socialist alternative can offer, – the element of merit. Desired results, achieved through effort and sacrifice, are dearer and sweeter to an individual than the same results achieved with others' help. To be frank, a highly moral and talented student would only have it this way. First, it gives him an opportunity to get precisely the kind of education he wants, – "it is your money, spend it as you wish" argument; second, a truly talented and moral individual would not want either his bar tab or his education to be taxed on another human being, – remember, it is not *government's* money, but a fellow taxpayer's.

Some of the most respected economists have suggested implementation of vouchers. True, a voucher would give its recipient greater freedom of choice than any other alternative currently in use. But still, what is a voucher but yet another euphemism for the money the government has collected by penalizing the taxpayer? This reminds me of the way chicken is most frequently eaten in the U.S. – deep fried. The process changes chicken's appearance to the point that it compels an average American consumer to forget where the meat came from; and when he sees a realistic-looking (and, of course, better tasting) chicken during his travel to South East Asia, he develops superiority complex, thinking that he is a civilized man and the Asians are bird-killing barbarians. – Boy, he is wrong! He has no clue that the Asian chicken had a much better life than her American colleague, free of hormones, antibiotics, fish meal and cages. On these grounds I am bound to say that no deep fried chicken and no voucher shall do for me, – it is no chicken and it is no voucher: on one hand, I see an animal first, tortured and then, butchered in a most unnatural and, hence, unrecognizable manner; and, on the other hand, I see the same old horse manure offered with a touch of sugar, as I see the society being manipulated into eating hormones and converted fishmeal.

This self-sustaining plan of higher education, where an individual is responsible for paying for his own education, will also serve as a natural filter preventing at least some significant number of talentless applicants from entering our colleges and universities, which, in turn, will raise standards of American education, as more students will be enrolling for education and *not* for drinking, partying, sports or basket weaving. And with this America will once again be able to produce *men* instead of hedonistic wimps or spoiled neurotics. The government also wins when economically disadvantaged and unprepared students decide not to pursue higher education. They will pursue a trade, and our society needs good tradesmen, just as much as it needs good statesmen and public servants. In this case the government will avoid sending, for free, an undeserved man into a university who would have flunked out or drunk his way through it anyway. The fact that education was not offered pro bono, prevented this individual from going down that parasitic path, which it seems to me many are treading nowadays, – if you would only look at our universities, its dorm rooms and its popular "culture".

We should never be in the position of a man living beyond his income. And it matters not whether we end up selling the last bits of our national assets our ancestors defended with the sword and shield in hand from invading empires; or we keep insisting that we cannot possibly earn more, and/or spend less, and in such a way manage to beg or to shimmy ourselves under the financial obligation through hook and crook; or, worse yet, we end up borrowing even more and with that we further perpetuate our serfdom to another country, a transnational bank or an "international" financial institution... That said, the road to freedom and prosperity must be chosen at a young age. It must start with getting used to the idea that, does not matter how talented and poor, when education is desired, each citizen *must* pay only for his own education.

In conclusion, I would like to remind you what Friedrich Hayek said, which, I believe, applies to the theme of this chapter: "We shall not grow wiser before we learn that much that we have done was very foolish."[163] And I am afraid that such is the case with higher education not only in Georgia or America, but all over the world. I do not know

---

[163] Hayek, F. A. (2007). *The Road to Serfdom*. The University of Chicago Press.

much about the world, but for Georgia and America this is the time to gather all our guts and admit that all that we have done in respect to financing higher education has been a giant mistake, – an act against the nature and injustice against all those taxpayers who have been burdened with paying for someone else's education. We must grow wiser as quickly as possible. For Georgia its geopolitical circumstances are so difficult that Georgians will be unable to survive without surpassing the others, among other things, in education. Americans, on the other hand, will not be able to maintain the most favorable global position of the world leader which they have held for the past hundred years.

CAPITALISM: A NATURAL FORM OF SELF-GOVERNANCE

What is modern democracy but a mere *opinion* of a nonessential majority? Would you ask the majority to decide what you need to be prescribed during your cancer treatment? How about something less vital, but by no means less complicated, such as fixing your car? Would you like to survey every dimwit and every knowledgeable man and woman around the block, and everyone in-between, or would you rather go straight to an expert – a car mechanic? Do you think that sheer *quantity* of *opinions* should overwhelm the sound voice of *truth*, even if it is a single voice on the face of the earth? I remember that voice. It was the only voice preaching in the desert. I heard it, and then I saw it silenced on the cross by none other than the democratic majority, and since then I decided to stop heeding to the dictating opinion of that ignorant and often brutal mob. As my dear and wise countryman, Thoreau would say, "When were the good and the brave ever in a majority?"[164] And then I would hear Socrates echo beyond the centuries, which, by the way, seem to obstruct the meeting of true good men throughout history, as they always seem to be ever so scarcely scattered throughout labyrinths of tense and dunes of time, "But my dear Crito, why should we pay so much attention to what 'most people' think?"[165] That same majority always discriminates against a genius. They cannot help it, – they are certainly opinionated, but know very little. Hence the conclusion: democracy is binding and limiting, as it binds you to cater to the opinion and fancy (rather than to the universal truth and benefit) of the majority, and that in itself limits your freedom of choice.

---

[164] Thoreau, H. D., Sanborn, F. B., Lazarashvili, Z. K. (2011). *American Heroes: Thoreau and Brown*. Georgian International University Press.
[165] Plato. (2005). *The Collected Dialogues of Plato: Including the Letters (Bollingen Series LXXI)*. Princeton University Press.

And why should we roll with the elite, i.e. aristocracy of any sort, as an alternative to that blind majority described above? Elite, if not always, at least from time to time is bound to be elitist and in the result, if not persecute us, at least bitterly disappoint us by being most inequitable, i.e. unfairly discriminating. Hence the conclusion: aristocracy, just like democracy, is also binding and limiting, as it binds you to cater to the opinion and fancy (rather than to the universal truth and benefit) of the elitist, but by no means wise, minority.

How about royalty? It seems to me that a King is a better alternative to the two forms of political government already mentioned, but that only if the chips of fortune are placed on the right guy. As I am a free man, I cannot leave my future, or the future of my fellow men, up to the fickle fortune, does not matter how good the odds. That same King, even if he is of the best stock, is bound to be most inequitable at least once. Recall biographies of the greatest Kings, and by that I mean most beneficent Kings in history, such as King David and King Solomon. They all, in spite of their God-given talent and power to administer justice, did unjust things sometimes to others, but more often to themselves. They could not help it, – by nature a man is a fallible creature. Hence the conclusion: royalty, just like democracy or elite, is also binding and limiting, as it binds you to cater to the opinion and fancy (rather than to the universal truth and benefit) of a powerful single individual. Now, if the individual is good, – and I must admit that there is a greater chance of a single special individual being good than of the majority or the minority – all is fine, but if he is not, the entire country is in deep trouble (forgive me using a euphemism just this once, but you all know perfectly well what I *really* mean by "trouble").

Things get much worse when socialists take over. They, just like all good historical demagogues, claim to benefit all, but profit only themselves. Now, imagine catering to such a tough crowd comprised of such "egalitarian" criminals, and that is the only option you have left for earning the daily bread. Hence the conclusion: socialism, just like democracy or elite or royalty, is also binding and limiting, as it binds you to cater to the opinion and fancy (rather than to the universal truth and benefit) of the powerful special interest group of hypocrites, who seem to preach by day and thieve by night.

So far we have not discussed the worst form of political governance – constitutional government. There you have a dingy and outdated legal instrument, called constitution, written by equally dingy and morally diseased old (and, thank goodness, extinct) men, which contemporary elitist minority worships beyond belief, and yet even within this elitist group no one seems to be able to agree on its essence. So they attempt varying and often opposing interpretations which to me is a most nonsensical gibberish, redundant prattle and useless gobbledygook in the first place. Judges, justices, prosecutors, lawyers, legal scholars, – all the "men" of the juridical science, – are running in circles, achieving no good; to quote the Book, "As a dog returneth to his vomit, so a fool returneth to his folly."[166] Hence the conclusion: constitutionalism, just like democracy or elite or royalty or socialism, is also binding and limiting, as it binds you to cater to the opinion and fancy (rather than to the universal truth and benefit) of the powerful special interest group of hypocrites, who seem to administer justice by default charging you an arm and a leg.

Capitalism is an alternative to all of these. It neither limits you, nor binds you in any way. Here you can cater to all: to the majority, to the minority, to a single man, to a demagogue who preaches socialism or to a hypocrite lawyer who tries to do injustice by advocating justice. You can open a Leftorium if it suits your lifestyle, as long as it is economically viable. Now, if you don't want to do any of these, that is also *perfectly* fine with capitalism. Do not participate in the marketplace. Be completely self-reliant. Do not cater to anyone, but yourself. Live on a parcel of land, plough and sow and reap the harvest for self-sustenance only. As long as you don't request anything from anyone else, no one else shall give you an ultimatum requesting something that is yours. And it is on these grounds I have stated that *capitalism is neither binding nor limiting*. In fact, all the truly great men of our common history, who were historically always persecuted, would have survived and even thrived in pure and competitive capitalism. Who threw Thoreau in prison? Who persecuted John Brown? Who attempted to enslave the American nation? NEVER capitalism, but always a democracy, elite, royalty, judiciary of some sort, and they all did it by engaging in collusive dealings with their elected or appointed governments. Georgians must carefully consider these facts.

Capitalism does not care about the color of your skin, or how superior or inferior anthropologically you *may* be. It does not take under consideration in its allocation of rewards anything, but merit as

---

[166] Bible, Proverbs 26:11.

recognized by the targeted market, not by majority, but rather by the distinct group which is of consideration in a given economic activity. It is up to *you* to choose the group, and that is something *no other* mode of political or economic governance, except capitalism, can offer continuously. And in the result, it does not unfairly discriminate, which means that the most meritorious, i.e. hardworking, talented, farsighted, courageous and vigorous succeed.

A FEW THINGS CAPITALISM CANNOT DO

Capitalism has a few deficiencies. For one, it fails to recognize when players engage in collusive dealings either among themselves or with the government. What can I say, no one is perfect and neither is the trusty friend of freedom and prosperity, – capitalism. And that is when a good government gets its window of opportunity to shine and to claim its five minutes of fame, by stepping in with the rule of law, and correcting the shenanigans collusively produced by the few rotten apples on both sides of the spectrum, – the government and the private sector.

Capitalism on its own is incapable of charity, – one of the most essential functions of life *sine qua non*. Some may argue to the contrary by producing a long list of capitalists turned-philanthropists. One, it is common knowledge, that the list is flawed, – many of these industrious individuals were charitable for vainglory, or to get a better tax treatment, or to use charity as a pulpit for public relations (PR) propaganda or other similar selfish ends. It is my opinion that these are utter insincerities and acts unbefitting a free man. They rarely stand up to the test of time. As Shakespeare said, "Time shall unfold what plighted cunning hides: Who covers faults, at last shame them derides". So the list indeed is much, *much* shorter than what it *seems*. Two, those genuinely charitable capitalists who get on that short list did charitable things not because they were capitalists, but precisely because they were human beings. They never lost touch either with their human nature or with humanity. Capitalism was the means by which they obtained their fortunes, but it had nothing to do with spending them charitably, for charity is a most counterproductive measure.

History conclusively demonstrates that this deficiency of capitalism, which it earnestly admits, is quite easily corrected by humaneness of humanity, and not by the government pickpocketing one citizen and gifting the plunder to another, – remember, there is no such thing as "government money", it is always "taxpayers' money", which the government received by overtaxing some in order to please others, and within this *redistribution of income* it managed to charge huge trustee fees for itself. Neither the government, nor capitalism can make men good. The one offers political security, the other offers economic freedom, – both mere trifles compared to genuine goodness and charity. It is up to individual men how they use these scarce resources, – their political and economic freedoms.

Making men morally good is the claim which capitalism does not make, but supporters of all the other forms of political and economic administration do. And that is yet another reason why I am more inclined to place my trust in capitalism than in any of the alternatives. As Aristotle says, "there is no room for excellence in any of their employments, whether they are mechanics or traders or laborers."[167] What good is freedom if it does not aim at good? Such freedom is merely a license, – tyranny of intemperance and excess at its best. And, surely, having a society or a nation, and worse yet, entire mankind of such licentious men, no matter how industrious, could not possibly be our ultimate aim, for, to quote Thoreau, "the philosophy and poetry and religion of such a mankind are not worth the dust of a puff ball. The hog that gets his living by rooting, stirring up the soil so, would be ashamed of such company."[168]

I have seen very little charity among men, regardless of their profession or affluence. But there is one good, which I more frequently observe among capitalists than among academics, scholars, lawyers, doctors, scientists, musicians, et cetera, and that is *humility*. I have noticed that a true capitalist keeps his head down, toils like a work horse, stays away from affairs of others, and humbles himself constantly lest he underestimates competition, miscalculates risk, mishandles investments and ruins himself, his family, his employees and his investors. I have also noticed that this humility encourages him to look for knowledge and seek the truth, just as much as he is seeking new technologies. I have also noticed that it is this humility which disposes him favorably to listening to contrary opinions, – he is not afraid to be proven wrong. Try finding this rare quality in any government, in any union, in any political party or nowadays even in an academia! He surrounds himself not with flattering demagogues, cheering propagandists, stagnant theoreticians, backbiting

---

[167] Aristotle. (2000). *Politics*. Dover Publications, Inc.
[168] Thoreau, H. D., Sanborn, F. B., Lazarashvili, Z. K. (2011). *American Heroes: Thoreau and Brown*. Georgian International University Press.

academics or suitable bureaucrats, but with clever individuals who are not afraid to speak the truth even when their truth contradicts convictions of their boss. He may allow some flattery at home, among his extended family (I have seen *that*), but *never* at his work. Capitalist does not try to *outtalk* anyone; he is trying to *outdo* everyone, and that too fair and square. He cannot afford having a superiority complex, – if that happens, he is ruined. Capitalist acknowledges his deficiencies both, in business and in scholarship. I heard one of them admitting in earnest: "I know no more of grammar than one of that farmer's calves".[169] This capitalist owned a tannery and engaged in international trade, until he was compelled to build the most freedom-producing enterprise in American history. And then I saw what a most learned historian said about this industrious man: "but he had what is essential in all grammars, — the power to make himself understood."[170] I have noticed that this humble attitude is ubiquitously present among the men of business and industry, but it is especially scarce in our academic and political institutions. And lest I am accused of unfair bias, I must offer one more proof of this noble capitalist humility. This was written by the man of eighty six, John D. Rockefeller, at the dusk of his most illustrious capitalist life:

> I was early taught to work as well as play,
> My life has been one long, happy holiday;
> Full of work and full of play –
> I dropped the worry on the way –
> And God was good to me everyday.[171]

It is evident that by being humble this capitalist man felt something no socialist ever felt, – his own minuteness and greatness of God. And I am *strongly* inclined to believe that such a man is more capable of charity than a pompous socialist ass who never held an honest job in his life, and, in the result, never discovered either his flaws or his humility, let alone the greatness of God.

Recognizing both, lack of charity and humility inherent in capitalism, the outstanding issue must be resolved, – if not through

---

[169] Thoreau, H. D., Sanborn, F. B., Lazarashvili, Z. K. (2011). *American Heroes: Thoreau and Brown*. Georgian International University Press.

[170] Thoreau, H. D., Sanborn, F. B., Lazarashvili, Z. K. (2011). *American Heroes: Thoreau and Brown*. Georgian International University Press. Also see: Sanborn, Franklin, Benjamin. (2010). *The Life and Letters of John Brown: Liberator of Kansas, and Martyr of Virginia*. Nabu Press.

[171] Chernow, Ron. (1999). *Titan: The Life of John D. Rockefeller, Sr.* Vintage.

capitalism, how do we make men morally good? I do not wish to answer this question here, but instead I will discuss how not to make men morally bad, and that is by not placing false hopes of achieving moral goodness through capitalism. As David Ricardo noted, "if a commodity were in no way useful, – in other words, if it could in no way contribute to our gratification, – it would be destitute of exchangeable value, however scarce it might be, or whatever quantity of labour might be necessary to procure it."[172] It is true that one cannot measure a man's goodness by the size of his wallet, just like it cannot be measured by the degree of democracy, scholarship, courage, physical strength or beauty present in him or in his fellow citizens. Goodness is outside of the scope of either practice of capitalism or theories of economics, and I like it this way.

When people start to overvalue the staple products of capitalism, – freedom and prosperity, – society starts to degenerate morally and eventually it disintegrates. The King of Judea, Herod the Great, if his legacy is measured by the standards of economic success, was one of the greatest kings Hebrew nation ever had, and yet in totality he was the worst king of that great country. What is the totality of which I speak? – Moral, honest of God, plain goodness. Herod built more synagogues and public buildings, and established more useful political and economic institutions than anyone else in history of Hebrew people, but he failed morally. Writings of the two most prominent and honorable Hebrew scholars and patriots, a most learned philosopher Philo of Alexandria and a most erudite historian Josephus (known in his native tongue as Yosef ben Matityahu) conclusively demonstrate this historical fact.

Furthermore, there was another man in Jewish history, named Herod, more commonly known as Agrippa, onto whom the crown was conferred by Gaius (Caligula) himself. As Josephus writes in his Antiquities, Book 19: "On the second day of the games he put on a robe woven entirely of silver, a remarkable fabric..." And then he continues: "His flatterers immediately shouted on all sides... 'Be gracious! Until now we have revered you as a man, but henceforth we confess that you are of more than mortal nature.' The king did not reprimand them or reject their blasphemous flattery." Soon after, this despicable "king",

---

[172] Ricardo, David. (2010). *On the Principles of Political Economy and Taxation*. Liberty Fund Inc.

Agrippa, saw an owl[173] and met his miserable death, before which, as reported by Josephus, he admitted: "Looking to his friends he said, 'I, your god, am now ordered to surrender my life, since fate has instantly disproved the lies you just uttered about me. He whom you called immortal is now being taken away to die.'"[174] Moral of the story is that *Capitalism is no Panacea*! You may honorably or dishonorably acquire a silver robe, but neither such robes nor capitalism can ensure either happiness or longevity, and people, who place their hopes in such necessary, but nevertheless fleeting superfluities, shall find themselves miserably disappointed.

There is plenty of merit in providing sustenance for bodily existence, whether of a single individual, a family, a nation or the entire humanity, and that is precisely what capitalism does, but unless we sustain ourselves morally, that is spiritually, we shall cease to exist as human beings. As Narayana wisely put it:

> "He truly lives, he does indeed,
> By whose life many will be living.
> Their own selves even crows can feed,
> From beak to belly morsels giving."[175]

I end this section with the words of our wise ancestor, Henry David Thoreau, who reminds us that we must strive beyond money-making not just somewhere in a distant future or at our deathbed, but right here and right now in our daily life: "When we want culture more than potatoes, and illumination more than sugar-plums, then the great resources of a world are taxed and drawn out, and the result, or staple production, is, not slaves, nor operatives, but men, — those rare fruits called heroes, saints, poets, philosophers, and redeemers."[176]

General foible of mankind is the pursuit of wealth to no end. Greed is brutish and therefore evil, and it vastly differs from INDUSTRY and FRUGALITY, which are human and therefore humane. And capitalism,

---

[173] Agrippa had been told by a fellow prisoner on Capri that when he saw an owl, he would be released from prison, which presumably happened, but a second owl would be a herald of imminent death.

[174] Josephus. (1980). *The Works of Josephus: Complete and Unabridged*. Hendrickson Publishers. Also see: Eusebius. (2007). *The Church History*. Kregel Academic & Professional.

[175] Narayana. (2007). *Hitopadesa*. Penguin Classics.

[176] Thoreau, H. D., Sanborn, F. B., Lazarashvili, Z. K. (2011). *American Heroes: Thoreau and Brown*. Georgian International University Press.

being a *human* enterprise, cannot regulate brutal, artificial, unnatural element of unchecked, immoral, criminal avarice, which is *not* human in its *indigenous* nature, – men were corrupted with it, but it did not originate in men. No invisible hand of a market has an ability to straighten out crooked designs and effects of a madman, – a farsighted crook and a methodical criminal, – a *human brute* obsessed with avarice. Such crookedness must be straightened out by the *universal* invisible hand and by men of *universal goodness*. Now, the *universal* invisible hand (by no means the same as either Adam Smith's invisible hand of the market, or the unnatural invisible hand of a demonic government) shall always do its share, and help the mankind. But the election of the men of universal goodness is something we have to do on our own. And unless we elect such men into government offices, we shall always have imperfect markets, as well as livelihoods. We shall all degenerate:

I recall reading one of the most ancient manuscripts, called *Avesta*. It is the main book of Zoroastrianism. And just like all PSEUDO-religions, – designed by men of unchecked greed and avarice, by methodical criminals and neurotic masterminds, for the sole purpose of manipulating and scamming the masses, – it too advocated material wealth over everything else, including goodness and freedom. I recall that according to this most ungodly book, the punishment for a man who breaks the first Mithra, i.e. a verbal contract would be 600 lashes: "Creator! He who breaks a Mithra (contract) in words; What is the punishment for it? Then answered Ahura-Mazda: Let them strike three hundred blows with the horse goad, three hundred with the Craosho-charana." And as soundness of business contracts increases from a verbal to a written form, and their scope rises from a negligible loss to a loss of land, the punishment goes all the way up to 2,000 lashes: "Creator! He who breaks a Mithra of the value of a tract of land; What is the punishment for it? Then answered Ahura-Mazda: Let them strike a thousand strokes with the horse-goad, a thousand with the Craosho-charana." Now, the fact that a man who breaks his contractual obligation is punished harshly is not necessarily a bad thing. What troubles me is the fact that such a man would be punish much more severely than a man who physically assaults and even kills another human being. Here is what Avesta law states on the most minor offense in that line of crime: "He who prepares to strike a man that is to him Agerepta; ...Creator! He who commits the Agerepta on a man; What is the punishment for it? Then answered Ahura-Mazda: Strike five strokes with the horse-goad, and five with the Craosho-charana." And here is what it has to say about a premeditated attempted murder: "Creator! He who wounds a man so that the blood flows; What is the punishment for it? Then answered Ahura-Mazda: Let them strike fifty strokes with the horse-goad, fifty with the Craosho-charana." By the time we read through the Fargard IV (Book IV) it becomes evident that penalties for breaking the contract law range from 600 to 2,000 lashes, while physically harming a human being (including a premeditated murder) entails significantly lesser punishments, ranging from 10 to only 100 lashes.[177] That's not capitalism, that's unchecked greed and sheer lunacy.

Greed is neurosis and excess. True, capitalism is no moral yardstick. It does not promote Socrates' teachings on the concept of Sophrosyne: "Nothing in excess", and "Know thyself".[178] But nevertheless it inadvertently makes men considerably better, as through constant competition, through hard work, and through due diligence required for success it saves men from pride, sloth and unchecked greed. As complete opposite of these greed compels men to plunder. When plunderers organize, they form an empire. With organized plunder their booty increases. They engage in overindulgence. In the result they eventually completely degenerate and plunderers become the plundered. History is full of examples when empires were taken over and trampled underfoot by other empires; their languages vanished or were mutilated to the point that the new has nothing in common with the old (take Greek, Latin or Persian, for example), and neither do the new people (anthropologically, as well as metaphysically speaking) with their ancient ancestors, – so great was the extent of their degeneration. Show me an empire, whether demised or extant, and I will show you the sure path of its incremental degeneration and inevitable destruction: Persians were taken over by the Seljuk Turks, Russians were taken over by Tatars and Turko-Mongols (this process is still in progress) of Khwarezm (Central Asia), Rome was taken over by Italians and Gauls, Egypt was taken over by Arabs, Greeks were taken over by the Osman Turks, Mongols were taken over by Russians, and the list goes on... and as a stark contrast to these empires, for the sake of simplicity and the least amount of controversy, look at Sardinians, – they are still Sardinians, *not* Italians. They are still standing, even in this world of universal ecumenism and cultural hodge-podge, where the right of first occupancy is just as irrelevant as the truth. Had creators of such empires engaged in capitalism, instead of plunder, they would have had a chance to achieve lasting greatness: hard work

---

[177] Bleeck, Arthur, Henry. (2001). *Avesta: The Religious Books of the Parsees*. Adamant Media Corporation.
[178] Plato. (2005). *The Collected Dialogues of Plato: Including the Letters (Bollingen Series LXXI)*. Princeton University Press.

required for success would have kept them busy, preventing them from becoming morally depraved; and competition would have kept them sharp and alert.

The end result of greed radically differs from the end result of capitalism. Greed aims at short-term economic success; capitalism provides an opportunity to achieve a lasting greatness. Greed uses injustice as its medium for achieving its goals. Capitalism relies on free competition and its incentives to allocate rewards. The end result of greed is self-destruction, as the plunderer is bound to become the plundered. The end result of capitalism is a life full of vivacity and healthy uncertainty leading to genuine prosperity. Still not convinced? Then I must describe the process of greedy existence step by step: once the unchecked greed settles in men, which is the gravest injustice one can do against himself, they become brutes; a congregation of such monsters violates the free market and transforms capitalism into a collusion of vicious and violent criminals, – special interest groups (they appear under different guises in different countries: organized mafia, politburo, plutocrats, cartels, national or international regulatory agencies, trade unions); these criminals hijack their government, and then the nation, – a perfectly just and fair enterprise, – is transformed into an empire; This empire, – a congregation of mam-eating men and serfs, – starts to tax and devour its neighboring nations; more international robberies generate more income; more income translates into more depravity and more degeneration; and it is thus that eventually even the greatest empires go bust! Their end is inevitable, but alas, such avaricious men and such greedy empires trample many good men and many fine countries during their vicious lifespan. I have seen entire nations eradicated by them, – the murder of an entire country, the Caucasian Albania, is one of the many unpunished criminal deeds of that *counterfeit-humanity* comprised of *counterfeit countries*, called empires, where justice is reduced to a piece of dingy legal paper; where quoting from the holy Book, or any book of truth for that matter, is irrelevance at best; where talking about universal justice is ridiculed and freedom of speech is fine, as long as you talk about either prices current or common gossip, but never about goodness, truth or God. Injustice, being the root and foundation of an empire, what else can be its fruit but sheer injustice? I remember that blessed man, St. Augustine of Hippo once say: "Justice being taken away, then what are kingdoms but great robberies? For what are robberies themselves, but little kingdoms?"[179] Yes, counterfeit countries with counterfeit freedoms and genuine injustices, comprising counterfeit-humanity, more so today than yesterday. – No wonder capitalism is on the verge of disappearing. And yet I believe that in the 21st century capitalism can defeat such madness, such tyranny and such imperialism, as even the greatest of plunders, in terms of money, falls short to what capitalism has to offer most peacefully and most honorably.

George Santayana's words about true patriotism and true industry still soothingly echo in the depths of my mind: "A man's feet should be planted in his country, but his eyes should survey the world."[180] Alas, the state of my vision differs from the state of my hearing, as currently I only see a legion of talented men whose feet are planted in the world, and their eyes are surveying their long-suffering native country in utmost indifference. They lock themselves up in an academia and are unwilling to speak up in defense of capitalism, – what a waste of their otherwise sound intelligence! Legacy of such "men" shall be only the dust of a puff ball, – and it matters *not* whether such indifferent "men" are Georgians or Americans.

SPECIAL INTEREST GROUPS

But what is the underlying reason for the imperfections of capitalism? The fact that capitalism is a natural force makes it a natural and integral part of nature. Nature in itself is altogether good, but by no means perfect. Nature cannot grasp issues of social nature, and neither can capitalism. Unjust laws and regulations, being offspring of purely social concoction, cannot be immediately sanded down by nature, although at the end nature shall prevail and rid the society of all unnatural laws and interfering regulations. The same way capitalism cannot immediately comprehend a criminal element, and apprehend, for example, a conspiring felon who engages in collusive dealings with other criminals both, in the market, and in the regulatory government, to extort the society by price-fixing or by limiting competitive elements at the market, and, hence, perpetuating its monopolistic position in order to continue his economic tyranny.

---

[179] Dods, Marcus (translator). St. Augustine of Hippo. (2000). *The City of God*. Modern Library.
[180] Santayana, George. (1921). *Little Essays Drawn from the Writings of George Santayana*. Charles Scribner's Sons.

Certain aspects of social coexistence must be coordinated by the people. But the people, being busy with everyday activities, are forced to elect representatives, so they may carry out justice by proxy. That is the original and most natural purpose of all modes of political government, – Kingship, aristocracy and democracy, and a few other crossbreeds that spring up in-between. The fact that sometimes bad men conspire and form a special interest group, forces the good to coordinate their effort as well, and form a government to protect themselves from the invasions of such unnatural sinister forces.

Sheer necessity forces free men to unite and defend themselves from the united evil, – special interest groups. In the past centuries the attack of such evil forces was military, today it's economic. Perhaps the essence of this argument can be best demonstrated with historical examples. The two Georgian people, namely, the Iberians (also known as Meskhis or Mushkis) and Colchis (also known as Laz or Chan) started to form statehoods and elected Kings in order to defend themselves from the invading special interest groups, tyrannical aggressors, – foreign invaders. Creation of the first fully united Georgian state served precisely that purpose. That was the reason why David III Kuropalates, presiding prince of Tao-Klarjeti (Meskheti)[181] and the most powerful ruler in the Caucasus at that time commenced the unification of all Georgian people. For that reason all Georgian people had already united once before, although the unification turned out to be temporary, in the previous chapter of Georgian history which took place in the era of pre-antiquity: to defend themselves against the Greeks who were invading Europe and its indigenous population from Asia. Proto-Georgian Trojans and Amazons thus once formed a powerful coalition, as homer described in his *Iliad*.

For the same reason, although at a later time, Greek people, who by then had established themselves in the Mediterranean by robbing the indigenous Europeans of much of the land, had to unite, first, against the Persians and, then, against the Turks. I will not bore you with Greco-

---

[181] Tao-Klarjeti, also known as Meskheti – the term conventionally used in modern history writings to describe the historic south-western Georgian principalities, the cradle of both, pre-Christian and Christian Iberian civilizations, now forming part of north-eastern Turkey and divided among the provinces of Erzurum, Artvin, Ardahan and Kars. Historically the area comprised of the following provinces: West of the Arsiani Mountains were Tao, Klarjeti and Shavsheti, to the east lay Samtskhe, Erusheti, Javakheti, Artaani and Kola. *See Appendix B at the end of the book for further reading.*

Turkish Wars, but one most illustrious example of Greek, and I believe world history must be given here, – astonishing deed of King Leonidas I and his 300 Spartans, 700 Thespians and 400 Thebans in the battle of Thermopylae serves as a most magnificent example of not mere men, but true heroes uniting and forming an impromptu and ad hoc Greek statehood on a short notice. This marvelous coalition of men of Greek heritage, as well as Greek ingenuity, stood up most effectively against the invading hordes of Xerxes I. That's *my* understanding of a genuine government and its purpose!

The notion of a state, historically speaking, is a relatively new concept brought on by the sheer necessity for people with the same anthropological origin, who have love of political and economic freedom, which they share as a common value, to defend themselves and their way of life from special interest groups, i.e. invaders, who are interested in disrupting that way of life either through immediate plundering or by imposing long-term serfdom.

Today's invading special interest group is more covert, and therefore more effective. It uses several camouflages and penetrates the targeted free societies in the guise of good. It goes by the following criminal aliases: "socialist", "liberal" (in the 20th and 21st centuries *only*), regulatory agency, labor union, guild, i.e. professional association (such as the American Medical Association), and the list goes on. Nota Bene! These are just a few aliases, but it has many other names to mask its true identity of a gangster. Why such harsh words? Allow me to explain:

All special interest groups have one cardinal objective, – to appropriate to themselves *exclusive* rights and liberties by depriving all the rest of *their* rights, in order to obtain an unfair advantage over free men, and that, in turn, in order to enslave the now disadvantaged free men by continuously depriving them of their resources both, inherited and earned. This is a *parasitic* relationship! And these are *parasitic* institutions!

Besides the above-noted original cardinal interest, today's special interest group started to develop additional aims, as corollary to its original success. One of them is to protect exclusivity of its membership. Another is to discourage free men from pursuing prosperity and accumulating wealth. For that purpose it has invented many mechanisms, but the best machinery so far is the graduated taxation. Yet another interest is to perpetuate itself physically, as being an exclusive club of inbreds, it constantly faces the danger of dying out, – thank God for nature and its invisible hand, which somehow does all she can to rid the society of all unnatural, parasitic social organisms! To evade the nature's punishment for the elitism, it breeds the substitutes for its dead members at both, public and private schools of higher education.

Worthy authors, including Milton Friedman, have addressed this issue in general, as well as in particular, describing evils of specific social interest groups, which are dismal creations of the past century, such as the American Medical Association, the American Bar Association, labor unions and others. The 21st century offers new mongrels, not yet discussed by the honorable and humble, and always erudite and true professors of the Austrian School or the most learned contemporary generation of scholars of the University of Chicago. Due to this apparent oversight, I am compelled to focus my examination on these new special interest groups.

Government, public and private monopolies created through collusion are all evil, but some have suggested that the latter is better than the two former forms of collusive malevolence and, therefore, admissible to a point. I *most respectfully* disagree. It matters little which sector is monopolizing. What matters is how the monopoly was created, – whether it was a natural formation from market forces and elements, or at least an expedient creation, or whether it was done by collusion to promote a special interest for one group of people on the expense of the others.

Without further delay, I will discuss the following topics: profession of an economist and pseudo-capitalism prevalent in some modern corporations. I will conclude my discussion describing the main aim of such collusions, – financial success for the inept, incompetent and, quite frankly, the maladroit few.

Economists

One holy and most learned father of Orthodox Christianity once described evil in this way: "The Devil constantly aping God". The same can be said about the economic evil. One of the aped elements in it is the process of initiation, which is enshrined in pseudo mysticism of advanced math, and many purposeless hurdles and useless obstacles.

And it is through such irrelevant considerations that our modern day economist is somehow lumped together... piece by piece.

You have to be neurotic or completely lack creativity to pass through the stages of initiation required for getting into the doctoral program in economics at the University of Pennsylvania and other "elite" mathematics factories. And if, per chance, some true genius, who, due to broadness of his talent, is well versed in higher (secondary) mathematics, – the subject as unrelated to the science of economics as the classical concert piano playing, – passes through labyrinths of sheer lunacy and gets into the program by the intellectual self-degradation, surely, by the time he graduates, he is bound to be molded into a conformist, dogmatic, jargon-loving, calculating statistical dimwit, – a pseudo-economist, who, precisely thanks to his "scientific" formulas and unrealistic formulations, is bound to come up with strange mass prescriptions, and misguide and eventually ruin his fellow men. I expect the day will came when such fine schools start making it a part of professional requirement for such an "economist" to wear a uniform mandatory for that profession, which would include a financial calculator, instead of a tie, hung around his neck and a slide rule as a walking stick, – necessary accessories to distinguish an out of work mathematician turned into an economist from the rest of the people. The idea is not too foreign or farfetched. Similar tomfoolery is demanded by many European juridical professions and institutions from judges and lawyers, – hoodwinks and counterfeits of that occupation.

To require an economist to learn advanced statistics and higher math is the same as to require knowledge of these subjects from a tailor. The only math a tailor needs to know in order to do his job well is basic arithmetic. I ask you, and so have asked a few other common sense men in history,[182] what relevance do quantitative methods have with measuring the inside leg from crutch down? What relevance does this have when discerning men's nature and social aspects of his behavior in a free economic environment? No wonder the lunatic idea of macroeconomic modeling seems like an appealing and lately even as an axiomatic concept to the "man" who knows nothing about consumer

---

[182] I am referring to an Irish (*not* English) satirist, essayist and political scientist, Jonathan Swift (1667-1745). The issue of academics tyrannizing the nation and discriminating against the truly talented, bright and able men by imposing mathematics as a scientific obstacle, is described in a wonderful sarcastic style by Swift in his famous satire, *Gulliver's Travels*. Swift, Jonathan. (1998). *Gulliver's Travels*. Oxford University Press, USA.

preferences, but knows almost everything there is to simulation models – our modern day economist! And indeed, such a man is not a scholar, but a mere simulator of scholasticism.

The foremost philosopher of our country once warned us, although, I am afraid, we did not hear him: "I would remind my countrymen that they are to be men first, and Americans only at a late and convenient hour. No matter how valuable law may be to protect your property, even to keep soul and body together, if it do not keep you and humanity together."[183] In a similar manner, today I remind my colleagues both, Georgians and Americans, that you are to be economists first, and mathematicians, banjo players, cheerleaders and basket weavers only at a late and convenient hour! There is more merit to a molecular gastronomist, as foolish as that invented trade is, than to today's economist. Math is present in everything, but that is no reason to commence studying of everything with mathematics. I do not see zoologists commencing their scholarly researches with a tick in every instance, even though a tick is ubiquitously present on almost every domestic animal. Kudos to today's zoologist! Good food is grown on, and, hence, to some degree is comprised of good manure, but I do not see chefs cooking up manure and discarding essential parts of the edible produce. Kudos to today's chefs! Having no special confidence in gastronomy, if the reader knows of such a strange chef (who insists on researching dung and cooking up manure), I'd urge the reader to match him up with a Keynesian "economist".

If admissions requirements must be made for a doctoral program in economics, why don't we choose the ones that have some relevance to the science and help to indicate some merit of an applicant? Instead of the standardized test of GMAT or GRE, or the prerequisites in mathematics and statistics, why don't we make it a requirement that a successful candidate has to substantiate at least one instance when he successfully and continuously ran an economic enterprise, however small, for a year? Or that he had put his career on hold in order to take care of the ailing grandmother or the Mentor? I shall explain: a future economist, who is aware that moral goodness has greater value than all economic values in the world combined, already knows plenty about the true nature of capitalism. Furthermore, such a man can never be a pseudo-egalitarian, for he has paid willingly and fair and square the cost

---

[183] Thoreau, H. D., Sanborn, F. B., Lazarashvili, Z. K. (2011). *American Heroes: Thoreau and Brown*. Georgian International University Press.

of charity out of his *own* pocket, without taxing his fellow men. In fact, when I read works of a famed professor of the University of Chicago and a Nobel Prize winning economist, Robert Lucas, I realized that a teacher or a nurse had greater total value than a prostitute, even though a prostitute's economic value was greater.[184] By the same token I learned that I could never accept the funds offered to me by socialists which would immediately require and result into my conversion to their gang (and I don't only speak figuratively here, – there was indeed such a case in my youth once), i.e. my prostitution. Indeed a gang! For the funds they offered me comprised of the money they had originally obtained by robbing another man whom I had not met yet. By the same token I learned that a fraternity, a school, a guild, a club or even a nation, which requires intellectual self-degradation or plundering another human being as a part of the initiation, is not worth joining. And that is precisely what today's universities require. Part of the payment has to be made up front, intellectual self-degradation that is, – you must know higher mathematics and believe in the power of either invented or irrelevant formulas. The second payment must be made by installments throughout your curriculum by taking nonsensical courses in statistics and advanced mathematics. The third payment must be continuously made after the graduation, – you must advocate robbing the talented and hard-working successful to pay off that blind majority of idiots, who, in turn, will award you a faculty position; you must also popularize your craft by preaching Keynesian, i.e. socialist economics with its multiplier, aggregate demand, spending, taxation, unsubstantiated hypotheses and flawed theories, – if you wish to obtain a tenure.

What shall I say? We are indeed in dire straits, my countrymen. We have been penetrated by parasites, who are engineering even more bloodsucking organisms, who, in turn, are leeching onto our entrails, devouring our national body from inside out. In fact, with all that leeching and scrounging that goes on in our intestines now for almost two centuries, it is a miracle that we still have some *guts* left!

Since science and human intelligence demonstrated absurdity of policies which all socialists wished to recommend and all communists tried to impose, these two most infamous marauding gangs of our modern history sought to invalidate the true science of economics and our logical intelligence, by inventing a new pseudo-science and by corrupting human intelligence with it. For that purpose they started to

---

[184] Lucas, Robert. (1997). *Market Economy*. Ministry of Finance of Georgia.

infiltrate not only our *courts* and *governments*, but also our *schools* and *universities*. And in this way almost the entire humanity was compelled to retire its logic once and for all. It was thus that mankind chose economic serfdom over economic freedom, – socialism over capitalism, and when it did not choose, it was forced into it at gunpoint, – as Russians did it to Georgia and the nations of the Caucasus, Czechs and the Baltic states, as Prussians did it to the rest of Germany, and as the Maoists did it to the Chinese and non-Chinese nations of what is today the People's Republic of China.

Socialist tyrants could not adduce the proof from economics that socialism was realizable, so they effectively infiltrated our Academia and reinvented several new disciplines of economics: Keynesian economics, normative economics, and the so called macroeconomics.

Socialist tyrants could not adduce the proof from logic that socialism was realizable, so they effectively infiltrated the society through public schools, universities, mass media, and other pulpits of propaganda, and reinvented new logic of consumerism which is *radically* contrary to capitalism, as consumerism completely ignores the natural economic necessity for capital goods and asserts that consumer goods can be created out of thin air. They emphasized spending and hedonism, and demonized thrift and industry. This flawed logic has led them to completely ignoring budget constraints of individual consumers on micro and of a nation or even of an entire continent (as it has recently happened in the EU) on macro levels. A handful of true economists did try to convince them otherwise with supply-side economics, but all in vain – as Georgians would say, *all good preachers need good listeners.*

Georgians and Americans are not immune to economic realities, and neither is the rest of the world. We have been duped into false sciences and false economic beliefs. We have been convinced to surrender our freedom – our "birthright for a mess of pottage"[185] – for the so called universal healthcare, for the so called social security, and for the so called public benefits. Today's false prophet is today's economist who has been cranked out at our academia. Just like his grandmaster, *mathematician* Keynes, he knows how to punch the numbers, but he lacks basic understanding of human nature. In fact, he lacks not just the *understanding* of human nature, but human nature *itself*. So he

---

[185] Genesis 25:31-34. "For bread and pottage of lentils" Essau sells his birthright to Jacob.

improvises: he improvises the economics, he improvises the science, he improvises the accounting, he improvises the truth and when the numbers still don't add up he invents his empty promises anew, – a new paradise through new government-funded programs, through new public spending, through new tax rebates, through new welfare cycles which are possible only through new forgery of money and through new plundering of the American nation.

So far I have only discussed the first step of the making of a modern "economist", – the admissions, i.e. initiation. As one of the greatest theologians of Orthodox Christianity, Pseudo-Dionysius the Areopagite describes, there are three steps to proper education: "we can reasonably say that purification, illumination, and perfection are all three the reception of an understanding of the Godhead".[186] Having the present example of American universities, the same way we may conclude that admissions, curriculum and practice are all three the reception of understanding of the *devil*, and the three-step process for creating its faithful servant, – *ignorance*. That considered, I am compelled to speak at least in few words with regard to curriculum and practice of the science of economics.

Why is there a coursework-based curriculum at a doctoral level? Who mandated and for what purposes this, historically speaking, new invention? Does this newly hatched requirement really raise standards of competence? Or is it merely a new vogue? Or does it serve an aim other than academic excellence? Let us answer these questions in turn.

Coursework-based curriculum is redundant, as all of these courses should have been included at master's level. An economist should especially understand concepts of efficiency and value of time. He should also realize that wasting time, this most precious of our resources, does not raise standards of either scholasticism or living. It appears to me that taking courses at a doctoral level is a lot of time lost and no competence gained. The trade-off is nonexistent, as it is not a situation that involves losing one quality or aspect of a thing in return for gaining another quality or aspect. Trade-off implies a decision to be made with full comprehension of both, upside and downside of a particular choice. Here we only have downside.

---

[186] Pseudo-Dionysius. (1988). *Pseudo-Dionysius: The Complete Works*. Paulist Press.

A doctoral degree used to be a research-based degree. Even the Soviet Union was ahead of us in that regard, – their doctorate (Ph.D.) or Doctor Habilitatus (Habilitation) required not a coursework, but pioneering theses (yes, in *plural*!). Moreover, Habilitation was highly preferred when applying for a faculty position, as it implied that the scholar was intellectually free-minded and had an ability to conduct an *independent* scholarly inquiry and to write *unsupervised* theses. I must explain this in greater detail: Habilitation is the highest academic qualification a scholar can achieve by his or her own pursuit in several European and Asian countries. Habilitation requires the candidate to write a professorial thesis (often known as a *Habilitationsschrift*, or Habilitation thesis) based on independent scholarship, reviewed by and defended before an academic committee in a process similar to that for the doctoral dissertation. However, the level of scholarship has to be considerably higher than that required for a research doctoral (Ph.D.) thesis in terms of quality and quantity, and must be accomplished *independently*, in contrast with a Ph.D. dissertation typically directed or guided by a faculty supervisor. In the sciences, publication of ten to more than thirty research articles is required during the habilitation period. Sometimes (as in the humanities) a major book publication is required before defense takes place. Usually teaching ability of the habilitation candidate is also evaluated. The outcome of a successful habilitation examination is a degree which stands as a sign for one's *ability* to contribute to the underlying academic discipline. I am compelled to repeat in a most alarming tone: alas, in this regard, *even the Soviets* were way ahead of us! We place emphases on experimental theories and crank out bookworm theoreticians; they placed emphases on the practice of trying and testing theories and, as a result, often produced brilliant scholars and scientists.

Adding coursework as the most essential base for a doctoral program is not only redundant, but it also destroys the most essential purpose of the program. A doctoral study in economic sciences both, in Georgia and in America used to be a rare scholastic opportunity offered only to exceptional applicants who had achieved high standing in economics or related disciplines, and had demonstrated remarkably strong aptitude and propensity for contributing to economic theory and performing advanced scholarly research in an economic field. In many premier European, middle-eastern and Asian academic institutions this still stands. But we have changed. And as I shall shortly demonstrate, this change is not a progress, but rather an utter and dangerous digression, which will ultimately result into a most dangerous regression.

I would argue wholeheartedly that all coursework must be abolished at a doctoral level, some special cases excluded, for example, when a philosopher wants to pursue a doctoral study in economics and, in spite of his philosophical brilliance, he lacks knowledge of basic economic disciplines. My colleagues would argue that this lowers standards of quality. I have already answered them in preceding paragraphs, but here I shall venture even further and go on an offensive. I say that having mandatory coursework vanquishes the one and only standard a doctoral program of economics should have as the requirement for graduation, – academic creativity, – an ability to produce a scholarly research which significantly contributes and advances economic science, which in turn contributes and advances economy, which in turn contributes and advances freedom and prosperity of mankind! Heavy curricula prevent this. They overemphasize the old and hinder a candidate from pursuing anything new. They promote academic stagnation, which is naturally followed with economic stagnation once such a graduate enters the labor force and starts issuing faulty opinions.

I have many reasons to believe that such a regression of all American doctoral programs in economics is not a chance occurrence, neither is it merely a vogue (although I believe that some are indeed engaged in it for that reason). It or rather its promoter has a well-calculated and menacing ulterior motive. I shall explain: scoundrels, untalented mathematicians and turned-economists, and dimwits aside, I have seen a great number of good men get into such programs simply because of their true love and devotion for capitalism and the science of economics. There are also those who realize evil of the system, but decide to join it nevertheless. Their argument is, if you can't beat them, join them. Both got ruined, but I, thank God and poverty, which compelled me to earn money and postpone getting graduate education, have narrowly escaped. The ones who got in, first, endured the degrading GMAT or GRE. Then came courses in math and statistics, attending which are self-mutilating endeavors to a true economist. Through such mutilation came the intellectual suicide and demise of their creative, truthful, laissez-faire, freedom-aspiring and beautiful economic minds. After graduation they were cooped up in tiny cubicles in government or academic offices. They started to propagate the same nonsense which they used to abhor, but nevertheless had ended up studying at school. That "liberal" propaganda robbed, plundered and killed in front of their eyes, – victims of the aggregate demand and welfare and tariffs and licensure and unions and graduated taxation were falling left and right in front of their eyes, which by that time had been already desensitized. They were not only dumb witnesses, but active participants in demolishing capitalism and free enterprise, as well as the Academia. I could give you names of at least two dozen brilliant men, former economists, patriots, philosophers and in every possible way once true friends and colleagues of mine, whom I knew well. They all ended up in this state, – on *both* sides of the Atlantic! Thoreau wrote about those men once: "After the first blush of sin comes its indifference; and from immoral it becomes, as it were, *un*moral..."[187]

Let's look at the founding father of the so called macroeconomics, John Maynard Keynes, oddly enough also known as the 1st Baron of Keynes. Would you look at his language! Look at his jargon! Look at his tongue full of pomp and circumstance! His scientific dialect! His critical vocabulary! His peacock speech! – Wise only in his own mind! What a pidgin between this "learned" man and his master, – masked ignorance! Allow me to explain and substantiate:

I should expect a more courteous, lucid, coherent and intelligible language from a hoodlum hooligan of West Philadelphia than this "brilliant" and highly acclaimed mind of the 20th century. The hooligan would be less polluted with slang and more endowed with *sense*, even if it is merely *common sense*, which is nowadays snubbed and rebuked, especially in academic circles. Keynes' language, – all jargon, but no sense. We need not examine fallacies of his so called concepts, as more worthy economists have already disproved Keynes. We only need to point out the striking similarity between this "man" and his modern follower, – an American "economist". They both mask their ignorance with this strange "academic" dialect. But I see no *dialectic* in such a *dialect*; and I discern not a single sound *thought* in their mode of *thinking*. Now, look at the language of Friedman, Hayek, Lucas, Sowell and, most important, look at the language of Ilia Chavchavadze. What lucid simplicity! What plain truth! What common sense! Clear, concise and harmonious as the most natural of musical instruments, – a spring running down from the Caucasus Mountains.

It is justice to our ears, because it does justice to the universal truth.

---

[187] Thoreau, H. D., Sanborn, F. B., Lazarashvili, Z. K. (2011). *American Heroes: Thoreau and Brown*. Georgian International University Press.

A man worthier than anyone now living in America, Henry David Thoreau wrote: "Justice is sweet and musical; but injustice is harsh and discordant. The judge still sits grinding at his organ, but it yields no music, and we hear only the sound of the handle. He believes that all the music resides in the handle, and the crowd toss him their coppers the same as before."[188] Today's economists are such judges, and Keynes presides as the supreme justice among them. They grind the organ of mathematics and jargon, and our society keeps tossing coins at them. But instead of chump change like in old days, we started to toss our national freedom and national economy to them, especially lately, since the 2008-2009 Keynesian Resurgence. "What a gang of criminals! What a horde of hypocrites! What a class of talentless 'men'!" – I kept thinking to myself, and that is when it dawned on me that the reason that hoodlum hooligan made more sense to me was because he was a petty criminal and something original, something native to human nature was still left intact in him, which his tongue expressed and his speech reflected, but in the case of Keynes and his modern followers we are dealing with experienced, highly expert, organized criminal masterminds who have created one grand enterprise, – academic mafia, and its members are only most ruthless and brutish seasoned felons.

We must further disprove Keynes and Keynesian thinking by demonstrating that they were completely out of line with economic realities, lest they further deceive American and Georgian nations.

Keynes, just like any good socialist, assumes that an economic environment is static. Based on this dangerously erroneous assumption, he starts to prescribe remedies only applicable to a static milieu. But the world in general, and economic world in particular, is a dynamic place. Nature itself is nothing but dynamism, and economic environment, being a big part of nature, automatically inherits this characteristic. I am compelled to think that, due to this original false assumption, a wrong opinion is produced, which in turn compels Keynes and the Keynesians to invent wrong remedies intended for a static, stationary and inactive system, which results in a catastrophe, – the socialist medicine, having adverse effect on the dynamic and active economy, brings it to the dismal peace and "balance", – static economic inertia, – stagnation, and as more worthy author once called it, the *"tyranny of the status quo."*[189] Economic data and history conclusively show that the remedies of the

---

[188] Thoreau, H. D., Sanborn, F. B., Lazarashvili, Z. K. (2011). *American Heroes: Thoreau and Brown.* Georgian International University Press.

[189] Friedman, Milton. (2002). *Capitalism and Freedom.* The University of Chicago Press.

Keynesian economics cure none of the underlying market imperfections. Instead, in the best case, the problems are merely conserved, and, in the worst case, made worse and perpetuated.

And in this evil incubator, – today's "academia", – today's "economists", – Keynesian hypocrites are mass hatched, so that by advocating false doctrines they, in turn, may mass-produce minions of slaves. With *this* kind of enlightenment our universities ruin men not only as professionals, but also as individuals, – not only did they crank out a bad economist, but also a bad citizen, as after graduation he is busily engaged in socialist propaganda, trying to poison the world. The domino effect does not quell here. Not only is this man a bad citizen, but also a bad human being, whose ultimate aim being pleasure and self-gratification at the expense of others, witnesses the slave trade taking place daily in front of his eyes. This fellow shall have only one ultimate end of which I shall not speak, for this is neither proper time nor venue for such moral discussions, which go eternity beyond realms of capitalism.

What shall we do? Today's conservative would argue not to interfere. But it is not interference which I am advocating, but rather an effort to share knowledge with our fellow men who are misleading others or themselves have been misled; I mean the "democrats" and their enslaved followers. There is a significant difference between coercion and persuasion. It is the latter which I encourage.

Conservatism is what it always was, – a sure support for the tyranny of the status quo. Although it often turned out to be an effective tool against socialist serfdom, as it tended to draw its values from historical past, and that past frequently *happened to be* better than the future. I empathize with this notion, *but* I disagree with its aggrandizing. It is an ideology befitting the good, but cowardly and uncreative men, – slaves who desire freedom, but will not lift a finger to acquire it. Or perhaps it is an ideology for the selfish, – egotists who have already secured freedom for themselves, but could care less what happens to the weak and the feebleminded. I would like to think that the former is true here. In which case, conservatism is a pessimistic, if not pathetic, mode of thinking and living. It is a moral stagnation, which, I agree, is better than moral degeneration, offered as an alternative to socialism, but it is still something quite unnatural, something quite less than what is required for a life of a free man.

We must refuse to conserve anything, especially our problems.

I remind my conservative friends to remember their original objective, – it is *laissez faire*, not *laissez fare raine*, i.e. *let do*, not *let do nothing*, which they initially intended. I recall reading in some annals of ancient history that "power makes the best of us forget our original intent". Have we degenerated to the point that it is not our power, but the power of the enemy which is currently making us forget our original intent? Has the tyranny of status quo, vigorously advocated by the socialist, taken a harbor in our mindset and stripped us of all the vigor and manly fiber our mind once possessed? What is *doing nothing* in this world of the fast-augmenting universal deceit, but doing something awful *for* it, – perpetuating the terrorizing autocracy of the present tense and avoiding the future? As Marcus Aurelius put it, "Injustice results as often from not doing as from doing."[190] It seems to me that fear is the only *tradition* modern *traditionalist* cares about, and that his *conservatism* is a mere euphemism for *conformism*. Sadly, he forgets that being *fearful* and being *careful*, besides some light euphony, have not an iota of common ground both, in theory, as well as in practice.

Rapid advancements in technology have made the world smaller both, in time, as well as in space, and are bound to make it smaller still. Previously being at par with evil, including the evil of socialism, was enough. Today a reactionary approach will prove to be an ineffective strategy. Today being on time is being too late. Today's defenders of freedom, and that includes free market capitalists, must go on the offensive. Merely staying current is no longer an option. Today's doctoral programs in economic sciences are far out of line with economic realities. They impose not the tyranny of *status quo*, as they did in the previous century, but the tyranny of *status falsus*, which shall soon undoubtedly translate into *status mors*.

It's not simpleminded barbarians that are inside our gates today, but rather an entire legion of trained, calculating and determined villains. This army has managed to camouflage itself as erudite elite, it has managed to acquire our trust, it has managed to acquire our vote of confidence, and now it runs our most essential institutions, – our universities, our hospitals, our governments and lately also our popular culture and economy. It trumpets socialist ignorance through sirens of mass media, movies and television. We the people, we the victims, we

---

[190] Aurelius, Marcus. (2002). *The Emperor's Handbook*. Scribner.

the *true* liberals have been engaged in wishful thinking for too long, – I would say since the 19th century. As that 19th century titan, Ilia Chavchavadze put it, "O my God! Constant sleep and unremitting slumber! How long until we shall all wake up?!"[191] Our bastion has become our prison, – it's still standing, but we have fallen in spirit, – as the enemy not only surrounds us, but he has already penetrated our hearts and minds, as well as our political borders, our motes and turrets, our steeples and towers without ever drawing a sword. And now he rules us from the inside. And in spite of this, we engage in wishful thinking. We are convinced that basic principles of microeconomics and verities revealed in the supply-side economics are so self-evident that no one will fail to comprehend them. Such wishful thinking has to be quelled. As Sun Tzu said: "The art of war teaches us to rely not on the likelihood of the enemy's not coming, but on our own readiness to receive him; not on the chance of his not attacking, but rather on the fact that we have made our position unassailable."[192] We were never ready for the Trojan Horse. I remember how, after a fruitless ten-year siege, the Greeks constructed a huge wooden horse, and hid a select force of thirty men inside. The Greeks pretended to sail away, and the Trojans pulled the horse into their city as a victory trophy. That night the Greek force crept out of the horse and opened the gates for the rest of the Greek army, which had sailed back under cover of night. The Greek army entered and destroyed the city of Troy, decisively ending the war.[193] And it *seems* that it was on this account that Sun Tzu said: "But a kingdom that has been destroyed can never come again into being; nor can the dead ever be brought back to life."[194]

Generally speaking, Sun Tzu was right, but there was this statistical anomaly, which among other things proves near uselessness of statistics, and attests to the amazing ability of these ancient proto-Iberians to achieve something nearly impossible, – even though Troy was destroyed, Trojans raised themselves from ashes, like the bird of Phoenix, and rebuilt their state stronger than ever, – it was Trojans, not Italians, who founded and ruled Rome. Do Georgians still have something in common with the Trojans, besides anthropology? Do Georgians and Americans have ability to rid their universities and their governments of pseudo-economists? I speak for both nations: – yes, *we* do!

---

[191] Lazarashvili, Z. K., Ihejirika, C. E., Chapidze, G. T., Stasen, G. P. (2011). *Pantheon of Political Philosophers*. Georgian International University Press.
[192] Sun Tzu. (2003). *The Art of War*. Barnes & Noble Classics.
[193] Homer. (1995). *The Iliad*. Barnes & Noble.
[194] Sun Tzu. (2003). *The Art of War*. Barnes & Noble Classics.

Another argument substantiating the fact that we cannot afford conservatism, and the reason why we must hurry and be more vigilant when dealing with the current academic pestilence is the sheer success of modern socialists in America, and, in turn, in Georgia. If previously the original generation of pseudo-academics, such as Keynes, were creating only an economic mythology, – merely an alternative conjecture, a hypothesis, so to say, a theoretical proposition, if I may add, *of lunacy*, today Keynes' followers have managed to validate such madness, and have elevated its status to an axiom. Modern Keynesians have created a pseudo-science out of Keynesian economics, which counterfeited the science of economics proper to the point that effectively Keynesian economics has become the science of economics, while all true economists are classed as heterodox, – the parasite has finally devoured its host body.

This effort was led by the high priest of pseudo-scholasticism of the 20th century, Paul Samuelson. Samuelson, by means of undue adherence to mathematics, perpetrated a myth that only the adherents of Keynesian economics, i.e. graduates of MIT, Harvard, the University of Pennsylvania and a few other North-Eastern schools of the same caliber, were expert enough to run the country. If Mister Samuelson were an honest doctor (pun intended), in an effort to explain Keynesian economics in his popular, but ever so inaccurate book, *Economics: An Introductory Analyses*, would have stated that Doctor Mathematician Keynes did not know a thing about the market and its two cardinal and essential elements, supply and demand; he knew nothing of deductive, logical reasoning which takes place everywhere in nature, including the market; and he certainly did not study consistency of macroeconomic events with the essential microeconomic behaviors and the ensuing theories. How could he? He was merely a mathematician, and a bad one at that.

But we *must* praise when and where praise is due, – one thing that these post-Keynesian pseudo-economists did better than the real economists was propaganda. The fact that Friedman, Hayek, Lucas and the Austrian and Neoclassical (New Classical) schools of thought, i.e. everybody and everything which is true and sane in economic sciences, are, at best, somewhat confined to academic obscurity, and, at worst, are anathematized, is the proof of the immense success of the Keynesians' propaganda. The fact that the University of Chicago has become the *only* New Haven (*alas alack*, pun intended) for true economists in America, speaks of the immense success of the Keynesian followers, – the pseudo-economists of our times.

Alas, this sort of evil is not unprecedented. For example, the sophist teachings of Gorgias, Nietzsche, Epicurus were promoted to such a point that at the commencement of the 20th century Sophism had effectively consumed Philosophy and affixed its righteous name to itself. I would also like to note that the old Epicureanism has been somewhat demonically resurrected. It is these modern Epicureans turned-economists who are now advocating for consumerism and ridicule the supply-side economics both, in our politics and our universities. When will we learn that it is most improper to call such people economists? And there are more examples of such *linguistic hijackings*: as Boethius witnessed one of many persecutions of philosophy by sophism, he was compelled to animate the voice of the oppressed philosophy in his writings: "As part of their loot they dragged me off, in spite of my protestations and resistance; they ripped apart the gown that I had woven with my own hands, and they departed bearing the ragged pieces which they had torn from it. They imagined that all of me had passed into their hands."[195] Their imaginings were indeed mere imaginations, not realities of life. Another even more horrifying example is that of the religion... I mean the precedents of Pharisees who, from time to time manage to prevail, affix the holy name of Christianity to themselves and appropriate the most fertile valleys of the lowland, while the true Christian and the true Christian church, – the true forethought, the truest Pro-Metheus of the day, – is chained at the peak of the mount Elbrus located somewhere far into the range of the Caucasus. As the Book teaches, "And no wonder, for even Satan disguises himself as an angel of light."[196] A few have been schooled in philosophy or Christianity or pre-Christian mysticism and esoteric history of Titans. Even fewer people have been educated in such wisdom, and even fewer have been properly initiated and truly enlightened in these mysteries. But still people should have some common sense left in them and speak up when it is due, – when evil linguistically hijacks a word which should only designate something good. I am afraid that if we sit idly and do nothing, in a single generation people will not know what a true economist is; and in two generations they will know nothing about being either an American or a Georgian, just as today very few know about Prometheus or the race of men he once represented.

---

[195] Boethius. (2008). *The Consolation of Philosophy*. Oxford University Press, USA.
[196] II Corinthians 11:14.

In light of the foregoing, I would humbly recommend studying economics not so much from schools, but from books of true economists, such as Hayek, Friedman, von Mises, Sowell, McConnell and Lucas... and especially from Ilia Chavchavadze. And if funds are scarce, or it is an inopportune time, learn it from nature itself, – observe both, human and dumb, that is metaphysical and physical, i.e. spiritual and wildlife nature. It does not counterfeit, – it does not have an ulterior motive, – it does not featherbed and it knows no slavery, – it does not encourage either economic fallacy or the subsequent economic serfdom, and when it runs out of its scarce resources it does not try to solve the problem simply by printing money.

Furthermore, I would be cautious of strange associations with strange requirements for initiation, such as a doctoral program in economics in America, as well as in Georgia. Be cautious of such a professional guild, organization, fraternity and especially a university, which, for or under the pretext of enlightenment, asks you to perform an intellectually self-degrading act worthy only of a degenerate. In fact, run *away* from such a university, such a fraternity, such a guild or organization. And once you are through with running, catch your breath, stand firmly on your feet and go back to destroy it, for it is an evil institution trying to mutate men's minds and souls into something unnatural and, therefore, evil. With this I temporarily conclude my discussion of one of many influential special interest groups in the United States, – modern economists, – as I would like to commence an inquiry into another powerful group, I call pseudo-capitalists. I shall pick up the theme of the profession of an economist in the ensuing chapter yet again.

Pseudo-capitalism

As I have already discussed elsewhere, two forms of monopoly should be comparatively easy to solve in the 21st century: natural and technical monopolies will be destroyed with innovations in technology, infrastructure and the forces of global competition which must follow, when we are ready to open our borders and do away with trade restrictions. Government monopoly too could be easily extinguished, – when people are morally and mentally ready, they will ask for (or rather fight for) a small government. Hence we are left with one last unnatural form of monopoly, – private monopoly which arose not through competition, meaning honest participation in the most natural economic competition judged by supply and demand and the price system, but by collusion either with the government or other pseudo-capitalists or both.

I am an ardent supporter of any corporation of honest men and women. I believe that free men, at least from time to time, indeed need to "incorporate", meaning to connect and to bond, in order to carry out useful aims unattainable by a single individual. Therefore, it must follow that forming a corporation is an expedient act and not a compulsory exploit. It is a historical fact that men often congregated, among other things, for economic reasons. I was compelled to give such a long historical prelude in order to demonstrate that the notion of a corporation is not at all foreign either to human nature or history, and that it is not a relatively new invention of English lordship, just as parliament is not.

Although unnatural monopoly may originate in nature, i.e. free market, it cannot prosper in there, – natural forces of the market do not allow it, as information on monopolistic profits disseminates quickly and soon new players engage in the game in order to take a piece of the pie. Special, i.e. monopoly privileges are granted by corrupt governments. Monopolistic privileges can be arranged in many forms, but the most sophisticated ways of rendering them are licensure, trade restrictions and graduated taxation, – all benefiting special interest group of an unnatural monopolist by limiting entries to the market in order to eliminate competition, which historically has been a prompt executioner of monopoly world over.

1. LICENSURE: Licensure limits the number of both, domestic and foreign entrants. It is one of the most effective tools for conducting an effective lobotomy on the market, as it completely gets rid of a most essential market element – freedom of labor, without which competition greatly suffers. But the evil of licensure does not stop here. Its ultimate goal is not only to alter the number, but also the quality of the labor force. Mandating a nationwide graduate record examination (GRE) or Graduate Management Admission Test (GMAT) or any other examination of this sort is the guarantee which ensures that only certain individuals with certain uncreative and most dull minds enter a certain occupational field. To this effect I have already discussed the profession of a modern "economist" in America. Once in a great while the filter fails and a talented applicant gets in, but for that he has already paid the price, – recognizing that the test was unjust, nevertheless he decided to engage in an intellectually self-degrading process and to pass the test in

order to get in. No matter how talented, such an individual now has a vital flaw, which will make it exceedingly difficult for him to live as a free man, – conformism. He is a subscriber to the notion, *if you can't beat them, join them*. As a result, in today's America we have the society of castes. We must admit that in this respect we are at par with the ancient Hindus, Persians, Egyptians and Mesopotamians.

Furthermore, I must relate a painful, but a least talked-about part of Georgian history in order to demonstrate counter-productive (if not politically dangerous) precedents of caste societies and guilds that stem from licensing. Armenians immigrated to Georgia in large numbers after their statehood was destroyed, first, by Persian and, then, by Seljuq[197] and eventually by Ottoman invaders. Georgia always extended its hand to the neighboring Christian Armenian people often in need of haven or military assistance. At the end of the 19th century and at the beginning of the 20th century Armenian refugees primarily populated large cities in Georgia, as they were and still are excellent artisans, but poor farmers. Their craftsmanship, especially in shoemaking, is outstanding. Some Armenian master-craftsmen in the turn of the century started to engage in a most discriminatory and unjust practice, – they would demand conversion to an Armenian last name from an apprentice of a non-Armenian origin. City of Telavi, located in Eastern Georgia is full of Georgians who were in this manner coerced into abandoning their Georgian last names and, with that their Georgian heritage. This example also demonstrates that licensing could be easily used as an effective device for cultural terrorism and hegemony, as well as ethnic discrimination, – the latter being only a minor transgression compared to the former two. I firmly believe that labor unions and associations do just that, but to a greater extent, – they endeavor to gut your humanity instead of nationality.

---

[197] Seljuq – a Turko-Persian Sunni Muslim dynasty that ruled parts of Central Asia and the Middle East from the 11th to 14th centuries. They established an empire, the Great Seljuq Empire, which at its height stretched from Anatolia through Persia and which was the target of the First Crusade. The dynasty had its origins in the Turkoman tribal confederations of Central Asia. After arriving in Persia, the Seljuqs embraced the Persian culture, adopting the Persian language as the official language of the government and language, and played an important role in the development of the Turko-Persian tradition which features Persian culture patronized by Turkic rulers. Today, they are remembered as great patrons of Persian culture, art, literature, and language and are regarded as the cultural ancestors of the Western Turks – the present-day inhabitants of Azerbaijan, Turkey, and Turkmenistan.

The same way it is applied to professional guilds, licensure can be applied to all other modes of business activity. Government can limit both, local and foreign competition by requiring these three forms of licensure: registration, certification and licensing. The government insists that such measures are necessary to ensure standards of quality. That is a most irrelevant consideration! Nowhere does evidence of any kind, whether empirical, or deductive, or historical support such a claim. What the empirical evidence overwhelming shows is that both, rational and irrational preferences of self-governing consumers ensure precisely that level of standard of quality which is most desired by and best suited for the market demand.

I remember the Soviet government trying to mandate their high standards by use of similar methods. As Soviet efforts were never in any way grounded in reality, but instead they represented phantasms of a handful of neurotic and powerful individuals, they were always in vain, destined for failure right from the start. And in terms of economics, standards demanded by Soviet planners had nothing to do with the market demand. For example:

Georgian winemaking has a rich history dating back thousands of years, with the earliest known production occurring around 8,000 years ago on the territory of modern-day Georgia. Through an extensive gene-mapping project in 2006, Dr. Patrick E. McGovern from the University of Pennsylvania and his colleagues analyzed the heritage of more than 110 modern grape cultivars, and narrowed their origin to a region in Georgia, where also wine residues were discovered on the inner surfaces of 8,000-year-old ceramic storage jars in Shulavari, Georgia.[198] The word "wine" originates from a Georgian word "gvino", which in turn ancient Romans popularized all over the world by dropping the hard-to-pronounce first letter "g" (using French phonetics, pronounced as letter "r", as in "Paris"). In fact, to this date, winemaking is the staple agricultural industry in Georgia, especially in its most fertile Kakheti region. Russians were well aware of this and cherished Georgian wine, as well as other alcoholic beverages, which Georgia specifically produced for the Russian market, namely, hard liquors which are popular among northern nations of Europe, but not among the Mediterranean and Caucasian people. Russian demand on Georgian wine and spirits was so

---

[198] McGovern, Patrick, E. (2007). *Ancient Wine: The Search for the Origins of Viniculture.* Princeton University Press. Also see: McGovern, Patrick, E. (2010). *Uncorking the Past: The Quest for Wine, Beer, and Other Alcoholic Beverages.* University of California Press.

high that, shortly after Georgia was conquered by Russia and forcibly incorporated into the Soviet Union in 1921, Russian demand on wine surpassed the maximum natural capacity of output in Georgia. The demand always remained higher than the supply in history of the U.S.S.R. Consumers cared for the quality and quantity of wine, and not the quality of packaging. In spite of many a Soviet mandate to make bottling and labeling more appealing, wine and spirits made in government facilities in Georgia remained true to the customers' demand, – inexpensive and, therefore, unappealing packaging, with high quality product inside. The Soviet politburo cared for its appearance, so that the shelves of Moscow and St. Petersburg supermarkets could put on a show for the visiting Western tourists, while the Russian consumer cared for its consumption qualities. Needless to say that the simple preferences of drunkard Russian consumers prevailed over the "farsighted" mandate of the highly aesthetical (but drunkard nevertheless) Soviet planners.

Even if we play the devil's advocate and believe that licensure itself is not a form of corruption, bias and nepotism, and that its original purpose is indeed to raise industry standards, we must admit that licensure will eventually open a door for all of that, meaning corruption, bias and nepotism. In such a case licensure becomes a serious infringement on freedom of individual citizens, as it encourages *some* and discourages *others* to pursue activities of their choice.

The sentiment expressed in the preceding paragraph is by no means random. I wish I could see, if not just results, at least just intentions in most government actions. I see plenty of room for improvement in the food and drug industries, which, a consumer having little expertise or time to investigate, are truly in need of some minimum national standards so that American and Georgian people, if not fed and cured, at least are not poisoned. This is one task that only the government could accomplish, but this is precisely the task the government refuses to do, or rather does not want to do it right.

One would think that food and drug manufacturers should have a vested interest in establishing a reputation for reliability and quality, but as the consumers' inquiry into food quality is quite casual, and, due to our busy lifestyles, our demanding jobs and families, hardly anyone is willing to devote time to investigating what we eat and drink, and even smaller number of individuals have either time or expertise to litigate or to go to the legislator and complain that most of the food in America contains fillers and preservatives unfit for human consumption, the mammoth manufacturer does what it has been doing for a long time, – it pays off the government and shoves the same old processed garbage in our face, which in turn makes us into human garbage disposers. As Aristotle puts it, "they find their employment pleasanter than the cares of government or office where no great gains can be made out of them." And then he continues: "A proof for this is the fact that even the ancient tyrannies were patiently endured by them... if they are allowed to work and are not deprived of their property."[199] The description is perfectly fitting for the modern consumer, – always busy, always undereducated, and always mule-like and tolerating.

It seems clear to me, that's where the government could step in effectively, as the market, the competitive forces and the consumers have all have failed. That's where it could get its five minutes of fame and demonstrate to the American people its purpose and its ability, and, quite frankly, justify its existence. When Kraft Foods invented processed cheese in the early 1900s, real (yes, indeed *real*, not merely *traditional*) cheese makers wanted the new "cheese" to be labeled as "embalmed cheese" by law. The U.S. government considered that term to be disparaging, and required that the product be labeled "process cheese."[200] Where was the government then? Where is the government now? When freedom is most endangered that is when the government becomes most scarce. And when our physical existence is in dire jeopardy, the government is worried about *disparaging*, that is disparaging our gluttony. So, we have effectively ended up with the two special interest groups, – the big government and the monopolistic corporation, and the American people ground in silence in-between. I can understand all the hush-hush of these two collusive monstrosities, but what beats me is the sheer muteness of the people.

In light of the foregoing, I must conclude that elimination of licensure will allow market forces to promote competition and get rid of certain unnatural monopolies and special interest groups most naturally.

2. TRADE RESTRICTIONS: limiting the inflow of foreign goods and services is another way to limit competition locally. Whenever, wherever and however such restrictions take place, in a case where no local rival exists, competition quells and monopoly arises. Tariffs are the

---

[199] Aristotle. (2000). *Politics*. Dover Publications, Inc.
[200] *Cheese* documentary on Modern Marvels, *History Channel* (November 22, 2007).

most benevolent in this wide-array of evil arsenal of economic weaponry, quotas and subsidies being the worst. What all trade restrictions do is that in effect they deprive local consumers, as well as the local monopolist, the benefit of competition. Consumers suffer because they are deprived of an alternative choice at the point of purchase. Local monopolist also suffers, as absence of competition dulls his skill and ability, stalls innovation and dampens his drive. He soon unlearns how to compete and, in order to prolong his dominance on the market, he quickly learns how to be an expert in collusion. He learns how to squeeze and how to coerce potential competition. Bullying is his cardinal production factor now, and not the *entrepreneurial ability* he once possessed.

I recall the words of young Socrates in Plato's *Statesman*: "It is quite clear that the arts as we know them would be annihilated and that they could never be resurrected because of this law which puts an embargo on all research. The result would be that life, which is hard enough as it is, would be quite impossible then and not to be endured."[201] It seems to me that we are living in the world of ultimate ignorance, as today's laws indeed have put their universal embargo on everything that is universally good and, therefore, universally essential for a free life, including competition. If Athens was faced with the extinction of its arts, we are faced with the extinction of our art of life, – free life that is. We pity caste victims somewhere in India, ignoring the fact that at least for the past eighty years we have been creating *the* most effective and a most evil caste system in the world right here, in America – by hampering the free American market and all of its participants with licensures, trade restrictions and penal taxation.

One of the most powerful special interest groups in the world, American Medical Association (A.M.A.), utilizes both, licensure and trade restrictions in order to remain in a monopolistic position in the United States. With licensing requirements it restricts number of entrants in American medical schools. With its Council on Medical Education and Hospitals it restricts number of medical schools, as well as number and quality of hospitals, as almost all hospitals are bound to hire only those licensed medical practitioners who graduate from a licensed American medical school, and of course such licensing both, in the case of a school and a medical professional, must be administered by the

---

[201] Plato. (2005). *The Collected Dialogues of Plato: Including the Letters (Bollingen Series LXXI)*. Princeton University Press. See Page 1070, *Statesman*.

A.M.A. And finally, it restricts number of foreign medical doctors entering the United States. With that it effectively restricts international trade of the most precious and most essential of all goods, that is, the trade of labor.

Americans have endured grave injustices perpetrated by special interest groups, especially in the medical field. So far the current medical system does not cause a lot of problems, – the rich receive medical coverage through their employer, the poor receive it through Medicaid. This is one case I fully justify the action of the poor, – I think we should all get on Medicaid and break the bank as soon as possible. The reason is this: less and less employers are offering *affordable* and *good* medical coverage. In fact, more and more employers are not offering it at all. One of the reasons why it is a norm today that payroll of a customer service manager at a retail store is deliberately kept under 35 hours per week is that an employer cannot afford offering medical coverage, – good or bad, affordable or not. The reason is simple, – it turns out that two special interest groups, – providers of medical services and providers of medical insurance, – have opposing special interests. As much as I dislike the insurance industry, in this case the blame must fall on the medical service providers. Their greed and inefficiency have inflated prices both, at hospitals and at medical offices. This has reached the point that not only good and affordable care is no longer available, but good and affordable insurance is also no longer available in the United States.

We live in critical times in that regard. I am convinced that soon sweeping changes will take place and the special interest groups in medical field will have to face a mass revolution authored not by some American government, some Washington, or some Lafayette, but by the American people. As useful and affordable healthcare and health insurance are less and less available, more and more people will try to get on Medicaid, this will either break the bank or the government will have to refuse more and more applicants. If it breaks the bank, the government will be forced to confront its own Frankenstein, – the AMA and all of its minions. This will not be a bloodless battle. If, on the other hand, the government decides to reject more and more Medicaid applications, more and more people will lose their loved ones. People are not as dumb and patient as you think. They will revolt. I know to an average American for now this seems like a farfetched conspiracy theory, as it has been quite some time since this country experienced internal turmoil on a large scale, and the mind, being a forgetful animal, tends to deceive itself by ignoring both, realities of the current environment, as well as historical precedents of the past. The environment is there, – it is in the final stage and will ripen soon, as the collusive dealing between medical professionals, their regulatory agencies, licensing institution and pharmaceutical companies reaches its peak, people's dissatisfaction will reach the zenith and the frustration of insurance companies will also reach the apex. As far as historical precedents are concerned, I would remind my American people that it was not that long ago when our nation was divided into two factions, both engaged in a ruthless war, one trying to slaughter the other. And finally, there is this third option, the so called universal healthcare which entails surrendering our *life* in order to extend our *lifespan*. What good is living without any life left in it? – That is free life which I meant.

At some point we have to realize the painful fact that our independence dwindles as our dependence on the government grows. For some reason I feel compelled to recall these famous words of the greatest naval commander in human history, and the greatest hero of Korean people, Admiral Yi Sun-shin:[202] "Those willing to die will live, and those willing to live will die." But long before Admiral Yi there was this truly universal Admiral who taught many that "whosoever will save his life shall lose it".[203] Alas, we have been losing it...

Is there a solution? Of course there is. But, of course, it is not government administered healthcare that will solve this problem. This is a serious issue which must be treated elsewhere in greater detail, but here I will only mention one thing in this regard: medical services cost a lot; the cost is high because there is no adequate supply of medical professionals; I believe that supply is limited both, naturally and artificially; We can increase supply of qualified medical professionals by importing them from foreign countries; We can eliminate artificial limitations by eliminating long-standing supremacy of the AMA in this

---

[202] Yi Sun-shin (1545-1598) – a Korean naval commander, famed for his victories against the Japanese navy during the Imjin War in the Joseon Dynasty, and is well-respected for his exemplary conduct on and off the battlefield not only by Koreans, but by Japanese Admirals as well. Perhaps his most remarkable military achievement occurred at the Battle of Myeongnyang. Outnumbered 333 ships to 13, and forced into a last stand with only his minimal fleet standing between the Japanese Army and Seoul, Yi delivered one of the most astonishing defeats in military history. Admiral Togo regarded Admiral Yi as his superior. At a party held in his honor, Togo took exception to a speech comparing him to Lord Nelson and Yi Sun-shin: "It may be proper to compare me with Nelson, but not with Korea's Yi Sun-sin, for he has no equal." Please see: Hawley, Samuel. (2005). *The Imjin War*. Royal Asiatic Society.
[203] Mathew 16:25.

country. Increased supply of medical professionals both, foreign and domestic, will foster competition, which in turn will increase quality and decrease prices both, in hospitals, as well as in private practice medical offices. At the end American consumers will benefit, and so will the insurance industry, and so will the government, as its expenditure on Medicaid subsequently and most naturally will decrease.

In light of the foregoing, I must conclude that elimination of trade restrictions will allow market forces to promote competition and get rid of certain unnatural monopolies and special interest groups most naturally.

3. GRADUATED TAXATION: this is the most potent tool in the hands of a powerful government to render the most talented citizens most powerless. It taxes most heavily and, consequently, most unfairly the best and the brightest in the nation, who are the best and the brightest *in deed* and *not in empty theorizing*. And not only do the able men suffer, but, in consequence, so do the rest of the people. As success is discouraged by imposing higher taxes on the successful, able men are either driven out of the country, as they may pursue better opportunities elsewhere, or are demoralized and rendered disheartened, – instead of rendering incentives for success, the government confiscates, – it taxes the successful at a progressively higher rate. Two questions: who will create new jobs if due to high taxes all industrious men are either paralyzed or driven out of the United States? And who will the government tax at that point?

If our government would only agree to read a basic book of microeconomics and understand that businesses treat most taxes as costs. Then it would realize that increase in taxes will increase production costs and reduce supply; and as supply dwindles jobs start to disappear, and the economy collapses.

Just glance at our government and you will at once realize why the good are squeezed and driven out. It is the government of inapt pseudo-scholars. Our future bureaucrat must have discovered his inaptitude at a very young age. Unable to *earn* his living, he first found a shelter in a choice "academia", and then in a government office. He is the graduate of Bureaucracy School of Politics and is no less eager to get rid of all the free and free-thinking men, as Stalin was in the Soviet Union. But I must admit that in *every* respect Stalin was a more tolerant tyrant. Although this is neither the right time, nor place fully to substantiate such a hypothesis, I will merely mention that unlike Stalin, our modern "democrat" encourages the intelligentsia to work for him by offering the cup of corruption and tardiness, – while Stalin merely deported or exterminated the best and the brightest, our modern day socialist is trying to corrupt them, – and *that's* the rub!

At some point we have to start calling things by their proper names: *penal taxation* will eventually result in yet another negative consequence – *tax evasion*. As able and clever industrious men realize that they are unjustly penalized, they will try to beat the system in its native game, – deception. I do not condone such an act. Such a deceit is an instrument of evil, no matter who wields it, whether it is an intelligent capitalist or a dimwitted bureaucrat. I believe that in the 21st century tax evasion will reach new zeniths and it will become a greater problem than ever before. As tax evasion is on the increase, the government, in turn, will impose more taxes to compensate for the lost revenue, – thinking that taxes imposed and revenues collected are in a linear relationship. This is yet another proof that all bureaucrats fail to understand basic economic concepts. They fail to comprehend that you can *tax and collect* only to a point. Frequent tax hikes will compel the taxpayers to perpetrate more tax evasion, which will throw the market with all of its elements and participants into a perpetual and deadly *cat and mouse* helical epidemic (I would not call it a game). I don't think the West fully understands, but that was the cardinal problem for Soviet bureaucrats. Perhaps the strength of this precedent can be best demonstrated with a simple example:

Telavi is the capital city of Kakheti region located in Eastern Georgia. The city was historically very capitalistic and the mindset was laissez-fair. In 1980s Telavi was experiencing a huge economic boom. Entrepreneurs, as well as some government members who privately engaged in free enterprise, were becoming increasingly rich. It is fashionable in Georgia to show the wealth primarily by living in a big house, and the length of your automobile also matters. Many such newly hatched millionaires faced income ceilings. Two tax regulations became especially problematic to them: one, a citizen could not own more than one automobile; two, a single family house could not have more than one floor. According to the Soviet internal revenue regulation, owning more than one car and living in a single family house with more than one floor would give an agent of the Soviet internal revenue service militia[204] a sufficient reason to start a full-scale investigation against a citizen.

But people are never as stupid as the government thinks. Georgians exercised their ingenuity and came up with a simple solution for their cars: I remember how my grandfather kept registering his top of the line Mercedes Benz under someone else's name. The house issue required a bit more creative thinking: first floor of my grandfather's house was dug underground to create an upscale basement and club house style entertainment, – this qualified as a basement under the Soviet construction code; the second floor was effectively the first floor, but it was deliberately built with low ceilings and was used for daily casual living, – due to low ceilings, this qualified as a storage space under the Soviet construction code; the third floor had cathedral ceilings and luxury at its best, – this qualified as the first and only floor under the Soviet construction code. The government could not do *a thing*.

Today's American tax collector, just like his Soviet colleague, tends to believe that taxes collected are in a linear relationship with taxes imposed. That is a sheer fallacy, it does not matter how you look at it, – statistics, historical analyses and deductive reasoning have proved most conclusively that when people are overtaxed they find loopholes, subsequently fewer taxes are collected and at the end the public good (and *not* the *government*) suffers; although to an extent public good also benefits inadvertently, as the tax evader, with his accumulated capital, starts creating new enterprises and, subsequently, new jobs.

As already mentioned, Aristotle stated that "if justice is the will of the majority, they will unjustly confiscate the property of the wealthy."[205] With the progressive taxation the government managed to create the ultimate special interest group, – a vicious majority comprised of the envious poor. It is this envious poor who, in turn, becomes the beggar and, in the result, the unwavering supporter of the big and plundering government. What the poor do not realize is that under the leadership of this government, under the penal, i.e. graduated taxation, they shall always remain poor and under the tyranny of the dismal status quo. Not only that, but there will be a day when they shall all starve, – what

---

[204] The Department for Fighting with Larceny of Socialist Property, formed in the Soviet Union as a police department of law enforcement part of the NKVD (People's Commission for Internal Affairs).

[205] Aristotle. (2000). *Politics*. Dover Publications, Inc.

happens when the wealthy taxpayers are also made poor? Who shall the government tax then?

It is self-evident that current graduated tax structure is paralyzing and counterproductive. It is a penal taxation. It punishes the successful and discourages men to pursue greatness. In contrast, elimination of the graduated taxation and implementation of a flat income tax would allow market forces to reinstate natural economic incentives and to promote competition, increase tax revenues, and get rid of the most unnatural monopoly and the most natural interest group most naturally, – the undue government and the *majority of the envious poor* by offering both the way to wealth instead of the way to plunder which they have so far pursued.

In the final analysis, it is evident that licensure, restrictions on trade and graduated taxation, as well as other unnatural and, therefore, unnecessary interferences are unnatural creations of the largest national monopoly, – the government. These interferences support special interest groups by unfairly discriminating against all other participants of the market. The cardinal aim and the ultimate end result of such actions is the creation of unnatural private monopolies through either eliminating or limiting competition. Heavy social costs, which arise in the consequence, are born by individuals individually and by the entire nation as a whole. Beyond the immediate financial injuries, such as limited choices, higher prices, and poor quality standards which monopolies always render, the public is left with the long-term impairment, – distrust. This is a new form of distrust aimed most rarely at the government, and most often at corporations. Loathing the government world around is nothing new, and at present I am not concerned with that. What concerns me is the general hatred of corporations and industrious men prevalent in the popular culture both, in America, as well as in Georgia. The reason for this popular sentiment is collusive dealings between the *always* dishonest government and *sometimes/some* dishonest corporations. Such precedents prompted the public to focus its anger at the corporations. Everyone always expects the government to be bad, but it is not everyone, and most certainly it is not always, that people expect corporations to be bad. Firms and companies that employ many of our neighbors, so to say, can't be all that villainous all the time. And *that's why* public anger is always greater against a dishonest corporation than against a dishonest government. This mindset, combined with some unfortunate precedents of American corporations engaging in collusive dealings, in turn, promoted a false-notion that all corporations are bad and, consequently, so is capitalism. Hatred of capitalism reverted people's trust back to that government which originally perpetrated this evil scheme. People start to place more trust than ever before in the government, hoping that it will regulate the market and help to weed out the bad apples, as well as some of the good ones; only to discover soon that, thanks to the government, all the good apples are discarded and the collusive bad ones are still left intact. The vicious circle of social engineering is now completed.

The reason people are so easily deceived and the heavy social tolls are so voluntarily accepted is because of two peculiar circumstances: one, the heavy costs are increased not at once, but incrementally; and two, people do not see their adverse effects immediately. As Aristotle notes, "The change does not take place all at once, and, therefore, is not observed; the mind is deceived, as in the fallacy which says that 'if each part is little, then the whole is little.'"[206]

One such deception is currently taking place in Georgia, – the mandatory teacher certification program composed by the *foreign* and imposed by the Georgian government. Anyone fluent in Georgian will easily perceive that the lingo, idioms, colloquialism and style of the language, as well as flawed pedagogic ideas expressed in this program, are not Georgian, but rather a crude, verbatim, carbon-copy and haphazard translation of a foreign tongue and a most foreign and obscene mentality. Beyond economic adversities, the current mandatory teacher certification program is bound to have dire political and social effects in Georgia. This program is full of foreign jargon and scientific nonsense. First, its foreign jargon is aimed at eradicating Georgian language and replacing it with barbarisms. It is easier to get rid of *barbarians* from inside the gates than *barbarisms* settled in your mother tongue. Barbarians *may* slaughter a nation physically, that's all; barbarisms, on the other hand, *shall* slaughter a nation's psyche, its intellect, its mode of thinking, its mindset, its essence, its spirit and its purity of expression. Second, the scientific nonsense trumpeted through this program is aimed at lobotomizing the nation. It is designed to eradicate and replace the time-tested pedagogic traditions and irrefutable philosophies of Ikalto, Bana, Gelati, Opiza, Khakhuli, and Fazisi[207] with the prattle and sophism of experimental pedagogy and its untested hypotheses. This is a *stark* warning to *all* Georgians: you must refuse learning foreign falsehoods

---

[206] Aristotle. (2000). *Politics*. Dover Publications, Inc.

[207] Names of notable ancient Georgian academies, some of them are still functioning.

and you must refuse unlearning your native truths. This is the last frontier, the last bastion, the final Rubicon. It can't be crossed, – I know a few nations who managed to recover from massacres and even genocides, but never once did I find a nation in world history which managed to have a comeback once its language and academia were polluted with foreign sophistry.

No nation can afford having either a macaronic language[208] or a macaronic mentality.

Considering the fact that Georgians ubiquitously are better disposed to philosophic poetry, rather than banal philosophies, for the sake of Georgian readers, I am compelled to end this chapter with a poem, pertinent as much to Georgians, as it is to all true liberty-loving Americans:

STAR-BEWILDERED

These tropic stars that burst with golden fire
Are not the little ones I used to know
That twinkled just above the village spire
And flickered friendly candles to the snow.

Those far New England stars knew apple trees
That danced in blowing pink skirts all night long;
Those stars looked in at barns and husking bees
And leaned to hear the farmers' cider-song.

But these strange lights hang orange in the sky,
Bright poisoned fruit spread out upon the blue
To lure the hearts of strangers passing by…
Surely these stars are not the ones I knew?[209]

---

[208] A macaronic language – a mixed language, a hodge-podge tongue, a muddled jargon characterized with hybrid words, barbarisms and bilingual puns. For example, Macaronic Latin is a jumbled jargon made up of vernacular words given Latin endings, or for Latin words mixed with the vernacular in a pastiche.

[209] Mathewson, Janet. (1939). *Poems*. Jewett City, Connecticut: Aunt Mable Young Buckingham Press.

MORE ON ECONOMICS AND ECONOMISTS

DESERT STRETCH

What sands are these the exploring mind has found?
What barren stretch of dunes and burning sky?
There is no sign to point to richer ground,
The philosophic sands, sun-dulled and dry,
Roll loosely under foot; and far and near
The thirsting mind sees nothing more than this –
The desert of dry wisdom, where appear
No springs of water, no green oasis.[210]

I am sure some will think, – what does poetry have to do with economics. I say, – *every*thing, as it shows the inevitable intellectual death that shall befall on all men who subscribe to any fallacious philosophy, including Keynesian economics. Furthermore, when I criticize Keynesian mathematics, it is not mathematics that I criticize, but its *undue*, and therefore *aimless* and mostly harmful use. Keynesian mathematics is flawed not because it is mathematics, but because it is the wrong use of this otherwise fine science, – it is utilized at an incongruous, undue and inappropriate time and venue. But as Keynes realized that math could not be used for achieving any truth in economics, he then employed it for self-aggrandizing. And it is on this basis that I am inclined to say that mathematics is a fine instrument fallen into bad hands, – have you not seen a good automobile used by a bad man, our very own government bureaucrat? The same applies to poetry, – when its objective is not merely to create some pretty prattle, but it rather aims at pursuing the universal truth, it is then not only poetry, but philosophy. Outside of American academia, historically speaking, poetry was the means by which truth was cloaked and transmitted throughout generations. Poets were early Christian theologians. And to this date, at least in the Orthodoxy, some of the best philosophy, Christology and theology are written in poetic verses. Psalms too are not mere twitting songs, but philosophy and theosophy in a most mystic form. That's why in Christianity such verses and the accompanying music are not called songs, but chants, and they are thoroughly studied in an academic subject, called hymnography. True poets are also good wordsmiths, –

---

[210] Mathewson, Janet. (1939). *Poems*. Jewett City, Connecticut: Aunt Mable Young Buckingham Press.

they enhance our language and philosophy, add new luster to it, while preserving its old beauty and ancient wisdom.

One of the ancient economists, Chanakya[211] once said, "One whose knowledge is confined to books, and whose wealth is in the possession of others, can use neither his knowledge nor the wealth when the need for them arises." I find his words perfectly applicable to the shenanigans today's "liberals" and "democrats" are trying relentlessly to carry out. But the fact that they use "economists" as means to their evil ends, is not only an injury to the universal truth and mankind, but it is also a bold impertinence, which requires, not only a logical, but an insolent remediation on my part, as an answer from a free man, – perhaps a bit of whiplash will help them to come to their senses. Allow me to explain:

It seems that knowledge for a modern American economist has been confined to academic books for too long, and to erroneous books at that, which resulted in his successful, first, learning and, then, propagating the wrong idea, which I shall heretofore describe. Today this idea threatens to destroy Georgia and America once and for all. Here is its essence: surrender control of your scarce and vital resources, including your talent, earnings, and your *entire future* to others. In return, you will get a featherbed and a pillow. Rest your pretty (but, of course, emptied) head on this pillow, fatten up your body like a Thanksgiving turkey (or perhaps like the human trash we often see hibernating in cubicles of a regulatory agency) on the welfare check of "equality", and grow as big as this featherbed (but *not* nature) shall allow.

I have a problem with that story. It is a sheer insult to every free man. First, no man needs a featherbed, and God did not place our head on our shoulders merely to put it on a pillow and sleep (or should have I said *slip*?) our lives away with it. It is this head with which we can think, compel our body to work and earn our daily bread. It is also capable of allocating, i.e. storing or spending, what it has earned. Second, I firmly believe that a man is the image of God, and there is one important privilege which comes with this, – to aspire and to accomplish (not to

---

[211] Chanakya (370-283 BC) – an adviser to the first Maurya Emperor Chandragupta (340-293 BC), and generally considered to be the architect of his rise to power. Traditionally, Chanakya is also identified by the names Kauṭilya and Vishnugupta, who authored the ancient Indian political treatise called Arthasastra. Chanakya has been considered as the pioneer of the field of economics and political science. In the Western world he has been referred to as The Indian Machiavelli, although Chanakya's works predate Machiavelli's by about 1,800 years.

dream, as some Utopian dimwit or an infomercial Heretic would make us believe) an infinity. Sir or Madam, whoever you are, do not try to choke this tangible (not theoretical or pensive) possibility out of me.

Perhaps the greatest mind France has ever produced, Victor Hugo – an ardent defender of freedom and freedom-loving men everywhere, including our own John Brown, the Abolitionist, as some like to call him, – poet, playwright, novelist, statesman and philosopher – yes, this same Victor Hugo in his surpassing novel, *The Man Who Laughs,* depicts an important and most shameful aspect of European life of not too distant past, when "men" called Comprachicos were engaged in physical engineering of people. The Comprachicos used to change the physical appearance of human beings by manipulating growing children in a similar way to the horticultural method of bonsai, – that is, *deliberate* mutilation. The most common methods said to be used in this practice included stunting children's growth by physical restraint, muzzling their faces to deform them, slitting their eyes, dislocating their joints, and malforming their bones. The resulting human monsters (appearance-wise *only*) made their living as mountebanks or were sold to lords and ladies to be used as pages or court jesters. Here is what Hugo says about this human engineering of the day: "The Comprachicos worked on man as the Chinese work on trees. A sort of fantastic stunted thing left their hands; it was ridiculous and wonderful. They could touch up a little being with such skill that its father could not have recognized it. Sometimes they left the spine straight and remade the face. Children destined for tumblers had their joints dislocated in a masterly manner; thus gymnasts were made. Not only did the Comprachicos take away his face from the child; they also took away his memory. At least, they took away all they could of it; the child had no consciousness of the mutilation to which he had been subjected. Of burnings by sulphur and incisions by the iron he remembered nothing. The Comprachicos deadened the little patient by means of a stupefying powder which was thought to be magical and which suppressed all pain."[212]

As a side note, I have to say, it burns my heart when I see a descendant, if not an apprentice, of this "cultured" and "civilized" "European" (yes, the quotation marks intended in all three cases) preaching to Georgians, whose ancestors ceaselessly gave up their lives for freedom and Christ, about tolerance, democratic values, international amnesty (as I am hardly an expert in the field, perhaps I forgot the right

---

[212] Hugo, Victor. (2010). *The Man Who Laughs.* Qontro Classic Books.

sequence of words in the last phrase, – sarcasm intended, *per usual*) and human rights.

What I find most repulsive in Comprachicos Hugo described is not that they mutilated bodies of innocent children, but the fact that they mutilated their minds: "Not only did the Comprachicos take away his face from the child; they also took away his memory." I believe that, generally speaking, our American memory has been completely eradicated, and Georgian memory is gasping. I am not a pessimist by *any* means, but in this case the facts speak louder than my hope and optimism, – great heroes, such as Thoreau and Brown, and besides them farsighted economists, such as Sowell, Friedman, Hayek, Lucas and a few other good men have tried to refresh American memory, but in vain. They are still bellowing at us, preaching to us, warning us of the imminent dangers of the modern Comprachicos, but we are still unable to recollect the true meaning of freedom, and we are still unwilling at least to point our finger at the mastermind criminal, our mutilator, our deceiver, Simon Magus of the last two centuries, – the modern architect of this dismal social experiment, – our socialist.

If the results of physical intervention in human life are so dismal and morose, imagine how much more sinister are the ones caused by the social engineering for which our "democrats" and our "liberals" are propagating. They may do as they please, – as much as I am eager, I would not throw them in a jail cell, although that would bring an immediate relief to mankind, but this relief must be *earned*, not *gifted*, – such is the bitter prescription of nature. But there is still one thing I can and shall do, and that is not to sit idly. Hugo did not sit idly when the Comprachicos mutilated children, John Brown did not sit idly when one part of this country's citizens enslaved the other, and neither shall I when I see a small number of dimwits licensed, first, at the top universities (and the opportunity which comes with it) of our country and, then, at cozy "jobs" (and power that comes with it) obtained in a government office, in a Washington think tank or, worse yet, in an international organization, usher not just my countrymen, but men *universally* into the *universal slavery* by mutilating their mind and their natural social-economic structure with it. "There will be snowflakes in Hell!" – I once heard a great New Englander, the last of the Mohicans of her ethnos exclaim in a high-spirited manner, like a true Yankee[213] – and I say it now: "there will be snowflakes in Hell before I, a free man, a man who

---

[213] Janet Mathewson is meant.

owes these two countries, – Georgia and America, – *all* that he is and *all* that he has, whatever trifle that may be, sit back and witness idly the mass mutilation which takes place daily right in front of me. Cowardice and bone-idleness is not my nature, – such was not the nature of any of my ancestors.

And there was another man, whose ancestry I in no way inherit, physically that is, or deserve, in a spiritual sense, but I'd gladly own it, if permitted either by his descendants or by the higher power; the man whose life is unprecedented in America and rarely matched or surpassed elsewhere now or in the historical past, who once solemnly and most truthfully stated the following: "Here, before God, in the presence of these witnesses, from this time, I consecrate my life to the destruction of slavery!"[214] That Founding Father of American salvation, if not of the American nation itself, was compelled to make the statement, because he saw that in his day in the name of justice grave injustices were done, and, in the result, his fellow men were suffering. Now we have slavery of a different kind, – the slave owner is no longer a hot-tempered man with a whip in his hand, the menacing mustache and sideburns on his face are gone, and so is a cigar stuck between his grisly teeth; he is a clean-shaven, calm and gentle man now, with an excellent government dental plan (paid by us, of course) and a pearl-white set of shiny teeth, and uses not a brute force, but rather a sweet and highly purposeful rhetoric full of euphemisms in order to give us a quick mental nudge and brainwash the nation into slavery. I present to you today's "democrat" – yesterday's socialist – the aborted zit, the blackhead, the slave owner of the past century, masked in a new set of clothes, and speedily discarded into our era – the 21st century.

And who do we see next to this modern day slaveholder as a trusty protégé, as an "able" foreman and, quite frankly, quite often as a pathetically funny and self-degrading sidekick? Well, it is none other than today's economist. This is the man who is skilled in the arithmetic nature of mathematics, but has no knowledge of the qualitative and, hence, real nature of numbers. His memory is *ample*, yet his reasoning is *simple*, and perhaps that is precisely why he always advocates *quantity* and despises *quality*, especially the human kind. He knows all the false theorems and counterfeit concepts, such as the aggregate demand. He knows all the nonessential and, quite frankly, invented, fictitious and

---

[214] Thoreau, H. D., Sanborn, F. B., Lazarashvili, Z. K. (2011). *American Heroes: Thoreau and Brown*. Georgian International University Press.

hence flawed formulas of finance, statistics and economics, but ask him to solve a simple essential equation of life and he is baffled. Ask him to find the value of X in it and he is puzzled: $1,000,000 \times 0 = X$. He missed the spirit of it, although he is learned in letters, as the Book would say. I shall explain: the spirit of the equation is that the million-dollar promises and wealth, which his boss, the modern day "liberal" politician is offering, come out to naught, as the fundamental premise of socialist wealth is the limiting condition of mandatory "equality", which requires public plundering of the wealthy, and surrendering of your freedom, and your past, current and future earning powers with that, to the government. These premises lead a man to slavery in literal sense, and symbolically, as it is depicted by the symbol of zero in this equation, they lead the sum X to a sheer zilch, nothingness, and nihilism.

"But the government is made up of wise and beneficent citizens", – the "economist" keeps pleading with me, like a Gipsy beggar. Even if he is an honest man, who has been himself deceived and misled, which I don't believe is the case, but still… if he is the unfortunate sucker trying to suck me into the same bull that he has been sucked into, I must not believe him, for I know that the Mentor of this protégé was an evil fellow, – the socialist slaveholder. It was *he* who put this unfortunate chap through a "public" school and then through an elitist university, and made him into what he is today, – an "economist".

Scenario one: the socialist has either brainwashed him to the point that he now in earnest supports socialism unwillingly and unwittingly; or scenario two: he owes the socialist for his "academic" "success" and now must "work" relentlessly to repay the old favor.

I have news for you, my learned "colleague": if it is the second scenario, and you are trying to repay the old favor, you are the living proof that there is no such thing as *free money* in the world, and you should be stripped of the honorable title of an economist on two cardinal grounds: first, on moral grounds, for you are knowingly conspiring and perpetuating what is legally, as well as morally, corruption; two, you are an idiot, for you could not utilize the science of economics even to your selfish advantage, as you miscalculated and duped yourself into a false belief of *free money*, – you did not understand the essence of the first chapter of McConnell's *Microeconomics*, which clearly teaches that "Scarce economic resources mean limited goods and services. Scarcity restricts options and demands choices. Because we 'can't have it all,' we must decide what we will have and what we must forgo".[215] Now you are forced to forgo not just money, but your birthright for that poor and overpriced education you once gladly received "for free", per *your* choice. I believe Charles Dickens once addressed you or your kind when he said: "All other swindlers upon earth are nothing to the self-swindlers, and with such pretences did I cheat myself."[216]

Now, if it is the scenario one, meaning you were brainwashed into this evil, once again you need to be stripped of all due honors which come with that sheepskin (I mean the diploma) you so proudly display on your office wall in a mahogany frame, for you have been deceived, duped and tricked into learning the false science, – Keynesian economics. If it is false knowledge you have received, it must then naturally follow that the corresponding diploma you possess is a counterfeit, and so are the privileges which come with it.

Worry not, mon "ami". I am not going to do any of what was mentioned above. As long as an iota of freedom still exists either in American conscience or in American consciousness, free market and American people will do it to you, once either your incompetence or your fraud is brought to light. I am a patient man. All I have to do is inform the people and then wait you out, – for once anger of the masses will be put to crucify Barabbas, and not Christ – the falsehood, and not the truth – the devil, and not the God:

"Time shall unfold what plighted cunning hides:
Who cover faults, at last shame them derides."[217]

I vividly recall the ending of one of the most emblematic American movies, *The Sting II*. Jake Hooker, played by Mac Davis, is asking his Mentor and (to an extent benevolent) master con artist, Fargo Gondorff, played by Jackie Gleason: "Fargo, whatever made you think I could beat Torres in the first place?"

Gleason gives his usual tilt-and-smile, and replies in a loving manner: "I don't know Jake, but you have a way of ignoring the reality of the things that always pulls you through."

---

[215] McConnell, C. R., Brue. S. L., Flynn. S. M. (2009). *Microeconomics*. McGraw-Hill.
[216] Dickens, Charles. (2010). *Great Expectations*. Ignatius Press.
[217] *King Lear* by William Shakespeare (Act I, Cordelia, Scene I). Please see: Shakespeare, William. (2005). *The Yale Shakespeare: Complete Works*. Barnes & Noble.

Moral of the story is that life is full of *pressing realities*, but such realities are only temporary, fleeting and transitory, especially when they are artificially induced in human existence, – socialism being one of them. Some pressing realities are quite natural, but they could be fleeting also, – poverty for example. I would like to call temporary realities, that are brought on artificially and unnaturally by collusion of devious and powerful men, *counterfeit realities*; and temporary realities that are brought on by nature, I would like to call *intermediary realities*, – I did not choose the term *intermediary* at random; it implies that ultimately nature aims at *the universal reality* for which sometimes intermediary arrangements are necessary. Both, counterfeit and intermediary realities are temporary and ephemeral, and therefore of little importance. We should not aim at either of these. Instead we should learn how to be farsighted, like our wise ancestor, Prometheus, and we should endeavor to aim at *the universal reality*, – the ultimate truth, – the *enduring actuality*. Granted, it is difficult to focus on a faraway future, when both, natural and artificial immediate presences force their will on us, but nevertheless we must keep our eye on the universal, on the ultimate, on the enduring truth, and not on mere opinions which happen to prevail *for now*. Most men cannot do this (as they are shortsighted), but *we* must, – the ultimate reality is not for the shortsighted or the fainthearted or the dimwitted, it is the reality of champions and visionaries; and I place among such champions and visionaries *all* industrious free market competitive capitalists.

Not somewhere in faraway history, but in our immediate lives we can find many pressing realities, some of them natural, i.e. intermediary, and some of them induced, i.e. counterfeit. For example, as it has been already mentioned, Keynesian economics has obliterated the true science of economics from American academia, which now often refers to true economics as "the Austrian School" or the supply-side economics, and defines it as a *heterodox* school of economic thought, while Keynesian gibberish is hailed as the *orthodox* economics. But we know that at last the universal truth shall prevail and Keynesianism will become just one of those anecdotal chapters full of fallacies we often find in history of economics, just like the Phillip's curve. One of the most pressing natural realities would be poverty. Socialist remedies, including redistribution of income, only perpetuate privation and never eradicate it. But we can overcome poverty by industry, guts, wisdom, hard work and frugality, and with that we can usher in an ultimate reality for Georgia and America, – freedom and prosperity.

It is typical of all counterfeit realities to be concerned with expediency, just as it is typical of all universal realities to be concerned with the ultimate truth, while intermediary realities, depending on wisdom and foresight of its participants, sometimes lean towards the expediency and sometimes tend to favor the truth, – I have seen many poor and uneducated men remained destitute and ignorant, but I have also seen many poor and uneducated men became wealthy and learned. It is a peculiar characteristic of all great men to pursue the truth, just as it is a peculiar characteristic of all petty people to pursue all that is immediately gratifying, i.e. the expediency, – those short-term goods which become the long-term evils. It is because of this that certain societies are inclined to raid and to plunder others, for the immediate gains seem expedient. In such societies truth becomes irrelevant. In fact, the two inseparable companions of the universal truth, *justice* and *good* become the subjects of mockery. As wise Socrates states in Plato's *Phaedrus*, "…they maintain, there is absolutely no need for the budding orator to concern himself with the truth about what is just or good conduct, nor indeed about who are just and good men whether by nature or education. In the courts of law nobody cares a rap for the truth about these matters, but only about what is plausible." And then he concludes: "Even actual facts ought sometimes not be stated, if they don't tally with probability; they should be replaced by what is probable, whether in prosecution or defense; whatever you say, you simply must pursue this probability they talk of, and can say good-by to the truth forever."[218] I am afraid that at least in our economics, if not in our morality, education, politics, laws, sciences, medicine and even in our God-given freedom, we have already said good-by to the truth for-*ever*, for our immediate gratifications we have extended the counterfeit reality with our falsehoods, and the universal reality and the universal truth, representing a most inconvenient company for most men, have been postponed until the eleventh hour, whenever that may be.

COMMON CULTURAL METAPHORS

In this section I intend to describe a few cultural metaphors. The reason for this is that these metaphors will be culturally acceptable to Georgian readers on the grounds of familiarity; but also because readers

---

[218] Plato. (2005). *The Collected Dialogues of Plato: Including the Letters (Bollingen Series LXXI)*. Princeton University Press.

of different cultural backgrounds will have an opportunity to learn about the unfamiliar ethnos, its folklore and popular culture.

I hardly know a Georgian of my or previous or subsequent generations within a forty-year timespan who is not familiar with a fable of two cousins, a wolf and a shepherd dog. It flows something like this: it is the dead of winter in Georgian country. Food is scarce in the mountains, so a wolf decides to visit his cousin, a shepherd dog who lives and works in the village located at the edge of the mountain range, – wolf's territory. The cousins are happy to see one another. The wolf notices a significant change in the dog who has become quite fat and fluffy. He asks his beloved cousin to explain the reason why he is so well taken care of. The dog tells him that the shepherd takes care of him. The wolf is no dummy. He is suspicious of free food (seems smarter than many men to me!) and pampering, wants to examine the small print and immediately throws him a follow up question, – what do you have to do in exchange? The dog explains to him that all he has to do is to howl and to scare off any stranger who tries to enter the pastures and harm the sheep. The wolf is fascinated and wants in on the deal. The dog is more than eager to extend the opportunity to his close relative. So they agree that the dog will ask his boss, the shepherd to employ the wolf. They meet the following evening. The answer is positive. They are both ecstatic! Not only is the answer positive, but the shepherd had advanced a boiled mutton quarter to welcome the new team member. They dine and decide that overnight the wolf will tie up all the loose ends in the woods and report for duty next morning. As the dog was seeing off his guest, at the gate the wolf noticed that hair on his cousin's neck was wearing off. He asked the reason. The dog tried to evade the question, but the wolf persisted. At the end the dog explained: "Well, cousin, it is a matter of no importance whatsoever, but I am balding because I have to wear a leash and a chain around my neck at night, once we get back from our daily trip to pastures. It is only for half a day, from dusk to dawn." The wolf looked at him bewildered and said: "My poor cousin, here I was yesterday looking up to you and trying to emulate your success. Here I am today and cannot but pity you. You have been fooled my friend! You have obtained the means to nourishing your body, but you have lost the spiritual manna – freedom – without which no man or no animal can truly live. I have to go now and to tell all our relatives out there in the woods to lament your demise and throw you a big funeral."

The universal truth that freedom is the universal requirement for life, – able, intelligent, and *manly* life that is, – is substantiated by the fact that wise men with different national and philosophical backgrounds, and from different epochs, have concluded their inquiry with identical conclusions supporting freedom and condemning slavery, even in such cases when slavery is financially somewhat rewarding and, therefore, in economic terms *seems* expedient. It was Confucius who said that "If a state is governed by the principles of reason, poverty and misery are subjects of shame; if a state is not governed by the principles of reason, riches and honors are the subjects of shame."[219] And then it was our very own Henry David Thoreau who centuries ago echoed that "A man may grow rich in Turkey even, if he will be in all respects a good subject of the Turkish government."[220] Are we no better than the Ottomans or their minions who have spilled the blood of the innocent universally, and through the "culture" of global robbery led the lives not befitting men, but leaches and parasites?

Here is another Georgian story which every first grader must read and thoroughly learn right after he finishes studying the Georgian alphabet. A nightingale's crooning had enchanted the King so much that he ordered to catch the nightingale with a lure. The chanting bird was brought to him in a bronze cage. The entire palace waited patiently, a few days went by, but the nightingale refused to croon. A vizier, wise only in his own conceit, the head of FHA[221] of his day, suggested to the King that the bird needed better housing and *then* it would chant. The King acquiesced. Surely enough the bureaucrat cranked out a silver cage, but the bird would not sing. The housing authority of his day suggested another stimulus upgrade, so a golden cage was produced, but the nightingale kept his silence. Then one long forgotten country philosopher was summoned. He looked at the nightingale and urged the King to let the bird fly away, lest it died. The King had no other choice, so he followed the philosopher's advice. The bird flew to the closest tree of the nearby forest, set on its branch and immediately started his crooning.

I have seen great many fishes (New Englanders, who speak the most eloquent and grammatically correct English, say fishes instead of fish – I defer to them in grammar, as well as in many other important aspects of life) being lured and caught by a relatively small number of men by use of tasty baits. The trick is such that the bait always covers the deadly

---

[219] Thoreau, Henry. (1970). *Henry David Thoreau: Walden and Other Writings*. Nelson Doubleday, Inc. Also see: Confucius. (1993). *The Essential Confucius*. Harper Collins.

[220] Thoreau, H. D., Sanborn, F. B., Lazarashvili, Z. K. (2011). *American Heroes: Thoreau and Brown*. Georgian International University Press.

[221] The Federal Housing Administration (F.H.A.).

hook and masks the bloody aftertaste. From now on, let not the same hook touch a single citizen of either Georgia or America. And it won't, if we remain vigilant and see dangers hidden in the socialist's lure.

Finally, I would like to conclude this section with a story from the book which is most dear to me, – the Orthodox Bible. Chapter 25 of the Book of Genesis ends with these words: "And Jacob said, 'Sell me this day thy birthright.' And Esau said, 'Behold, I am at the point to die: and what profit shall this birthright do to me?' And Jacob said, 'Swear to me this day;' and he swore unto him: and he sold his birthright unto Jacob. Then Jacob gave Esau bread and pottage of lentils; and he did eat and drink, and rose up, and went his way: thus Esau despised his birthright."[222] Esau's fate was not as dire as ours, – true, he sold his life, his invaluable birthright, his freedom and opportunity for greatness, but at least we know that it was sold into good hands as it was bought by Jacob, but the buyer of our Georgian and American birthrights is no wise man. He is an evil hypocrite who wholeheartedly desires our serfdom and our destruction. His name, I hope you have guessed already, is the modern day "democrat" – the old socialist. Do not sell your freedom for pottage of any kind. Do not sell it to a socialist for his promises. Do not sell it to a capitalist either. We should all affix a three-line label on it:

"MADE IN HEAVEN. INVALUABLE. NEVER FOR SALE."

CONCLUSION

There is an insurmountable, but nowadays almost universally ignored, difference between predestination and fatalism. Predestination, at least in an Orthodox Christian sense, is anchored on a healthy belief, which itself is based on quite a real fact of life, that God's grace, as well as man's free will are required for success. Fatalism, on the other hand, advocates that Fate governs all human existence and there is nothing that a man can do to avoid the predetermined outcome. Georgians have no right to degenerate to the level of fatalism. Neither can they follow the heretical doctrine so ubiquitously present in today's Western world, that an individual's free will is *all* that is required for success. Such a free will, when estranged from God, is a mere license, not courage, not bravery, not independence, and, most certainly, not freedom. The Georgian way is the way of Christianity, – let God's will be done and let

---

[222] Genesis 25:31-34.

us simultaneously exercise our will. I firmly believe that God has already done his will, – he has granted us a most beautiful land, he has given us hands and feet to work with and intelligence to work them with. Furthermore, I strongly believe that he continues to exercise his will to help us when help is due. It is our turn now. And if work is our part in the grand scheme of this universe, let us do it diligently, and might as well let us do it in the environment which is most fair, which does not punish the talented, the brave and the hardworking, which encumbers nobody's freedom and liberty, and requires no monthly, quarterly or annual sacrifice as it is natural and, therefore, a self-sustaining enterprise, – capitalism.

I would suggest to my countrymen not to underestimate what capitalism has to offer compared to every other alternative known to men to date. I am compelled to remind them once again to be just as least trusting toward democracy, when it demands a payment from them in the form of a tax increase, as they are toward communism. I would also like to plea with them to try to be self-reliant as much as circumstances allow, and I urge them not to depend on countries which anchor their economic or political policies on either of those two political modes. History is full of examples of contests between democracy and communism. It is a rerun of an old drama with a hint of comic irony. The grand finale is always the same, – democratic and communist empires always win, but a small freedom-loving country is squashed between the two goliaths. The staple production of such showdowns is always dismal for the middle man. In the best case, history is left with North and South Korea as its residual "benefit", – a devastating split of one brave nation, now with two heads, and, *quite* frankly, I do not know which puppet head is less evil, the one with greater diversity of clothes, but more limited diversity of slaves, or the other with greater diversity of slaves, but with a less diverse wardrobe. This is an example of the best case scenario. But in the worst case you get Laos, – a beautiful mountainous country which was never in any war either with the U.S. or the U.S.S.R., but, nevertheless, where the U.S. and the U.S.S.R. dropped more bombs than in Germany and Japan combined during the World War II. Such are the joint gifts of democracy and socialism. Capitalism, on the other hand, shall never gift you anything, and in return you shan't gift anything back either, and I like it this way! So do, for example, the Vietnamese, – in only ten years capitalism has managed to rebuild what communism and democracy had managed to destroy in twenty.

SELF-RELIANCE shall bring SELF-GOVERNANCE.

"Vivere Militare Est" – "To live is to fight" (Seneca the Younger), "Militia Est Vita Hominis" – "The life of man upon earth is a warfare" (Book of Job 7:1), "Si Vis Pacem, Para Bellum" – "If you wish for peace, prepare for war" (Publius Flavius Vegetius Renatus). These are stark, but undeniable facts of life. Our ancestors did well by working relentlessly towards an essential goal of defending and sustaining their country by use of the methods which their times demanded, – I mean military warfare. But our times are different from theirs. Today's environment demands something completely different. It demands economic success. Back in those days our ancestor bravely picked up his sword and shield to do his duty well. We must pick up the sword and shield of a different kind. Nations who do not successfully engage in today's warfare, – economic competition, which is purely economic, not military, – will become extinct. Nations who choose economic welfare over economic warfare will dissolve.

Mussolini was dead wrong when he said that "Blood alone moves the wheels of history."[223] And more so was Martin Luther, saying "No one need think that the world can be ruled without blood. The civil sword shall and must be red and bloody."[224] Hasty and thoughtless words of influential men have a tendency to produce rash and injudicious actions, and, in turn, such actions often result in quick and speedy catastrophes for mankind. I'd like to ask Mr. Luther, why is it that the world *needs* to be ruled in the first place? And why is it that it always must be ruled either by a big-belly bigot or a big-headed hypocrite? I would like to make a seemingly small alteration in Luther's wording and state simply that "No one need think that the world can be ruled (period!)." And as far as history goes, I would say that it is not merely *moving* with which we should concern ourselves, but rather with *moving forward*. And this forward movement requires not necessarily *some* blood, but the fuel more precious and rare than the biological plasma of *random* men. It requires sweat, and that too not just of any kind, but the sweat accompanied with foresight, hard work, industry and frugality which always moved, always moves and always shall move the wheels of history *forward*! And if sometimes it is blood which indeed moves the wheels of history, it is not the blood of rhetorical hypocrites, invading serfs and random slaves, but the blood of true martyrs, saints, patriots and redeemers. To paraphrase Tertullian, "The blood of the martyrs is

---

[223] A popular excerpt from the speech given by Mussolini in Parma on December 13, 1914, advocating Italian entry into World War I.
[224] Luther, Martin. (1947). *Von Kauflandlung und Wucher*. Neckar-Verl.

the seed of the church",[225] – and I would extend his thought and say that it is *this* blood that is also the seed of the entire man-kind.

Georgians cannot be the ostriches and the dodos of today's world, – ignoring pressing realities by nostalgically pining for the days of yore. The world has changed, – you get almost nowhere by wielding a sword. It is industry through free enterprise we must now wield, and wield it better than *any*one else, for the competition in this line of war is fiercer than on a battle field. The good news is that today's battlefield and the labor which it requires are more honorable than the battlefields and toils of the old days. Another good thing is that today's battlefield, just like the old one, is based on merit and not on equality, – you are not one on one with the enemy, but neither was your ancestor, and still success on the field is a function of your toil, quickness of mind, courage, knowledge, industry and foresight.

We, the today's Georgians and today's Americans must learn quickly and then act even quicker, keeping in mind that "You will never live long enough to learn everything that you need to know to succeed".[226] We must work relentlessly to rid ourselves of the evil of serfdom and its cause, – the undue government and its undue obstructing of our Georgian and American free markets. But before that, we must get rid of all the socialist mentality which, due to the lengthy and effective "liberal" propaganda coming from TV, media and formal "education", has settled in our minds, and causes us to experience constant drowsiness when on a few occasions we come across some fundamental facts of life and discover basic economic truths. We have been sleeping for too long. One more short nap may result in a complete annihilation of American and Georgian freedoms and livelihoods. If that happens, be assured that our descendants will look at their family trees not with reverence, but with disgust, thinking, if not saying: "So many men, so little purpose".

True, we have a difficult task ahead of us, but difficulty is the excuse which history shall never accept. As Napoleon once said, "History is the version of past events that people have decided to agree

---

[225] Tertullian's original expression is often paraphrased in this form. Please see: Tertullian. Sider, Robert, D. (2001). *Christian and Pagan in the Roman Empire: The Witness of Tertullian*. Catholic University of America Press.
[226] Franklin, Benjamin. (2006). *The Way to Wealth and Other Writings on Finance*. Sterling Publishing Co., Inc.

upon".[227] In this regard, I ask my contemporary countrymen: What are *we* agreeing upon? What's the version *we* want to imprint as our footsteps and fingerprints on the history of mankind? Surely, I would be ashamed to leave fingerprints of a plundering criminal! And I would certainly be embarrassed to cast timid footprints of a wimp! It seems clear to me that the only honorable path left for me, as well as for my nation, is the path of industry, innovation, competition, frugality and laissez-faire capitalism.

Do we not desire to be known as such men, such historical, and I would even say *historic* ambassadors of mankind, about whom generations shall say: "All they had was the product of their labor..." For how long must we hide our deficiencies and our foibles? For how long must we be ashamed of having been poor? How much longer must we handle our economy with mittens or rubber gloves, – featherbedding or surgically engineering our nation? And how much longer must we keep our noses to the grindstone, – working all we can and buying all we can? Have we ever tried SAVING *all we can*? And how about tithing and helping all we can?

I must explain why I feel such an urge to convince Georgians and Americans to sustain and to further their economic freedom: even though freedom is in decline in the entire world, and that includes Georgia and the United States, one may yet call Georgians and Americans free in comparison to the Russians and the Chinese, where individual existence is confined to the long-existing social tyranny and citizenship has very little to do with individualism and individual freedom.

Once again, I am convinced in the idea I have already expressed in a previous paragraph: *we are yet to declare our independence.*

My dear and beloved countrymen, whether we like it or not, these are the pressing realities of our times, and the sooner we capitalize on them, the better it shall be for each one of us individually and, in a cumulative sense, better it shall be for our once, and still to be, great nation, Iberia.

---

[227] Wellman, Jerry, L. (2009). *Organizational Learning: How Companies and Institutions Manage and Apply Knowledge*. Palgrave Macmillan.

POST SCRIPTUM:

"I have heard of some great Man, whose Rule it was with regard to Offices, *Never to ask for them*, and *never to refuse them*: To which I have always added in my own Practice, *Never to resign them*."[228] Holding two moral, and at the same time *most practical* full time offices, one as a Georgian, the other as a Yankee, I was compelled to speak the truth, as uttering any falsehood, however sweet and seemingly expedient, is not permitted under these two employments, and such a misconduct would have been equal to my resignation. Furthermore, one peculiar common character of holding these two offices is that, once you accept the appointments, it is impossible to resign them. Such are high honors and duties of being a Georgian and a Yankee. So you see my predicament when I say that I was *compelled* to speak the truth. Moreover, I seek no other employment, I ask for no other commission and no greater position from anyone, than what I have already received from these two great nations. Not only that, but often I get a feeling that I have been vastly overpaid.

---

[228] Franklin, Benjamin. (2006). *The Way to Wealth and Other Writings on Finance.* Sterling Publishing Co., Inc.

BIBLIOGRAPHY

Aristotle. (2000). *Politics*. Dover Publications, Inc.

Aurelius, Marcus. (2002). *The Emperor's Handbook*. Scribner.

Bastiat, Frederic. (2010). *The Law*. Tribeca Books.

Bleeck, Arthur, Henry. (2001). *Avesta: The Religious Books of the Parsees*. Adamant Media Corporation.

Boethius. (2008). *The Consolation of Philosophy*. Oxford University Press, USA.

Chavchavadze, Ilia. (1984). *Compositions*. Sabchota Sakartvelo.

Chernow, Ron. (1999). *Titan: The Life of John D. Rockefeller, Sr*. Vintage.

Cicero. (2008). *On Obligations*. Oxford University Press, USA.

Cicero. (2009). *Political Speeches*. Oxford University Press, USA.

Cicero. (2009). *The Republic and the Laws*. Oxford University Press, USA.

Confucius. (1993). *The Essential Confucius*. Harper Collins.

Dickens, Charles. (2010). *Great Expectations*. Ignatius Press.

Dods, Marcus (translator). St. Augustine of Hippo. (2000). *The City of God*. Modern Library.

Doyle, Arthur, Conan. (2004). *The Complete Sherlock Holmes*. Barnes & Noble Classics.

Epictetus. *Discourses. Book III*.

Eusebius. (2007). *The Church History*. Kregel Academic & Professional.

Friedman, Milton. (2002). *Capitalism and Freedom*. The University of Chicago Press.

Friedman, Milton. (1990). *Free to Choose: A Personal Statement*. Mariner Books.

Hawley, Samuel. (2005). *The Imjin War*. Royal Asiatic Society.

Hayek, F. A. (2007). *The Road to Serfdom*. The University of Chicago Press.

Hayek, F. A. (2011). *The Constitution of Liberty*. The University of Chicago Press.

Hayek, Friedrich, A. (1976). *Law, Legislation and Liberty. Volume 2. The Mirage of Social Justice*. The University of Chicago Press.

Hayek, Friedrich, A. (1976). *Law, Legislation and Liberty. Volume 3. The Mirage of Social Justice*. The University of Chicago Press.

Homer. (1995). *The Iliad*. Barnes & Noble.

Homer. *Odyssey. Book IV*.

Hugo, Victor. (2010). *The Man Who Laughs*. Qontro Classic Books.

Josephus. (1980). *The Works of Josephus: Complete and Unabridged*. Hendrickson Publishers.

Kierkegaard, Soren. (1956). *Purity of Heart: Is to Will One Thing*. HarperOne.

Lazarashvili, Z. K., Ihejirika, C. E., Chapidze, G. T., Stasen, G. P. (2011). *Pantheon of Political Philosophers*. Georgian International University Press.

Lucas, Robert. (1997). *Market Economy*. Ministry of Finance of Georgia.

Luther, Martin. (1947). *Von Kauflandlung und Wucher*. Neckar-Verl.

Machiavelli, Niccolo. (2001). *The Art of War*. Da Capo Press.

Mathewson, Janet. (1962). *Michael Torey*. Garden City, New York: Doubleday & Company, Inc.

Mathewson, Janet. (1939). *Poems*. Jewett City, Connecticut: Aunt Mable Young Buckingham Press.

McConnell, C. R., Brue. S. L., Flynn. S. M. (2009). *Microeconomics*. McGraw-Hill.

McGovern, Patrick, E. (2007). *Ancient Wine: The Search for the Origins of Viniculture*. Princeton University Press.

McGovern, Patrick, E. (2010). *Uncorking the Past: The Quest for Wine, Beer, and Other Alcoholic Beverages*. University of California Press.

Mises, Ludwig, von. (2010). *Liberalism*. Ludwig von Mises Institute.

Narayana. (2007). *Hitopadesa*. Penguin Classics.

Nietzsche, Friedrich. (1995). *Thus Spoke Zarathustra*. The Modern Library.

Olivelle, Patrick (translator). (2008). *Upanisads*. Oxford University Press, USA.

Pascal, Blaise. (1999). *Pensees and Other Writings*. Oxford University Press.

Philo of Alexandria. (2005). *The Works of Philo*. Hendrickson Publishers.

Plato. (2005). *The Collected Dialogues of Plato: Including the Letters (Bollingen Series LXXI)*. Princeton University Press.

Pseudo-Dionysius. (1988). *Pseudo-Dionysius: The Complete Works*. Paulist Press.

Ricardo, David. (2010). *On the Principles of Political Economy and Taxation*. Liberty Fund Inc.

Ricardo, David. (2010). *The Works of David Ricardo*. General Books LLC.

Sanborn, Franklin, Benjamin. (2010). *The Life and Letters of John Brown: Liberator of Kansas, and Martyr of Virginia*. Nabu Press.

Santayana, George. Cardiff, Ira. (1964). *The Wisdom of George Santayana: Atoms of Thought*. Citadel Press.

Santayana, George. (1921). *Little Essays Drawn from the Writings of George Santayana*. Charles Scribner's Sons.
Schumpeter, Joseph. (1962). *Capitalism, Socialism and Democracy*. New York: Harper & Row.

Schumpeter. (1954). *History of Economic Analysis*. Oxford University Press.

Shakespeare, William. (2005). *The Yale Shakespeare: Complete Works*. Barnes & Noble.

Smith, Adam. (1991, original 1776). *The Wealth of Nations*. Everymans Library.

Sowell, Thomas. (1999). *Barbarians Inside the Gates*. Hoover Institution Press.

Sowell, Thomas. (2006). *Ever Wonder Why?* Hoover Institution Press.

Sowell, Tomas. (2007). *A Conflict of Visions*. Basic Books.

Sun Tzu. (2003). *The Art of War*. Barnes & Noble Classics.

Swift, Jonathan. (1998). *Gulliver's Travels*. Oxford University Press, USA.

Tertullian. Sider, Robert, D. (2001). *Christian and Pagan in the Roman Empire: The Witness of Tertullian*. Catholic University of America Press.

Thompson, Robert W. (1996). *Rewriting Caucasian History: The Medieval Armenian Adaptation of the Georgian Chronicles: The Original Georgian Texts and the Armenian Adaptation*. Oxford Oriental Monographs. Oxford University Press.

Thoreau, Henry. (1970). *Henry David Thoreau: Walden and Other Writings*. Nelson Doubleday, Inc.

Thoreau, H. D., Sanborn, F. B., Lazarashvili, Z. K. (2011). *American Heroes: Thoreau and Brown*. Georgian International University Press.

Wellman, Jerry, L. (2009). *Organizational Learning: How Companies and Institutions Manage and Apply Knowledge*. Palgrave Macmillan.

APPENDIX A

The Lost Opening Paragraph

I originally intended to commence my thesis with this paragraph now shown below, but a dear friend, always a well-wisher, an ardent supporter of freedom and laissez-faire capitalism, gave me a sound *practical* advice to start the thesis with another paragraph, more appealing to potential readers. It was in this way that I was compelled to act contrary to my conviction. Nevertheless, I decided to include the "lost" opening paragraph in this appendix, as I believe it is relevant not only to laissez-faire capitalism, but to the very essence of human existence:

"I am under a strong impression that some, if not all nations aspire to be good. As a result, they value freedom and prosperity over serfdom and limited opportunities it offers to prosper *honorably*. Being to a large extent familiar with Georgian history leaves no doubt in my mind that Georgia always was and currently is such a nation. Some important, but long forgotten aspects of American history suggest the same propensity about this country as well, although presently I see little evidence of such aspirations among the American people. Speaking from a personal standpoint, that is most deplorable and painful to me. But I tell myself, as well as my neighbor, that however little and stale, the evidence is still there; and that with proper love and care even the smallest of musty acorns has a definitive chance to develop into a magnificent oak tree, yet again."

APPENDIX B

Excerpts from Georgian History

One Hundred Thousand Martyrs of Tbilisi

Georgia is a most unique country. In all of our common human history it is exceedingly rare to come across a nation so devoted to freedom, independence and self-governance, and that too for a very, *very* long time. This I must briefly, but effectively substantiate, lest accused of unjust partiality and unfair bias by the reader who is not familiar with Georgia and Georgian people.

When Jalal ad-Din Mingburnu, the leading tyrant of his time and the last ruler of the Khwarezmid Empire[229] invaded Tbilisi, the capital city of Georgia in 1226, demolished the cupola of the Sioni cathedral,[230] set up his throne in its stead, and ordered icons of Jesus and Theotokos to be brought out from the church and placed at the foot of the bridge, and then set conditions that Georgians who would choose conformity and step on these icons, symbolically condemning their God and their liberty with it, would receive the gift of life and, on top of that, a substantial financial compensation in a form of a complete tax relief, and the ones who would not, should be decapitated, all one hundred thousand Georgians chose to

---

[229] Khwarezmid Empire – central Asian empire with relatively short longevity. It was founded by the Khwarazmians, also known as Khwarazmids. Dynasty of Khwarazm Shahs or Khwarezm-Shah dynasty was a Persianate Sunni Muslim dynasty of Turkic origin. They ruled Greater Iran in the High Middle Ages, in the period of about 1077 to 1231, first, as vassals of the Seljuqs, Kara-Khitan, and, later, as independent rulers, up until the Mongol invasions of the 13th century. The dynasty was founded by Anush Tigin Gharchai, a former slave of the Seljuq sultans, who was appointed as the governor of Khwarezm. His son, Qutb ad-Din Muhammad I, became the first hereditary Shah of Khwarezm.

[230] The Sioni Cathedral of the Dormition – a Georgian Orthodox Cathedral in Tbilisi, the capital of Georgia. Following a medieval Georgian tradition of naming churches after particular places in the Holy Land, the Sioni Cathedral bears the name of Mount Zion at Jerusalem. It is commonly known as the "Tbilisi Sioni" to distinguish it from several other churches across Georgia bearing the name *Sioni*. The Tbilisi Sioni Cathedral is situated in historic *Sionis Kucha* (Sioni Street) in downtown Tbilisi, with its eastern facade fronting the right embankment of the Mtkvari River. It was initially built in the 6th-7th centuries. Since then, it has been destroyed by foreign invaders and reconstructed several times. The current church is based on a 13th-century version with some changes from the 17th to 19th centuries. The Sioni Cathedral was the main Georgian Orthodox Cathedral and the seat of Catholicos-Patriarch of All Georgia until the Holy Trinity Cathedral was consecrated in 2004.

remain faithful to their God, as well as to their freedom. This was no deed of a lone hero – this was a deed of an entire heroic nation, not per parliamentary decree or a King's order, but per its free will. Hence the one hundred thousand martyrs which Georgian Orthodox Church now venerates, whose if not veneration, at least admiration I recommend to all freedom-loving men regardless of nationality.

Tao-Klarjeti – The Cradle of the Iberian Civilization

Tao-Klarjeti, also known as Meskheti is the term conventionally used in modern history to describe the historic south-western Georgian principalities, the cradle of both, pre-Christian and Christian Iberian civilizations, now forming parts of north-eastern Turkey and divided among the provinces of Erzurum, Artvin, Ardahan and Kars. Historically the area comprised of the following Georgian provinces (to this date populated by ethnic Georgians): West of the Arsiani Mountains were Tao, Klarjeti and Shavsheti, to the east lay Samtskhe, Erusheti, Javakheti, Artaani and Kola. The landscape is characterized by mountains and the river-systems of Chorokhi and Mtkvari. Tao-Klarjeti's geographical position between the great Empires of the East and the West, and the fact that one branch of the Silk Road ran through its territory, meant that it was subject to a constant stream of diverging influences. Tao-Klarjeti was ruled by the Bagrationi dynasty, the royal family of Georgia which originally descended from that region, – yet one more reason why Tao-Klarjeti played the *most* crucial role in the unification of all Georgian states into a single feudal Kingdom in 1008. Alongside the magnificent nature, the architectural monuments of Tao-Klarjeti – Georgian Orthodox churches, monasteries, bridges and castles – function as tourist attractions today, but many monuments are endangered, since nothing is done for their preservation. Also, there have been cases of deliberate destruction and vandalism from the Turkish side, for instance, in Opiza, Bana and Tbeti. Armenians, on the other hand, have been long engaged in cultural and historical terrorism, – erasing Georgian frescos and Georgian inscriptions on the ancient churches, and inscribing graffiti in their native alphabet in order to usurp cultural heritage of this not only important, but vital region for Georgian nation, from which Georgian language, alphabet, Christianity, royal dynasty, monastic culture, literature, theology and philosophy take origin *and* sustenance – the cradle and alma mater of Georgian civilization.

Petritsoni Monastery

Petritsoni Monastery is an important monument of Christian architecture and one of the largest and oldest Eastern Orthodox monasteries in Eastern Europe. It is located on the right bank of the Chepelare River, 189 km from Sofia and 10 km south of Asenovgrad, and is directly subordinate to the Holy Synod of the Bulgarian Orthodox Church. The monastery is known and appreciated for the unique combination of Georgian, Byzantine and Bulgarian cultures, united by the common faith. The monastery was founded as an Iberian Orthodox monastery in 1083 by Prince Grigol the son of Bakuriani (also known in Greek as Gregory Pakourianos), a prominent Georgian statesman and military commander in the Byzantine service. In 1204 the Petritsoni Monasteri was vandalized and robbed by Catholic Crusaders. The Cathedral Church of the Virgin Mary (dating from 1604) is the place where a valuable icon of the Virgin Mary Eleusa is kept, which was brought from Georgia in 1310. According to the legend, the icon is wonder-working, attracting many pilgrims. This church was built in the place of the monastery's oldest church destroyed by Turks. The building has survived to this day in its original structure of a three-aisled, cruciform domed basilica with three pentagonal apses. A silver-gilded cross rising from the dome bears this ancient original inscription in Georgian: "Always win!" The monastery was known for its contributions to Christian and Neo-Platonist philosophies. Its school of philosophy was led in the 11th and 12th centuries by Ioane Petritsi, who was a Georgian Neoplatonic philosopher, best known for his translations of Proclus, along with an extensive commentary. In later sources, he is also referred to as Ioane Chimchimeli. He translated Aristotle, Proclus, Nemesius, Ammonius Hermiae, components of the Bible, hagiography, and some other pieces. Of his original works, an extensive commentary to Proclus and Neoplatonism are the most important. But he also composed ascetic and mystic poetry, and hymns.

Monastery of the Cross

Monastery of the Cross is a monastery near the Nayot neighborhood of Jerusalem, Israel. It is located in the Valley of the Cross, below the Israel Museum and the Knesset. The monastery was built in the 11th century, during the reign of King Bagrat IV of Georgia by a Georgian Giorgi-Prokhore of Shavsheti. It is believed that the site was originally consecrated in the 4th century under the instruction of the Roman emperor Constantine the Great, who later gave the site to the Georgian King Mirian III of Iberia. Legend has it that the monastery was erected on the burial spot of Adam's head from which grew the tree that gave its wood to the cross on which Christ was crucified. A fresco of the legendary Georgian poet Shota Rustveli (Rustaveli) on a column inside the church was defaced in June 2004 by "unknown" *vandals*. The face and part of the accompanying inscription were scratched out. Georgia officially complained to Israel after the incident. Similar incidents occurred in the monastery in 1970s and 1980s. The Georgian inscriptions were painted over and replaced by Greek ones. In the 1901 photograph the Council of Archangels has Georgian inscriptions, but in the 1960 photographs the inscriptions are Greek; after cleaning the paintings, the original Georgian inscriptions emerged once again. The same happened in the case of the Anapeston. In many places (e.g. near the figures of St. Luke and St. Prochore) the outline of Georgian letters are clearly seen under the Greek inscription that is there now; in the 1980s the Greek Patriarchate had the frescoes 'restored' or, to be more precise, they were repainted very crudely with oil paints to acquire a more 'complete aspect', as a result of which many features of the original Georgian paintings have been lost.

Holy Monastery of Ivirion

Holy Monastery of Iviron is an Eastern Orthodox monastery at the monastic state of Mount Athos in Greece. The monastery was built under the supervision of Ioane (Ioannes in Greek) the Iberian and Tornike (Tornikios in Greek) between 980-983 AD and housed Iberian clergy and priests. The monastery ranks third in the hierarchy of the Athonite monasteries. The library of Iviron monastery contains 2,000 manuscripts, 15 liturgical scrolls, and 20,000 books, most of which are in Georgian, Greek, Hebrew and Latin. The name Iviron originated from the ancient Georgian Kingdom of Iberia (Iveria) where the master architect of the monastery Ioannes was from, and so were all of its original founders and historical inhabitants. The monastery has the relics of more canonized saints than any other on Mount Athos. The Panagia Portaitissa, the famous 9th century icon, is also located at Iviron. The monastery was once the leading school of Christian and Neo-Platonist philosophy and theology in the world. Among its prominent scholars was Euthymius the Athonite – a renowned Georgian philosopher and scholar, also known as Eufimius the Abasgian or St. Euthymius the Georgian. Fluent in Georgian, Greek and other languages, he translated many religious treatises and philosophical works. Among his major works was the translation of "Sibrdzne Balavarisa" ("Wisdom of Balahvari") – a Christianized version of episodes from the life of Gautama Buddha that became very popular in Medieval Europe as the story of Barlaam and Josaphat. Of equal importance was Euthymius' work to prepare Georgian translations of various Greek philosophical, ecclesiastical and legal discourses. Another famous scholar of the school was Giorgi Mtatsmindeli (George the Hagiorite in Greek) (1009-1065) – a Georgian monk, religious writer, and translator, who spearheaded the activities of Georgian monastic communities in the Byzantine Empire. His epithets *Mtatsmindeli* and *Atoneli*, meaning "of the Holy Mountain" (Hagiorite) and "of Athos" (Athonite) respectively, are a reference to his association with the Iviron monastery on Mount Athos, where he served as hegumen. One of the most influential Christian churchmen of medieval Georgia, George acted as an arbitrator and facilitator of cross-cultural engagement between his native country and the Byzantine Empire. He extensively translated the Fathers of the Church, the Psalms, works of exegesis and synaxaria from Greek – some things which had not previously existed in Georgian – revised many others, and improved the translations of one of his predecessors, Euthymius of Athos, to whom, and also to Ioane (John) of Athos, George dedicated his most important original work "The Vitae of John and Euthymius". Active also in Georgia, he helped to regulate local canon law, and brought his young compatriots to be educated at Athos. His defense of the autocephaly of the Georgian Orthodox church, when it was questioned by the Patriarch of Antioch, made him one of the most venerated Saints in Georgia. He featured prominently during the Great Schism between the Eastern and Western Christendom, being one of the few Eastern churchmen who defended the separated Western brethren.

APPENDIX C

Excerpts on Russian Tyranny from
Liberalism by Ludwig von Mises
Original US publication in April 1962

Chapter 3
Subchapter 11
Russia

The law-abiding citizen by his labor serves both himself and his fellow man and thereby integrates himself peacefully into the social order. The robber, on the other hand, is intent, not on honest toil, but on the forcible appropriation of the fruits of others' labor. For thousands of years the world had to submit to the yoke of military conquerors and feudal lords who simply took for granted that the products of the industry of other men existed for them to consume. The evolution of mankind towards civilization and the strengthening of social bonds required, first of all, overcoming the intellectual and physical influence of the military and feudal castes that aspired to rule the world and the substitution of the ideal of the bourgeois for that of the hereditary lord. The supplanting of the militaristic ideal, which esteems only the warrior and despises honest labor, has not, by any means, even yet been completely achieved. In every nation there are still individuals whose minds are altogether taken up with the ideas and images of the militaristic ages. There are nations in which transient atavistic impulses toward plunder and violence, which one would have presumed to have long since been mastered, still break out and once more gain ascendancy. But, by and large, one can say of the nations of the white race that today inhabit central and western Europe and America that the mentality that Herbert Spencer called "militaristic" has been displaced by that to which he gave the name "industrial." Today there is only *one* great nation that steadfastly adheres to the militaristic ideal, viz., the Russians.

Of course, even among the Russian people there are some who do not share this attitude. It is only to be regretted that they have not been able to prevail over their compatriots. Ever since Russia was first in a position to exercise an influence on European politics, it has continually behaved like a robber who lies in wait for the moment when he can pounce upon his victim and plunder him of his possessions. At no time did the Russian Czars acknowledge any other limits to the expansion of their empire than those dictated by the force of circumstances. The position of the Bolsheviks in regard to the problem of the territorial expansion of their dominions is not a whit different. They too acknowledge no other rule than that, in the conquest of new lands, one may and indeed must go as far as one dares, with due regard to one's resources. The fortunate circumstances that saved civilization from being destroyed by the Russians was the fact that the nations of Europe were strong enough to be able successfully to stand off the onslaught of the hordes of Russian barbarians. The experiences of the Russians in the Napoleonic Wars, the Crimean War, and the Turkish campaign of 1877-78 showed them that, in spite of the great number of their soldiers, their army is unable to seize the offensive against Europe. The World War merely confirmed this.

More dangerous than the bayonets and cannon are the weapons of the mind. To be sure, the response that the ideas of the Russians found in Europe was due, in the first place, to the fact that Europe itself was already full of these ideas before they came out of Russia. Indeed, it would perhaps be more nearly correct to say that these Russian ideas themselves were not originally Russian, however much they may have suited the character of the Russian people, but that they were borrowed by the Russians from Europe. So great is the intellectual sterility of the Russians that they were never able to formulate for themselves the expression of their own inmost nature.

Liberalism,[231] which is based completely on science and whose policies represent nothing but the application of the results of science, must be on its guard not to make unscientific value judgments. Value judgments stand outside of science and are always purely subjective. One cannot, therefore, classify nations according to their worth and speak of them as worthy or less worthy. Consequently, the question whether or not the Russians are inferior lies completely outside the scope of our consideration. We do not at all contend that they are so. What we maintain is only that they do not *wish* to enter into the scheme of human social cooperation. In relation to human society and the community of

---

[231] Classical, pre 20th century liberalism is meant – the belief in the importance of liberty, freedom and independence. Classical liberalism upholds the laissez-faire, free and natural economics – competitive capitalism, as well as the rule of law and minimum government involvement. Classical liberalism is the philosophy committed to protecting the human birthright – freedom. The term "classical liberalism" is applied in retrospect to distinguish the original, 19th-century liberalism from the newer pseudo-liberalism – the so called social liberalism.

nations their position is that of a people intent on nothing but the consumption of what others have accumulated. People among whom the ideas of Dostoyevsky, Tolstoy, and Lenin are a living force cannot produce a lasting social organization. They must revert to a condition of complete barbarism. Russia is endowed far more richly by nature with fertility of soil and mineral resources of all kinds than is the United States. If the Russians had pursued the same capitalistic policy as the Americans, they would today be the richest people in the world. Despotism, imperialism, and Bolshevism have made them the poorest. Now they are seeking capital and credits from all over the world.

Once this is recognized, it clearly follows what must be the guiding principle of the policy of the civilized nations toward Russia. Let the Russians be Russians. Let them do what they want in their own country. But do not let them pass beyond the boundaries of their own land to destroy European civilization. This is not to say, of course, that the importation and translation of Russian writings ought to be prohibited. Neurotics may enjoy them as much as they wish; the healthy will, in any case, eschew them. Nor does this mean that the Russians ought to be prohibited from spreading their propaganda and distributing bribes the way the Czars did throughout the world. If modern civilization were unable to defend itself against the attacks of hirelings, then it could not, in any case, remain in existence much longer. This is not to say, either, that Americans or Europeans ought to be prevented from visiting Russia if they are attracted to it. Let them view at first hand, at their own risk and on their own responsibility, the land of mass murder and mass misery. Nor does this mean that capitalists ought to be prevented from granting loans to the Soviets or otherwise to invest capital in Russia. If they are foolish enough to believe that they will ever see any part of it again, let them make the venture.

But the governments of Europe and America must stop promoting Soviet destructionism by paying premiums for exports to Soviet Russia and thereby furthering the Russian Soviet system by financial contributions. Let them stop propagandizing for emigration and the export of capital to Soviet Russia.

Whether or not the Russian people are to discard the Soviet system is for them to settle among themselves. The land of the knout and the prison-camp no longer poses a threat to the world today. With all their will to war and destruction, the Russians are no longer capable seriously of imperiling the peace of Europe. One may therefore safely let them alone. The only thing that needs to be resisted is any tendency on our part to support or promote the destructionist policy of the Soviets.

Elsewhere in his *Liberalism* Ludwig von Mises writes:

If public opinion today favors capital investment in Russia, the liberal may endeavor to explain that it is as intelligent to invest capital in a land whose government openly proclaims as the ultimate goal of its policy the expropriation of all capital as it would be to dump goods into the sea.

ILIA CHAVCHAVADZE

WHAT IS THERE TO TELL YOU?
WHAT IS THERE TO COMFORT YOU WITH?

Yet another new year rolls in!.. Do we have a reason to congratulate ourselves, my fellow Georgians? Is there anything of old which we would like to retain, or anything new we would like to wish and wait for? Lately we've been looking around only to discover that at present we have done nothing to be proud of, or to give us some cause at least for a regretful exclamation: "O, the minute of rapture, how brief you were!" We are looking forward and yet in tomorrow's fog I cannot discern a single reason for comfort, or anything which would compel us to say: "Let the day of joy come!.." What is there to tell you? What is there to comfort you with?

Would you really suggest following the same old Holiday routine and faded etiquette? Shall I per usual nod at you politely, as it befits a proper guest, and announce: "Now that I have set my foot across your threshold, God bless you and your household!"[232] How far do you intend to ride on the coat tails of God's blessing, my friend? Perhaps it is time for you to shimmy yourself around, move a muscle or two and, just this once, rely on your labor, rather than on God's blessing? The blessing itself is thoroughly good, but why blame the poor blessing when its recipient, the human being, so abundantly blessed by God, is too lazy to water its roots, to prune its branches, to bud its sprouts, to care and to tend to it. God bestowed on us all the blessing that was due, and said that the rest was up to us – our manliness and our ability. What manliness can you boast of lately?.. What is there to tell you? What is there to comfort you with?

God never harmed us; God never held back from us; God never shorted us; If there is a spot or two on the face of the earth which could be said, – Christ God has showered with natural abundance, – Georgia is not the least among them, I assure you. God has already given us all that a man alone cannot attain, but must necessarily come about through God's might. We hold this beautiful land in our hands, which, when beheld, compels even foreigners to exclaim: "Nowhere is there Georgia

---

[232] Referring to a popular Georgian tradition practiced during New Year, called "Mekvleoba" ("Tracing").

like this, in no other corner of the world can it be found".[233] And from what I see, in this heavenly country only a Georgian is failing – his soul is ceasing, his heart is fainting, his body is wasting away... What is there to tell you? What is there to comfort you with?

We possess such woods and rivers, mountains and planes, soils and waters, fresh air and climates that, whatever the heart desires, we are blessed with all that is necessary for earning, accumulating and enjoying wealth. As the saying goes, even the bird's milk could be obtained here, as long as you are willing to move a muscle, to work, to cheer and to keep your chin up, and as long as you don't allow your stomach and your fancy to run your life and to become your tyrannical masters. Know that today power is obtained through work, toil and accumulating, saving, managing, thrift, on as needed bases, and by no means through that insatiable appetite which our fancy and our desire invent.[234] And are we those men who possess such a power? What is there to tell you? What is there to comfort you with?

What horrific misfortunes, what invading enemies, what bloodsheds, what grinding teeth or grinding stones of geopolitical windmills, you name it, we suffered them all, and yet we have weathered them all, we have braved them all, we have managed to sustain our bodily life, as well as our national existence, our country. Leng-Timurs[235] bathed us in our own blood, but still we survived and revived.

---

[233] Quoted from a popular poem *Sadgegrdzelo* (*A Toast*) by Grigol Orbeliani (1804-1883) – a Georgian Romanticist poet and a most decorated soldier in the Imperial Russian service. One of the most colorful figures in the 19th-century Georgian culture, Orbeliani is noted for his patriotic poetry, lamenting Georgia's lost past and independent monarchy. At the same time, he spent decades in the Russian military service, rising through ranks to highest positions in the imperial administration in the Caucasus. Orbeliani's mutual relations with the new generation of Georgian intellectuals were ambiguous. This new movement, dubbed as "the sons", spearheaded by Ilia Chavchavadze, was critical of "the fathers" – old Georgian nobility who had pledged their allegiance to the Tsar, instead of being concerned with Georgia's success and independence. Orbeliani was praised by Chavchavadze as presiding over "the strength and wealth of our verse", but his 1871 jubilee was met by the younger generation in cold silence. In the 1860s, Orbeliani tried to stand aside from the quarrels between "the sons and the fathers", but he could not refrain from attacking the new generation in a caustic rhymed response published in 1874. This did not prevent him, however, from being alone in acclaiming the melodramatic prose of one of the "sons", Alexander Kazbegi, in 1881.

[234] Note that this is an argument for the supply-side economics St. Ilia made long before the supply-side economics was conceived by any American economist.

[235] Timur Leng (1336-1405) – historically known as Tamerlane in English, was a fourteenth-century conqueror of West, South and Central Asia, and the founder of the Timurid dynasty (1370-1405) in Central Asia, and great, great grandfather of Babur, the

Shah Abbases[236] made us tear our own children with our own teeth, but still we regained consciousness and restored our life. Agha Muhammad Khans[237] made us bite the dust, and did not leave a single stone standing as they slaughtered us, as they massacred us, and still we got back on our feet. We endured Greece, Rome, Mongols, Arabs, Osman-Turks, Persians, Christian Heretics and Muslim aggressors, and, although the flag of Georgia was torn by lance tips, arrows and bullets, and soaked in our own blood, nevertheless we managed to hold on to it tight. We never let go of it, we never dropped it for others to carry it away, we never let anyone to curse and to desecrate it. It would be a shame, now, wouldn't

---

founder of the Mughal Dynasty, which survived as the Mughal Empire in India until 1857. Timur's campaigns caused vast destruction everywhere. In a form of rectification, in 1400 Timur invaded Christian Georgia. Of the surviving population, more than 60,000 of the local people were captured as slaves, and many districts were completely depopulated. Georgia, a Christian kingdom in the Caucasus, was subjected, between 1386 and 1404, to several disastrous invasions by the Islamic armies of Turko-Mongol conqueror Timur, whose vast empire stretched, at its greatest extent, from Central Asia into Anatolia. These conflicts were intimately linked with the wars between Timur and Tokhtamysh, the last khan of the Golden Horde and Timur's major rival for control over the Islamic world. Timur officially proclaimed his invasions to be Jihad against the region's non-Muslims. In the first of at least seven invasions, Timur sacked Georgia's capital, Tbilisi, and captured the king Bagrat V in 1386. Georgian resistance prompted a renewed attack by the Turko-Mongol armies. Bagrat's son and successor, George VII, put up a stiff resistance and had to spend much of his reign (1395-1405) fighting the Timurid invasions. Timur personally led most of these raids to subdue the recalcitrant Georgian monarch. Although he was not able to establish a firm control over Georgia, the country suffered a blow from which it never recovered. By the time George VII was forced to accept Timur's terms of peace and agree to pay tribute, he was a master of little more than gutted towns, ravaged countryside and a shattered monarchy.

[236] Shah Abbas I (1571-1629) – Shah of Iran, and generally considered the greatest ruler of the Safavid dynasty. Shah Abbas was one of the most tyrannical dictators in history. He accomplished more than any other Shah for Iran by robbing and devastating its neighboring countries. Shah Abbas had special admiration for Georgian people as superior warriors, but at the same time he had special hatred for them as uncompromising, faithful Christians. In 1614-15, Abbas suppressed a rebellion by the Christian Georgians of Kakheti, killing 60-70,000 and deporting over 100,000 Georgian peasants to Iran. He later had the Georgian Queen Ketevan tortured to death when she refused to renounce Christianity. Portions of her relics were clandestinely taken by the St. Augustine Portuguese Catholic missioners, eyewitnesses of her martyrdom, to Georgia where they were interred at the Alaverdi Cathedral. The rest of her remains are reported to have been buried at the St. Augustine Church in Goa, India.

[237] Agha Mohammad Khan (1742-1797) – the chief of the Qajar tribe, succeeding his father Mohammad Hassan Khan, who was killed on the orders of Adil Shah. He became the Shah of Persia in 1794 and established the Qajar dynasty. In 1795 he ravaged Georgia, and almost completely burned down Tbilisi – he was a eunuch who believed that mineral baths of Tbilisi, which have certain medicinal qualities, would restore him. It is said that he was so disappointed that he decided to burn down Tbilisi out of sheer rage. Incidentally, he was assassinated by a Georgian palace servant named Sadeq in 1797.

it, if today we let moths to eat it and mice to gnaw it away!.. And that is precisely what the future seems to hold for us. What is there to tell you? What is there to comfort you with?

Christ-God was crucified for the world and we too were crucified for Christ in this world. We opened the chest of our tiny country, and on it, as on a solid rock, we built the Holy Seat for Christianity, we used our bones as stones and our blood as lime to cement it, and the gates of Hell never prevailed against it.[238] We were slaughtered and massacred, but we willingly sacrificed our lives and our families. Even though evil was bent against good, with all its multitude, we remained upright and won the most uneven battles. We gave up our bodies to save our souls and we, although a small and handful nation, managed to retain Christianity, in this tiny country, which with justifiable dignity and delight we call our motherland, our fatherland. Would it not be a pity if this nation died out! Would it not be a pity if this lion were devoured by mosquitoes from inside out! Would it not be a pity to leave its lifeless body for jackals and foxes to gnaw at it, as if it were a cadaver or a corpse! Why? What for? For which crime?.. What is there to tell you? What is there to comfort you with?

As we were able to do all of that, the question must naturally follow, – how were we able to do it? What saved us? How did we survive when being crucified for Christ? What made us to persevere, to revive and to live for the sake of our country as we were tortured and bled? The answer is knowledge – we knew what was required and when it was required. We knew what were the demands of the time. We knew what would serve as a castle and fortress, as a sword and shield in that particular era. When courage was needed, we showed courage. When sword was needed, we became blacksmiths. When the art of war was needed, we studied the art of war. And that's what enabled us, that's what saved us, that's what carried us through!.. We were chiseled according to the workbench of those times; we were proofed in the fire of that age; we were forged into solid steel in the steel mill of that epoch. "We had softness of sheepskin" – as Christians, "and hardness of forged metal"[239] – as warriors and patriots. With that we carried ourselves

---

[238] Mathew 16:18.

[239] *The Knight in the Panther's Skin* is an epic poem, consisting of over 1600 *shairi* quatrains, was written in the 12th century by the Georgian epic-poet Shota Rustveli, who was a Prince and Treasurer at the royal court of Queen Tamar of Georgia. *The Knight in the Panther's Skin* is often seen as Georgia's national epic. The poem has been highly

through thick and thin, as we knew whatever was required by that time, as we knew all the due methods, all the fitting ways, all the measures, all the knowledge, all the courage and all the toil suitable and appropriate to that time. That time is gone now: sword has become dull, courage has been cancelled. Nowadays it is more fitting to put our sword away somewhere in the back of a shelf, as it is no longer an adequate weapon of the day; Instead we must pick up either an abacus or a plough, or a lathe of a mill, or wires of a machinery. Battlefield courage and spilling blood is no longer of use; today it is courage of labor and spilling sweat that are useful and beneficial. Furthermore, today the world belongs to the one who toils and knows trades, its secrets and its proper methodologies; today the world belongs to the one who cherishes the fruits of his labor and knows how to save. Today the power belongs only to such a man, who is endeavoring, trying and industrious, and is diligent and studious, both, in his spirit, as well as in his body, that is, in his knowledge, as well as in his labor.[240] And do we possess such goodness and such talents, suitable for today's times? What is there to tell you? What is there to comfort you with?

A sword-clad enemy could not make us surrender or take by force our country. We have endured such sword-clad enemies, and we have survived them all. We kept our country, its land and its name and managed to preserve posterity, and never let anyone to sequester our race in a tomb. Those who came by sword never got the best of us, but the enemy of the future who comes with toil and labor, with knowledge and method, shall overrun us, shall take away our standing ground right under our feet, shall erase our name, shall annihilate us, and with that the name of the Georgian nation will be expunged from existence, and others shall take over the ownership of our beautiful country and occupy it as an abandoned throne. No one of us will be able to withstand a knowledgeable and methodical invader, unless we counter him with our own knowledge and our own method. But are we ready for all of this? Or does it seem that at least we know the dangers and we are preparing for all of this?.. What is there to tell you? What is there to comfort you with?

Life is still a war, not only the pouring of blood, but the pouring of sweat, a bloodless war, peaceful and placid. This war knows no bugle or trumpet. It sows and reaps quietly without any such bugling or

---

praised by literary critics for its language and dramatic effect. The poem was first printed in 1712, in Tbilisi. Chavchavadze is quoting line 1149.

[240] Note that this is yet another argument for the supply-side economics St. Ilia made long before the supply-side economics was conceived by any American economist.

trumpeting. It is nothing like a torrential rainfall, which in a furious manner carries away chunks of highlands and lowlands with it, tosses and twists the soil, bends and destroys all in its path, but it is rather like "a quiet rain which brings forth the fruit".[241] It engages neither in vandalism nor in robbery. Such things are not written in its nature, unless the man himself drips such venomous foreign notions into it, unless the man himself poisons and taints its nature. This is a war of labor, and just like labor – it is a fair and honest thing, and just as honorable an activity, just as admirable and praiseworthy as the war of guns and swords in the days of yore. Courage required for this war is of finer fiber than the courage required for the bloody battles of the past. As a Georgian farmer used to say, when you'd give him a chance to speak the truth and share his most concise and always pertinent wisdom, – a hardworking laborer is thrice the man of a courageous warrior. Forget the farmer!.. This present day is telling us precisely that. Our contemporaneous day preaches this wisdom to us, but do we hear it? Alas, we do not!.. So then, what is there to tell you? What is there to comfort you with?

We do not know – who we used to be, we do not see – what we are now, we do not discern – what it is that we shall be in the future! We have covered our ears with cotton balls and our eyes with our hands. We neither see nor hear anything. We, all the Georgians, have a vast trench in front of us, and yet we are not even aware of it. We are standing in front of this trench, one nudge – and we shall all get smashed up in it. And the depth of this trench is so great and the bottom of it is so bottomless that even eagles and buzzards won't be able to discover us, won't be able to grasp our bones to gnaw and to nibble at them. So here we are all blowing hot smoke, buzzing "I can pull that out of my sock" like flies most ineffectively,[242] soon to be forced to face the reality of the fact that no good is accomplished either with such smoke or such buzzing. Perhaps that's because buzzing all flies can, but only bees sustain.[243] New Year, if you indeed possess special powers, then please ajar our eyes, dump all that cotton out of our ears, help us learn from the little bee all the courageous habits befitting our times, so that at least the

---

[241] Chavchavadze is quoting from one of his most important literary works, *Otaraant Widow*.

[242] Chavchavadze uses a popular Georgian proverb, "The world belongs to me and my trenchcoat". The proverb is used for boasting. Considering the highly idiomatic nature of the proverb, I decided to translate by spirit, rather than by letter, and used a similar popular American saying.

[243] A popular Georgian aphorism.

generation after us does not have to say: What is there to tell you? What is there to comfort you with?

[1897. 31 December]

GEORGIAN INTERNATIONAL UNIVERSITY PRESS

AMERICAN HEROES

Zviad Kliment
Lazarashvili

HENRY DAVID THOREAU: ESSAYS

Henry David Thoreau,
Lazarashvili

MICHAEL TOREY

Janet Mathewson

A MATTER OF PRIDE

Janet Mathewson

POLITICAL THEORY MADE SIMPLE

Lazarashvili, Ihejirika,
Steel

PANTHEON OF POLITICAL PHILOSOPHERS
FIRST EDITION

Ihejirika, Lazarashvili,
Chapidze

FREEDOM AND PROSPERITY
IN THE 21ST CENTURY

Stasen, Lazarashvili,
Chapidze, Ihejirika,
Ramishvili

FIFTEEN POETS

Lazarashvili, Stasen

NEW ENGLAND POETRY

Janet Mathewson

GIU PRESS CLASSICS

Literature
Philosophy
Hagiography
American History
Political Science
Orthodox Theology
Georgian Literature
Psychology
Law
Education
Pedagogy
Economics
Finance
Management
Marketing

Visit us on the web:
www.GIUAmerica.org